Only in My America
By Colonel Robert F. Warren (USMC, Ret.)

Copyright ©2021 by William D. Warren

All rights reserved. No part of this book may be reproduced or transmitted in any form or by any means, electronic or mechanical, including photocopying, recording, or by any information storage and retrieval system, without permission in writing from the copyright holder.

Printed in the United States of America

Bob's family is very thankful for Skip Rains' permission to use and reproduce the cover image, which he painted for Bob in 1987.

ISBN: 978-1-09838-342-8

This book is dedicated to Millie;
my loyal and loving wife of 65 years.

Contents

Introduction 1
Chapter 1: The Early Years 3
    Our Telephone 7
    The Ingraham One-Room School 9
    Adoptions 11
    Daily Farm Life 13
    The Benton Harbor Fruit Market 16
    Grain Threshing 18
    Other Work Around the Farm 20
Chapter 2: High School & College 25
    Coloma High School 25
    Covert High School 26
    Meeting Millie 27
    Palisades Park 31
    Michigan State College 33
    Military Service 1942 35
    Civilian Pilot Training at Austin Lake 36
    First Solo Flight 42
    Meanwhile with Millie 43
    Returning to Michigan State College 45
Chapter 3: Preflight and Primary Flight Training 47
    Iowa Preflight School 47
    Naval Air Station (NAS), Ottumwa, Iowa 52
    Night Flight Training 57

Carrier on the Prairie	57
Engagement to Millie at "Autumn-wa," Iowa	59
NAS, Corpus Christi, Texas	59
The King Ranch	60
NAS, Cuddihy	61
NAS, Corpus Christi (Mainside)	63
My First Flight Challenges	66
The Value of Flying the SNJ	67
Naval Aviator Wings	68
Chapter 4: Advanced Flight Training	**71**
NAS, Cecil Field, Florida	71
Time with Millie	76
MCAS, Cherry Point	77
NAS, Vero Beach	79
Millie and Marriage	81
Hellcat Flight Training	83
Returning to Cherry Point	84
Chapter 5: World War II Pacific Deployments Begin	**89**
MCAS, EL CENTRO, CALIFORNIA	89
MCAS, Ewa, Hawaii	91
Ulithi Atoll Staging Area	94
Chapter 6: Amphibious Assault on Okinawa	**97**
The Attack Plan	97
USS *SITKOH BAY* (CVE-86)	97
Kamikaze Attack on the USS *Achernar* (AKA-53)	99
Okinawan Tombs	101
Daily Combat Flights	102
Night Combat Air Patrols (CAP)	104

Accidents, Casualties, Injuries, and the Aftermath 108

Living in a Forward Area 111

Operation Iceberg 113

NAS, Agana, Guam 115

Chapter 7: Saipan Operations – World War II Victory 117

Battle Highlights Saipan and Tinian 117

Japanese Surrender 126

Detachment Returns to Guam 127

Return to the United States (Land of the Big PXs) 129

Chapter 8: Career Decision – Quantico Transfer 131

Options and Decision 131

Request for Active Duty Assignment 133

Return to Active Duty.. 135

The Crossroads of the Marine Corps 135

Quantico Town and the Main Base.. 136

Air-Infantry School 137

Family Move to Washington, D.C. 140

School Carpool 142

Chapter 9: Cherry Point Photo Squadron 143

Background 143

Marine Photo Reconnaissance Squadron (VMP-354)................ 145

Photo Squadron Training at MCAS, Cherry Point 147

Chapter 10: USS Siboney - Caribbean Deployment 149

My Barrier Crash 150

Naval Station, Guantanamo Bay, Cuba 154

Return from Caribbean Deployment 155

The Fly Home Program 160

Marine Air Group (MAG) Staff Assignment 163

  Lieutenant Colonel Marion Carl, USMC 164

  Reburial Detail in Chicago 165

Chapter 11: Transition to Helicopters... 169

  Free Ballooning at Lakehurst 173

  Pooling Ignorance 177

Chapter 12: Santa Ana - Camp Pendleton - San Diego 181

  Transfer to California 181

  Marine Corps Air Facility (MCAF), Santa Ana, California 183

  Marine Corps Base Camp Pendleton 187

Chapter 13: Arrival in Korea 193

  Squadron Positioning for Combat... 193

  Squadron Rear Echelon Location 194

  Forward Echelon Location 195

  South Korean Laborers.. 198

  First Combat Mission 199

  U.S. Navy Hospital Ships 199

  The Experimental Mission... 202

  Subsequent Missions 203

  Summing up September 1951 204

  The Construction of Revetments 205

  October 1951 206

  Operation Bumblebee... 207

  Support for a Republic of Korea Company 208

  Operation Bushbeater 209

  Operation Rabbit Hunt.. 210

  November 1951 212

  Operation Switch 214

  Thanksgiving Day Celebration... 214

  December 1951 215

  Christmas Card from Old Korea 223

Chapter 14: Korea Winter and Spring Operations 225

  USO Show 226

  January 1952 226

  The Battleship USS *Wisconsin* 227

  Operation Ripple 229

  Armistice Meetings at Panmunjom 230

  Downed Pilot Rescue Mission 231

  Move Across Korea 233

  The Panmunjom Armistice Site 235

  The Armistice Negotiators 236

Chapter 15: 1952 Return From Korea 239

  Joyful Family Reunion 239

  Headquarters and Maintenance Squadron 242

  Marine Air Base Squadron (MABS) 242

  Second Flight Across the United States 244

  Non-Commissioned Officer (NCO) Leadership School 245

Chapter 16: Aide to General Schilt 249

  Interview and Selection 249

  Aide Selection Announcement 250

  General Schilt's First Helicopter Instruction Flight 251

  Serving at El Toro 253

  General Schilt's Career, and My History with Him 255

    General Schilt's Medal of Honor 256

    Marine Air Reserve Training Command 256

    Staff Pilot, Captain Kelvin Bailey 260

    Repeated Flights to Indian Springs 261

  The Atomic Bomb Explosion Experience 262

  MCAS, Yuma, Arizona 263

  The Gadsden Land Purchase 264

  St. Paul Winter Carnival 264

  Another Interesting Far East Trip 265

  President Syngman Rhee 266

Chapter 17: Transfer to Washington, D.C. 269

  The Navy Annex 273

  Aide Duties in Washington 274

  Naval War College 277

  Lunch with Igor Sikorsky 277

  Heavy Lift Helicopter Shopping 278

  Assessing Readiness 279

  Helicopter Flying at MCAS, Quantico 279

Chapter 18: Trip to Europe 283

  Lord Louis Mountbatten 283

  The Hague 284

  Italy 285

  Naples, Madrid, and Morocco 285

  The Azores 286

Chapter 19: General Schilt's Final Far East Trip 287

  Helicopter and KC-130 Shopping 288

  General Schilt's Retirement 293

  Major Kelvin Bailey 294

  Marine Lieutenant General Verne J. McCaul 295

Chapter 20: Transfer to California 297

  Helicopter Transport for President Eisenhower 298

  Rocket Engine Tests and Artificial Clouds 303

Visiting Parents 304
Purple Thanksgiving Turkey 305

Chapter 21: Philippines Operations 307
To the Philippines and Back 307
Severe Storm at Sea 307
Performing All Manner of Things 308
A Large Navy Flotilla 310
Luzon Ship-To-Shore Landing Exercise 310
Return to Japan 311
Manning the Rails 312

Chapter 22: Helicopter Squadron Command 315
Flag and Bible Marines 315
Fatal Crash 318

Chapter 23: Oppama, Japan 321
Reassignment to the Far East 321
Aircraft Carrier USS *Ranger* (CV-61) 322
Captain Paul D. Buie, USN 324
Submarine USS *Ronquil* (SS-396) 325
Dive, Dive, Dive 327

Chapter 24: First Orders to Laos 329
Laos Overview 331
Arrival in Vientiane 332
Return to Japan 335

Chapter 25: Second Orders to Laos 337
U.S. Embassy in Laos 337
Vientiane Airfield Helicopter Operations 339

Chapter 26: Spouse Visit to Japan 345
Preparing for Millie's Visit 345

  Visit to Kyoto 347

  Mt. Fujiama 349

  Sendai, Japan 350

  CINCPAC Helicopter Transport 353

  Air Group Commander Change 354

Chapter 27: Transfer to Okinawa 355

  Tachikawa Air Force Base - Japan 355

  Welcome to Okinawa 355

  WW II Okinawa Reminiscing 357

  Return Home 358

Chapter 28: Quantico Education Center 361

  Arrival Good News 361

  Range of Aviation Branch Instruction 362

  Lustron Houses 364

  The Basic School 365

  The AWS Junior Course 367

    Lieutenant General Roy S. Geiger 367

  The AWS Senior School 369

Chapter 29: Joy of Quantico Duty 375

  Crossroads of the Marine Corps 375

  A Unique Little Town 375

  Dependent Schools 376

  Dependent School Activities 377

    Daughter, Jeanne Warren 377

    Son, Bill Warren 378

    Quantico High School Football Team 378

  The U.S. Air Force Aero Club 381

  QHS Senior Nick Fritz 383

- Our Family Visits to Quantico 385
- The Teen Club 386
- Major General Lewis Walt, USMC.. 387
- End of Quantico Duty... 388

Chapter 30: MCAS, Beaufort to Spain.. 393
- Brief History of MCAS, Beaufort 393
- Operation Steel Pike In Spain... 394
- SATS Construction.. 396
- The Fresh Water Pump Woes 398
- Return to Beaufort... 399

Chapter 31: Transition to Jets 401
- The Jet-Powered F9F Cougar 401
- Flying the TF9F-J.. 404
- Jet Transition Flights 406
- Cross-Country Flight.. 408
- The Tail-Chase 409
- Instrument Flight 411

Chapter 32: Change of Squadron Command 415
- Change of Command Party 416
- Change of Command Honored Guests 416
- Traditional Changing of Command 417

Chapter 33: Jet Squadron Training 419
- Getting VMA-331 Organized 419
- First All Pilot's Meeting 420
- A4-E Skyhawk History 421
- Skyhawk Familiarization and Training Flights 422

Chapter 34: Puerto Rico Deployment 427
- Naval Station Roosevelt Roads, Ponce, Puerto Rico 427

    Surprise Arrival of VMF-451 432

    Return to Beaufort 435

Chapter 35: Jet Squadron TransLants 443

    East-Toward the Rising Sun... 443

    Larissa Air Base 446

    U.S. Air Force War Reserve Equipment 447

    Naval Station, Rota, Spain... 451

    Translant West-Toward the Setting Sun 452

Chapter 36: Beaufort to Cherry Point 457

    Change of Station Orders... 457

    Promotion and Staff Assignment 459

    Temporary Orders to Europe 461

    Munich, Germany 462

    General George S. Patton Hotel.. 462

    Oberammergau... 463

    The Conference 464

    Garmisch-Partenkirchen 464

    Conference End - Return to the USA 465

    Year 1967 466

Chapter 37: Transfer to Vietnam 469

    Recent Vietnam Political Background.. 470

    United States-South Vietnamese Military Relationships 470

Chapter 38: III MAF Assignment 475

    Reporting to Lieutenant General Walt... 475

    My III MAF Assignment 475

    Daily 0700 III MAF Staff Briefings... 479

    CIA Pilatus PC-6 Turbo Porter Airplane 481

    DMZ Refugee Crisis 482

Chapter 39: Distinguished Visitors 487
  General and Mrs. Omar Bradley 487
  Scout-Sniper Platoon Visit 497
  Other Briefing Tent Occupants 498
  Refugee Camp Visit 499
Chapter 40: Australia R & R Leave 507
  Charles Kingsford Smith 508
  Sydney Welcome Center 509
  Sidney, Australia 511
Chapter 41: 1968 Tet Offensive 515
  Background-Introduction of U.S. Forces Vietnam 516
  "Arc Light" Missions 517
Chapter 42: End of Vietnam Tour Events 525
  Event One: Ambassador Koren's Retirement 525
  Event Two: Arrival of the *Helgoland* 528
  Event Three: The Elephants of Tra bong 531
  Event IV: Junketing Politicians 535
  Event V: Departure from Vietnam 537
Chapter 43: Final Career Transfer 543
  Marine Helicopter Air Group Fifty Six (MAG-56) 546
  MAG-56 Mission 549
  Army-Trained Marine Helicopter Pilots 552
  Annual Rifle Range Qualification 553
  Thousands of Field Jackets 554
  General Lewis Walt Visit 556
  Retirement Decision 557

Chapter 44: Retirement 559
Chapter 45: My Son's Career Synopsis 561
    Introduction 561
    Bill Warren's USMC Career – In His Own Words 561
Epilogue 577
Family Pictures 581
Acknowledgements 589
Appendix Items 591
Index 619
Notes 633

Introduction

Motivation for writing this story came from my two children, their spouses and from close relatives and friends. When I related the names of prominent people I had met during my career as a Marine Corps Aviator, in three wars, they urged me to write my description of those, and other encounters, and thus provide a historical record for my descendants. When I commenced writing it quickly became apparent that my story could have happened Only in My America.

Where else could an orphaned farm kid have the good fortune to be adopted, and raised as their own, by family relatives; then, be educated and trained to serve my country as a fighter pilot in WW II, a helicopter pilot in Korea, and in Vietnam, serve as the Chief Of Staff to the State Department Director for Civil Operations? Where else would I be offered commands of both a Marine Helicopter squadron and later, a Marine Jet Attack squadron; then command an Air Group with seven squadrons, manned by hundreds of highly skilled, enlisted Marines who always earned my appreciation and respect? Where else could I have transported the President of the United States in a Marine Helicopter; or, met other notables, including South Korean President Syngman Rhee in his Seoul office, and Lord Louis Mountbatten in London?

Throughout this narrative, I have tried to include bits of historical information, so the reader may have a better understanding of events as I described them. For instance, why was I twice ordered to Laos, traveling with two passports? And why was I ordered to Saipan, in charge of a night-fighter detachment, a year after that island had been captured? To my readers, I hope answers to these questions, and many others, lead you to enjoy this tale of happiness, love and dedicated service, that could have begun Only in My America.

Chapter 1: The Early Years

My life began on 10 December 1923 near the little rural village of Riverside, Michigan. My father was Walter Fred Kuzian and my mother was Angeline Louise (Allen) Kuzian. My parents named me Robert Frank Kuzian; probably after one of my father's brothers named Frank Kuzian. My mother and father were married on 24 December 1920. My older brother, Walter Fred Kuzian, Jr. was born on 2 May 1921.

My father had been drafted into the U.S. Army in 1917. He served in France during WWI and was discharged in 1919.

My father's parents were John Kuzian and Mary (Urie) Kuzian who emigrated from Poland. My father was born on 4 December 1894 in Baltimore, Maryland. My mother was born in 1901 and her parents were Edward "Jack" and Daisy Allen who lived locally near Riverside, Michigan. At age twenty-five my mother Angeline Kuzian died from complications of appendicitis and peritonitis. She is buried in the Hagar Township Cemetery, near Riverside, Michigan. My father died of a cardiac arrest on 13 January 1964 in the small mountain town of Bangor, California. He is buried in the San Bruno Veterans National Cemetery, near the San Francisco International Airport.

After the passing of our mother, our father faced a real dilemma. What was he to do with two small children; one still a baby? Under those circumstances, he probably did the best he could by taking my brother and me to our Aunt Ruth and Uncle Tom Warren's farm home, located about four miles north of the small town of Coloma, Michigan and about ten miles from his Riverside home. He was certain that his two boys would be warm and well fed there in the large Warren farmhouse. I think the Warrens expected our father to contribute something to help provide for our welfare. However, he didn't. Instead, he promptly and completely disappeared! No one in our family knew of his whereabouts for the next sixty years. When recalled to active duty in the 1980s, I unexpectedly learned many details of his life; including his travels to Louisiana, Nebraska, and later to California, where he died.

```
WALTER F
KUZIAN
NORTH DAKOTA
COOK CO L 23 INF
2 DIVISION
WORLD WAR I
DECEMBER 4 1893
JANUARY 13 1964
```

The Warren farm consisted of sixty acres; with the front twenty acres devoted to small crops including tomatoes, cucumbers, strawberries, watermelons, cantaloupes, raspberries, string beans, and lima beans. My Aunt Ruth also planted, and maintained, a very large and productive garden.

The front twenty acres also had all of the farm buildings, including a barn where the animals were housed and fed. The barn included space for two vehicles and had an overhead haymow and bins for grain storage. The farm structures included the large farmhouse with an adjacent windmill, a free-standing two-car garage, and several small chicken houses; sometimes referred to as brooder houses, or chicken coops. There was also a ten-acre orchard, where apple, cherry, plum, peach, and pear trees were grown, alongside several rows of Concord grapes.

The back forty acres were treeless; planted with the grain crops needed to feed the horses, cows, pigs, and chickens. The barn, house, and garage all had vertical lightning rods attached atop each building, and grounded by a one-half inch mesh cable extending into the ground. Tom and Ruth Warren had two children named Helen and George, who were ten and eight years old.

To suddenly have the number of children living in their home doubled was a major concern for our Aunt Ruth and Uncle Tom. But, they were a kind and giving couple who accepted and treated my brother and me as full members of their family. As the only baby, I probably enjoyed, and demanded, a lot of special attention; a.k.a., being spoiled.

Growing up, we were disciplined fairly, and treated very well. Throughout my life I've felt that one of the reasons I have enjoyed excellent health was because I ate so much good, nourishing food when I was growing up on that farm. I can recall picking and eating many delicious foods that were all very good for growing children.

I don't remember that the Warrens had much cash, but they always managed to provide an abundance of good food. During the summer when we were picking and harvesting, Aunt Ruth Warren and her daughter, Helen, were busy canning, to ensure that we had enough food to last through the next winter. Their large basement had multiple bins and shelves. The bins held cabbages, apples, and root crops, including potatoes, carrots, beets, rutabagas, and turnips. The fruit cellar shelves held rows of glass Mason jars, filled with colorful canned fruits and vegetables that provided food for the winter months.

Bob Warren at six months old

Ruth and Thomas Warren in 1969

During the school year, I recall trudging three fourths of a mile to our one-classroom Ingraham School. Before our township schools were consolidated, small schools were constructed about two miles apart throughout the township. Building small schools ensured that school children lived no farther than a mile from a school. Many farms adjacent to our route to school had fruit trees and vineyards. We always felt free to stop and pick apples, pears, plums, and grapes, on our way to school. That roadside fruit often supplemented the sandwich lunches we carried in small brown paper sacks.

Our kitchen icebox had a compartment on top; large enough to hold a large block of ice. We bought ice blocks from a commercial ice storage facility, located a couple of miles from our farm. During winter months, ice blocks had been cut into various sizes from the nearby Little Paw Paw Lake with a long metal ice saw. The ice blocks were stored in a building, with wood sawdust between the blocks of ice. When an ice block was delivered by a truck, and placed into the top of our icebox, the melting block lasted long enough to keep milk and other foods preserved for several days.

Our Telephone

We had a fifteen inch by ten-inch wooden telephone hung against our dining room wall. Our telephone number was 1-2F-21. We answered the telephone when we heard two long bell rings, followed by one short ring (the last two of our telephone numbers). Our telephone was on a party line; shared with five neighbors, each having a different telephone bell-ringing sequence. The telephone was built into a shiny golden oak box, with two round bells at the top-front of the box, and a six-inch adjustable (up and down only) mouthpiece, protruding several inches in front of the telephone box face. A wired, five-inch, handheld receiver hung on a cradle, on the left side of the box.

When our ringing bell sequence was recognized, the call was answered by removing the receiver from its cradle. With the weight of a receiver removed, the spring-loaded cradle raised, making connection with the caller's telephone. To hear a caller, the receiver had to be held against the listener's ear.

A slanted wooden tray, designed to hold a small telephone book, was built into the lower front of the box. A hand signaling crank was mounted on the right side of the telephone box. The crank was used to call the local Michigan Bell Telephone Company switchboard operator, or to call others on the party line, using their ringing bell sequence. Long distance calls had to be made through the switchboard operator. The telephone box bore the Western Electric Company trademark. Gossip sessions among the neighboring women, using the shared party line seemed to be a popular, relaxing afternoon pastime.

Warren farm house, Coloma, MI, 1960

The Ingraham One-Room School

Walking three fourths of a mile to the Ingraham rural school was a lot of fun. In the winter we often pulled our sleds, and a toboggan, and gave rides to the smaller children of families along our route to school. The sled of choice was the Flexible Flyer, because it had wide metal runners, and it was very sturdy.

After school, we often stopped on our way home to dig caves into the large roadside snow banks created by blowing snow; and on our sleds, we coasted down the hilly road home. On winter evenings, the older neighborhood kids would often gather at one of several nearby shallow ponds; build a bonfire on the ice, and enjoy skating, with frequent warming stops next to the fire. Our metal ice skates were held firmly against our shoes, using adjustable shoe sole clamps, and belt-like leather ankle straps. Our curfew was at 10:00 p.m. sharp.

Ingraham was a typical township one-room rural school house; of which there were many built at that time. The school had a single large classroom, a high bell tower rising over one end of the school structure; adjacent to it was a water well with a manually operated pump handle. A small, unheated, detached building housed school supplies, equipment, and the dry wood needed to fuel the classroom stove. The school lacked indoor plumbing. Boy and Girl privies were built at one end of the school. Fresh drinking water was hand-pumped into a metal bucket, and students shared the same long-handled metal water dipper, when drinking from the bucket.

The back two-thirds of the classroom were furnished with permanent desks. Each desk had a seat. At the front of the classroom, chairs were arranged in a semicircle. When called by the teacher, students from that class would stand, and quietly move to the front of the classroom, and sit in their semicircle seats. Students from a different school grade, who had just finished their class, would return to their seats; moving along the opposite side of the classroom.

I clearly recall the teacher loudly saying, "Third graders, rise and pass." Our teacher, Mr. Forrest E. Totten , taught all eight grades. I feel that attending a one-room school had a distinct advantage, as younger students learned from hearing the recitations of students in the higher grades. Accordingly, the one-classroom students received an excellent, basic primary education.

In our family, my older brother became a Northwest Orient Airlines Captain, and I retired a Marine Corps Colonel. In later years my older brother often asked, "I wonder whatever happened to Mr. Forrest E. Totten?" We never forgot our amazing teacher, who was highly intelligent, and a teacher who was respected by both his students, and their parents. He had the ability to organize every aspect of student activity in the Ingraham School. Students were taught to clean the blackboard, carry stove wood and water, hand crank the eraser-cleaning machine, and pull the long rope that rang the school bell to start each school day, and to end lunch and recess periods.

A picture of George Washington, a United States flag, and a large round pendulum school clock were displayed at the front of the classroom, along with a large blackboard; which was built with a chalk and eraser tray, along the blackboard bottom. Just above the entire length of the blackboard, permanent alphabet letters, in both capital and lower case, were affixed.

Each school day started with a student leading the Pledge of Allegiance to the Flag. During recess periods, Mr. Totten would organize and supervise various outdoor games which required some vigorous activity. Lunch periods were thirty minutes long. Again, the school bell would ring, and the students would promptly return to the classroom, and commence their class work. Each school day had only a limited number of hours for Mr. Totten to teach all eight grades. Mr. Totten managed those school hours very well.

Each school year ended with a school picnic, which was held in the school yard. Homemade vanilla ice cream, prepared by several parents, using their hand-cranked ice cream freezers, was served to all. Passing diplomas were presented, grade by grade, to most students. But, if students did not receive passing grades, they were required to repeat that grade the next school year. Each school year started in September, and ended in May of the following year. Graduating eighth graders anxiously looked forward to attending Coloma High School the next year. Ingraham School is no longer used; however, the school still stands at its original location on North Coloma Road.

Ingraham School, Coloma, MI, 1960

Adoptions

From the late 1920s, and into the 1930s, our Nation was in a serious financial depression that affected almost everyone. The Warrens, like most other farmers, had difficulty selling their products. The cost of raising four children became a critical family financial problem for the Warrens. Accordingly, they had to place one of the Kuzian children up for adoption.

My older brother was chosen, and he was adopted by Dick and Lucille Dean; members of the Dean's Dairy family in Berrien Springs, Michigan. The Deans let my brother select his new name. He changed it from Walter Fred Kuzian, Jr., to William F. Dean. At the same time, the Warrens adopted me; changing only my last name, to Warren. Thus, at ages eleven and eight, two blood brothers had different last names; Billy Dean and Bobby Warren. I think those adoptions proved beneficial for both of us; although we grew up separated from each other. My older brother went from being a poor farm kid, to one of some privilege, afforded by the Dean Dairy family wealth. For instance, my brother attended a prestigious boy's school on the Leelanau Peninsula; near Traverse City, Michigan.

By comparison, my childhood seemed rather dull. In retrospect, however, my life was very full. In the summer, I wore bib overalls, and like most of my neighborhood friends and cousins, we worked and played barefooted. The Warrens had a unique way of making sure we had new school clothes each year. They paid us for working, but retained most of the money to purchase our new school clothes; allowing us to keep a small percentage of our earnings as personal spending money. I was able to retain enough of the money I earned picking strawberries at home, to purchase a used Western Flyer Bicycle for five dollars.

We spent countless hours during the summer, poring over the Sears Roebuck, and Montgomery Ward catalogs, looking for items we would need to start school. We compared the cost of items we wanted, against what we could afford from each escrow account held by our parents. Extensive detailed calculation was done during that process. The new clothes selected for me, purchased through those mail order catalogs, included new bib overalls, shirts, socks, long winter underwear, sweaters, gloves, caps, and jackets. Opening the packages of new clothes was always exciting.

A gift I always wanted for Christmas was a pair of high-top shoes. They were leather shoes, which laced up to the lower mid-calf of your legs. A really exciting feature of the shoes for me, as a young boy, was that one of the shoes had a knife pocket stitched on the side. A small jackknife was included with the new shoes. Much to my delight, I received a pair.

Daily Farm Life

Each day started early, with the lighting of kerosene lanterns. My Uncle Tom Warren, and his son, George, carried the lanterns to the barn. Five or six cows were herded into the barn; where the cows put their heads through open stanchions, and started eating grain in a long trough. The stanchions were then closed around their necks, limiting their movement while being milked. Milking machines had not yet been invented; our cows were milked by hand. A small amount of fresh milk was squirted directly into the mouths of the patiently waiting barn cats. Pails of fresh milk were poured into larger milk cans, and cooled outside of the barn, using long metal stirring rods. Daily, the full milk cans were carried to the edge of the road, where the driver of a large milk truck would stop and load the cans, and leave a handwritten receipt, along with clean milk cans for use the next day. Our full milk cans were trucked to a commercial dairy.

Meanwhile, Aunt Ruth Warren and her daughter, Helen, would start a fire in the wood-burning kitchen stove, and start preparing breakfast which usually consisted of oatmeal, eggs, toast, and crisp bacon; or pancakes with home-churned butter, maple syrup, in-season fruit and fresh milk. The kitchen stoves (ranges) had one large baking oven, and two smaller overhead ovens, used to keep food warm until served. By time we ate breakfast, we had worked over an hour, and were very hungry.

Warm water was provided by a large tea kettle taken from the hot stove, or from the water tank built into the stove, next to the fire box. Before eating, we poured warm water into a small wash basin, added soap, washed, and then dried our hands on a shared towel. One of the most pleasant memories of my childhood is of those tasty and filling breakfasts.

Weekly baths were taken on Saturday evenings, in front of the warm kitchen stove, with the oven door open. Warm, clean bath water was poured into a large, round, metal laundry tub that became our family Saturday night bathtub; which was emptied after individual baths.

The Warrens also established a chicken business on their farm; primarily run by my Aunt Ruth. The double-car garage was modified to accommodate a large, five thousand-egg incubator, with a heater, required to keep the incubating eggs at the proper hatching temperature. Chicken eggs required an incubating period of three weeks; turkey eggs require four weeks; while goose eggs require five weeks.

The eggs were placed on incubator tray rollers, and had to be rolled. At the end of each roller, there was a round-toothed gear, which meshed with a long matching-geared rod that extended the full length of the incubator. When the rod was moved, hundreds of eggs, which were resting on rollers, were turned; thereby simulating the egg-turning actions of a setting hen. The rod was moved with a simple crank; turning several hundred eggs at one time. The eggs were turned every three hours, and our family members shared that duty, day and night, during the hatching season.

Turning eggs stopped, when the eggs started to hatch. The fuzzy little chicks were removed from the incubator, and placed into cardboard boxes. Each box had four sections, a lid, and small coin-sized air holes. The boxes of little chicks were then delivered to local customers, or the chicks were mailed greater distances, by the U.S. Postal Service. The chicks to be raised on our farm were moved into a brooder house; where they could eat, drink, and were kept warm, under a heated, overhead metal shroud.

Our chickens were White Leghorns, Rhode Island Reds, and black Barred Rocks. We always raised a small flock of turkeys too. My Aunt Ruth would raise the chicks until they weighed about three pounds; then butcher and sell them to steady customers, who drove to our farm, anxious to purchase tender young chickens, which were cleaned and ready for frying.

My Aunt Ruth always planted a large garden. She would hoe weeds, and harvest the beans, carrots, cabbages, rutabagas, kale, turnips, sweet corn, and other vegetables; not grown elsewhere on the farm. Some were eaten, or canned, and if grown in abundance, were often sold to her chicken-buying customers. Most of the products grown on our farm were sold at an open-air market, located in Benton Harbor, Michigan; which was about twenty miles from our farm.

The ripening season of various farm products required considerable coordination to get a truckload ready for market; two or more truckloads, each week. My Uncle Tom drove his 1926 Model-T Ford truck to the market, and I was often sent with him. I suspect that was calculated to keep me away from being a noisy, underfoot pest.

Trips to the market were always exciting for me. Years later, when my duties in Vietnam often involved assisting Vietnamese farmers with growing and marketing their products, I felt that my farm background helped me immeasurably. For instance, at one of his early morning staff meetings at his III MAF headquarters in Da Nang, Lieutenant General Cushman asked me when rice would be harvested in Quang Ngai Province. I knew the answer. (A later chapter of my story is devoted to my thirteen-month tour of duty in Vietnam, during which I spent almost all of my time helping civilian Vietnamese, including farmers.)

The Benton Harbor Fruit Market

The Benton Harbor, Michigan outdoor fruit market was built on a long, spacious, open-air quadrangle, in which there were many long, chalk-marked, selling lanes. After paying $1.00 to enter the market, a farmer would be directed to one of several lanes. Covered loading platforms bordered the length of each side of the market. The produce buyers would back their large semi-trailers to a numbered loading space, outside of the loading platforms. After selling, a farmer unloaded his produce at the corresponding-numbered platform. Thus, farm products purchased could easily be moved from a farmer's truck, across the narrow loading platform, and directly into the waiting buyer's semi-trailer.

During the selling process, buyers, who were mostly from Chicago, used a small, forked, metal wrench to pry crate covers off, for closer produce inspection. All bartering and price negotiation took place at the farmer's vehicle, while still in a selling lane. When a buyer and the farmer agreed on a price, the buyer would direct the farmer to the proper unloading shed, where the previously agreed upon price was paid in cash. If the entire load was not purchased, a farmer could again enter a selling lane, at no additional charge, because the buyers usually bought a single product.

After all our truckloads of produce were sold, my Uncle Tom Warren would stop at a drug store in Benton Harbor where large ice cream cones were the store specialty. If the selling price for the produce had been good, we always stopped; and he would purchase two cones, which we really enjoyed eating, while driving home. When we returned to the farm, Aunt Ruth Warren was anxiously waiting to learn the price of each product sold. She and my cousins, Helen and George, were usually busy; preparing the next load to be trucked to the Benton Harbor fruit market.

The cycle of picking, packing, transporting, and selling, went on during the harvesting season; which on our farm, lasted from June through October. Our farm produce was always taken to market in new wooden crates or baskets; purchased from a commercial basket factory in Coloma, and hand stamped with the Warren name, and their Rural Route number. The Warren address was RR-2, Coloma, Michigan.

During the summer, and early fall months, it was necessary to hire migrant workers, most of who were from Haiti. Uncle Tom would hire several workers from a labor pool in Coloma. They would sleep overnights in the barn hayloft, and at daybreak, they were up and ready to pick apples, tomatoes, grapes, and other farm crops. Aunt Ruth Warren, who was a kind soul, would prepare and take a big breakfast to those workers, because she knew they hadn't eaten anything that morning.

Those acts of kindness were so typical of Aunt Ruth. She was tough, but also very warm-hearted; smart, considerate, fair, and a wonderful person. She was the family matriarch; the engine that shrewdly kept all family activities coordinated and running smoothly. In addition, she baked superb pies, and made delicious strawberry shortcake!

Grain Threshing

A major harvesting event took place at our farm during October of each year. When grain was ready for threshing, the neighborhood farmers would band together and assist each other. Those farmers arrived at the designated farm early, with their horses and wagons, ready to go into the grain fields and load the shocks of grain that had been previously cut with a machine called a binder. The binder mechanically tied each grain shock (bundles) with binder twine. When loaded, they drove their wagons alongside the threshing machine; owned and operated by Mack Grant, a local Coloma man.

Mr. Grant arrived at our farm, driving his big Huber tractor down the road, pulling his large threshing machine. I was fascinated when watching him un-hitch the threshing machine from his tractor, alongside our barn. He would then turn his tractor around, and facing the threshing machine, would align his tractor, about thirty feet from it. He then manually connected a ten-inch-wide driving belt between the driving pulley of his tractor, and the matching threshing machine pulley. After putting a half twist in the belt to keep it from flopping, he would tighten the belt, by reversing his tractor slowly, until the belt was tight. Next, he set the tractor brake, and shifted power to his tractor belt pulley.

Meanwhile, the first wagon, loaded with grain shocks, approached the threshing machine. Mack Grant would sit on his tractor, and watch the farmers, using long handled pitchforks, feed the grain shocks from their wagon into the threshing machine; and simultaneously, the machine would blow straw out of the rear of the machine; quickly building a stack of straw.

This amazing choreographic event represented a stage-like production. Only here, the actors were skilled farmers, directed by the ever-watching Mack Grant, sitting atop his tractor. The threshing machine had a hopper to receive the separated grain, and feed it into an attached metal chute, to carry the grain to the opened burlap sacks. When filled, the sacks would be unhooked from the chute, and carried into the barn; where they were then emptied into a grain bin.

I worked at those inside bins. I received the open burlap sacks - each weighing about fifty pounds - and tossed the grain, (usually wheat or oats) from the opened burlap sacks, into the correct grain bin. This hard work no doubt contributed to my excellent physical condition; and the job taught me teamwork, and to accept a degree of responsibility. I was proud to have a role in the threshing process. I was equally thankful to work safely away from that noisy tractor, with the dangerous rapidly moving threshing machine belt; which at times frightened horses.

Threshing at our farm usually took half of a day. Traditionally, on threshing day, the lady of the house prepared a noontime dinner for all neighboring farmers, who had assisted my Uncle Tom in threshing that day. They all knew who served the best noontime dinners. Aunt Ruth always fed them very well. So, the visiting farmers were very pleased to eat at our farmhouse. And, why not? The dinner consisted of delicious fried chicken, mashed potatoes and milk gravy, several fresh garden vegetables, with hot, home-baked bread, topped with butter and homemade jam. The dessert was freshly baked apple or pumpkin pie, topped with whipped cream, and served with hot coffee.

Uncle Tom was very proud to watch his farmer friends enjoy the sumptuous dinner, evidenced by his self-satisfied facial expression, and a twinkle in his eye, reflecting pride in his wife's expert cooking. The threshing participants anticipated that a superb noontime meal would always be served at the Warren farmhouse and they were never disappointed. I took boyish pride, when sitting among those farmers, and with Mack Grant, at the noon dinner.

When the threshing was completed at our farm, Mack Grant again hitched his threshing machine to his tractor, and drove to another farm, where the whole threshing process would be repeated. But, my participation in threshing was limited to our farm.

Other Work Around the Farm

As the family children grew older, we were each given increased responsibilities; thereby making us feel like very proud, farm work contributors. In my early teens, I was permitted to harness our team of two horses, and hitch them to whatever farm implements were to be used that day; be it a plow, harrow, hay rake, wagon, or the grain cutting binder. I would drive the team to an open field, and start work.

I learned to rest the horses periodically, and to make certain they had plenty of drinking water. After quitting time, I had to be sure that their barn mangers were full of hay and grain. At the end of their working day, I also had to un-harness and groom the horses, with a special curry comb, and a hand-held brush with stiff bristles. The horses seemed to enjoy the grooming. After several productive years, Uncle Tom bought a new Allis Chalmers tractor; painted the distinctive, bright orange, Allis Chalmers company color. Hooray! Most of my days spent looking at the wrong end of a horse were over!

Bob and his dog, Coloma, MI, 1935

My older cousin, Helen, took over some of her mother's duties, including house cleaning, canning, cooking, and sewing. At times she found it necessary to apply some much-needed discipline to me. On one winter day, Helen told me that if I did not stop one of my annoying antics, she would throw me into a backyard snow bank. I didn't, and she did! That got my attention quickly.

One of the things Aunt Ruth did to make financial ends meet, was to make and sell hooked rugs. The material used was tough chicken feed sacks, which were purchased from the Purina and Nappanee chicken feed companies, full of feed. The feed came in tightly stitched cloth bags, colorfully dyed with bright company lettering. When emptied, the chicken feed bags were washed, torn into narrow strips, and sewn end-to-end. The colorful long cloth strips were then hooked into an oval rug, using a straight three eighth inch round, dowel-like wooden hook, eight to ten inches long. When properly notched at one end, the hook was made. The rugs were brightly colored, oval shaped, and almost indestructible. Hooking rugs was one of the many things my Aunt Ruth Warren did in her spare time. She was, indeed, a hardworking, resourceful, and intelligent lady.

Helen Warren, 1933

George H. Warren, 1935

Chapter 2: High School & College

Coloma High School

During my high school freshman year, I rode my bicycle five miles to Coloma High School. On my route to school, I passed many farms. The Grootendorst's Flower Farm was spectacular in color, during the summer, and the early fall months. Approaching town, I rode down a hill, across the Little Paw Paw River bridge, and then up the hill on the opposite side of the river, where the North Coloma Road became Coloma's main street.

In earlier days, Coloma was first named Gilson's Shingle-Diggins, later Dickersville, and finally, Coloma. Coloma is the name of a fragrant flower that grew on the hills of California. Coloma was named by Stephen R. Gilson who had traveled to California, where he lived in the village of Coloma, during the gold rush. Returning to Dickersville, he renamed the community, Coloma.

Daily, I pedaled through Coloma, passing Doctor Khotler's In-Home Clinic, Claude Mast's Gasoline Station, and Charlie Shoup's Carpenter Shop. Then, I rode past Verne Grant's 5 & 10 cent Store, across the Pere Marquette Railroad tracks that, at ninety degrees, crossed Coloma's main street, passing Scott's Drug Store and the State Bank of Coloma. At this point, I rode on to the newly constructed Coloma High School. My Western Flyer bicycle, which I had purchased for five dollars, provided my daily transportation to and from Coloma High School for several months.

Then, on one Spring day, when riding too fast, I turned into a friend's driveway. My bicycle wheels lost traction on some loose gravel, and the bicycle slid from under me. I fell with the bicycle, breaking a bone in my lower right leg; probably when it was hit by the bicycle drive chain sprocket. After being taken home, Dr. Khotler was summoned. He came to our house, and set my leg. He then fashioned a thick plaster cast, encompassing the full length of my leg, from thigh to toes; where it remained for six weeks. I hobbled about on crutches until my broken shin bone knitted, and the leg cast was removed. I never again attended Coloma High School, except to play basketball and baseball games against my former Coloma High School classmates.

Covert High School

My resourceful Aunt Ruth Warren, decided that I should not ride my bicycle to school any further. She had my school records, including my passing freshman grades, transferred to the Covert Consolidated High School. Covert was a smaller town than was Coloma, and our farm was equal distance from each school. However, Covert had consolidated its schools, and had purchased a fleet of ten new REO Speed Wagon School Buses, and built a large, rounded-roof school bus garage.

Mr. George Packard was the head school bus driver. He was responsible for school bus maintenance, and for bus route scheduling. I could now ride to high school after walking only a block from our farmhouse, to a school bus stop located at the end of Coloma North Road, where it ended at the Van Buren County line. The student compartment of each bus was of wood construction; giving a long box-like appearance, with small windows along each side. Students entered and exited at the rear of the school bus, through a hinged door opened and closed by a responsible older student.

The forward interior of each bus opened into the driver's compartment. Students had no individual seats, thus requiring them to sit on long wooden benches built along each side of the bus. Each bus was painted a shiny dark brown color, and had a long, COVERT CONSOLIDATED SCHOOL sign, painted in six-inch gold colors lengthwise on the outside of each bus. The school buses had no other caution signs or warning lights. One of the school buses was also used to transport high school basketball and baseball teams to and from neighboring high schools for games, which were usually on Fridays.

I transferred to Covert Consolidated High School as a freshman, and attended there until I graduated with my twenty-four-member class in 1941. Based upon its student population, Covert was designated a Class "D" High School, which is the smallest high school designation assigned in the State of Michigan. While a student at Covert High School, I earned varsity letters in both basketball and baseball. I proudly wore my gold and blue varsity letter "C" on my blue school sweater. The Covert High School student population was too small to field a varsity football team.

The school did not have a kindergarten class. Children started school in first grade, and progressed through twelfth grade, in the same three-story red brick school building. My older siblings had graduated from Covert High School; Helen in 1933, and George in 1935. I graduated in 1941. The Covert Consolidated High School colors were blue and gold. The school mascot was a bulldog, and I still use that fact sometimes, to verify my computer password.

Meeting Millie

Soon after transferring to Covert High, I met a cute little classmate named Millie Weber. She became my best friend throughout our remaining high school years.

Her dad, Rudy Weber, served on the Covert School Board (without pay) for several years. He was very well-respected as a capable carpenter, and home builder. During the early 1920s, he had been an accomplished left-handed baseball pitcher for several professional minor league teams; including in Tulsa, Oklahoma, and Peoria, Illinois. Based on his pitching ability, he was signed to a

Major League baseball contract with the Chicago Cubs. His contract terms specified a seasonal salary of three thousand, five hundred dollars, plus an additional fifty dollars for each game he pitched. A copy of his contract with the Chicago Cubs is now on display in the Covert Township Library. He traveled with the Cubs baseball team to Pasadena, then to Catalina Island, located off the coast of Southern California, for baseball Spring training. The Chicago Cubs baseball team owner was Mr. P. K. Wrigley of Wrigley's chewing gum fame. The iconic home of the Chicago Cubs Major League Baseball team still carries his name, Wrigley Field.

The Peoria (IL) Tractors minor league team in the Illinois, Indiana, Iowa League, 1920. Rudy Weber, back row, on the left.

    The after-school basketball and baseball practices often caused me to miss my school bus ride home. So, I had to walk or hitch-hike home; a distance of approximately five miles. However, Mr. Rudy Weber, who loved sports, usually stopped to watch our practice sessions, and then he generously offered our team members rides home in his Ford pickup truck. I think he sensed that I was very fond of his daughter. So perhaps he was also evaluating me, a.k.a. "watching."

Millie Weber, age 16

I invited Millie to attend the Covert High School proms during both our Junior and Senior High School years. I recall how pretty she looked in her full-length white dress, that her mother and grandmother had sewn for her. Over it, she wore a long sleeve jacket. I borrowed my parent's 1933 Chevrolet Sedan, and drove to the proms, which were held in our High School gymnasium. Allowing me to use their car to take Millie to the proms, was a major concession on my parents' part. I had learned to drive at a much younger age; having driven my parents' 1926 "Model T" Ford truck around our farm. By comparison, the Chevrolet Sedan was real luxury.

Bob and Millie going to the Covert High School Prom (1941)

Millie and Bob, Covert High School (1941)

Another big event for me happened during my teenage years, when one day, a yellow Taylor Cub training airplane circled overhead, and then landed on the back forty acres of our farm. The pilot was my older brother, Bill Dean, who had learned to fly at Lee Roskay's Flying School in Niles, Michigan. Niles was located about thirty miles south of our farm, and just across the Michigan/Indiana border from South Bend, Indiana. I got a lot of bragging rights, having an older brother who was an airplane pilot. Accordingly, he became my hero. In those days, having a relative who was a pilot, was really a big deal. That event, no doubt, sparked my interest to later follow my brother, to become an airplane pilot.

Palisades Park

Following high school graduation in May 1941, I moved to a privately-owned, upscale resort community called Palisades Park. The community was in Covert Township, on the eastern shore of Lake Michigan; directly across Lake Michigan from Chicago. I roomed there with my high school classmate, Jim Overhuel, at his mother's residence, over the grocery and convenience store she owned and operated.

Millie also moved to a Palisades Park resort hotel, called the Sturdevant Lodge. She lived and worked there as a waitress, along with several of her female classmates.

I was hired by a man who owned a milk delivery truck and a gravel truck. His name was Tony Canoni, a local Covert man of Italian descent; whose principal efforts were maintaining the several miles of gravel roads throughout Palisades Park. He also ran a milk delivery route, serving the Palisades Park homeowners. He hired me to drive his milk delivery truck, and he drove the gravel truck. Tony Canoni had a knack for hiring dependable people, and I believe he felt that way about me. Tony had only a fourth-grade formal education, but he was honest, clever, and very street-smart. He later developed a very lucrative construction business. Many years later, I read in a West Coast newspaper that the Canoni Construction Company of South Haven, Michigan had been awarded a sixteen million dollar contract to remove an entire Southern California waste dump.

During WWII, Tony's company expanded rapidly; building shipping docks in San Francisco Bay, and airfields and highways throughout the country; all started by a very savvy gravel truck owner, and I like to think, by the kid who made deliveries in his milk truck. I've always been very proud of my early association with Tony Canoni.

I spent a wonderful summer in 1941 at beautiful Palisades Park, working for Tony Canoni, living rent free with my best high school buddy, and near my girlfriend who lived and worked nearby at the Sturdevant Lodge.

Her dad, Rudy Weber, was in Palisades Park almost every day; building or repairing residents' expensive houses. Sometimes, he received some rather unusual requests. For instance, he once received a call from a resident, telling Rudy that the resident had purchased a large wooden Purple Martin birdhouse in Minnesota, and was having it shipped to Palisades Park. Rudy Weber was asked to purchase a sturdy long wooden pole, attach the birdhouse atop it, and set the pole vertically in the ground on the property. He then was to call the resident, when the Purple Martins arrived, and moved into, their individual birdhouse apartments.

At Palisades Park I had a wonderful employer, who trusted me to operate his milk delivery service. Life was so good that I secretly wished the summer of 1941 would never end. But, unfortunately it did, when the wealthy resort homeowners arranged for Rudy Weber to shutter, and otherwise winterize their houses, before they moved back to their permanent homes; most to Chicago. That beautiful Palisades Park is now the site of a nuclear power plant. Progress? Go figure.

Michigan State College

During the summer, I had enrolled in Michigan State College, located in East Lansing, Michigan. At that same time, Millie Weber's older brother, Walt Weber, was starting his third year at Michigan State. He was pursuing a degree in agriculture. Michigan State then had five thousand six hundred students and it was sometimes referred to as "The Cow College."

Walt Weber provided me with a good insight into what my college life would be like. But, I still had no appreciation for the size of the college classes. My high school graduating class numbered twenty-four and many of the lectures at Michigan State had several hundred students packed into one lecture hall. I often had to scramble to find a seat.

At Michigan State College, I lived in a male student dormitory, named Abbot Hall. To pay my dormitory rent, tuition, books, and other student financial obligations, I took a job working in the on-campus dairy. Specifically, I joined a crew that operated the dairy's glass milk bottle washing machine. Here's how it worked: Six one-quart glass bottles at a time were fed into one end of the dairy's very large washing machine conveyor, and simultaneously, six clean bottles would emerge at the other end and be placed into clean wooden milk crates. The crates were then taken to another section of the dairy. After being filled with fresh milk, the clean glass bottles were capped with a round wax paper cap seal. Some empty bottles had the caps re-inserted into the empty bottles and these had to be removed before washing. We used short ice picks to penetrate the caps, and flip them from the empty bottles. During slack periods, we aimed and threw the ice picks end-over-end at the empty wooden crates. We had unofficial contests, to see who was the most skilled ice pick thrower.

The job required arrival and work starting every morning at six a.m. Payment for the job was adequate to meet my college expenses. However, the job had one major drawback. The job was a seven-day-a-week job, and just like dairy farming everywhere, the cows had to be fed and milked daily, using milking machines. Accordingly, the dairy also had to operate daily, which meant I had no free time to do anything except study and attend classes. On weekends the bottles still had to be washed, leaving me no free days - none!

After a few months, I tired of that time-demanding schedule, and applied for a job in downtown Lansing. I was hired to monitor the emergency call center at the Consumers Power Electric Company. An occasional severe storm would cause an electric power outage, or a home fire would require that I call out the electric company's emergency repair crew. Otherwise, it was usually a quiet, calm, and peaceful job atmosphere, which allowed me to study while working. My daily shifts were from six p.m. until midnight. I rode a city bus six miles each way between the East Lansing college campus and downtown Lansing. In addition, I had every other weekend free. So, I usually hitch-hiked home and back; a distance of about one hundred ten miles each way. Or, I went to see Millie, who was still attending business college, forty miles closer, in Kalamazoo.

Getting a ride when hitch-hiking was easy. We stood alongside a highway edge, next to our suitcase with a large green and white "S" decal on its side, indicating that we were Michigan State students. I was returning from a visit home on 7 December 1941, and between Battle Creek and Lansing, I caught a ride with a traveling businessman. He had his car radio turned on, and suddenly the program was interrupted by a flash news message: The U.S. Navy Base at Pearl Harbor in Hawaii had been attacked by enemy Japanese aircraft!

At that time, I really had little appreciation for the effect that attack would have on the rest of my life. Very soon, however, I learned that it would have a very profound and lasting effect. I finished my freshman year at Michigan State College, in June 1942.

I returned home; where I took several part time jobs, trying to save as much money as possible to meet my college expenses for the next year. I vividly recall that one of my temporary jobs was shoveling coal over the six-foot side of a metal railroad coal car, using a large scoop shovel. In two days, I emptied the coal car, by shoveling several tons of coal into the coal bin of the Michigan Shore Lumber and Supply Company in South Haven. Such work would probably now be termed labor-intensive, but I was very strong, and glad to prove I could do it.

I also considered traveling to Alaska, where fish canning companies offered their newly hired employees' railroad and ship tickets to and from Alaska. Those canning companies paid their temporary seasonal employees very well. I calculated that in three months, I could have earned enough money to pay my expenses for my next entire college year. But, at age eighteen, I had to register for the military draft, and that sharply changed all thoughts regarding my college education, and my future.

Military Service 1942

Realizing that I was strong, healthy, unmarried, and having no serious family hardships, it was just a matter of time, before I received my notice to report somewhere for military training. I quickly explored several options. My first choice, probably inspired by my older brother, Bill Dean, was to serve as a military pilot. I contacted a U.S. Army Air Corps recruiter who told me that I qualified for pilot training, with the caveat that I would have to pass the Army's flight physical examination. Exploring further, I learned that the U.S. Army intended to expand its troop-carrying glider program. I discussed this with the Army recruiter who told me that he could not guarantee what type of an aircraft I would fly, be it fighters, bombers, training planes, or gliders. There was no way I wanted to fly, or even ride in, any airplane without an engine. Gliders? No thanks!

So, I contacted a U.S. Navy recruiter about the Navy's pilot training program. He assured me, that Naval aviation had no gliders in its aircraft inventory, nor was any such program planned or anticipated. After passing another flight physical examination, I joined the Navy Aviation V-5 pilot training program. I was ordered to Detroit, where I was sworn in as an aviation cadet in what was called the Naval Aviation V-5 Program.

The initial phase of the program provided for flight instruction at a Civilian Pilot Training (CPT) facility. This training was to determine, early on, just who really did or did not want to fly, and to also quickly eliminate cadets, who for various reasons, simply could not be taught to fly. The V-5 program also had the provision, that if a cadet failed any phase of pilot training, he would be retained in the Navy, with the enlisted rank of Seaman Second Class. This elimination process was to spare the Navy the expense of sending all its aviation cadets to formal preflight schools, established at one of five major universities. Not knowing whether some cadets really wanted to fly, or could even be taught to fly, the Navy wisely first assigned all new aviation cadets to relatively inexpensive CPT schools.

Civilian Pilot Training at Austin Lake

The cadets were organized, placed in groups of ten or less, and ordered to a designated local CPT school, where they were issued khaki uniforms with no rank insignia. My cadet group was ordered to the CPT school located at the Western State Teachers

College, in Kalamazoo, Michigan. Our flight instruction was at the small Austin Lake Airport, which was located a few miles south of Kalamazoo. We were billeted in the college dormitory, ate meals in the college student cafeteria, and were bussed daily to and from the Austin Lake airfield. We received no pay.

Before starting flight instruction, we attended ground school for a week, in college classrooms. We learned the basic aircraft forces of lift, thrust, and drag. We also studied weather patterns; including the names of various cloud formations, and what each formation meant, insofar as flying was concerned. The danger of thunderstorms was always stressed. We learned about gas tank capacities, and the various airspeed, altitude, rate of climb, compass, and aircraft engine instruments, which were mounted on small wooden blocks on classroom tables.

Aircraft safety precautions were stressed constantly. Before we started to fly, we were aware of the dangers of whirling aircraft propellers. We were shown pictures of the signs painted on the superstructures of large aircraft carriers, which read: "BEWARE OF PROPELLERS."

After a week-long ground school in the college classrooms, we were bused to Austin Lake, where we would begin flight instruction. The small, grass-surfaced airport was owned by Mr. Irving Woodham, a Fixed Base Operator (FBO) who met our bus, and welcomed us. He then introduced us to our assigned civilian pilot flight instructors. My instructor was Howard Shakaski who, like all others flight instructors teaching Navy cadets, had to be a Certified CPT Instructor. I found out later that my older brother, Bill Dean, was a CPT Certified flight instructor at the Stockert Flying School, in South Bend, Indiana.

Each instructor was assigned two cadets. My instructor led us to one of six spanking-new Aeronca Champion civilian training airplanes. They had recently been flown to Austin Lake from the

Aeronca manufacturing plant in Middleton, Ohio. All six had identical single high wings. Each was painted bright blue, with large black civilian identification numbers painted on top and underneath the wing. Each was powered by a four-cylinder, sixty-five HP engine.

The two pilot seats (cockpits) were arranged in tandem. We were told that the flight instructors would occupy the front cockpit, and students, the rear. Each cockpit had identical flight controls, consisting of a centered control stick, rudder pedals, throttles, and instruments. The single ignition switch was placed so that it could be reached from either cockpit.

Our group of cadets spent at least two hours watching the outside airplane control surfaces move, when the corresponding cockpit controls were moved. Our instructor explained the function of tail elevators and rudders, and the wing ailerons. We took turns moving the controls, while seated in the rear cockpit. We were instructed to make sure the ignition switch was in the "Off" position, and then loudly call out, "Switch Off," every time we entered the cockpit.

The single gasoline gauge was a stiff vertical wire, protruding through the top of the wing. The gasoline tank was mounted inside the top aircraft wing, and it was filled from the top. The gauge wire was fastened to a float inside the gasoline tank, and protruded vertically, threading through a small hole on top of the wing. In this position, the wire could easily be viewed from either cockpit, to check the amount of gasoline remaining in the tank.

Our first day at Austin Lake ended with no flying. As we boarded the bus for our ride back to our college dormitory, all the cadets were very quiet, as we tried to remember all we had learned that day about the airplane, and the many safety rules that were emphasized. Probably for the first time, we realized that flying was an undertaking not to be taken lightly. During the evening, many of us drifted back to our ground school classroom, to once again study the various instruments we had just seen mounted in a real airplane cockpit for the first time. I went to sleep that night, realizing that "Switch Off" meant exactly that, and with visions of whirling propeller dangers.

  The second day, when we got off our bus at Austin Lake, the entire instructor staff was waiting to meet us. We were told we would review all we learned the previous day. We then learned how to safely start the engine. With one instructor in the front cockpit, another instructor demonstrated how the engines were hand cranked. But, before touching the propeller, he called, "Switch off." The instructor inside confirmed that the switch was in the "Off" position, and then loudly repeated, "Switch Off." He also ensured that the engine throttle was slightly cracked open. The cranking instructor then approached the airplane directly, from the front; making sure that his body would always be outside the turning plane propeller. Against engine compression, he turned the propeller several times, causing a small amount of gasoline to be injected into each of the four cylinders. He then positioned one propeller blade high and to his left, and then stepped back and called, "Contact!" The inside instructor switched the ignition to the "On" position and loudly responded, "Contact!"

  Hearing that, the cranking instructor stepped forward, and gripped the top of the high blade with both hands. To establish momentum and power, he kicked his right foot forward; then swung his entire body down and away from the airplane propeller. Thus, in a single motion, he pulled the blade sharply down, and released his grip, while swinging his entire body safely down and away from the now running engine, and its dangerous whirling propeller. We had been instructed to always approach an airplane from behind the wing, when its engine was running. We practiced this several times, taking turns pulling ropes attached to triangle-shaped blocks (chocks), from in front of the two main landing gear wheels.

Now the airplane, with chocks pulled, and with both instructor and student in their cockpits, was free to taxi to the end of the runway, before taking off. For the first few instructional flights, the student followed through by holding the controls and throttle lightly, while the instructor taxied and took off and loudly, over the engine noise, explained what he was doing, and why he was doing it. In one day, each of our cadets had his initial instructional flight. On their bus ride back to Kalamazoo that afternoon, there was constant and loud chatter by the cadets, as all tried to describe their first training flight.

After days of quiet instruction, we had all been surprised at how noisy the engine was. We also learned a cardinal flying rule that day: *If your engine fails during takeoff, land straight ahead into the wind.* Do not try to turn back to the airfield, because you will quickly run out of altitude and airspeed; the airplane will stall; it will crash, and probably kill you. During my later instruction flights, when I was taking off, my instructor would often suddenly chop the throttle back to the idle position, simulating engine failure, to test my immediate reaction. He would then quickly add throttle, and let me continue the takeoff climb.

During the first few instructional flights, we would take off, leave the airfield traffic pattern, and climb to an altitude of three thousand feet. The instructor would then completely take control, and demonstrate both power-off and power-on stalls, *caused by too little airflow over the wing,* noting the airspeed when each stall occurred.

Next, after stalling the airplane, he would demonstrate tailspins, and spin recovery technique, explaining that the airplane rudder was the only effective control when the airplane was spinning in a stalled condition. Therefore, to recover from a tailspin, the pilot must first stop the spin by applying full opposite rudder, and then the pilot sharply must drop the nose of the airplane to regain flying speed. After those maneuvers were demonstrated several times, my instructor told me, "Take us home."

Having no appreciation for how far we had flown, or where we were, quickly taught me to always be aware of my location in relation to our home Austin Lake airfield. Further, I learned to check the fuel gauge often, so that I would always know how much fuel was remaining. When approaching the home airfield for landing, I had to remember to look for the airfield windsock that gave wind direction and wind speed. Upon entering the landing pattern, I had to maintain specific altitudes, airspeeds, glides, and approach directions. After landing, parking the airplane, and exiting the cockpits, my instructor would review all that we had done on that flight. I soon realized that flying required long pre-flight and post-flight briefings; and that flying was going to be very noisy!

On subsequent flights, I was permitted to control the airplane almost completely, as the instructor verbally corrected what I was doing. He pointed out landmarks around the airfield, thus making me very aware of where we were in relation to our home airport. I was taught to look for the airfield windsock to check surface wind direction and speed and to use the airplane compass to follow established directions, and to keep the airplane on a straight course. In addition, I was warned to always to keep an eye on the fuel gauge.

Our two daily training flights were each an hour long. When approaching the airport for landing, I was taught to enter the pattern at an altitude of one thousand feet Above Ground Level (AGL), and that the correct angle to intercept the downwind leg of the landing pattern was forty-five degrees. After completing a right turn of another forty-five degrees, we correctly joined the landing downwind leg, paralleling the runway, and then passed the airport boundary, while maintaining one thousand feet AGL. Then, we made a ninety-degree left turn to the landing pattern base leg, while simultaneously throttling back, and descending to five hundred feet.

Proper airspeed was maintained, while still descending, and again turning left, lining up with the runway on the final approach leg, and still descending toward the landing runway. When over the landing runway, the throttle was completely reduced (chopped), as the airplane floated just above the landing runway, losing airspeed until the wing lost lift, and the plane settled (touched down) on the runway. The landing roll out direction on the runway was maintained by steering with the rudder, which also operated a steerable tail wheel.

After landing, the aircraft was taxied to its parking spot. The engine was stopped while idling, by turning the ignition switch off. My instructor and I then exited our cockpits, and made sure the airplane was properly tied down, and the wheels were chocked before we left the flight line.

First Solo Flight

After several days of instruction away from the airfield, my instructor told me that we would stay in the airport flight pattern during the next flight. After each landing touchdown, the throttle was opened, as I accomplished touch-and-go landings and takeoffs. Following the third landing, we stopped, and he got out; telling me to taxi to the takeoff end of the runway, takeoff, stay in the pattern, land, and stop near where he was standing.

The one thing I remember most about that - my first solo flight - was how empty the airplane seemed, without the instructor in the front cockpit. I was alone, all by myself in that airplane! That solo flight was scary stuff.

After landing, and stopping near him as directed, he came over to my cockpit, shook my hand and congratulated me for making my first solo flight. Even today, the thrill of that great day remains very clear among my many flying memories. Our CPT flight training at Kalamazoo lasted only five weeks.

Meanwhile with Millie

After graduating from high school and spending a wonderful summer at Palisades Park, Millie moved to Kalamazoo, where she enrolled at Maher's Business College. One of her classmates was Betty Vischer; whose parents were celery farmers, living in the township of Portage, near the Kalamazoo airport, and only a few miles from Austin Lake. The Vischers invited Millie to move into their home with their daughter Betty, so that they could attend business college classes together, and Millie could assist with celery planting and harvesting.

Among the Vischer's farm implement inventory was a small celery planting machine, which was powered by a small gasoline engine. When operating properly, the machine followed a guide wire stretched tightly across large flat celery planting fields. The machine had two seats for the occupant planters, who rode low over the ground while feeding small celery shoots from a large seedling tray, into the two planting wheel receptacles. The planting wheels rotated into the soil a few inches, leaving the small celery shoots planted in two straight rows across the field. Each field-crossing took about an hour.

Occasionally, the stretched guide wire would loosen, because the end anchors did not remain tight. That happened one day, when Millie and Betty were the planting machine operators. The wire no longer kept the machine on a straight course, and now, free from its guide wire, it selected its own direction across the planting field. Unaware of a slight change in direction, they happily rode along, planting and talking, without a care in the world. The unguided machine continued planting in the wrong direction, until noticed by Mr. Vischer, who shouted for them to stop. While he repositioned the machine, and tightened its guide wire, the girls were told to pull up all the celery shoots that had been planted in the wrong direction. They were mildly admonished by Mr. Vischer, who suggested that they pay more attention to the planting machine, and less time discussing their business college machines, or more likely, their recent dates. However, Mr. Vischer was probably secretly amused, understanding his hired hands were two carefree, giggling girls.

Bob and Millie, Austin Lake airfield, 1942

    Millie and Betty visited the Austin Lake airport often, and became acquainted with the other cadets; one of whom was Harold "Hal" Hawkins from Kalamazoo, who I didn't see again until stationed on the island of Saipan in 1945. I was not permitted to fly with passengers, because doing so was prohibited by Navy regulations. Too, I was a very inexperienced pilot who had yet to receive a private pilot's license. However, I proudly showed them the airplanes, and enthusiastically described some of my harrowing flying experiences. They also met several of our instructors; one of whom was Sandy Allen, who took Millie flying in a smaller Aeronca that was powered by a small, two-cylinder, thirty-seven horsepower (HP) engine. The side-by-side, two cockpit design created an unusual shape, and accordingly, that Aeronca C-2 was nicknamed "The Flying Bathtub".

Returning to Michigan State College

Those wonderful days ended abruptly, when I finished my CPT training at Austin Lake, and received new orders to attend a more advanced CPT school at Michigan State College, in East Lansing. The school consisted of only flying, with no ground school classes. Again, I lived in a student dormitory, and ate in the college cafeteria.

Except for flying, I returned to my very familiar Michigan State College campus surroundings. Our flying lessons were taught at the Lansing, Michigan Airport, in Waco UPF-7 biplanes, which had two open cockpits. Years later, in May 2011, I was enshrined into the Michigan Aviation Hall of Fame, in Kalamazoo, along with Clayton J. Brukner. Brukner had started, and owned the company that designed and built the Waco UPF-7 biplanes, as well as other Waco models.

Flying in open cockpits in Michigan in November and December is cold, and required wearing a warm sheepskin lined flying suit, sheepskin lined boots, helmet, and gloves. In the school, basic acrobatic maneuvers, including inverted flight, slow rolls, and loops were demonstrated and practiced. Two-plane formation flights also taught me that flying next to another airplane could be done safely.

The CPT Advanced Course at Lansing lasted only three weeks. From there, I was ordered to again report to the U.S. Navy Induction Center at Detroit, by 31 December 1942. That slight delay gave me time to return home, celebrate Christmas, and say goodbye to my family, to Millie and her family, and to other friends, before following my orders to attend the U.S. Navy Preflight School, at the University of Iowa.

Chapter 3: Preflight and Primary Flight Training

Iowa Preflight School

On 31 December 1942, along with many other cadet CPT graduates, I again reported to the U.S. Navy Induction Center in Detroit. After receiving Naval Aviation Cadet identification cards, we were issued dark blue U.S. Navy Officer Uniforms with no rank insignia, an overcoat, and a hat with a gold colored metal anchor centered above the visor of the hat. The list of uniform issued items included black uniform shoes, black socks and neckties, white shirts, and under clothing. Mailing boxes were provided, to send our civilian clothing home, and we were paid our first seventy-five dollar monthly Aviation Cadet pay.

Proudly wearing our new uniforms, we boarded a Pere Marquette Railroad train, with a destination of Chicago; and then continued on to the Navy Preflight School in Iowa City. As the train passed through my home town of Coloma, I got a glimpse of Scott's Drug Store, Vern Grant's 5 & 10 Cent Store, and the familiar basket factory. The train then passed through the next village of Riverside, where I was born.

Arriving in Chicago, we joined hundreds of uniformed Navy cadets, arriving from other Midwestern induction centers. Following a delay of several hours, we boarded another train, bound for Iowa City. On arrival, we were transported by U.S. Navy buses to a student dormitory on the University of Iowa campus.

Four cadets were assigned to a room. We were provided postcards to be mailed home, informing our families that we had arrived safely, and to provide our Preflight School mailing address. Navy Preflight Schools had been established at four major universities, and one college. In addition to Iowa (Iowa City), the others were in Georgia (Athens), North Carolina (Chapel Hill), and California (St. Mary's) and Washington (Seattle).

Bob Warren, Navy Preflight School, Univ. of Iowa, 1943

Preflight school lasted three months. One-half of each day was devoted to academics, and the other half to calisthenics, including marching (close order drill). All cadets boxed, played football, wrestled, and swam in the University's indoor swimming pool. The swimming instructor was the University's swimming coach, named Bardo. His favorite admonishment to cadets as he paced back and forth along the pool edge was, "If you can't swim, go to the bottom of the pool and do pushups." The cadets christened the swimming pool "Bardo's Beach".

In addition to swimming, water exercises included jumping into the deep end of the pool fully clothed, and then removing our trousers. While treading water, we tied knots in the lower trouser legs then flipped them over our heads to capture air. Holding the wet trousers at the waist to prevent air from escaping, we were taught use them as a floatation device.

Our water exercise instruction also required jumping into the pool wearing a standard yellow Naval Aviator's "Mae West" life jacket. The jacket had two sections; and one, or both sections could be inflated, by pulling cords that released gas from two small metal cylinders; each instantly inflating one half of the jacket. Additionally, we were taught to inflate the life jacket manually, by blowing air through two small rubber tubes; each attached to one section of the life jacket.

The rigors of college football were considered perfect for cadet wartime physical preparation. Several college football athletes and coaches were recruited as preflight school instructors. For instance, the former University of Michigan football team captain, Forest Evashevski, was a commissioned U.S. Navy Lieutenant, and he played on the Iowa Pre-Flight Seahawks football team in 1942. The Seahawks football team was initially coached by former University of Minnesota football coach Bernie Bierman, who had been commissioned a Lieutenant Colonel in the Marine Corps Reserve, and then assigned to head the entire Iowa Preflight School athletic program. The Seahawks football team records were: in 1942: 7–3 (coach Bierman); in 1943: 9–1 (coach Faurot); in 1944: 10–1 (coach Meagher). The Seahawks played against other Big-10 football teams, and other service academy teams as well. Forest Evashevski later coached the University of Iowa football team from 1952-1960. His Iowa Hawkeyes football teams won the Rose Bowl game twice; in 1957, and in 1959. When I attended the Iowa Navy Preflight School, Forest Evashevski was my football and wrestling coach.

The academics half of each day was spent in university classrooms, studying basic celestial navigation, learning and practicing Morse Code, using actual telegraph keys and large detached shipboard blinker lights. Aircraft navigation was taught by using flat plotting boards that were fifteen inches square. In flight, the plotting boards were fitted under the cockpit instrument panel. When slid into a special slot below the instrument panel, the plotting boards were automatically locked into position by small spring-loaded latches. Those latches prevented the plotting board from sliding back into the pilot's lap during the violent aircraft carrier catapult takeoff accelerations. After takeoff, the plotting boards could be pulled from their special slots for navigational use. During operations, the plotting boards were considered the personal property of each pilot. We were encouraged to insert a small picture of a loved one under the see-through plotting board surface; with the intent of reminding us to always check our navigation.

Known navigation data was written on the plotting boards during simulated mission briefings, in the Pilot Ready Room. In addition, the correct wind speed, the ship's course, and the ship's Speed of Advance (SOA) were written on the plotting boards, just before the loudspeaker ordered, "Pilots, man your planes". We were taught that the wind direction could be calculated by observing the sea surface whitecaps. We learned that the foam from breaking ocean whitecaps always slid down the backside of a breaking wave into the prevailing wind, thus providing near correct surface wind direction. From observing the number of whitecaps, pilots could quite accurately calculate wind speed. When properly used, a plotting board assisted returning pilots in finding their aircraft carrier, which typically had steamed many miles since their takeoff. Thus, the practical value of pre-plotting the ship's SOA, the ship's course, and underway steaming direction became an obvious step in the prevention of ditching at sea, by lost returning pilots.

To ensure that the necessary wind speed down the flight deck was achieved, aircraft carriers always launched aircraft into the wind. Learning to use a plotting board, in the safety of a preflight school classroom, greatly assisted future Naval aviators in solving actual moving base problems. At this point, I realized that the knowledge gained in the preflight school classrooms, was becoming deadly serious.

In other classes, we were taught recognition of enemy Japanese, German, and Italian aircraft and ships. Mixed silhouettes of friendly and enemy ships and aircraft were flashed on a movie screen for a few seconds. When we recognized a ship or aircraft, we loudly shouted out, "Friendly!" or "Enemy!"

All of our Preflight School studies related to Naval warfare. Navy terminology and jargon was taught, and used, including: forward, aft, ladders, corpsman, mess deck, coxswain, log out, midships, capstans, hawsers, wardroom, fantail, stern, bow, tugs, Captain's Mast, flight deck, arresting hooks, hangar deck, galley, and the locations of the ship's bridge, brig, flag plot, pre-fly, and sick bay. For me, the most confusing Navy terminology was, "Lay before the mast, all the eight o'clock reports." I could only make a feeble attempt to explain that shipboard order, so I'll just skip it.

We also learned that Marines were forbidden by Navy Regulations to ever command U.S. Navy vessels. Even the landing craft, transporting Marines to a hostile landing beach, were driven by enlisted U.S. Navy Coxswains. However, armed Amphibian Tractors (AMTRACS) were driven by Marines because, after reaching the landing beach, the AMTRACS could then be driven over the beach to maneuver and fight on dry land.

Social life for cadets was extremely limited, as classes were held six days a week, with a two-hour study period each evening. On Sundays, cadets could leave the campus to attend the church of their choice. If they didn't have one, they quickly "got religion," and declared their religious preference, just to have a valid excuse to leave the campus on Sunday to attend church services, and to enjoy some Iowa City sights, which usually included University of Iowa co-eds.

On Sunday afternoons, tea dances were held for the cadets in the campus field house. Girls who desired to attend were required to sign up during the week prior, and were required to ride Navy buses to and from the campus field house. The girls were not permitted to leave the dance area of the field house for any reason. Probably for the protection of all participants, the tea dances were sternly chaperoned. Despite all the restrictive rules, the tea dances were very popular. Live dance music was provided; thereby making the dances very enjoyable for both the girls, and their cadet dancing partners.

Until aviation cadets had completed training, and received their gold Naval Aviator Wings, and commissions as Navy Ensigns, or as Marine Corps Second Lieutenants, they were not permitted to marry. The consequences of violating that rule, were swift and guaranteed. A newly married cadet would be immediately dropped from further aviation flight training, and quickly transferred elsewhere, to continue service as a Navy enlisted seaman.

Upon completion, Preflight School had no formal ending. We simply left our dormitory rooms clean, inspected, and ready for the next arriving battalion (class). I was in the 17th battalion.

Naval Air Station (NAS), Ottumwa, Iowa

Many Preflight School graduates were ordered to board trains, transporting them to Primary Flight Training Naval Air Stations, including New Orleans, Louisiana; Norman, Oklahoma; Hutchison and Olathe, Kansas; Livermore, California; and Pasco, Washington. My orders were to proceed, via a Navy bus, to the Naval Air Station at Ottumwa, Iowa, which was a distance of about one hundred miles. I wondered if I would ever leave Iowa and see an ocean, because here I was in the middle of the United States, as far from salt water as I could possibly get.

Upon arrival at the Ottumwa Naval Air Station (NAS), I noted that construction had not yet been fully completed; but limited flight training had already begun. I was in the second group of cadets arriving for flight training. The base (NAS, Ottumwa) had been formally commissioned by the Secretary of the Navy, Frank Knox only a few weeks before I arrived.

Everything was new; including a large, round asphalt takeoff and landing mat, that served as an all-directions temporary aircraft runway. A large, colorful windsock, lighted at night, established proper takeoff and landing directions. After moving into a new two-story cadet barracks, we were issued one-piece khaki flying suits, helmets and goggles, leather flight jackets, and thin soft leather flight gloves. We were taken to the flight line, where we viewed rows of yellow Stearman-Boeing N2S training biplanes, neatly lined up, wing tip to wing tip. Each had "U.S. Navy" painted in large black letters on top of the right-wing surface, and under the bottom of the lower left wing. Before climbing into our airplane, we had to sign the yellow sheet, indicating that we had inspected, and accepted, that airplane for flight. Upon return from a flight, any aircraft discrepancies were noted on the same yellow sheet.

Behind that flight line, a row of low, gray, wooden sheds had been built to store packed, ready-for-use parachutes, alongside more sheds that housed aircraft maintenance and equipment. Red fire extinguishers, resting on two-wheel dollies, were positioned the entire length of the flight line - one for each airplane.

Parachutes were repacked periodically, in a distant, temperature-controlled, on-base parachute loft, with a two-story tower at one end. Inside the tower, open parachutes were hung and inspected by enlisted parachute riggers, who had completed training at the U.S. Navy Parachute Riggers School at NAS, Lakehurst, New Jersey. After inspection, repairing, and repacking, the parachutes - each with a harness attached - were transported back to the flight line parachute shack, ready again for issue to pilots. Parachute and harness, including the all-important metal rip cord grip, became a single unit, with the chute hanging low in back.

Watching a pilot walk toward his airplane, with a low-hanging packed parachute bumping his rear with each step he took, was comical. After reaching his plane, the pilot stepped up onto the lower left wing, and gripping a handle on the top wing, stepped into the open cockpit, and stood upright, facing forward. When he then sat in the cockpit, the parachute lowered into the seat pan; becoming his seat cushion. While lowering himself, his feet moved forward, and rested lightly on the adjustable rudder pedals. The pilot then connected two straps, extending from the center of his parachute harness, over his legs, to snaps on each side of his parachute harness. Next, the pilot pulled the two sides of his upper harness together, and snapped them in front of his chest. The pilot then strapped himself to the airplane, by pulling tight, and locking a wide safety belt tightly across his lap. The pilot and the airplane now became a single entity, ready to fly.

One-way communication from instructor to student was accomplished through a flexible rubber tube, called a gosport. When I started flying at Ottumwa, Iowa on 14 April 1943, I did not realize that exactly one year from that date, Millie and I would be married at Vero Beach, Florida.

The flight training program at NAS, Ottumwa was standardized, and purposely challenging. The program moved a cadet along rapidly, flying the sturdy Stearman N2S "Yellow Peril" biplanes, with two open cockpits. Each Lycoming two hundred twenty-five HP radial engine was started, by an enlisted plane captain inserting a crank into a matching slot behind the left side of the engine, where it engaged a heavy inertial wheel, and clockwise cranking began. When that hidden, inertial wheel was determined to be fast enough, the crank was removed, and the plane captain moved away from the engine, past the airplane wingtip. When the pilot saw that the area near the engine was clear, he turned on the double ignition switch, and engaged the inertial wheel to start the engine. The engines almost always started, but if not, the pilot turned off the ignition switches and the inertial wheel had to be cranked again; much to the displeasure of the enlisted plane captain, who again had to do the cranking.

NAS, Ottumwa had an aircraft control tower. However, the N2S Stearmans had no radios. So, airport control from the tower was accomplished by very bright Aldis lamps, which emitted a bright green, red, or white light. The colors, steady or flashing, had different meanings to aircraft in flight or on the ground. For instance, a steady green light from the tower to an approaching aircraft, meant that an aircraft was cleared to land. The pilot would acknowledge the lamp instruction by rocking the aircraft wings, or at night, by blinking the aircraft navigation lights.

Following several solo flights, we were taught combat flying formations, acrobatics, and night flying. We learned that aircraft navigation lights were red on the left, green on the right, and white at the tail; no doubt copied from standard surface ship lighting. The Iowa spring weather was balmy, and the instructors were excellent. I had all Navy instructors, mostly Ensigns and Lieutenants, Junior Grade, ranks corresponding to 2nd and 1st Lieutenants in the Marine Corps and the Army. After three instructional flights, I soloed, and felt good about finally flying a real U.S. Navy airplane.

The flight training program at NAS, Ottumwa was well planned. Soon after solo flights, our instructors started teaching us acrobatics. Some would be rather violent, including entering and recovering from tailspins. The spins, loops, Immelmann turns, and all other maneuvers required anticipation, and coordination of engine and flight controls. Most maneuvers pulled a few Gs on the aircraft; but not enough to cause pilot blackout. I quickly became used to flying inverted, and hanging from my strong seat belt; which kept me inside the cockpit. Flying inverted had to be of very short duration, because the engine fuel tank was in the top wing above the engine, which was gravity-fed. Inverted flight quickly starved the engine, and it would first sputter, and then quit running.

    I quickly became accustomed to two-plane, then four-plane formation flying. Now, the training planes I had flown at Kalamazoo were, by comparison to the more powerful and sturdy N2S, rather flimsy little airplanes. The Stearman N2S was fabric covered, but considered to be a tough bird; built to sustain several Gs. The plane was known as an honest airplane, as it had no unusual flying characteristics, and did exactly what the pilot expected. Over ten thousand of them were built for our Armed Forces, during WWII.

    Wapello County, Iowa had many pig farms, and one of my instructors took great delight in diving low over those farms. He loved to watch the pigs scatter and run. He thought that was great fun; although I doubt the farmers were very amused.

    One of the maneuvers taught, and one that that I really enjoyed, was called "slips to a circle." The maneuver was taught, in case a pilot needed to lose altitude quickly, for an emergency landing, in the event of, for instance an engine failure. To practice, the pilot would approach a desired landing spot, purposely higher than normal. Then, after chopping the engine throttle back to idle to simulate engine failure, the pilot would cross control. That is, the rudder would be pushed completely in one direction, and the control stick fully deflected in the opposite direction. This action pushed the side of the airplane fuselage against the prevailing wind. To prevent a stall, safe airspeed had to be maintained. Part of the wing was blanked out, causing some lower wing lift loss. The net result created the slip. To practice "slips to a circle," we were taught to approach the suitable landing field, pick a spot ahead and into the prevailing wind, slipping the aircraft until treetops or other obstacles were avoided, and then stop the slip. If done right, a successful engine-failed, dead-stick landing was made on a marked surface circle.

Night Flight Training

On April 14, 1943 I had my first flight in the Stearman N2S, and by the end of April, I had logged twenty-one flight hours on sixteen flights. During May, I logged fifty-five flight hours on thirty-three flights. The flight training syllabus included three night flights.

I took off with an instructor on my first night flight. All planes had their red, green, and white navigation (running) lights turned on. On my first night flight, the instructor told me to stay in the airfield pattern, establish a safe interval with other planes, and watch the tower for a green light, before making each landing. While making the first two established pattern circuits, I could feel him moving the controls, from the other cockpit. He then climbed out, and told me that I had done just fine. He directed me to fly around in pattern, three more times, land, and then taxi back to the flight line; where the plane captain directed me to the proper flight line parking spot, using two handheld flashlights.

My next two flights were night solo flights. I enjoyed night flying at Ottumwa because the night air was usually still; which made for smooth night flying. I did considerably more night flying before WWII ended.

Carrier on the Prairie

NAS, Ottumwa was also known as the "carrier on the prairie." An Ottumwa lady, Elsie Mae Cofer, authored a book with that title. At one time, the Base had about three thousand five hundred personnel assigned, including cadets. One, who later became well known, was a Naval Officer named Richard Nixon. Another cadet who trained at Ottumwa, was Scott Carpenter who went on to become a Navy test pilot. He was also a pioneer on the Mercury Astronaut Project and the second American to orbit the earth; after John Glenn. Another NAS, Ottumwa-trained cadet became the Navy's first black pilot. His name was Jessie Brown. Flying from the aircraft carrier USS *Leyte*, he made the ultimate sacrifice in North Korea, following a successful wheels-up landing in his damaged F4U Corsair. The weather was bitterly cold. He was trapped in the cockpit, and died of his injuries, and exposure to the extreme cold temperatures.

When flying, I noticed that a streamline train would make a brief daily afternoon stop at Ottumwa. I learned it was the Burlington Zephyr, which shuttled daily between Chicago and Denver, with stops at Ottumwa each way. Thereafter, I requested to get on the flight schedule on Friday mornings. This schedule allowed me to start my off-base liberty on Friday afternoons, and not report in until Monday morning. I would board that Burlington Zephyr, ride to Chicago, transfer to the South Shore Electric Railroad, and ride to Michigan City, Indiana, following stops at the East Chicago, and the Gary, Indiana stations. I called ahead to let Millie know when I would be arriving, so that I would be met and driven home to nearby Southern Michigan, where I spent most of the weekend. On Sunday, I would reverse course, arriving back at Ottumwa on Sunday evening. Seeing Millie, and my family, was much better than attending the rather boring tea dances, scheduled each Sunday afternoon. Most of the girls who attended those dances were employed by the J. T. Morrell Meat Packing Company, in Ottumwa, and their hair always had some stockyard fragrance.

Engagement to Millie at "Autumn-wa," Iowa

After I made that trip home by train a couple of times, I suggested to Millie that she come to Ottumwa, and surprisingly, she did! In Chicago, she asked a ticket agent for a ticket to "Autumn-wa, Iowa." He laughed, and told her how you were supposed to pronounce it. The weekend she arrived at "Autumn-wa" she stayed from Friday evening, until Monday. We became engaged, knowing of course that we could not get married while I was still a cadet. I had saved most of my monthly seventy-five dollar paychecks, and was pretty confident that she would accept my marriage proposal. I used some of my savings to purchase an engagement ring for her in Iowa City. The diamond was quite small, but she wore it for years, until I replaced that ring on our twenty-fifth wedding anniversary with a new ring that had much larger stones. By then, I was a Lieutenant Colonel on active duty, and could afford a larger diamond ring. I bought the new ring at a jewelry store in the Fashion Island Mall in Newport Beach, California from Claire Gilman, the wife of a Marine Corps pilot friend of mine, Major George "Gizmo" Gilman. The ring was made of two interlocked rings, which were set beautifully. Millie wore the rings, with her wedding band, for the rest of her life. After she passed away on 8 January 2010, I gave her rings to our daughter Jeanne, and she still enjoys wearing them.

My final flight at Ottumwa was a night flight, on 28 May 1943. Soon thereafter, I was ordered to NAS, Corpus Christi, Texas, for more advanced flight training.

NAS, Corpus Christi, Texas

From Ottumwa, I rode an antiquated train to Dallas. I am not sure when that steam engine train was built, but the cars still had tapestries and tassels. The train looked like something dating back to the Civil War. We stopped in towns, long enough for us to eat at local restaurants, while the steam engine took on water from a trackside water tank. Rumor had it that our troop train was so slow, that we had to stop, so the faster freight trains could pass. While riding from Ottumwa, Iowa to Dallas, Texas, we took turns sitting outside on the rear platform of the last car; two at a time, we dangled our feet. We really enjoyed the ride; although it seemed to take forever to get away from Iowa, and finally to Dallas, after passing through the rural farms and ranches in Iowa, Missouri, Kansas, Oklahoma, and Texas.

Upon arrival in Dallas, we boarded The Sunbeam, a more modern train with a diesel engine that offered a very pleasant ride to Corpus Christi, where we arrived on 4 July 1943. We were still wearing our winter uniforms from Ottumwa, as specified in our orders. The weather at Corpus Christi was very hot and humid, so we quickly changed into our lighter and cooler khaki uniforms.

Processing at the NAS, Corpus Christi took several days. After processing, along with many other cadets, I was sent on a Navy bus, to an outlying airfield called NAS, Cuddihy. The other outlying Corpus Christi NASs were Cabaniss and Beeville. The NAS, Corpus Christi was the Central Headquarters, commanded by a Rear Admiral, who directed the cadet training syllabus for all outlying airfields in the Corpus Christi area. Otherwise, each outlying airfield operated as an independent NAS.

The King Ranch

The central headquarters NAS was commonly referred to as Mainside. Mainside was actually located in nearby Kingsville, Texas, which was named after Captain Richard King, who founded the King Ranch.

The King Ranch covered nearly one thousand three hundred square miles; which is an area larger than the entire state of Rhode Island. The ranch sprawled over three Texas counties. The eight hundred twenty-five-thousand-acre ranch was acquired from the Spanish, and through other land grants by Captain King and his several partners. They initially set up a cattle camp on Santa Gertrudis Creek in South Texas. The final purchase began in 1853 when they bought the adjacent fifteen thousand five-hundred-acre Spanish Land Grant Rincon de Santa Gertrudis, on Santa Gertrudis Creek. They also acquired a Mexican Land Grant of another fifty-three thousand acres. During the late 1850s, King and his business partners acquired even more holdings. Captain King had previously been in the steamboat business; where he received the title of Captain. While conducting one of his cattle operations (forays) into Mexico, he brought back an entire Mexican village of one hundred Mexican workers, their wives, children, cattle, horses, and all else they owned. Most of those Mexican families have remained on the King Ranch. Now, generations later, they are indispensable in operating the vast King Ranch, and have become highly respected, very knowledgeable and well-paid ranch hands.

NAS, Cuddihy

I was sent to NAS, Cuddihy, which was approximately ten miles southeast of Corpus Christi. Flying there was a major step up in my flying experience. I now started flying metal, low-wing SNV monoplanes that offered great visibility in all directions, through its sliding open or closed plexiglass canopy. The U.S. Armed Services bought over eleven thousand of these airplanes, to meet the pilot training needs of the U.S. Army Air Corps and the Navy; making it one of the most important advanced training aircraft in the United States during WWII. The Army designated it the BT-13, and the Navy version was the SNV. The plane was designed and built by the Vultee Aircraft Company of Inglewood, California.

The SNV had a fixed landing gear, and the sliding plexiglass canopy covered both tandem cockpits. The plane was powered by a four hundred fifty HP radial engine. The engine had an electric starter, and each airplane had a multi-channel radio for the two-way communications required for the positive tower-to-aircraft-control needed to control faster aircraft, as well as providing communication with other airplanes. The radio was designed to permit internal communication (intercom) between an instructor and his cadet student. No more one-way communication gosports!

The SNV had a two-position controllable, two-blade metal propeller; which was new to me. The plane had two pitch (bite) positions. Take-offs, requiring maximum engine power, and were accomplished with the propeller operating in low pitch. When safe altitude was reached, the propeller was switched to the high pitch position, which allowed the pilot to reduce engine speeds. When landing, low pitch was selected, as a wave off was always possible, and the aircraft would again require full power.

The SNV had duel controls in its enclosed tandem cockpits. When flying solo, the pilot sat in the front cockpit. The SNV was another very honest airplane, that responded to whatever its pilot directed. I enjoyed the challenge of flying a heavier and faster airplane, though it had fixed (non-retractable) landing gear. Each SNV had a single fuel tank, with a capacity of one hundred twenty gallons of aviation gasoline. A fuel gauge was located on each cockpit instrument panel. No more floating wire fuel gauges. My first flight in the SNV at Cuddihy was on 12 July 1943, and my first night flight was on 23 July.

NAS, Cuddihy Field had several hangars. The hangars were primarily used for required aircraft maintenance checks, which followed a schedule of prescribed numbers of flying hours, and the hangars were sometimes used for minor repairs. The aircraft were parked outside the hangars, on the flight line. The SNV cruised at over one hundred fifty mph. This particular plane was used to increase the flying experience of cadets in an airplane that was more powerful, faster, and heavier. I learned acrobatics that required more altitude and flew in many two- and four-plane combat formations. Flying at NAS, Cuddihy challenged cadets to hone their flying skills. I had no engine failures, or other flying difficulties, during the two months I spent at NAS, Cuddihy. Several nearby mile-square fields, which were hard surfaced (Texas-dry) were used for practice landings. The Navy received four thousand, of the eleven thousand Vultee SNV trainers that were built. I flew the SNV for forty-three hours, while stationed at NAS, Cuddihy. After my last flight in the SNV on 1 September 1943, I was transferred back to Mainside, for more advanced flight training in the SNJ Advanced Trainer.

NAS, Corpus Christi (Mainside)

Before flying the SNJ Mainside, all cadets were required to fly an old Navy N3N biplane; the original "Yellow Peril." This plane preceded the Stearman N2S by several years, and had been built at the Naval Aircraft Factory in Philadelphia. The plane looked similar to the bi-wing Stearman N2S, but was much older than the N2S I had flown earlier that year at Ottumwa. The reason all cadets were required to fly the N3N was because of the inverted spin possibility when flying more advanced airplanes like the SNJ. In an inverted spin, the pilot is outside the spin, being held inside the cockpit by his tight safety belt In a normal spin, the pilot is inside of the spin, and is forced down into the cockpit. When flying certain heavier airplanes, it was possible to enter a violent inverted spin without warning. So, recognizing, and practicing recovery from inverted spins in the old N3N could be taught in relative safety, and at much lower altitudes.

While flying the old N3N, entering then recovering from inverted spins was relatively simple, but landing the N3N afterward was another matter. My instructor and I took off in the N3N and he demonstrated inverted spins. Then I practiced inverted spin entries and recoveries. While away from Mainside, at an outlying airfield, my instructor practiced several landings, as the N3N was also very prone to ground loops. Accordingly, my instructor wanted to practice some landings, away from Mainside. A ground loop occurs during landing touchdown, when one wing suddenly rises high, and the opposite lower wing tip scrapes along the runway surface, damaging it. The airplane then pivots around (ground loops) on the runway, and ends up facing the opposite direction; often coasting backward.

After my instructor practiced several normal landings at an outlying airfield, he became confident that he could land safely back at Mainside. But, upon touchdown at Mainside, the old "Yellow Peril" stubbornly ground looped in full view of all who were watching. I have no doubt that my instructor told everyone that his student was flying during that ground loop, thereby preventing some embarrassing explanations for him. The old N3Ns ground looped so often that bent wooden skids, about four feet long, were attached on the underside of both lower wing tips. If the airplane did ground loop, it usually damaged only an easily replaceable wooden skid; thereby preventing major wingtip damage repair. My inverted spin flight instruction in the N3N was on 7 October 1943. In one day, my flying experience in the N3N started and ended. The inverted spin practice, followed by our Mainside ground loop, made it one hell of an exciting airplane ride for me.

Following my N3N inverted spin instruction, I was introduced to a beautiful, sleek low-wing monoplane—the SNJ. The

Navy called it the SNJ, while the Army called it the A-T6 (Texan) and the British called it the Harvard. The SNJ was my first experience flying an airplane with retractable landing gear. North American Aviation factories in California, Texas, and Canada produced fifteen thousand four hundred ninety-five of these airplanes. The plane was powered by a six hundred HP Pratt & Whitney radial engine, with a two-blade variable pitch propeller, and a sliding plexiglass canopy over both front and rear cockpits.

The SNJ was the first airplane I had flown with wing flaps that permitted lower landing speeds. The retractable wheels and wing flaps were controlled from the cockpit. This plane was also the first airplane I flew that had a thirty-caliber machine gun. The airplane was designed in the late 1930s, and went through several different phases while being built. For instance, some Navy SNJs had upgraded multi-channel (frequency) radios, and others were fitted with arresting hooks, to permit aircraft carrier landings. Other models had a single, forward-firing thirty-caliber machine gun mounted in front of the pilot's wind screen. The machine gun fired through the propeller of the plane, but its firing was synchronized so that the machine gun bullets would not hit the propeller. If it ever did, supposedly each would go through the same hole in the propeller.

The SNJ was a superior training airplane. The Canadians built the SNJ (Harvard) in Montreal for the British Royal Air Force, and the Australian and New Zealand Air Forces. Many British Royal Air Force students were sent to bases in Oklahoma for training, before the United States officially entered the wars against Germany and Japan.

My older brother, Bill Dean, was hired as a civilian pilot prior to WWII, to teach British cadets to fly both the BT-13/SNV and the AT-6/SNJ at airfields in Oklahoma. In an ironic twist, we both flew two of same military training airplanes; Bill, as a civilian instructor pilot, and I, several years later, as a Naval Aviation Cadet.

The SNJ had a limited high G-force capability but not enough to cause pilot blackout. Pilot blackouts occur when high G (Gravity) forces are experienced, causing decreased blood flow to the pilot's brain. First, his vision will narrow, and then if the high G-force is sustained long enough, he will lose complete consciousness. The limited G-forces experienced when flying the SNJ, made wearing anti-blackout (G-suits) unnecessary.

My First Flight Challenges

To activate the SNJ retractable landing gear, the pilot would move the wheel lever up or down, and then push a hydraulic pump lever that released hydraulic fluid under high pressure, to raise or lower the landing gear (wheels). I failed my first acrobatic check in the SNJ. The checkride procedure was to have the cadet perform the acrobatic maneuvers, solo, over Mainside, while the instructor watched from the ground. As I completed my maneuvers, I thought the airplane seemed rather sluggish when performing the required loops, rolls, and other acrobatics. When I prepared to land, I reached for the landing gear handle to lower the landing gear to put the wheels down, but "Oops" the handle was already down! I had flown my entire acrobatic check ride with the wheels down, which explained why the airplane seemed sluggish. When I landed, the angry instructor asked, "What the hell were you trying to do up there?" That was the only down check I received during my entire flight training experience. My instructor sent me right back up for second check flight. On that second check flight, I remembered to raise the wheels, and I received an acrobatic up check.

I also had some trouble scoring hits on gunnery training flights. On those flights, one plane would tow a white heavy fabric target sleeve that was about thirty feet long and three feet in diameter; somewhat resembling a large airfield windsock. The sleeve was towed behind another SNJ, by a two-thousand-foot line. To score and record hits, the bullet tips were dipped into different color paint for each firing airplane. When a bullet went through the white fabric target, it left its color at each bullet hole. Counting the colored holes made it easy to identify hits for each firing aircraft. I had shot poorly on most of my gunnery training flights. However, on qualification day, when hit scores were recorded, I riddled that target sleeve. The other cadets, as well as my instructor, were amazed that I had scored so high.

The Value of Flying the SNJ

The SNJ had all the systems and characteristics necessary to prepare cadets for flying real combat aircraft. The plane was real joy to fly. We practiced combat formation flying. In preparing to land, our flight would approach over the landing field, at a specified altitude, flying in a close right echelon. Then, the first airplane to land would break sharply to the left (port). After five seconds, and one plane at a time, the remaining SNJs would break away, or peel off from the formation, at exactly ten second intervals. The ten-second timing established proper distances between the landing airplanes, and made the flight look very sharp and well disciplined.

At NAS, Corpus Christi Mainside, our flight training syllabus required intense instrument flying. The instructors would put the cadet under a removable hood, and have him fly patterns and maneuvers, to demonstrate capability to properly control the airplane while flying on instruments, and to recover (on instruments) from extreme aircraft attitudes. Instrument training served me well later, when I was assigned to a night-fighter squadron. On 28 October 1943, I flew my last flight at NAS, Corpus Christi Mainside.

Naval Aviator Wings

On 30 October 1943, I received my Naval Aviator Gold Wings, and my Marine Corps Second Lieutenant Commission. I don't really know why I opted for the Marine Corps instead of the Navy, as both branches required completion of the same flight training. However, at Cuddihy Field, I had been assigned Marine Corps flight instructors. For the first time, I noticed a certain swagger and confident manner on the part of the Marine flight instructors. One day a Marine Corps Major asked me if I had requested a Marine Corps commission. I told him that, so far, I hadn't thought much about it. He suggested that I do it, and I did. When the list of graduating cadets was published, I knew for certain that I was going to be commissioned a Naval Aviator with gold wings, and a Marine Corps Second Lieutenant rank, rather than a Navy Ensign. Both ranks were paid the same amount of money. When promoted from Aviation Cadet to Second Lieutenant, my monthly pay increased from seventy-five dollars, to over four hundred dollars; which I thought was just great.

Of course, there were a few new things I had not yet learned. For instance, as an officer, I had to purchase my Marine Corps uniforms, and pay for my meals. I hadn't considered either, because as cadets, we were given everything. Instead of being able to wear my Navy uniform, which I had as a cadet, I had to buy new ones, as the Marine Corps wore entirely different uniforms.

The officer who pinned on my wings was a highly decorated Marine Corps dive-bomber pilot, who had just returned from combat in the South Pacific. His name was Lieutenant Colonel Richard C. Mangrum, USMC. He later rose to the rank of Major General in the Marine Corps, and during my military career, I got to know him quite well. He was a tall, handsome Marine Corps officer, who sported a small, thin mustache.

When Colonel Mangrum approached, and pinned those gold Naval Aviator wings on me, it was a joyful time. I was no longer an Aviation Cadet, but a full-blown Naval Aviator, and a commissioned officer in the United States Marine Corps. Our graduating class formed four ranks to have our class picture taken, which was included in the bound book called the *Slipstream*. A similar class picture had been taken on 9 June 1943, and included in my copy of the *Slipstream* is a picture of a newly commissioned Ensign named George Herbert Walker Bush who, of course, later became the President of The United States. At age 19, I wasn't used to all the salutes I started receiving, and of course, returning. I called Millie, and told her that I had completed flight training, and had received my wings and my commission. She told me how proud she was of me. I really appreciated her support, and I told her that I hoped to see her before too long.

A good friend of mine, who received his wings and commission on the same day, was Second Lieutenant Charles F. "Chuck" Temple. We stood together for our graduation class picture. We became close friends at Corpus Christi, and when ordered, we traveled together to the next assignment in Florida. I remember that his mother came to the graduation, and saw Chuck get his gold Naval Aviator wings. We rode a train to Florida, and we stopped in Shreveport, Louisiana where we stayed overnight at Barksdale Field, a U.S. Army Air Corps base. We went to an Officer's Club, for the first time.

From Shreveport, we rode on to Florida, arrived at the southeast corner of Florida, and reported to another air station located at a city called Opa-locka. Officially, it was NAS, Miami, Florida. We flew two more months at Miami. Flying there was quite intense, and demanding. However, we were still flying only SNJ advanced trainers. I felt that we were there to build up more flying experience, by increasing our total flight hours. I was extremely grateful to learn that, at NAS, Miami, they had just stopped using a dangerous and worthless airplane, called the F2A Brewster Buffalo. The plane was a short, stubby, underpowered, low-wing monoplane, that often came apart in the air, for no apparent reason. Nearly every time it faced the Japanese in combat at Wake Island in the Pacific, the plane was shot down. I was used to flying reliable and dependable airplanes. Therefore, I wanted no part of flying the Brewster Buffalo F2A. The plane crashed so often that it earned its grim reputation as an "Ensign Eliminator." On 10 December 1943, I celebrated my twentieth Birthday, and having finished training at NAS, Miami, I received orders to NAS, Cecil Field, near Jacksonville, Florida.

Chapter 4: Advanced Flight Training

NAS, Cecil Field, Florida

From NAS, Miami, I was ordered directly to NAS, Cecil Field; an outlying airfield that operated under the command of NAS, Jacksonville, which was located forty miles southeast of Jacksonville, Florida. At NAS, Cecil Field, I learned to fly SBD (Dauntless) Dive Bombers. The SBD was the first combat aircraft that I had flown, thus far in my flight training.

Manufactured by the Douglas Aircraft plants in El Segundo, California and Tulsa, Oklahoma, pilots had been flying the SBD for years, in the WWII Pacific Theater; using it to attack Japanese ships, and to support allied troop amphibious landings from Guadalcanal to the Philippines Islands. Undoubtedly, the single most important contribution of this plane to the American war effort came during the Battle of Midway in June 1942, when U.S. aircraft carriers launched their SBD dive bombers, which destroyed and sank all four of the opposing Japanese aircraft carriers; three in just six minutes.

From Pearl Harbor through April 1944, pilots had flown the SBD over a million operational hours. The battle record of this plane shows, that in addition to using the plane to sink six Japanese aircraft carriers, the plane was used to sink fourteen Japanese cruisers, six Japanese destroyers, and fifteen enemy transport and cargo ships. The SBD also saw combat action during the Allied landings in North Africa in 1942, flying from the USS *Ranger* and escort carriers. A few months later SBDs, flying from the USS *Ranger*, attacked Nazi German shipping in Bodo, Norway.

The SBD was produced from 1940–1944. The total number built was five thousand nine hundred thirty-six. The fighter was designed by a Douglas Aircraft engineer named Ed Heinemann from

Michigan who years later, in 1989, was enshrined into the Michigan Aviation Hall of Fame.

The SBD was designed with two unique features. One was a yoke, which was permanently attached, and hinged, under the SBD fuselage. The yoke was located just behind the airplane's twelve hundred HP Wright Cyclone engine, and was just a bit wider than a five-hundred-pound bomb. When a bomb, carried inside, and attached to the yoke, was dropped, the yoke swung down and away from the SBD fuselage, flinging the bomb far enough away to miss the propeller of the plane during a dive.

The second unique feature of the SBD was its perforated flaps. In a dive, when the split flaps were opened, the aircraft speed was limited to about two hundred thirty knots. The split flaps served as dive brakes. A pilot could dive vertically, and have ample time to aim at enemy ships, or enemy land targets. Pilots could fire with precise accuracy. This advantage was a major reason for its amazing success in the Battle of Midway, and against many other enemy ships, during other battles as well. Perforations in the split flaps prevented tail buffeting; which allowed great aircraft stability in dives, when the split flaps were open.

Twin thirty caliber machine guns were mounted behind the rear cockpit, pointing aft. The rear cockpit seat could be turned completely around, enabling the rear seat gunner to fire at any enemy aircraft approaching the SBD from behind. Or, when flying in tight formation, the twin machine guns of several SBDs could be massed, and brought to bear on one or more attacking enemy aircraft.

During takeoffs, the rear seat gunner faced forward in his cockpit. He then turned his seat around, and facing the rear, unlimbered his twin machine guns and fed belted ammunition into them. He could guard the rear of his SBD by facing aft throughout each mission. In preparation for landing, he unloaded the ammunition, and stowed the machine guns, before turning his seat to face forward. I've always admired the courage of those rear seat gunners, especially when they had to ride backwards, during very steep dive-bombing runs.

During its combat service, the SBD proved to be an excellent dive bomber. The plane possessed good handling characteristics, long range maneuverability, a potent bomb load, great diving stability, and ruggedness. In addition, the plane carried good defensive armament, both fore and aft. However, in 1944 the Navy stopped SBD production, and placed emphasis on the heavier, more powerful, faster, and longer-range Curtiss SB2C dive bomber. Replacing the SBDs, The SB2C made for excellent, advanced pilot training in a proven combat aircraft.

However, the Marine Corps decided to go in a different direction. The flight syllabus at NAS, Cecil Field was changed from training dive bomber pilots, to training fighter pilots. As a Marine Corps pilot, I practiced in an SBD, but did not fly the SBD with a rear seat gunner, because the pilots reporting for training at Cecil Field were ordered there to specifically learn fighter pilot tactics. Most of our flights at Cecil Field were over the nearby Atlantic Ocean; using one of several aircraft gunnery ranges under the control of NAS, Jacksonville. While nearing one of many off-shore live firing gunnery ranges, our flight approached its assigned gunnery range at an altitude of eight thousand feet. Our instructor would report to the Range Control personnel by radio. Range Control would assign flights to one of several gunnery ranges, and clear to commence live firing at our towed target. Our instructor would lead the flight through one of several different live firing runs.

One live firing run was the "High-Side Run" which required the firing aircraft to approach the target two thousand feet above and to one side, and then turn, and dive steeply at the towed target. We used the aircraft gun sight to establish proper lead, and then opened fire at the target sleeve at angles of more than thirty degrees. The "High-Side Run" produced a no G-force dive, but the dive was steep; causing the firing aircraft to pull out several thousand feet below the target. Each pilot, at the start of his live firing run, would broadcast his call sign by radio, followed by the announcement "Rolling In," to start his firing, and would again report his call sign, followed by the announcement "Level and climbing" as his SBD pulled out of the dive, climbed, and passed the tow plane. The next pilot could then safely commence his firing run.

Another run—called a "Level or Side Run"—was to approach the tow aircraft on the opposite course, off to one side, but at the same altitude. After passing the tow plane in the opposite direction, the firing aircraft would immediately turn hard toward the target. Standing the airplane on one wing, the pilot made a high-G turn toward the target, firing when in range, at a full ninety-degree deflection. The long leads required placing the firing aircraft gun sight far ahead of the target sleeve, almost at the tow plane. But, the high-G forces, and the opposing speeds, would cause the bullets to arrive at the target far to the rear of the tow plane, and hopefully they would hit the towed sleeve. Those firing runs, no doubt caused some anxiety on the part of the tow plane pilot, who could see each aircraft start a firing run with its nose pointing right at him, and he knew that each aircraft had its guns charged and firing.

One day, our flight of four was cleared to our assigned gunnery range, and led by our instructor, we commenced making overhead gunnery runs. This run required approaching the target two thousand feet overhead and on an opposite course of the tow plane. The pilot had to then roll inverted, and sharply dive down at the towed target, and when in range, commence firing. Pullout from the steep dives would carry the firing aircraft several thousand feet below the tow plane. We didn't know what happened to our instructor on his first overhead run, but after completing the firing run, his aircraft did not recover from its steep dive, and continued straight down, crashing into the ocean. The tow plane pilot quickly took charge, and ordered our flight to cease further gunnery runs. Next, he reported the crash to Jacksonville Range Control. The tow plane pilot then directed our flight to join him, and follow him back to Cecil Field, where he dropped the sleeve, and our flight landed safely. This crash was the first fatal crash that I witnessed. Our flight members had to describe our experiences on the day our flight instructor crashed, and was killed, to a formal Aircraft Accident Board.

While we gained experience in flying the SBD, our flights were plagued with ground accidents. When landing any airplane, the pilot has to look constantly ahead from the cockpit. Meanwhile, in the SBD he had to blindly fumble with his left hand to find and select other controls that were all mounted on the same cockpit throttle quadrant. One controlled the engine throttle; another raised and lowered wing flaps; while another activated the split flaps. The propeller pitch control and the fuel mixture control were also mounted on the throttle quadrant. The landing gear lever was positioned near all the other cockpit controls. Until a pilot became familiar with those SBD controls, it was easy to grasp and activate the wrong control. Occasionally, while landing his SBD, a pilot would raise the landing gear, instead of raising the landing wing flaps. Of course, the mistake would retract (raise) the wheels, and the airplane would settle and skid to a stop on the runway surface; bending the propeller and causing extensive damage to the belly of the SBD.

Before each SBD flight, the pilot had to check the two-man inflatable life raft. The raft was carried internally, behind the gunner's rear cockpit, in a large, round, life raft access tube. To inspect it, the pilot had to open the raft access door, reach inside the tube, and blindly grasp a life raft strap, to pull it from the airplane for inspection. Grasping the life raft <u>inflation</u> strap was easy, and when pulled, it inflated the raft, while it was still inside the aircraft. The inflated raft damaged some of the aircraft metal skin, by popping rivets. Also, the raft had to be deflated before it could be removed; which meant punching holes in several compartments of the raft, thereby destroying it.

Time with Millie

Completing out fighter pilot syllabus at NAS, Cecil Field would predictably take over two months. Knowing that, and because Millie and I had become engaged the year before at Ottumwa, Iowa, I called and invited her to come to Florida. She and her high school friend, Charlotte Jensen, immediately came to Jacksonville. My buddy, Lieutenant Chuck Temple, and I rented a room where the girls would stay, from a lady who lived in Jacksonville, whose husband was serving overseas. To supplement her income, she rented a room in her house. Chuck and I could be there only on weekends. So, the girls got to know their landlady, Mozell Schous, very well.

Mozell was not much older than Millie and Charlotte, and she realized that we wanted to be together, as much as possible. She invited the four of us to dinner at her house every Sunday. Mozell always served a chicken dinner, which the girls helped prepare. Mozell was always included in the fun of our many impromptu parties, which started immediately upon our Friday evening arrivals from Cecil Field. While there, Chuck Temple and Charlotte Jensen became close friends. Accordingly, the four of us always had a great time during our free weekends. After two months, Chuck Temple and I completed our flight training at Cecil Field. We, regretfully, then had to say "good-bye" to Millie and

Charlotte, who returned to Michigan by train, and we were transferred to our first Marine Corps Air Station (MCAS).

MCAS, Cherry Point

Our six flight members, who had trained together at Cecil Field, all reported to MCAS, Cherry Point, North Carolina; which had been constructed along the Neuse River in the tidewater area of eastern North Carolina. The temporary living conditions at Cherry Point were downright miserable. We were billeted in small, wooden, square Dallas huts; with six pilots per hut. The weather was rainy and cold. The individual Dallas huts were each heated with one free-standing stove that was placed in the center of the hut. The stove chimney extended above the stove, and through the hut roof. Several times each night, a Marine would open the hut door unannounced, and carrying a full coal scuttle, would enter the hut. The Marine would open the stove lid, and noisily dump chunks of coal with coal dust, directly into the stove fire. Soot would rise through the chimney, but some would also rise through the open stove lid; settling on everything inside the hut, including our new uniforms.

We were administratively attached to Aircraft and Engineering Squadron Nine (AES-9). AES-9 was a holding squadron for pilots awaiting assignment to one of the many fighter squadrons training for combat at Cherry Point. While waiting, our flying hours were very limited.

One day, when I was at the squadron headquarters hangar, I noticed a sign-up sheet on the bulkhead (wall) that solicited pilots for night-fighter training at NAS, Vero Beach, Florida. I knew that our entire flight squadron, who had trained together at NAS, Cecil Field, all missed Florida; especially the warmer weather. Confident that they would all want to return to Florida, and without their knowledge, I placed all their names on the list of pilots volunteering for night-fighter training.

As I was writing names on the list, I noticed a Marine Colonel watching me. He approached and introduced himself. He was Marine Colonel E. A. Montgomery, who was in charge of organizing and training night-fighter squadrons for combat, at MCAS, Cherry Point. I learned later that the Marine Corps had sent him to England, to learn how the British Royal Air Force had organized, managed, and trained its night-fighter program. He then returned to organize and train Marine Corps night-fighter squadrons, at MCAS, Cherry Point. His first step was to select the pilots, and then send them to NAS, Vero Beach, Florida to learn to fly the Navy's latest fighter airplane, the Grumman F6F Hellcat, that Marine Corps pilots would fly in their night-fighter squadron.

During our conversation, I told him that the names I had added to the list were all close friends, with whom I had flown ever since we had received our Gold Wings; which had been all of an impressive period of about three months. He explained that the night-fighter version of the Hellcat would be designated the F6F-3N, and that it would be equipped with a radar system. So far, the first F6F-3N had not yet arrived at Cherry Point. Colonel Montgomery told me that the pilots on the list would receive their orders to NAS, Vero Beach within a few days. I hurried back to our Dallas hut, and told my friends that we were all returning to Florida, to fly the Navy's newest fighter plane at Vero Beach. I assured them that they were all going, as I had just seen the list. What I didn't tell them was that I had "volunteered" them, when I put their names on that list. Unless they read this story, they may never know how they were so carefully selected.

NAS, Vero Beach

We departed Cherry Point on 21 March 1945, in a Marine transport airplane, and flew non-stop to NAS, Vero Beach, Florida. Upon arrival, we were billeted in very nice two-story wooden quarters, which had been recently built, in a citrus orchard.

Many of the citrus trees remained. Picking ripe fruit from an orange or grapefruit tree growing adjacent to our quarters was easy. I recall picking delicious grapefruit, and carefully mashing them by hand; and after cutting a small hole in the stem end, I would lie on my bunk, place the hole in the grapefruit against my mouth, and squeeze the fruit; which forced the fresh juice directly into my mouth. That delicious Indian River fruit is still quite well-known today. The small city of Vero Beach is the County Seat of Indian River County. For years, following WWII, the Los Angeles Dodgers baseball team traveled to Vero Beach and used the former Naval Air Station for their baseball spring training site.

Flying at Vero Beach was delightful. We all quickly checked out in the single-piloted Grumman F6F-3N fighter airplane, which was designed to outperform the nimble Japanese fighter plane known as the Zero. Over five thousand U.S. Navy/Marine Corps F6F Hellcats were produced by the Grumman Aircraft plant located at Bethpage, Long Island, New York. This plane quickly became the Navy's first line fighter, replacing the smaller and slower Grumman F4F Wildcat. Powered by a supercharged two thousand HP Pratt & Whitney engine, the F6F Hellcat shot down more (over five thousand) enemy airplanes, than did any other U.S. produced fighter plane in WWII; including its predecessors, the F4F Wildcat, the North American P-51 Mustang, the Chance-Vought F4U Corsair, the Lockheed P-38 Lightning, the Republic P-47 Thunderbolt, and the Curtiss P-40 Warhawk. In addition, the F6F Hellcat kills included thirteen German aircraft while flying from British aircraft carriers in Southern France and Norway.

The Hellcats starred during the battle called "The Great Mariana Turkey Shoot," which took place near the Mariana islands of Guam, Tinian, and Saipan. The first day of the battle, in June 1944, the Hellcats shot down three hundred forty-six Japanese aircraft, with a loss of only twenty-three Hellcats. By the end of the three-day or four-day battle, the Hellcats scored four hundred eighty Japanese air-to-air kills. The Hellcats we flew at Vero Beach were not equipped with radar. Accordingly, they were used just for pilot checkout, and to accumulate day fighter experience, and to learn a few day fighter tactics, before we returned to Cherry Point for assignment to a night-fighter squadron.

F6F training at NAS, Vero Beach, FL (1944)
Bob Warren, standing 1st on the left;
Chuck Temple, standing 1st on the right.

Millie and Marriage

Knowing that we would be in Vero Beach for about two months, I called Millie, and asked her to come down to Vero Beach and marry me. She told me later, that my call caused quite a stir in the Weber household. Her father did not object to our marriage, but he was adamant about wanting us to wait until WWII was over. On the other hand, her mother supported her desire to travel to Florida and marry me. She listened to her Mom, and immediately left for Florida by train. I met her at the Vero Beach train station.

At Vero Beach, Millie and I married on 14 April 1944. I was twenty years old, and Millie celebrated her twentieth Birthday the day before we married.

Millie and Bob, Vero Beach, FL (1944)

I had already obtained a marriage license, and we were married in the office of Justice of the Peace, Otis Cobb, in the Indian River County Courthouse. Millie's bridesmaid was our landlady, Mrs. Cliff Phillips, and Chuck Temple was my best man. I had been granted a day off from flying, to get married. Millie and I had rented a small, one-bedroom detached apartment near the end of one of the NAS, Vero Beach runways. The apartment was a nice and cozy little place, that was just right for newlyweds. Our transportation consisted of two bicycles. I rented one, and our landlady loaned one to Millie. Again, like in Jacksonville, our landlady's husband was serving overseas. She received some additional income by renting their little detached one-bedroom apartment to us. On our wedding night, all night long, pilots who knew we had just married, decided to help us celebrate our marriage. They took off, keeping their Hellcat propellers in noisy low pitch, and at full throttle, while flying over (Buzzing!) our little apartment. Thank you very much, guys, for all your unwanted help!

I remember Millie having some trouble cooking. I asked her to cook some chicken gizzards. I hadn't eaten them since leaving my home in Michigan, and I thought chicken gizzards would be very tasty. When I tried to eat the gizzards, they were only partially cooked - still raw - and I could not eat them. Millie cried, and exclaimed, "I don't think you like my cooking." I certainly loved her; but I thought she had left some of her cooking skills in Michigan, with her mother and grandmother, who were both excellent cooks.

Otherwise, married life at Vero Beach was wonderful. We rode our bicycles around town, and back and forth to the base. My training flights were from noon until midnight, six days a week, with an hour off each evening for dinner. Millie would pedal her bicycle to the nearby air station, and join me for dinner (no more raw chicken gizzards). After dinner, she would pedal her bicycle out of the air station main gate, and ride back home. The air station main gate sentries soon recognized her, and waved her through without stopping her to check her new military dependent ID Card. I flew until midnight, and then I rode my bicycle home.

Every morning, at nine o'clock, a Navy bus would pass our house carrying military personnel, including dependents, back and forth to the beach. I arranged for the bus to stop at our house. The "bus" was actually a tractor and a semi-trailer, configured to carry people. We called it a cattle car. Our house was very close to the air station, and only a ten-minute bus ride from the beach. If we were outside waiting, the bus would stop, and take us to the beach every morning, up to six days a week. We could swim, and have a wonderful time for a couple of hours. Sharply at 11:00 a.m., the bus would depart the beach, and we rode it back to our rented house. This schedule allowed time for me to shower, put on my uniform, eat a quick lunch, and ride my bicycle back to the base by noon.

Hellcat Flight Training

Our flight training was designed for pilots to become familiar with the F6F Grumman Hellcat. The Hellcat was a very honest and forgiving airplane; doing exactly what its pilot expected, without any surprises. Our training syllabus at Vero Beach was evenly divided between day and night flights.

On a night training flight, a pilot named Eddie Gaudette experienced complete engine failure, right after takeoff. He had no choice but to land straight ahead, into in a nearby swamp. He was not injured, but after getting out of his airplane, and wading and crawling out of the swamp, he was wet, and covered with slime and gunk. He spotted the lights a farmhouse, walked to it, and knocked on the door. A small girl opened the door and screamed, when she saw a slime covered creature from the swamp standing there. After the family learned that he was a pilot, and had just landed his plane in the swamp, they kindly gave him a ride back to the air station.

During the daytime, we were taught fighter tactics. We would go out with four fighter planes and learn how to shoot down an attacking enemy aircraft. When attacked, we were taught to split several thousand yards apart, and then proceed on the same course. When the enemy pilot chose which side of the split he would attack, we turned toward the other two Hellcats to shoot down the attacking plane. That maneuvering tactic was known as "The Thach Weave," named after a famous Navy pilot named John Thach.

At night, we flew. The flights went smoother and easier, because it was a different kind of flying. Night time flying at NAS, Vero Beach was largely devoted to night over-water navigation. Sometimes, arriving home at night became confusing, when we did not return to Vero Beach, but to a similar airfield along Florida's Atlantic Coast. At night, airfield runway lights appear much the same. Occasionally, a returning night-fighter pilot would make a mistake, and land at the Melbourne or Banana River military airfields; thinking it was Vero Beach. After landing, looking around, and realizing that he had landed at a strange airfield, he quickly took off and landed at Vero Beach, where he should have been, had he flown the flight exactly as briefed.

Returning to Cherry Point

My final flight at Vero Beach was on 2 May 1944. From there, I returned to Cherry Point, North Carolina, and joined my first night-fighter squadron, VMF (N)-543, which became my first squadron training for combat. Combat training started in May 1944 at Cherry Point, and lasted until 22 September 1944. During that time, Millie had moved to Cherry Point. We didn't have on-base housing. So, we rented a house about fifteen miles away on Evans Street in Morehead City, North Carolina. Chuck Temple had also married, and lived in the house adjacent to ours. The two of us bought a car - a 1941 Ford V8 with a sixty HP engine - from my sister and brother-in-law, Helen and Eugene McKean. We drove the Ford to and from MCAS, Cherry Point. We shared our Evans Street location with another Marine Corps Pilot; the former movie star Tyrone Power, and his wife.

Major Claude J. Carlson was the very popular commanding officer of our night-fighter squadron. Earlier in the war, he served in the infantry; but then went through flight training. He was a wonderful leader, and was pleasant, helpful, and approachable. Although senior to all of us, he had no more flying experience than we did.

When preparing to fly, the Major kept fiddling with the oxygen shut off system in the airplane; believing that you could meter its use, by slightly turning it off. However, that was a bad procedure, because the oxygen system was designed to give the pilot the correct amount of oxygen. We all knew that, before a flight, all we had to do was ensure the oxygen system on/off valve was turned on. It was called a Diluter/Demand System that always gave a pilot the correct amount of oxygen. We all knew that his oxygen saving theory was wrong; but didn't feel, as Lieutenants, that we dared tell him about his flawed procedure. If anyone should tell him, it should have been Executive Officer, Claire "C" Chamberlain; who also held the rank of Major.

As the squadron commander, Major Carlson insisted on test flying each new Hellcat, when it was delivered to our squadron. His last test flight included climbing to high altitude, and testing all the controls and systems. On that test flight, Major Carlson crashed and was killed. We could only surmise that he was fiddling with that oxygen bottle valve, while flying at high altitude. If so, he probably experienced anoxia (a condition caused by a lack of oxygen), and while unconscious, his Hellcat made a small crater where it crashed.

Losing our respected and popular leader was a traumatic event for our squadron.

The squadron Executive Officer, Major Chamberlain, who had returned from the South Pacific after completing a combat tour, became our new VMF (N)-543 commanding officer. He was a poor leader, who sort of "winged" things, and made decisions as he went along. He played favorites; and except for flying, showed few leadership skills. He commanded our squadron through its entire combat tour in Okinawa. One of the wild things Major Chamberlain did at Cherry Point: while on liberty to Washington D. C., he met and married a girl on the spot, and brought her back to Cherry Point. Her name was Patti Chamberlain. Lucky for us, she was a very nice person, and well-liked by everyone in the squadron.

The twenty-four airplanes we received in our squadron at Cherry Point were the F6F-3N Grumman Hellcat night-fighters. Each was equipped with a radar intercept system. The sending and receiving antennas were in a bulging, fiberglass housing, near the end of the Hellcat's right wing. Those image-producing radar antennas fed enemy aircraft distance, altitude, and other information to a cathode ray tube, centered in the Hellcat instrument panel. Using a cockpit radar control knob, the pilot could select sixty, thirty, five, and one-mile radar ranges; which was great for closing to positions behind enemy aircraft (bogeys), and excellent for navigation.

At the sixty-mile range, the pilot could identify land, rivers, and seacoasts on that small cathode ray tube. The display was almost like reading a map. Shorter ranges were selected when making a bogey intercept; selecting the one-mile range for the final intercept. When closing in on the bogey aircraft within one mile, two little side-by-side blips moved from top to bottom on the radar scope. The pilot couldn't really see the bogey airplane very close ahead of him. Sometimes, it was very close, as the Hellcat flew into, and would be buffeted around by, the bogey slipstream before seeing him. We were issued heavy binoculars; which helped our night vision. They helped the Hellcat pilot to see the bogey aircraft. But using them had some serious downsides; as they compounded the already busy Hellcat pilot's problems. First, holding them took one of the pilot's hands away from the throttle control, leaving him no way to control his closing speed. Second, the binoculars were heavy, and hung around our necks. In bumpy air, we had to hold the binoculars against our chests; to keep them from flying around in the Hellcat cockpit.

2nd Lt. Bob Warren in the cockpit of a F6F Hellcat,
MCAS Cherry Point, NC (1944)

    The training at Cherry Point was extensive; lasting through late September 1944. At that time, we knew we were about to leave on the first leg of our journey to combat, somewhere in the Pacific Theater. Millie went home, and I flew my airplane, with the rest of the squadron from Cherry Point, to MCAS, El Centro, California. Getting there took two days. We made several refueling stops along the way. We were headed for MCAS, El Toro, California, but while refueling at Barksdale Army Airfield in Shreveport, Louisiana, we got a message changing our destination to MCAS, El Centro, California; located about one hundred miles east of San Diego.

Chuck Temple (L) and Bob Warren (R), Morehead City, NC (1944)

Chapter 5: World War II Pacific Deployments Begin

MCAS, EL CENTRO, CALIFORNIA

Upon arrival at MCAS, El Centro, I was surprised to see a female Marine, directing us to our flight line parking spots. That was the first time I saw a female Marine working on the flight line. They were now sharing flight line duties at Naval Air Stations, with their Navy (Wave) counterparts.

When I learned that our squadron was going to be at El Centro for two months, I called Millie, and she was on the first available train to California. When she arrived at El Centro, I was not there to meet her, because I had flown a Hellcat to NAS, North Island, in San Diego, for two days, to have six rocket rails installed on the airplane. We flew our squadron Hellcats to NAS, North Island, one at a time, to get that work done. It was simply my turn.

When Millie arrived at the El Centro train station, she recognized one of our squadron pilots, whom she had met at Cherry Point. They hitch-hiked together about ten miles to the Naval Air Station; where I had reserved a Quonset hut. Rows of Quonset hut apartments were all the same, except for an identifying number painted over the door. Each hut had two furnished apartments. Each apartment contained a little kitchenette, a living room, two bedrooms, and a single bathroom with a shower. They were furnished with electric refrigerators and stoves. Dishes, cookware, flatware, and lamps were also provided. Windows lighted all rooms.

Early one morning there was a lot of commotion outside of our Quonset hut apartment. We went outside, and learned that there had been a fire inside a Quonset apartment located just two rows from ours. When we arrived, we learned the fire had been in a

Quonset assigned to one of our squadron senior Staff Non-commissioned officers. He escaped, wearing his undershirt and some green uniform trousers. His wife was wearing her bathrobe. Millie asked them to come to our Quonset apartment, where she would fix breakfast for them. But, Millie accidentally brought them to a Quonset located one row from ours. When Millie opened the door, and the NCO and his wife entered, some startled lady was in her kitchen, fixing breakfast. They all had to back out, and followed Millie as she re-navigated and found our Quonset apartment. Except for a Quonset hut number, they were identical in size, color, and configuration.

Some of our unmarried squadron pilots met several airline hostesses who were living in Hollywood. They invited them to El Centro, and the ladies stayed with us for a few days, in our spare bedroom. We had a hilarious time hosting several impromptu parties. We also traveled to El Centro, and across the U.S./Mexican border to the Mexican city of Mexicali. Our squadron used the El Centro High School gymnasium for basketball and other sporting activities. The community always demonstrated great hospitality to the military personnel stationed at "their" Naval Air Station.

At El Centro, we concentrated on, and honed our night-fighter intercept skills. I flew almost fifty hours during the short time our squadron was based at El Centro. Our training flight area extended over most of the Imperial Valley from El Centro, west about 50 miles, then north to Palm Springs; passing over the landlocked Salton Sea, east to the Chocolate Mountain gunnery ranges, then south to the US/Mexican border. The dry desert weather was ideal for night-fighter training. El Centro is located near the south end of the Imperial Valley, where most of the lettuce, consumed in the United States was, and still is, grown. We thoroughly enjoyed our duty at El Centro. However, we realized that it was our final permanent stop before combat deployment overseas.

Our squadron remained at El Centro until December 4, 1944. Then it was ordered to move to the MCAS at Miramar, located only a few miles north of San Diego. We paused there briefly before flying our airplanes on to NAS, North Island, where they were loaded dockside onto an aircraft carrier. At North Island, the aircraft carriers were tied up to the air station piers, making it easy to simply hoist the planes aboard. Our airplanes were part of a mixed load of several types of airplanes, also loaded at dockside. Our next stop was Pearl Harbor, Hawaii.

Millie followed me to Miramar. A few days later, when we started flying our airplanes to San Diego, we said "Goodbye," knowing I would most likely not see her again until after WW II ended. She arranged to share a ride with another squadron wife who was driving back to the Midwest. Millie rode with her to Ft. Sill, Oklahoma, where her brother, Walter Weber and sister-in-law, Marnie Weber were living. Walt was an Army 2nd Lieutenant, attending field artillery school at Ft. Sill before being sent overseas to the Pacific. After staying two weeks, Millie rode the train to Chicago, then on home to Michigan.

MCAS, Ewa, Hawaii

We left from North Island aboard a small aircraft carrier. I quickly got seasick, as we were leaving San Diego Harbor, and still passing Point Loma, before entering the Pacific Ocean. The ship was very crowded. We had no rooms or beds, but instead, slept on canvas cots in the ship's passageways. Sailors performing their duties had to inch their way around us. It was a very uncomfortable five day trip to Pearl Harbor. After arriving, our F6F Hellcats were off loaded by hoisting them ashore at a small airstrip in the middle of Pearl Harbor, named Ford Island.

We then flew our airplanes to MCAS, EWA (pronounced Eva); a few miles from Ford Island. MCAS, EWA, was adjacent to NAS, Barbers Point. The two air stations were connected by a taxiway. MCAS, Ewa was surrounded by sugar cane fields. A sugar mill operated nearby.

At NAS, Barbers Point, newly developed Ground Controlled Approach (GCA) equipment was being tested. GCA is a small, radar controlled approach system that provided terminal guidance to landing aircraft; right down to the threshold of a landing runway. One of the last instructions given to the pilot using GCA was always, "Check your gear (wheels) down and locked". It was a wonderful system to help an approaching aircraft during inclement weather.

Most of our flying at EWA was at night; and following our flights, we had no place to eat. NAS, Barbers Point had a round-the-clock mess hall; but Marine pilots were not permitted to eat there. We quickly solved that problem by purchasing black neckties (worn by Navy Officers) and replacing our khaki neckties (worn by Marine Officers), we ate as U.S. Navy officers. In preparation for the necktie switch, we also had to tuck our caps into our belts, making sure the Marine Corps emblem was inside, so it could not be seen. Thereafter, we thoroughly enjoyed eating at the NAS, Barbers Point mess hall. Such innovation was sometimes necessary to achieve our goals. Accordingly, Marines sometimes resorted to "creative," a.k.a. "sneaky" practices.

One of the last things we were able to enjoy before our squadron left for the Western Pacific, was to fly to Hilo, a city located on Hawaii; the largest of several islands in the Hawaii Island chain. Hawaii is often referred to as "the Big Island." We were flown from Ewa to Hilo on a twin engine medium bomber, known as the Martin JM. The Army Air Corps called it a B-26, and it was widely used in Europe. Our JM pilot was First Lieutenant Charlie Lutz. We flew to Hilo on 23 December, and back to EWA on 26 December. I rode in the nose gunner's seat, located in the plexiglass enclosed nose of the airplane. From that vantage point, I was able to get a beautiful view of several other islands making up the Hawaiian Island chain.

After leaving from MCAS, Ewa, located on the island of Oahu, we flew past the islands of Maui, Lanai, and Molokai, before landing at Hilo. Two very active volcanoes, named Mauna Loa and Mauna Kea; each sharply and beautifully rising over thirteen thousand, six hundred feet remain active, and often erupt; creating extensive new lava beds. We thoroughly enjoyed our last liberty trip to Hilo. We swam, rode horses, visited some newly formed lava beds and took a lot of pictures. Those were some of the last pictures taken with several of our pilots, who were killed or wounded during the forthcoming battle for Okinawa.

During the first week of March, 1945, our squadron prepared for departure from Hawaii, to proceed to the Ulithi atoll staging area, before going to Okinawa. I was able to get one last look at Hawaii on 2 March, 1945 when I flew a Hellcat on a three hour flight, non-stop to Hilo and back. Then we started flying our squadron aircraft back to Ford Island, in preparation for hoisting them aboard the USS *Sitkoh Bay*; the aircraft carrier that would transport our squadron to a massive staging area near the Ulithi atoll in the Caroline Islands.

One by one, our squadron Hellcats were "spotted' on the ship's catapult. All of our pilots took turns sitting in the Hellcat cockpit through a simulated catapult launch. That included flaps down, propeller in low pitch, and applying full throttle to the engine, while responding to the hand signals from the ship's catapult hookup crew, and finally the launch officer who would direct catapult launch. All that was missing during a simulated launch was the cable that, during an actual catapult launch, would be attached to hooks, permanently fastened beneath each Hellcat wing.

During an actual launch, the cables would reach from the aircraft, sharply down to flight deck level. The center of the cable was first attached to the shuttle. Crewman, each holding an end of the cable, would move as far as possible to each side. Next, the airplane would quickly taxi a few feet forward until it reached a point almost directly above the shuttle, before the two crewmen holding the ends of the cable, moved in behind the dangerous propeller and attached both cable ends to the aircraft under-wing hooks. Just prior to having his aircraft catapulted, the pilot would hold the throttle wide open, and would then reach farther forward and grasp the grab handle; to prevent the pilot jerking the throttle closed during launch. Just before the catapult shot, the pilot would move his head back against a small padded cushion, so his head would not be slammed back when the catapult fired. Again, we were practicing for our upcoming catapult launch from the USS *Sitkoh Bay*, upon arrival at Okinawa.

Ulithi Atoll Staging Area

During the first week of March, 1945, we sailed from Pearl Harbor toward Okinawa, first joining a massive fleet assembly near the Ulithi atoll. Ulithi is located three hundred, fifty miles southwest of Guam; eight hundred, fifty miles east of the Philippines; and thirteen hundred miles south of Tokyo. Our squadron planes shared the flight deck of the USS *Sitkoh Bay*, with VMF-312, a Marine Corps day fighter squadron, equipped with F4U Corsairs. At the Ulithi atoll staging area, our ship anchored among several hundred other ships; including fifteen aircraft carriers, thirteen battleships, twenty-eight cruisers, one hundred six destroyers, and hundreds of tankers and cargo ships, loaded with thousands of troops, and tons of fuel and equipment. The Ulithi atoll provided a twenty by ten mile deep water anchorage. The ships were staging (assembling) for landings on Okinawa; to be followed by the invasion of the Japanese mainland. I expect that no one will ever again witness such a massive display of naval power assembling for two invasions.

The single runway at Ulithi was too short to land a high performance fighter plane safely; so a high speed turn off taxiway was built at each end of the single thirty-two hundred foot runway. VMF (N)-542, a sister night-fighter squadron, had been sent to Ulithi a few months before our arrival. It was hoped that, when landing, if the trade winds were strong enough, the Hellcats would slow down enough to finish their landing roll on the single short, water-to-water thirty-two hundred foot runway. But, if not, the landing Hellcats turned onto a wide, high speed taxiway, to finish their landing rollout.

VMF(N) 542 was also going to participate in the invasion of Okinawa. Their Hellcats were placed on powered barges one at a time, then chugged to an aircraft carrier anchored close by; where they were hoisted from the barge to the carrier flight deck. Squadron enlisted Marines ran the powered barges.

There was another short runway on Mog Mog, one of the Ulithi atoll islands. The Navy had constructed vast facilities for men on liberty to enjoy themselves on Mog Mog. There were four baseball diamonds, makeshift outdoor taverns serving beer, and sandy swimming beaches; each with signs showing those on liberty where to go. Shore liberty was very well organized, for thousands of sailors and troops. I will never forget seeing the tremendous collection of ships spread over miles and miles of ocean. There were ships of every description. And, I was privileged to see it all from our ship, and then, from the air. Those were truly awesome and memorable sights.

Our squadron enlisted men, plus the squadron Executive Officer, Major William P. "Mitch" Mitchell, and several other squadron officers, left Pearl Harbor aboard the USS *Achernar* (AKA-53), an amphibious cargo attack ship. The *Achernar* sailed directly from Pearl Harbor, passing the Palau Islands, to the Philippine Island of Leyte. Leyte was the first island attacked by General Douglas MacArthur's forces carrying out his promised return to the Philippines. Soon after wading ashore with the Philippine President Sergio Osmena, MacArthur broadcast by radio, world-wide, "People of the Philippines, I have returned!" Soon thereafter, the Marines would chant, "With the help of God, and a few Marines, MacArthur returned to the Philippines".

The most anxious VMF(N)-543 Marine to go ashore when the USS *Achernar* anchored at Leyte was our squadron Executive Officer, Major Mitchell. While in Australia, during a previous South Pacific combat tour, Mitch met, and fell in love with, a beautiful U. S. Army nurse named Margaret. Her hospital unit had followed the war north, and she was now stationed about eighteen miles from Tacloban airfield on the Island of Leyte. Mitch found her there, and during the USS *Achernar*'s short stay at Leyte, Margaret and Mitch were married. I was told they spent their very short honeymoon in a small, nearby recreation area, called Belly Acres.

Chapter 6: Amphibious Assault on Okinawa

The Attack Plan

The amphibious assault on Okinawa by the U.S. 10th Army, led by Lieutenant General Simon Bolivar Buckner, Jr., would begin with landings on Easter Sunday, 1 April, 1945. The initial landings would be made on the west side of Okinawa; to first capture Yontan and Kadena airfields. The Marine and Army troops would then drive across Okinawa, thereby effectively severing Okinawa at one of its narrowest points. That would open a three mile wide sector, completely across the Island. The U.S. Army Divisions would turn south to established blocking and other defensive positions; to prevent the strong Japanese forces, known to be concentrated on the lower one third of Okinawa, from attacking north.

Both Marine Divisions would turn north, and capture the less defended northern two thirds of Okinawa. Ie Shima Island, located off the northwest coast of Okinawa, would be captured in a separate landing operation by the U.S. Army, 77th Division. The Marines 1st Division occupied the northern two thirds of Okinawa, and would provide replacements for the Marine's 6th Division, which would move south, and fight alongside units of the U.S. Army until the Japanese forces surrendered.

USS *SITKOH BAY* (CVE-86)

The flight echelon of my night-fighter squadron, VMF(N)-543, equipped with twenty-four F6F (Hellcats) shared the *Sitkoh Bay* flight deck and hangar spaces with an embarked Marine Corps day fighter squadron, VMF-312, equipped with twenty-four Chance-Vought F4U (Corsairs). They were called "the Checkerboards," because the engine cowlings on their Corsair noses were all painted in a distinctive blue and white checkerboard pattern. Our Hellcats had our Nighthawk Squadron insignia painted on both sides of each aircraft.

F6F-3N Hellcats ready for take off from the USS *Sitkoh Bay*

On 1 April 1945, the *Sitkoh Bay* approached Okinawa from the west, and launched its two squadrons. Approaching Okinawa at eight-thousand feet, we could see two smoke lines, about three miles apart, all the way across Okinawa. Gunfire, and other explosive smoke marked the frontlines north (Marines), and frontlines south (Army). Okinawa is an island about seventy miles long, with widths ranging from three miles to about twelve miles. In between those two smoke-marked frontlines were two existing Japanese airfields, Yontan and Kadena. Our squadron went to Kadena, where we were assigned to MAG-33 (Marine Air Group-33 at Kadena Airfield). After takeoff from the *Sitkoh Bay*, VMF-312 (the "Checkerboards") flew ashore, and landed at Yontan where, as planned, they joined MAG-31.

Kamikaze Attack on the USS *Achernar* (AKA-53)

Sailing a few miles west of the Okinawa landing beaches, the amphibious transport ship, USS *Achernar*, was steaming in large circles, creating smoke to make herself, and other ships, difficult to see. The *Achernar* was moving closer to the landing beaches, to commence unloading our squadron equipment and supplies; including trucks loaded with boxed rations, fresh drinking water, shelter tents, drummed aviation gasoline fuel, hand-cranked gasoline refueling pumps, and aircraft engine oil. The ground echelon of our squadron, loaded on the *Achernar*, was to have our squadron ready for operations, with the support and supplies needed for several days, following arrival of our Hellcats.

To check the general condition of the single runway Kadena Airfield, where our squadron would build a camp, and soon thereafter, conduct flight operations, my close friend, 2nd Lieutenant Chuck Temple, and other officers, were sent ashore from the *Achernar* in one of the ship's landing craft, to conduct a quick airfield reconnaissance, and return to the ship with their assessments of airfield conditions. They landed with the second wave of Marine infantrymen on 1 April 1945, and returned to the ship the same day. They said that fighting was still taking place at the north side of Kadena airstrip. So, when they returned, their assessments and recommendations were very limited.

However, the information mattered little, because the next day, 2 April 1945, the *Achernar*, still steaming in circles and making smoke to reduce visibility, was attacked and severely damaged, when hit by a Japanese Kamakazi aircraft. Ship casualties numbered five killed, and forty-one wounded. Amazingly, there were no Marine casualties; although the number of ship's crew and embarked squadron Marines was nearly equal.

Groups of Marines and sailors fought to extinguish fires, conducted repairs to the ship's deck plates, and re-rigged the cranes and booms necessary for unloading the embarked squadron. After being hit by the attacking Japanese aircraft, the *Achernar* limped to the nearby Kerama Retto anchorage, where the ship's damage control and repairs could more safely continue. A burial detail was sent ashore to bury the five dead sailors. By the 5th of April, the unloaded squadron supplies started arriving at the north side of the single Kadena Airfield runway, where the VMF(N)-543 flight line, personnel tents, and operating areas had been planned.

When the squadron airplanes arrived at Kadena from the USS *Sitkoh Bay* on 9 April, there was a lot frenzied airfield activity, but very little organization. The Navy Construction Battalion (SeaBee) personnel had been working for several days, attempting to ready the airstrip for flight operations. Some runway improvements had been made, and all of our Hellcats landed safely. However, when attempting to taxi, and find a suitable parking area, some of our Hellcats had a wheel sink through the soft coral and shell surface. When that happened, the engine had to be shut down, and the airplane pulled from the mud.

As more equipment and supplies arrived from the *Achernar*, organization slowly took shape. On the first day the Hellcats landed at Kadena, perimeter guard posts were selected and sentries posted, daily passwords were revealed, and a squadron armory was established and guarded. Tents to house and shelter critical material had been erected, and latrines had been dug. By nightfall on 9 April 1945, it was decided to limit the size of the perimeter security, by having the pilots and other officers provide their own security outside of the small airfield perimeter.

Okinawan Tombs

Across Okinawa, strange tombs dotted the landscape. They had been built over centuries, by families, to provide burial sites, and to honor their deceased relatives. The tombs were often described by wartime combatants as "perfect foxholes." The walls were thick; constructed of a cement material, and built into the sides of hills. Each tomb was seashell-shaped, and approximately twenty feet wide, twenty feet high, and thirty feet deep. Each tomb front had a flat wall, with an access hole (and a same-size stone), that allowed the remains of the deceased to be placed within the tomb. The hole could then be covered over with the stone. The tombs were domed, giving them a turtle-like appearance, when viewed from above.

At the front of each tomb was a porch, which provided a place where a family could gather to mourn, and to honor the deceased, before placing the family member inside the tomb. It was on these "porches" that pilots and other officers would try to sleep, while providing our own security, outside of the airfield perimeter. There would be four officers assigned per tomb; each standing guard for two-hour watches. Three pilots would sleep outside the tomb, but within the small tomb "front porch;" partially surrounded by a three foot high concrete wall. The fourth pilot would stand guard, armed with a Thompson submachine gun. However, pilots got little sleep because of the constant anti-aircraft fire from both the nearby ships' shore batteries. We wore our steel helmets, as the jagged material from the exploding shells overhead, continually rained down on us. After two rather sleepless nights, we ceased using the tombs, as the size of squadron perimeter security area was expanded.

Daily Combat Flights

Most of the U.S. airplanes on Okinawa were Marine Corps airplanes. The Marines had several fighter squadrons; made up of F4U Corsairs, which we called the "Bent-Wing Monster." The Japanese called the plane "Whistling Death," due to the distinctive sound the engine made when on high-speed descent. The airplane was a beautiful fighter, with an inverted gull wing. In comparison, our F6F Hellcats were configured for night intercepts, using the APS-6 radar. The radar bulb, housing the radar antennas, was on the right wing. Each of the air groups had a combination of these airplanes.

VMF(N) 543 Nighthawks; Kadena Air Base, Okinawa (1945)
Bob Warren, kneeling, 3rd from right

In addition to flying daytime combat air patrols, and looking for the enemy, our squadron had to do close air support for the troops on the ground. Providing air cover was the reason the ratio of day fighters to night-fighters was so different. At night, we didn't do any close air support for the troops. Since then, technology has improved the ability to provide support for the troops at night.

For the first two to three weeks, conditions in our squadron area were grim. On the other side of the Kadena airstrip a day fighter squadron, the VMF-323 "Death Rattlers," were doing quite well. VMF-323 scored heavily each day against the Japanese aircraft attempting to hit our U.S. Navy ships. Other day fighter squadrons based at Yontan scored equally as well, including the VMF-312 "Checkerboards" who had flown off the USS *Sitkoh Bay* on the same day we did.

The Death Rattlers were commanded by a twenty-four-year-old Major, named George Axtell, the youngest commanding officer of a Marine fighter squadron, during WWII. In one thirty-day period, his Death Rattler squadron shot down ninety Japanese enemy aircraft. Major Axtell became an ace (shooting down five or more enemy airplanes) on a single flight. His wingman, Lieutenant William "Bill" Hood, a friend of mine from Benton Harbor, Michigan, also became an ace. Several additional pilots in that squadron became aces, because of the fierce air battle that occurred while defending ships from attacking Kamikaze. Conditions on the ground were worse.

George Axtell led his squadron from Okinawa, to the island of Kyushu in southern Japan; then led them back to Kadena airfield. With gas tanks almost empty, he couldn't quite reach Kadena. He landed on the little island of Ie-Shima, located just off the northwest coast of Okinawa. The Japanese defended that island quite fiercely, until it was captured by the U.S. Army 27th Division. Ernie Pyle, a famous war correspondent from Europe, was killed at Ie-Shima. He is buried in the beautiful, National Memorial Cemetery of the Pacific, at Punchbowl Crater, in Honolulu, on the island of Ohau in Hawaii.

VMF-323, and the other Okinawa-based day fighter squadrons, deserved all the attention and accolades they received; including a visit from the Commandant of the Marine Corps. George Axtell retired many years later, wearing the three stars of a Lieutenant General.

Night Combat Air Patrols (CAP)

The single Kadena runway slowly improved. However, on night take-offs, our Hellcats would roll through unseen muddy, soft spots in the runway, slowing the aircraft enough that the pilot would rock forward in the cockpit. Therefore, it was decided to fly our aircraft the short distance (about three miles) to the Yontan airfield each evening, and fly our night missions from there. Yontan had several runways that were in much better repair, than the one at Kadena. Yontan also had a raised operating control tower, which Kadena lacked.

Flying our night missions from Yontan caused serious crowding. The Yontan runway lights were turned on just before takeoff, and turned off as soon as our night-fighters took off. The runway lights were purposely hooded to make them impossible to be seen from above. So, landing aircraft had to look for approach lights that made a V pattern, leading to the hooded runway lights which could then be seen during low landing approaches. During frequent Japanese air raids, all lights were extinguished, making it impossible to land at Yontan. When that happened, our Hellcat night-fighters, returning from a mission, had to divert, and land at Ie Shima Island, and wait for dawn. I had to divert several times.

Most of the missions assigned to our squadron were night heckler missions, for a couple of reasons: First, our night heckler missions were of much longer duration, than were the close-in Combat Air Patrol (CAP) missions. The congested air traffic at Yontan was markedly reduced with our squadron aircraft away for several hours. Second, our commanding officer was junior in rank from all of the other night-fighter squadron commanders flying from Okinawa. So, he could not argue for more CAP missions that offered more opportunities to shoot down enemy planes. However, on occasion, we were assigned CAP missions.

Our flights were a combination of heckler missions and night combat air patrols, where we would go out into various sectors, and just loiter, until we heard from the ground radar stations, directing us toward an enemy aircraft approaching Okinawa. We would then chase after the bogey.

We would fly to a Japanese-held island, called Ishagaki, located off Formosa, or we would fly north between Okinawa and Japan, to a large Japanese naval base on the island of Amami Oshima; located midway between Okinawa and the Japanese homeland. We often flew those night heckler missions alone. Sometimes I would fly low over the base, with the Hellcat propeller in low pitch, to create the loudest noise possible. Often, I would fly over the Japanese installations, and drop a bomb. Sometimes I would fire a rocket. When a rocket left the Hellcat, the rocket motor burn was blinding, and I would temporarily lose my night vision. Sometimes, our squadron doctor would give us small, empty, medicinal brandy bottles. Occasionally, I would roll back the cockpit hatch, and throw those little brandy bottles out. They would whistle coming down, and might keep the Japanese awake. Night heckler missions were always very interesting.

When we would go out on combat air patrol, often there would be two Hellcats. Between two aircraft, you were assured of having one good radar system. If possible, we would fly two Hellcats together, on each night CAP; but often, we had to fly those CAP missions alone.

One night, late in May, 1945, I was fortunate to be assigned one of those rare CAP missions. My CAP station was from thirty to fifty miles to the north of Okinawa, where I was to loiter at an altitude of twenty thousand feet, under control of one of our Marine Corps ground-based radar stations on Okinawa. I was still climbing north, through eighteen thousand feet, when I was suddenly vectored (turned) back toward Okinawa. The radar station had detected a bogey (an enemy aircraft) heading south toward Okinawa and flying at an altitude of eight hundred feet. We had previously been briefed that the Japanese were flying a flag officer (General or Admiral) to and from the enemy southern sector of Okinawa, in a twin-engine flying boat that was given the Allied Forces nickname "Emily."

My immediate action was to turn south, and descend rapidly; trying to quickly lose about seventeen thousand feet. I immediately throttled back, and reduced my airspeed to one hundred thirty knots. At that airspeed, I could safely lower my aircraft flaps and wheels, to induce maximum drag, causing my Hellcat to descend at a much faster rate. I adjusted my radar range to one mile, and picked up the blip of the bogey airplane moving rapidly down my cockpit radar scope. This was soon followed by the violent rocking motion of my Hellcat, flying through the unseen bogey aircraft's slipstream. I stopped my descent by raising the Hellcat's wheels and flaps, then adding engine power. But, when I added power, by advancing the throttle, my Hellcat engine coughed and quit.

During that long descent, I had forgotten to move the fuel mixture control from Full Rich to Automatic Lean, causing my Hellcat's engine to "load up" with an excessive amount of fuel. At the same time I spotted the engine flame patterns of the bogey aircraft, flying slightly higher and to the left of my position. I became one very busy, and very concerned night-fighter pilot. I quickly assessed my predicament. At first it seemed hopeless, because I was flying in an aircraft with a dead engine, in complete darkness over the East China Sea, and at an altitude too low to bail out.

The bogey aircraft quickly became the lesser of my concerns until my Hellcat engine suddenly coughed, and began running again. It seemed like I had a dead engine for several minutes but, actually, it was only about five to ten seconds. Now, once again, I could concentrate on the bogey aircraft, whose flame patterns I could still see. I pushed both of the cockpit-controlled machine charging handles, thereby charging all six fifty-caliber machine guns simultaneously; three mounted on each wing. While maneuvering to get behind the bogey aircraft, I passed close to his tail section; then lined up directly behind him, with all six machine guns ready to fire, and my gun sight red pipper (dot) directly on the bogey aircraft.

All I had to do now was to squeeze the red firing button on the Hellcat cockpit control stick grip, sending that bogey, with its nine man crew to Hell. But, remembering my view of his tail section, a few minutes earlier, I had a nagging feeling that there was something familiar about that bogey airplane so, I didn't fire. Instead, I flew around and looked at the tail section once again. To my knowledge, there was only one aircraft that had its twin tail surface sections shaped like a lady's fingernail. It was the U.S. Navy twin-engine "flying boat," designated the Martin PBM Mariner. That was my "bogey" aircraft!

The controlling radar station did not know why the PBM was showing as an enemy plane on their radar. We could only surmise that it's IFF (Identification-Friend or Foe) System switch was turned OFF or, that its IFF was not working properly. Regardless, I was shaking, and I thanked God that I took a second look at that PBM. Again, I turned north, and climbed back to my designated CAP Station; very thankful for those aircraft recognition classes I had attended during my Iowa Preflight School tenure. The rest of that flight was uneventful, and I landed back at Yontan a couple of hours later.

Accidents, Casualties, Injuries, and the Aftermath

On 17 April 1945, one of our pilots, Second Lieutenant Allen Schutter took off from Yontan on a scheduled night mission. A second squadron pilot, Second Lieutenant Edwin T. "Ivy" Iverson was to take off; then join up with Al Schutter's Hellcat wing; then proceed on their two-plane mission. While Lieutenant Iverson was taking off, a pilot from another night-fighter squadron mistakenly taxied onto the live runway. Lieutenant Iverson's night-fighter, at full takeoff speed, hit the taxiing airplane, fatally injuring both pilots.

On another night in April, Yontan had been bombed. After the air raid was over, I took off; and my friend, Lieutenant Chuck Temple was to immediately follow, and join up on my wing, for our assigned two-plane mission. After I was airborne, and he did not show up to join me, I called the Yontan control tower to report that my wingman had not joined up, on my wing. The tower told me to contact our controlling radar station, and to proceed on my mission alone. I did not know what happened to Chuck until after I later landed, back at Yontan. The terrible news is described as follows; and it still pains me to write about my seriously injured close friend.

After the Japanese bombing raid on Yontan was over, and most of the anti-aircraft fire had ceased, no one knew that there was a bomb hole in the active runway. I took off, and somehow missed the bomb hole. Chuck Temple was not as fortunate. He hit the bomb hole; throwing his Hellcat off the runway, and it plowed through a parked TBF (torpedo bomber), cutting it in half and setting both Chuck's Hellcat, and the parked TBF on fire. Chuck was still in the cockpit of his burning Hellcat.

Our squadron flight surgeon, Navy Lieutenant Commander Richard E. "Doc" Kelley, had told us that if we were ever on fire, we should take a deep breath to quickly end our life. Chuck tried to do that; but he was still wearing his oxygen mask, as breathing oxygen was supposed to improve a pilot's night vision. So, instead of breathing fire, Chuck got a gulp of oxygen. It revived him enough to kick his way out of his burning Hellcat. He then crawled several yards, before he collapsed. "Doc" Kelley was there immediately, and laid down beside the burning aircraft next to Chuck, thereby shielding Chuck's body from the machine gun rounds that were now "cooking off' in Chuck's burning Hellcat. For that act of bravery, "Doc" Kelley was later decorated with a medal "For unswerving disregard for his own safety, maintaining the highest traditions of the Naval Service" (paraphrased). From there Chuck was taken to a field hospital for immediate burn treatment, and preparation for Air Evacuation.

At first light the following day, I found Chuck, bandaged and lying on a stretcher on the floor of a bombed out school building that had no walls; awaiting air evacuation to a rear area hospital. Chucks arms were heavily bandaged; and crossed over his chest. His face had only minor burns, because his head had been protected by his oxygen mask, and by his helmet and goggles. Except for his head, and bandaged arms, Chuck's body was completed covered with blankets. He was conscious, and told me that he would return to the squadron in a couple of weeks. It was obvious that he was heavily sedated for pain, and therefore not completely rational. I knew that his injuries were severe, and that he would require a long period of recovery and rehabilitation. I did not see my best friend again until after WWII ended.

Chuck Temple's F6F Hellcat crash, Yontan Airfield, Okinawa (1945)

Chuck was evacuated by air, to a hospital on Guam, where he stayed for over two weeks. He was then air evacuated to Hawaii for treatment in the Aiea Naval Hospital, before returning to the United States, for treatment in several West Coast hospitals. This was all related to me later; as I had lost track of Chuck after he was evacuated from Okinawa. I really missed him; but was overjoyed to learn after WWII, that he had recovered from his injuries. He was assigned to MCAS, El Toro, California, returned to flight status, and flew F4U Corsairs there, in a day fighter squadron.

We had many other pilot losses, before we left Okinawa. Lieutenant "Rocky" Steele was shot down on 9 June, by Corsair day fighters, north of Okinawa. Lieutenant Bruce Bonner was killed, when he crashed at Kadena; he was buried in a military cemetery on Okinawa. Captain "Gus" Arndt disappeared one night on a night heckler mission, and never returned. Lieutenant Charles "Chuck" Engman was shot down twice, in one twenty-four-hour period; once during daylight hours, and the second at night, when he and a Japanese pilot who also had been shot down, were splashing around near each other in the water. Both pilots were rescued, and taken aboard a U.S. Navy cruiser.

The activity at Yontan was intense, with events happening quickly. For instance, one evening when one of our squadron pilots, Captain Jim Etheridge, was taking off, four enemy fighter planes flew very low, at full speed, across the airfield. Captain Etheredge's Hellcat had just left the ground, and the Hellcat's wheels were still retracting, when Jim turned and shot one of the enemy fighters down, in a full deflection shot (shooting at ninety degrees). Jim then flew through intense "friendly" fire, from the Navy ships offshore, and landed his crippled Hellcat; which had an engine cylinder shot off. The very reliable Pratt & Whitney two thousand HP radial engine was smoking heavily; but still running. Jim's Hellcat was so badly damaged, that it had to be stricken from the records. Luckily, Jim was unhurt during his flight; which lasted less than ten minutes. Jim's mission was thrill-filled, indeed!

Living in a Forward Area

Eating boxed K-Rations was bland and uninteresting, with the possible exception of the small cans of peaches. One day, Lieutenant Al Schutter and I noticed some steam rising across the Kadena runway in the VMF-323 operating area. We surmised that a hot breakfast was being served over there, so, we quickly found our metal mess kits, and aluminum canteen cups. Crossing the Kadena runway, we dodged aircraft taking off, and soon found the chow line that inched along the top of a terrace, toward the steam rising from the boiling water. We planned to disinfect our mess kits, metal knife, fork, and spoon, and canteen cup by dipping them into the barrel of boiling water. To cool the metal, we would wave them in the air. Next, we planned to move to the hot chow line where food would be ladled into the disinfected mess.

Al Schutter and I were waiting in line, until we were about thirty feet from reaching the first barrel of boiling water. Suddenly, two Japanese artillery rounds screamed low over our heads, and exploded just beyond the hot chow line. The whole line of those waiting for a hot breakfast went down the side of the terrace, resembling a human waterfall, to the next level below. Incoming artillery rounds are very frightening, as you can hear the rounds coming, but not for long enough to take cover, or even to crouch down. Al and I had a quick two-man squadron pilots meeting on the lower terrace level, in which we agreed that we did not really need hot chow that morning after all, by shouting, "Let's get the hell out of here." The Japanese were firing artillery from guns hidden in cave entrances, about five miles south of Kadena. Al and I raced back across the Kadena runway to safety. We thought the Japanese artillery piece might have been aiming at the rising steam from the hot chow line.

Lt. Bob Warren, Kadena airfield, Okinawa (April 1945)

The firing soon stopped, and things started to return to normal for us. In about a week, we had our own hot chow line, and a canvas eating shelter. Our skin had yellowed, from taking Atabrine tablets daily, to prevent malaria. We used our steel helmets as washbasins for shaving and bathing. We could not skip shaving, as a beard would cause our oxygen masks to leak. We cut each other's hair; using only paper cutting type scissors and razors. Lacking any barber skills, our haircuts were lopsided, notched, or both. After a few weeks we were a motley looking gaggle of squadron pilots.

Operation Iceberg

By May we were getting weary. We flew at night and couldn't develop regular sleeping patterns. We were taking part in the largest amphibious operation in the Pacific - the invasion of Okinawa, which was named "Operation Iceberg," as it represented the United States' entrance into their strategic operations in the Pacific region – just the tip of the "iceberg." The Japanese were desperate; as Okinawa is only three hundred fifty miles from the Japanese mainland, and losing the battle for Okinawa would surely spell defeat for Japan. Operation Iceberg was led by Lieutenant General Buckner, until he was killed on 18 June 1945, while observing Marine combat operations in Southern Okinawa. A Japanese incoming artillery round hit a nearby rock, and exploded. Rock fragments from that explosion hit General Buckner in the head, killing him instantly. He died because he was not wearing his steel helmet

The next senior general officer on site was Major General Roy Geiger; the IIIAC commanding general. Geiger was a Marine Corps aviator, and an amphibious warfare expert. Geiger immediately assumed command of the 10th U.S. Army, and was immediately promoted to Lieutenant General, becoming the first and only Marine, and the first and only aviator, ever to command a numbered American Army division, in the field.

The 10th Army included the 7th, 27th, 77th, and 96th Army Divisions, and the 1st and 6th Marine Divisions. Overall, two hundred eighty-seven thousand soldiers, sailors, and marines made up the 10th U.S. Army, which operated under overall Amphibious Task Force (U.S. Navy) Command.

General MacArthur, Supreme Commander for Allied Powers, rushed his old Army associate, General Jonathan "Skinny" Wainwright, to Okinawa, to take command of the 10th US. Army. General Wainwright had formerly been left on Corregidor Island, to surrender Philippine and American forces to the Japanese, after General MacArthur had left by PT Boat; having been ordered to Australia, by President Roosevelt. However, before General Wainwright could arrive and take command of the 10th Army, the Japanese surrendered at a brief ceremony near Kadena airfield. The Japanese forces defending Okinawa were commanded by General Mitsuru Ushijima. His Chief of Staff was Lieutenant General Isamu Cho. Those two senior Japanese Commanders committed Hari-kari (ritual suicide), when the surrender of their forces became imminent.

During June 1945, our squadron started receiving replacement pilots. The night flying schedule we had to maintain, flying from Yontan, plus day fighter operations at Kadena, left little opportunity for our pilots to rest. Accordingly, we had become exhausted, and were anxious to see the replacement pilots arrive. Finally, on 20 July, all of our original pilots departed on a Marine Corps Curtiss Commando (R5C) transport aircraft for a six-hour flight to Clark Field in the Philippine Islands. I slept on the aircraft deck during the entire flight; not knowing that the R5C had completed the flight on just one engine. After repair to the failed engine, and refueling at Clark Field, our transport aircraft flew another six hours, to the Island of Peleliu. Many of our replacement pilots at Okinawa came from VMF(N)-541 on Peleliu Island. So, one-half of our squadron pilots remained at Peleliu, and the other half proceeded on to the U.S. Island territory of Guam, on a flight that took another four and one-half hours. I was in the half that was ordered to Guam.

NAS, Agana, Guam

Upon arrival, we were assigned to VMF(N)-534, stationed at Naval Air Station Agana, on Guam. It was good to be on United States owned territory again, where we were able to get a decent haircut, and enjoy some excellent food. We lived in tents at Agana. But, my time at Agana airfield was short lived. VMF(N)-534 was tasked to send a four-plane, four-pilot detachment, with support personnel, to the Island of Saipan; located about one hundred and twenty miles North of Guam. As the senior 1st Lieutenant, I was ordered to lead that detachment to Saipan.

Chapter 7: Saipan Operations – World War II Victory

A few days after arriving at Guam, I led four F6F Hellcat night-fighter aircraft to the island of Saipan; the largest island in the Mariana Island chain. Saipan was the first island in the chain to be captured; followed by Tinian, then Guam; in the Navy's island-hopping strategy known as "Operation Forager." Saipan is located only five miles from the adjacent island of Tinian. The island of Saipan is less than six miles wide; and only twelve miles long. Between Tinian and Guam was the smaller island of Rota; which was never invaded by Allied forces, but was surrendered one hour after the official surrender of Japan.

We were directed to operate from Kagman (sometimes called East Field) on Saipan. The single-runway airfield was located on the Kagman Peninsula, on the eastern side of Saipan. Four pilots and twenty-one enlisted Marines made up our squadron's Saipan detachment. As the senior Marine First Lieutenant, I was in charge of the squadron's Saipan detachment. The other pilots were Lieutenants Carl Davis from Montana, Allen Schutter from Michigan and "Tex" Simmons.

Battle Highlights Saipan and Tinian

Saipan had been captured by American military forces a year before we arrived. Eight thousand troops from the 2nd Marine Division (2NDMARDIV) stormed the beaches on the western side of Saipan, from three hundred landing craft on 15 June 1944. The fighting was furious, and the Marines suffered over two thousand casualties the first day. As the battle raged for several days, the Marines were able to reach a major objective, on 25 June, by fighting their way to the one thousand five-hundred fifty foot top of Mt. Tapochau.

Taking this island high-point eliminated an observation point the Japanese were using to cause carnage on the landing beaches, and in the valleys below. The Marines and Army troops then pushed north toward Marpi Point, located on the northern tip of Saipan. At Marpi Point, thousands of brainwashed Japanese civilians jumped off the Marpi Point cliffs into the sea, and onto rocks hundreds of feet below; often carrying their children to their deaths. Over twenty-two thousand Japanese civilians died; most by jumping off the high cliffs, and some by other suicidal actions. Japanese defenders charged the advancing American troops, in a last fanatical attempt to kill as many of them as possible, with rifles and fixed bayonets. Those Japanese troops were killed by the hundreds, by cross machine gun and rifle fire, and by artillery rounds fused to explode only a few hundred yards in front of the firing guns, directly into the fanatical massed Japanese Banzai charges.

The battle to capture Saipan ended on 9 July 1944. The two senior Japanese commanders, Lieutenant General Yoshitsugu Saito and Admiral Chuichi Nagumo committed ritual suicide (Hari-kari) in caves, as the battle ended. In just twenty-nine days, American troop casualties numbered three thousand killed, and thirteen thousand wounded. While a few wounded Japanese were captured, and a few Japanese hid out until Japan surrendered, the majority of the thirty thousand Japanese garrison defenders were killed.

The Marine Corps commander at the Battle of Saipan was Lieutenant General Holland M. "Howlin' Mad" Smith, who later commanded the three Marine divisions that captured Iwo Jima. The Fleet Marine Pacific Headquarters in Hawaii is named Camp H. M. Smith. Sadly, General Smith was not invited to attend and witness the Japanese surrender aboard the battleship, USS *Missouri*, in Tokyo Bay. Shame on U.S. Navy Admiral Chester Nimitiz. As the brilliant Marine Corps commander of many WWII Naval forces in the Pacific, how could your fighting Marine General, who so courageously and successfully defeated the fanatical Japanese defenders on both Saipan and Iwo Jima, be so rudely ignored? Just what was your problem with General Smith, your highly respected Marine Corps combat leader? That is a subject worthy of study by future military historians.

On 16 July 1944 Naval bombardment of the small island of Tinian began. Tinian was populated by fifteen thousand Japanese, and two thousand Korean civilians. Tinian was defended by nine thousand Japanese troops. Unique in amphibious operations, Marine Corps artillery joined the Naval bombardment, by firing from one island (Saipan), destroying targets on another island (Tinian), only five miles away. On 24 July 1944, troops of the 4th Marine Division (4THMARDIV) landed on the island of Tinian, followed by the 2nd Marine Division (2NDMARDIV), landing the next day.

Resistance on Tinian continued until 10 August. Of the nine thousand Japanese defenders, less than four hundred survived. American troop casualties on Tinian were seven hundred fifty, with one hundred five killed. Following its capture, Tinian became an important base for further operations in the Pacific campaign. Camps were built for fifty thousand troops. Fifteen thousand Navy Seabees turned the island into the busiest airfield of the war. The Seabees build six - seven thousand, nine hundred-foot runways to support B-29 (Superfortress) bombers attacking targets in the Philippines, and the Ryukyu Islands (which included Okinawa), and ultimately, the Japanese homeland.

Our role on Saipan was to identify damaged Army Air Corp B-29's returning from their long-range bombing raids to the Japanese homeland. We also defended against any possible night air attacks against the B-29 bases on Saipan and Tinian. Following those B-29 raids, our Hellcats were usually vectored west to accompany the stream of B-29s returning from their missions. Seeing fifty or more B-29s strung out for miles on their final approach to the runways on both Tinian and Saipan was a common sight. We also worked with searchlight crews by flying low across the B-29 airfields. To prevent being blinded by those searchlights, we lowered our cockpit seats and turned up our instruments, so that they glowed bright red, and in effect, flew low across the airfields on instruments. Earlier attempts to expose their aircraft to searchlights, resulted in crashes of several Army Air Corps P-38 fighter aircraft, when pilots were blinded by the searchlights.

When we arrived at Kagman Airfield on Saipan, we were the only flying unit based there. The Navy controlled the airfield, which included a very large parking area for new replacement aircraft - F6F Hellcats, Curtiss SB2C Helldivers, TBM Avengers (torpedo planes), F4U Corsairs, and small OY-1 Artillery Spotters; all maintained in ready-to-fly condition, waiting to be delivered, mainly to aircraft carriers.

Large, twin-engine Marine Curtiss C-46 Commando transport aircraft occasionally used Kagman Airfield to deliver supplies and equipment to the 2nd Marine Division that was bivouacked nearby. Those transport aircraft had a squadron detachment at Isley Field, which was a B-29 base on Saipan. One of the C-46 pilots was Marine Lieutenant Harold "Hal" Hawkins, my friend from Michigan, who I had not seen since our CPT association at Kalamazoo and Austin Lake airfields, where we both initially learned to fly airplanes. Without requesting authorization from anyone, I let Hal Hawkins fly one of our F6F Hellcats. Having been used to the long wings of a C-46 transport, he looked out of the Hellcat cockpit, and viewing its short wings exclaimed, "No wings!" Another Marine pilot in that same C-46 squadron was my former Morehead City, North Carolina down-the-street neighbor, movie actor, and Marine Lieutenant, Tyrone Power.

We often watched the high tails of the B-29 bombers start taxiing into position for takeoff from Saipan during the late afternoons. After takeoff, we watched the B-29s cross Magicienne Bay, flying over water and past our airfield, without gaining any altitude, due to their heavy bomb loads, and the weight of the fuel each carried. Those takeoffs would last until after dark. We could also see even more B-29s taking off from Tinian Island. It was truly an amazing display of air power.

We knew they would eventually turn north and pass over Iwo Jima, on their route to bomb Japanese homeland targets. We never witnessed any B-29 takeoff problems. However, we always noted that several Navy seaplanes flew along the B-29 takeoff routes, ready to provide Air/Sea Rescue services, if required. Iwo Jima was located at midpoint on the B-29s one thousand, two hundred mile routes, to and from Japan. The capture of Iwo Jima eliminated the capability of Japanese fighter aircraft based there of attacking the B-29s flying to Japan; and from attacking our forces in the Marianas. Hundreds of damaged B-29s made emergency landings on Iwo Jima, while returning from their raids over Japan. Landing on Iwo Jima saved thousands of B-29 crew members' lives.

Iwo Jima was captured at the tremendous cost of twenty-six thousand casualties; including over seven thousand Marines killed in an operation that lasted only thirty-six days, on an island that is two miles wide, and about five miles long. Iwo Jima was one of the bloodiest battles in the WWII Pacific theater, and was the only battle in the Pacific theater where the attacking Marine casualties exceeded those of the Japanese defenders. The Japanese fought from underground, from twenty-six miles of tunnels throughout the island.

Prior to our arrival at Saipan, major changes in the command structure were made in order to prepare and provide logistical backup for the invasion of mainland Japan. The U.S. Army command on Saipan was named the Western Pacific Base Command, and by the date we arrived, had already constructed and moved into its very large new headquarters on Mt. Tapochau. A large U.S. Army hospital was part of the new headquarters Saipan complex.

One of our Saipan detachment pilots was Lieutenant Carl Davis of Dillon, Montana. The senior enlisted (Top Sergeant) in the Western Pacific Base Command was Roy Forrester, son of a rancher; also from Dillon, Montana. Roy had graduated from Duke University and was offered, but declined, a commission in the U.S. Army. He chose instead to be a career enlisted man, rising quickly to his senior enlisted rank. Roy, in well-known top sergeant fashion, really knew how to get things done. He was a mover and a shaker in every sense. For Instance, he convinced the command mess sergeant that the four Marine night-fighter pilots stationed at Kagman Airfield should be served steaks every Sunday evening.

Following one Sunday evening steak dinner, Roy also arranged to have the motor pool sergeant supervise our installation of a Chevrolet engine in a Japanese landing craft that had been captured undamaged, but was minus an engine. The motor pool sergeant was also charged with supervising our modifying a water trailer, to transport the former Japanese landing craft to the beach for recreational purposes; more specifically, to the section of the beach reserved for the hospital nurses. That was all accomplished within a week, and was available the following Sunday for the enjoyment of the nurses; and of course, for some off-duty Marine night-fighter pilots who after all, had provided the critical trailer hitch, making it possible to move the boat to the nurse-section beach. Duty on Saipan was just great for our night-fighter detachment.

To support our detachment, we had been provided a truck, a jeep, and a weapons carrier. The Dodge weapons carrier was larger than a jeep but smaller than a cargo truck. The weapons carrier could be described as a jumbo pickup truck, with a canvas covered bed. We assigned the jeep and the truck to our enlisted men, and the pilots were assigned the weapons carrier. In two and one-half months our Dodge weapons carrier was driven over two thousand, five hundred miles; which is remarkable, because Saipan is only twelve miles long. Our detachment had no mail service, so every day except Sunday, one of our pilots flew to Guam to get the mail for our detachment.

    One of my concerns was the morale of our enlisted men, who never got to leave Saipan. Our Hellcats were single seat fighters. So, I asked to borrow one of the TBM torpedo bombers parked in the pool of aircraft at Kagman Airfield, to transport a few of our enlisted men to Guam. It was a large single-engine, carrier aircraft. The TBM and the TBF were the same airplane except that the TBF was built by Grumman, on Long Island, and the TBM was built by General Motors. In addition to the pilot, the TBM had three crew stations.

    When I asked to borrow a TBM, I was asked if I had flown one before. I stated that to the best of my recollection I had flown it about thirty hours. My recollection was seriously flawed (I lied), because I had never flown a TBM or a TBF. When I was granted permission to borrow a TBM, I thought that I should at least make a solo flight to Guam to gain knowledge regarding the flying characteristics of that airplane, before transporting any passengers. I quizzed the Navy flight line mechanic extensively, about The TBM wing folding and locking operations, making certain that its wings were locked before takeoff.

    I also prepared the enlisted men for the flight by teaching them how to buckle on a parachute harness, how to attach the parachute to the harness, and how to pull the parachute rip cord to open the parachute, after bailout. They were obviously ready to go, so I got them aside and explained that I had never flown that airplane so they probably should wait until I made at least one solo flight. They scoffed at the idea, stating that they had to go as they were the winners of a contest. When I demanded, "What contest?" they explained that a contest was held among all the enlisted men, to determine who would be the first to fly with me to Guam and return. I quickly gave in, and I told them to get aboard, and how to use the crew inter-communications system.

 I started the engine and made certain that the wings were spread and locked, before calling the airfield control tower, requesting taxi and takeoff clearances. The flight was uneventful. The TBM in flight was solid as a rock; albeit the controls seemed somewhat stiff and heavy, when compared to those of our more nimble Hellcats. The TBM cockpit was roomy, and complete with two retractable armrests. I flew low over Rota, so the men could view a Japanese-held island, and so they would have some beer drinking, bragging rights, after they returned to Saipan, describing their flight over an enemy Japanese-held island.

 Landing the TBM was very easy. With flaps and wheels down, and the propeller in low pitch, I held the approach speed at eighty-five knots. Touchdown was gentle. When I raised the flaps, the airplane settled solidly, and tracked straight down the Agana airfield runway. I waited on Guam as long as possible; giving my passengers as much time as possible to shoot the bull, and have a bottle or two of beer with their squadron buddies on Guam.

 After loading our mail, and making certain that the return flight to Guam could be completed before darkness, I flew the TBM back to Kagman Airfield on Saipan, and landed. The last names of my passengers were Fosmark, Peacock and Poschel. I hope they can read this account of that day I'll never forget because, in that small way, I could express some appreciation for what all those talented enlisted Marines did for our pilots. Those Marines were, and still are the unsung heroes of Marine Corps Aviation. They were Marines in every way; always present at our detachment daily, early morning muster.

Each day, one of our pilots was the designated Officer Of the Day. In military formation, he received the muster report from the detachment's senior sergeant. He announced the schedule for that day, including daily aircraft maintenance, the name of the standby pilot, and other pertinent information, such as work schedules, and always the daily mail delivery time. Following Saturday morning muster, close order drill was held for thirty minutes; followed by rifle, and detachment area, inspections. Liberty commenced at noon on Saturday, and lasted through Sunday, for those not on duty. The men were permitted to drive the truck and/or the jeep to the beach, or to visit areas of interest; returning before dark. They were always armed, as we knew there were still a few Japanese soldier holdouts, hiding in caves, and in other inaccessible areas on Saipan.

The weather around the Mariana Islands was warm, balmy, and generally very pleasant. We were very comfortable; living in our hillside tents, overlooking Magicienne Bay. The weather offered no unusual hazardous conditions. Often, when flying in the daytime, we saw waterspouts reaching down from a two thousand five hundred, to three thousand foot cloud base, to the sea surface; where a pronounced cavity in the water could be seen. That cavity was caused by the water being pulled up to the cloud, thus causing a long snake-like waterspout. We would fly around those waterspouts, and we resisted the temptation to cut one by flying through it. Our fear was that the water might swamp our Hellcat engine. The waterspouts dissipated after sunset, so they presented no flying hazards at night.

One evening when I was the duty pilot, I was directed to "scramble" (takeoff immediately) as a bogey aircraft had been detected on radar, about one hundred miles east of Saipan, flying west toward Saipan, at eight thousand feet. I flew toward the unidentified bogey for about forty-five minutes, until I detected a thunderstorm dead ahead. I thought that perhaps it was the thunderstorm that was being detected on the radar, rather than an unidentified "bogey." I realized I was wrong, when suddenly, popping out of the storm area, I saw a large aircraft, flying with all of its running and cabin lights on. It looked like a flying hotel. When I flew closer I saw that it was a very large, four-engine, twin-tail, U.S. Navy PB2Y Coronado flying boat. I flew alongside it, blinking my navigation lights, so that the PB2Y pilots would know that they had friendly company flying nearby. I flew with that large flying boat back to Saipan, where it descended and landed in the water at the Tanapag Harbor seaplane base. I returned, and landed at Kagman Airfield.

Japanese Surrender

Early in August 1945, we began hearing rumors concerning the end of WWII. We observed an increase in B-29 raids from Isley Field and from Tinian Island. At the same time, we listened to news broadcasts concerning various ultimatums being issued to Japan, demanding surrender. We knew nothing about the two atom bombs which would target Hiroshima and Nagasaki, that were loaded in a special area, built by Navy Construction Battalions (SeaBees), on nearby Tinian Island. We learned later that atom bomb loading pits were dug, because the clearance between the B-29 fuselage belly, and the ground, would not provide the clearance necessary to taxi over the bombs to be loaded. By placing the atom bombs in the pits first, the B-29s were able to taxi over the pits, with their bomb bay doors open. The bombs were then winched up, and into, the open B-29 bomb bays.

Later, we learned that an atom bomb had been dropped on Hiroshima; and that Japanese Emperor Hirohito, following the second atomic bomb exploding over Nagasaki, would accept terms of surrender. Realizing the futility of further combat, he had overruled the militaristic Prime Minister, General Hideki Tojo, and his determination to have the Japanese military fight on. General Tojo resigned a week later. B-29 flying missions continued, following the news that the war with Japan was over. But now, their missions were to drop food, and other supplies, to the known Prisoner of War (POW) Camps and locations; and to drop leaflets to tell the POWs that the Japanese had surrendered, and that food and medical help was on the way.

Detachment Returns to Guam

A few days after the official surrender of Japan, five Japanese soldiers simply walked to Kagman Airfield, and surrendered. They had been hiding in caves on Saipan, for a year. They were taken away by military police. It became obvious that there was no longer a real reason to maintain a night-fighter detachment on Saipan. Accordingly, we expected orders to return to Guam were imminent. Two weeks passed, before we received official orders, transferring our detachment back to Guam. Meanwhile, we continued our daily mail flights.

I took advantage of this waiting period, to check out, and fly a carrier-based Curtiss SB2C Helldiver. I flew one to Guam, and back to Saipan, on 31 August 1945. I also flew the TBM several more times, as well as the two-seat OY-1 Sentinel, on local flights. On 14 August, the day of the surrender ceremony aboard the USS *Missouri* in Tokyo Bay, I flew an OY-1 on a one-hour sightseeing flight around Saipan and Tinian. My passenger was a U.S. Army nurse, named Myers. The OY-1 was a small high-wing airplane, manufactured by the Stinson Aircraft Company, near Detroit. The plane was used for artillery spotting and casualty transport. Powered by a six-cylinder Lycoming, one hundred eighty-five HP engine, its maximum speed was one hundred thirty-five miles per hour. Those small airplanes were fun to fly but they were slow to respond to power changes. It seemed that when I advanced or retarded the OY-1 throttle, all that seemed to happen, was a change in engine noise. On 12 September 1945, our detachment officially returned to Guam.

The orders to return to Guam specified that we leave our three vehicles on Saipan. We had to say goodbye to our detachment's skilled enlisted men, as they boarded a Marine C-46 transport, and left Saipan for Guam. While flying past the island of Rota for the last time, we saw a U.S. Navy ship anchored there; and an American flag was flying over an inland building. I imagined that the Japanese citizens of Rota were happy that their island was no longer being used for B-29 bombing practice, and that the machine gunning from our Hellcats had stopped.

On Saturdays we would fly two of our Hellcats back to Saipan. On 22 September, Lieutenant Al Schutter and I flew to Saipan, and remained there until our return to Guam on 24 September. When approaching Saipan, we would dive down and buzz the beach, to let our friends know we had arrived. They would drive to Kagman Airfield to meet us, and we would all return to the beach.

On 7 October Al Schutter and I flew to Saipan again. After buzzing the beach, we landed at Kagman Airfield. I was summoned to the commanding officer's office. He said to me, "Well, Warren, they finally caught you." I was surprised, as I had no idea that an admiral had moved into quarters adjacent to the nurses' beach. Al and I were directed to submit an explanatory letter, stating why we had buzzed the beach. Our letter weakly supported our actions, by stating that we were not trying to impress anyone, by our reduction in altitude, and increase in speed, but that we only wanted to notify our friends that we had arrived.

Al Schutter and I returned to Guam the next day and I never again flew to Saipan, during that WWII tour of duty. Instead, a few days later, we embarked on a much longer trip, in another direction, when we boarded a Navy transport ship for our return to San Diego.

I never knew what happened to our letter until years later, when I was reviewing my record at Headquarters, U.S Marine Corps. There, in my records folder, was a copy of that feeble letter. By then I had been promoted several times. Therefore, I assume that those promotion boards concluded: "What else should we expect from a young Marine Corps combat fighter pilot?"

Return to the United States (Land of the Big PXs)

The trip home from Guam's Apra Harbor, to San Diego, took three weeks. The ship was very crowded, and we were limited to two meals a day. No one really cared, as we were excited that the war was over, and we were going home! During the return trip to San Diego, there was continual gambling among the returnees from all the U.S Armed services. Poker appeared to be the card game of choice. No doubt thousands of back-pay dollars changed hands, by the time we arrived in San Diego.

Our reception when our ship docked in San Diego, was well planned, and could only be described as superb. We were treated to a variety of patriotic music, by a Navy band, playing at dockside. The entire dock was filled with people, including Welcoming Committee Members from San Diego, who really went all-out, to express their appreciation for our war efforts. The returning servicemen were treated royally, when we walked down the ship's gangplanks. After speeches, and many expressions of thanks on the dock, the returning Marine Corps enlisted men rode buses to the nearby San

Diego Marine Corps Recruit Depot. Returning Marine Corps Aviation personnel - mostly pilots - boarded buses, and rode to MCAS, Miramar, twelve miles north of San Diego.

Millie and Bob, San Diego (1945)

Chapter 8: Career Decision – Quantico Transfer

At MCAS, Miramar I was billeted in comfortable quarters, and told to report for processing the following morning. The processing was well-organized, and very brief. Basically, we were asked whether or not we wanted to remain on active duty; be discharged from the Marine Corps immediately; or be placed on ninety-day terminal leave, with the option of applying within the ninety-day period, for return to active duty. I selected the ninety-day terminal leave option. To me, it was a wise option, because I was understandably tired of war.

I merely wanted to return home to be with my family again, with little thought toward the future. I really didn't know what I wanted to accomplish. Following processing, which included receiving all of my back pay, I caught a military flight to MCAS, Eagle Mountain Lake, Texas. From there, I flew home to Michigan, on a commercial airline.

My mother, Ruth Warren, who had had been treated for years for high blood pressure, astounded her doctor when her blood pressure returned to normal. He was somewhat puzzled, until she told him that she finally relaxed, because her son had just returned safely from overseas. My mother quickly planned a "bridal" shower for Millie. She felt there had been no time to honor Millie as a bride, before or after we were married, and she wanted to do that properly.

Options and Decision

After a few weeks together, Millie and I gave serious thought to our future; specifically, how we would be able to earn a living, and raise a family. We considered my returning to college, but ruled that out, as it promised three more years of financial struggle. We also considered joining Millie's dad, Rudy Weber, in the construction business. I also considered a commercial flying career, and contacted my brother, Bill Dean, who was an airline captain with Northwest Airlines. He recommended that I get a commercial pilot's instrument rating. I obtained a Commercial Pilot's License, No.122024, which showed that I was qualified in single, and multi-engine aircraft, and that I had a flight instructor rating. I continued to fly at the local Benton Harbor airport.

Bill Dean, Northwest Airlines Captain (1959)

I had to drive to Grand Rapids Airport to earn my instrument flying qualification, as that was the nearest flight school offering that training. After only a few flights in an instrumented Stinson high-wing monoplane, I easily passed the instrument rating flight test. An instrument rating was then added to my commercial pilot's license. At the Benton Harbor Airport, I often took members of my family flying with me, including Millie's parents, and my sister. It became costly, as I had to pay, out-of-pocket, from my saved military pay, for all those non-military flying hours. We lived with

Millie's parents, who always made us feel welcome; but we were anxious to become self-sufficient, and to manage on our own.

After many hours of discussions, Millie and I concluded that staying in the Marine Corps was the best option for us. I had an excellent military reputation, evidenced by my combat record at Okinawa, and my selection to lead our night-fighter detachment on Saipan. I had served in two WWII Pacific Theater combat actions, and had received combat decorations for both; all while I was still only twenty-one years old. In addition, I had been promoted to First Lieutenant.

During our decision process, I received a letter from my older brother, Bill Dean, telling me that, if I desired to, I would be hired to fly for Northwest Airlines. Deep down, I knew that I really didn't want to be an airline pilot. I thought it would become very monotonous, over time, to fly as a co-pilot, whose principal duties for years would be to make the required radio calls, raise and lower the aircraft landing gear, and to hold the throttles in the full open position after takeoffs. Whoopee! Dullness and boredom would be guaranteed for years!

I did know that, as an airline pilot, I would likely make considerably more money, than I would as a military pilot. However, I felt that the excitement - the thrill of flying military airplanes - would offer a constant challenge. In addition, because I was a Naval Aviator, the possibility of making arrested landings on aircraft carriers existed (and would later come to pass). All these conditions far outweighed any airline pilot monetary considerations. Accordingly, we decided to request a Marine Corps career.

Request for Active Duty Assignment

In response to my request for orders to active duty, I was surprised that my first orders directed me to report, in uniform, to an interview (screening) board in Chicago. Chicago is only about a hundred miles from where we were living with Millie's parents, in southern Michigan. At the start of my interview, the senior member of the five-member board explained the purpose of the screening board; that the interview was to determine if my appearance, my responses to questions, and my overall demeanor, appeared suitable enough for the board to recommend approval of my request to return to active duty. If my request was not approved, I would be told, and I would receive an honorable discharge from the Marine Corps.

The board meeting was then called to order. The setting was very informal and conversational, but the serious purpose was very evident. The board wanted me to express my views, and I did so by my responses to a series of their questions. First, I was asked to briefly describe my combat experiences at Okinawa, and on Saipan. At one point, a board member questioned the need for pilots to receive additional pay for flying. My firm response was that the life insurance actuarial tables plainly showed the flight pay was indeed warranted. I think the purpose of that question was only to test my reaction to the question. The interview was cordial, and lasted about one hour. The board then took a short recess, to vote in private, on my suitability. The senior board member convened the board again, and announced that the board had recommended me for active duty assignment. The members all congratulated me. I was told that my orders to active duty would be forthcoming. I was dismissed and told to go home, and await further orders from Headquarters, U.S. Marine Corps.

With the assurance of a regular income, Millie and I bought a beautiful, new, light green and gray, four door Packard sedan, for $1,875. Our car was the fifth new car that the Packard dealer in St. Joseph, Michigan, Mr. Warren Clark, had received after WWII ended.

Return to Active Duty

My orders to active duty were to attend the Air-Infantry School at the Quantico, (MCB Quantico) Virginia Marine Corps Base. Quantico is located about thirty miles south of Washington, D.C. My orders also stated that I would continue in a flight status as a Naval Aviator. I was ordered to report to Quantico no later than 15 August 1946. Millie was now pregnant, and due to deliver our baby in November. We decided that she would remain comfortably in Michigan, with her parents, until after our baby was born.

In addition, Millie's brother, Walt Weber, had returned from the Philippine Islands, and had been discharged from the Army. He and his wife, Marnie, returned to Michigan, where they settled in the Benton Harbor area permanently. They were now the proud parents of a newborn girl they named Patricia.

Early in August, I drove our new Packard to Quantico, Virginia; a distance of seven hundred miles. I drove east across Indiana, Ohio, and into Pennsylvania. Southeast of Pittsburgh, at New Stanton, I started driving though the Appalachian Mountains on the new Pennsylvania Turnpike, for one hundred ten miles, exiting at Breezewood. I then drove south to Quantico; passing through the Maryland cities of Hancock, Frederick, Hagerstown, and Washington, D.C. The Marine Corps Base at Quantico, Virginia is located on the western shore of the Potomac River; only thirty miles south of Washington, D.C. I thoroughly enjoyed this very pleasant seven-hundred-mile trip, in our new automobile.

The Crossroads of the Marine Corps

The Marine Corps Commandant established Marine Barracks Quantico on 14 May 1917. Since that time, Quantico has initiated Marine Corps doctrine, concepts, and amphibious equipment. The Marine Corps, and other branches of our armed services, sometimes look to Quantico to lead in developing technological advancements, as well as other creative and innovative advancements for present and future wars. Quantico is the academic platform for the Corps; from Officers Candidates School, to multiple higher academic education levels. Major General Smedley Butler, who twice was awarded the Medal of Honor, described the Marine Barracks at Quantico, as "a great university." During their careers, Marine Officers can expect to attend several levels of warfighting schools at Quantico. The Marine Barracks Quantico is truly the crossroads of the Marine Corps. Attendance at one of several schools will provide, in addition to professional knowledge, an education in the rich and proud Marine Corps heritage; and I gained more of both during my first few weeks at the Air-Infantry School.

Quantico Town and the Main Base

The tiny town of Quantico is unique in that the town is completely surrounded by the Marine Corps Base. The town is actually more of an enclave, than a town; with a population of less than five hundred people, and about one hundred forty dwellings, and only ten streets. The area encompasses one tenth of a square mile. Its main thoroughfare is Potomac Avenue, which leads from the Marine Base Main Gate, across the busy Richmond, Fredericksburg and Potomac Railroad tracks, to the town; which boasted nine barber shops, and as many dry cleaners. Several Marine Corps Uniform shops, a restaurant, and a bank are the other principal businesses, along the few blocks of Potomac Avenue. Jokingly, people say the town offers three Hs: haircuts, hamburgers and hangars. The main route through to Quantico's main base is Barnett Avenue, which parallels the railroad tracks through the base.

The main base is also home to the Quantico Marine Corps Air Station; located between the same railroad tracks and the Potomac River. The Marine Corps Basic School, the FBI Academy and several large, live firing ranges and impact areas, are all located west of U.S. Highway 1, which connects Richmond, Virginia with Washington, D.C. Overall, Quantico, including the town, covers fifty-five thousand acres.

Air-Infantry School

During the six-month course we were taught the proud history of the Marine Corps, and the necessity of continuing Amphibious Warfare expertise. Our course work included a wide variety of subjects appropriate for Marine Lieutenants. I learned early on, that the Marine Corps viewed me first as a Marine officer, and at a distant second, a Marine Corps pilot. We attended classes in Geiger Hall, a very functional new, tan brick building, which was only used by the Air-Infantry School. The building was named after Lieutenant General Roy Geiger, who was the Deputy Commander of the U.S. 10th Army, during the 1945 Assault on Okinawa. When the 10th U.S. Army commander, Lieutenant General Simon Buckner, Jr. was killed, General Geiger assumed command of the 10th Army; making him the only Marine in history to have commanded a field army. He was a highly respected Marine Corps pilot, and a proven amphibious warfare expert.

While attending classes at Geiger Hall, I came to realize that the main purpose of Marine Aviation was to provide air support for troops on the ground, i.e., Marines. I became familiar with the term Close Air Support (CAS). The procedures to properly use CAS were developed by Marine infantry officers, and Marine aviators, in the 1920s, during the "banana wars" in Central America; which were fought to protect America's interests in the region. The bond between ground and air, cemented in those "banana wars," has existed ever since. What I could not have known during my time in Air-Infantry school, was that six years later, I would serve as Aide-de-Camp to Major General Christian Schilt; one of those 1920 pioneer Marine Corps pilots, who had been awarded the Congressional Medal of Honor, for heroic flights in those "banana wars."

Attendance at the Air-Infantry School proved to be a very rewarding experience for me; and for most of my classmates as well. The number of attending students was evenly split between junior Marine Corps ground Officers, and junior Marine Corps pilots. The close association of air and ground lieutenants at the Air Infantry course, forged many valuable career-long friendships.

Most of our instructors were Marine captains but, unlike the students, the instructors were predominantly infantry officers. One of those instructors, who I will never forget, was Captain Martin "Stormy" Sexton. In one of his classes, he stressed the value of using surprise in combat. He then "surprised" the entire class when, suddenly a concealed .30 caliber machine gun, fed with blank ammunition, opened fire inside the classroom. Our entire class hit the deck; trying to dive under our desks, as most of us had recently been engaged in combat operations. Accordingly, we were very familiar with the sound, and effect, of machine gun fire. With that, Captain Sexton ended his class on the value of surprise; as there was no need for further instruction on the subject.

The aviators in the class were required to maintain their flying proficiency, by logging at least four hours per month. Air-Infantry School pilot students had to vie for flight time at MCAS, Quantico, with all the other aviators attending higher level schools, and with school staff member aviators as well. The air station provided training airplanes; including small, utility, twin-engine, twin-tailed Beechcraft SNB s. We often referred to the SNBs as the "little twin-engine bug smashers." Advanced SNJ trainers, and the small OY-1 "grasshoppers," were all available at MCAS, Quantico for school student flying. The airplanes all had dual controls; therefore, two pilots could log proficiency hours on a single flight. All Air-Infantry School aviator students had to fly after school hours, on weekends, or at night. School students at Quantico could fly on only local flights; cross country flying was not permitted.

One morning we were bused to the large base theater, where we joined students gathered from the various other schools for some "special education." The special education started, when the Base Commanding General, Lieutenant General Clifton B. Cates, introduced Five-star Admiral of the Fleet, William F. "Bull" Halsey, Jr. During the introduction, General Cates stated that Admiral Halsey was the honored guest at a dinner, the previous evening. General Cates said that during the cocktail party that preceded the dinner, he noted that most of the ladies present, had gathered around the honored guest. Admiral Halsey quickly responded, saying, "That's what happens when a new animal enters the zoo." At the end of his outstanding presentation, Admiral Halsey insisted that he meet us individually, and shook our hands. Later in this chronicle, I'll describe some of my brief associations with three more Five-star Navy, and Army flag officers; Admiral Chester Nimitz, General Dwight Eisenhower, and General Omar Bradley.

On 4 November 1946, our son, Bill, was born in Mercy Hospital in Benton Harbor Michigan. Immediately following our last class at Quantico, on 8 November, another classmate, Lieutenant Francis "Rocky" Opeka, and I, drove my Packard, non-stop to Muncie, Indiana where his wife, Marcy, had also recently given birth to their first baby. From Muncie, I drove alone to Michigan, to visit Millie, and our new son. While there, on Saturday, we took our new son home. The time was a joyous one for our family, and many said that the baby looked like me. When Doctor Thorpe, who delivered our baby, heard that remark, he said, "Well, that's convenient."

Early on Sunday morning, I started driving back to Quantico, with a stop in Muncie, where I again met my friend "Rocky" Opeka. From Muncie, we drove back to Quantico; arriving in time for our first class on Monday morning, following our breakneck weekend driving trip of over one thousand four hundred miles.

In anticipation of driving to Michigan during the Christmas Holidays, and bringing Millie and our baby back with me, I rented a house on Wisconsin Avenue, in Northwest Washington, D.C. Our landlady seemed somewhat eccentric, as she would rent her house only to military officers, or to members of the Washington Senators professional baseball team. We were granted Christmas leave, officially extending from 23 December 1946 through 3 January 1947; a leave of twelve days. However, by adding an off-duty weekend to each end of the Christmas leave, our total absence from Quantico would be sixteen days.

When classes ended on 20 December, I started the drive back to Michigan. Again, my friend Rocky Opeka and another classmate, Bob Crone, also rode with me. We shared the driving; and except for fuel, food, and rest stops, we drove straight through to Michigan. Rocky Opeka and Bob Crone resided in the Illinois cities of Des Plaines and Rockford; both near Chicago. Rocky's father had driven to Michigan to meet his son; and he also drove Bob Crone to his family home in Rockford.

Family Move to Washington, D.C.

We had a very joyful Christmas, with many of our relatives and friends. During the days following Christmas, we packed our 1946 Packard sedan with Millie's clothes, a full range of new baby supplies, and the household appliances Millie had received at her bridal shower, plus our Christmas gifts. After tearful goodbyes to our families; with our new baby snug in a large basket, on the backseat of our 1946 Packard sedan, we departed Michigan for the long drive back to the house I had rented in Washington, D.C. Our traveling experiences were considerably different now; as we had to take our baby into restaurants, and ask that his bottle be heated, before he could be fed.

The trip went well, until we passed Pittsburgh; driving on a road leading to the Pennsylvania Turnpike. At Greensburg, the large, semi-tractor-trailer we were following stopped, just ahead of us. The road had icy spots, but the semi rig, with its multiple wheels, had no trouble stopping. We did; and our Packard slid on an icy section of the road, into the back of the stopped semi-trailer. Our front bumper was lower than the rear of the semi-trailer. So, the impact damage was above the Packard bumper, to the grill, radiator, front fenders, and the hood. Fortunately, we were driving very slowly; but still, the damage rendered our car not driveable. The real worry was that the impact was severe enough to tip baby Bill's basket on its side, and catapult him forward out of the basket, onto the rear seat floor. Other than a small bruise near his eye, he had no other injuries.

We decided that I would stay in Greensburg, to get the Packard repaired; and Millie would catch a train to Washington, D.C. I called my sister, Helen McKean, who lived with her husband, Eugene "Gene," and their two small children, Don and Nancy, in the Washington suburb of Falls Church, Virginia. Helen and Gene met Millie, when she arrived at Washington's Union Station, and drove Millie and Bill to their Falls Church home. They were both dirty, and a pitiful sight. Bill's baby blanket and basket contents were filthy with coal soot from the train.

Repairs to our Packard took just a few days as, largely, only body work and painting were required, and then I left immediately for my sister's Falls Church home. The next day, I drove with my family to the house I had rented. Our trip was finally complete; with two days remaining on my extended Christmas leave.

School Carpool

Three of my Air-Infantry school classmates also resided in Washington, D.C. They had established a carpool to Quantico. Each weekday, the driver for that day would meet the non-driving pool members at Washington's 14th Street bridge, and then drive south on Highway 1 to Quantico. They were happy to have me join their driving pool. On the days I didn't drive, I rode a city streetcar down Wisconsin Avenue to the 14th Street Bridge. Except for the very early reveilles, the daily ride to Quantico, passing Ft. Belvoir, then the towns of Woodbridge, Dumfries, and Triangle, became routine; and were generally enjoyable.

The two-story house I rented on Wisconsin Avenue was well-located near a large shopping center. It had a hot water heating system. Water was heated by a wood/coal furnace in the basement of the house; and the hot water was piped to radiators in each room. We fueled the furnace with wood that I purchased. A small, free standing, one-car garage was in a narrow alley behind the house. The garage had been built for cars much smaller that our Packard. To drive into the garage, I had to drive down a narrow alley and then turn sharply into the garage. The maneuver always required several back and forth turns to align the Packard with the garage. On days that I didn't drive to Quantico, Millie would often put Bill in the car, and drive downtown to Hecht's Department Store, where she would meet my sister for an enjoyable lunch, and shopping. During March 1947, I completed Air-Infantry school at Quantico and was transferred to the Second Marine Aircraft Wing at Cherry Point, North Carolina, for "Duty Involving Flying."

Chapter 9: Cherry Point Photo Squadron

Background

In July 1941, the U.S. Congress appropriated fifteen million dollars for clearing eight thousand acres of farmland, timberland, and swamps, in preparation for the building of a Marine Corps Air Station near Havelock, North Carolina. Clearing involved extensive drainage and malaria control. Construction began in November 1941; just days prior to the attack on Pearl Harbor. The facility was commissioned on 20 May 1942, and named Marine Corps Air Station, Cherry Point; after a local post office situated among some cherry trees. Its primary WWII mission was to train squadrons of Marine pilots, and aviation qualified enlisted Marines, preparing for combat in the Pacific theater. My WWII night-fighter squadron, VMF(N)-543, trained at Cherry Point, for the eventual combat, overseas.

When Millie and I arrived at Cherry Point from Quantico, with Bill, our five-month-old son, we learned that on-base housing was not available for married Second Lieutenants. We then drove to Morehead City; where we rented a house on Evans Street. Morehead City is about 20 miles distance from MCAS, Cherry Point. Our next-door neighbors were Percy and Roxy Holland. Percy Holland was a charter fishing boat Captain and Roxy Holland was a school teacher. They were wonderful down-home people. Bill took his first steps in their kitchen. Roxy would look at him and say, "He's some kind of cute, I reckon." Eventually, we were able to move into a Quonset hut apartment, on the Cherry Point Air Station. We lived there for over two years. Our daughter, Jeanne Kay, was born on 3 July 1950 at the Cherry Point Air Station Hospital. Percy Holland would say to Millie and me, "Y'all may be Yankees, but that youngin's (Jeanne Kay) a Tar Heel." I reckon he was right.

Bob and Bill Warren, Cherry Point, NC (1947)

Bill Warren's 1st Birthday Party (4 Nov 1947)

Marine Photo Reconnaissance Squadron (VMP-354)

My orders from Quantico to Cherry Point were Permanent Change of Station (PCS) orders. The orders further specified that I was to report to the Third Marine Aircraft Wing (3rd MAW) for "duty involving flying." At the 3rd MAW, I was sent to Marine Air Group 14 (MAG-14) which, along with MAG-11, were the two major subordinate flying commands in the 3rd MAW. I was assigned to MAG-14, because I was a veteran night-fighter pilot, and MAG-14 had two night-fighter squadrons. One flew F6F Hellcats, and the other, radar equipped F7F Tigercats. The night-fighter Tigercat had twin engines, and tandem cockpit seats; one for the pilot, and behind, one for the radar operator.

When I reported to MAG-14, I was told that neither of the night-fighter squadrons had any pilot vacancies; but, that the Photo Reconnaissance Squadron, VMP-354, had F7F Tigercats; and had pilot vacancies. Accordingly, I was assigned to VMP-354, which was commanded by a very capable combat Marine pilot, Major Harlen E. "Tex" Hood. The squadron flew three types of combat aircraft - single-engine F6F Hellcats, single-engine F4U Corsairs, and twin-engine, single-seat cockpit, F7F Tigercats - all modified to accommodate installation of large aerial cameras, having focal lengths of up to twenty-four inches.

My assignment to the photo squadron proved to be a wonderful assignment for me, as I got to fly the familiar Hellcat, plus I also flew, and qualified in, the F4U Corsair, and the F7F Tigercat. Flying two types of squadron aircraft in a single day wasn't unusual; and occasionally I flew all three. All of those airplanes were powered by very reliable Pratt & Whitney R-2800, two thousand HP engines. Hellcats and Corsairs each had six wing-mounted .50 caliber machine guns. The F7Fs had four of the same caliber machine guns, all mounted in the aircraft nose. All three had rocket rails attached under their wings.

Our daily photo training flights in those aircraft were realistic. Rolls of aerial camera film we shot would be carefully analyzed during the post-flight briefings. Our pre-briefed targets were bridges, shipyards, railroads, road junctions, and selected airfields, and fuel farms; all within one hundred miles of Cherry Point. All aerial cameras were located in the fuselage of the plane. The Hellcats carried three cameras: one vertical camera, and two oblique cameras; one mounted on each side. The F4U Corsair had a single, vertical, aerial camera. The F7F Tigercat carried all three cameras. With two - two thousand HP engines, the Tigercat was fast, and a real joy to fly; but it had been proven to be unsuitable for aircraft carrier operations. Thus, the Hellcat, with three cameras, was the most versatile photo airplane in the squadron.

Often, two photo pilots, Flying Hellcat photo planes, would be temporarily attached to a twenty-four plane F4U Corsair fighter squadron, aboard a CVE (Jeep) aircraft carrier for deployments to the Mediterranean Sea for six months, or to the Caribbean Sea for three months. More often, our photo squadron deployed to the Roosevelt Roads Naval Station, located on the east end of Puerto Rico, with only the F7F Tigercats. The small island of Vieques - only five miles from Roosevelt Roads – was the site of many, and varied, ground targets. Our squadron training at Roosevelt Roads included aerial gunnery, firing at a towed sleeve, strafing ground targets on Vieques Island, and firing a single High Velocity Aircraft Rocket (HVAR), which was eleven inches in diameter.

When aimed and fired, the eleven-inch HVAR left the Tigercat, attached to a lanyard, which prevented the rocket from firing, until it was well clear of the firing aircraft; preventing the exhaust blast from damaging the firing aircraft. The eleven-inch HVAR could penetrate a target made with several feet of reinforced concrete. These types of live ordnance training were never done by our squadron, at our home Cherry Point base.

Photo Squadron Training at MCAS, Cherry Point

In June 1947, my VMP-354 squadron commanding officer, Major Harlen E. "Tex" Hood, told me that I would be temporarily assigned to Marine Fighter Squadron 225 (VMF-225) for a three-month deployment to the Caribbean Sea area, aboard a small aircraft carrier, the USS *Siboney*. Going along with me, would be my good friend and fellow squadron pilot, Lieutenant Francis "Rocky" Opeka.

We immediately started practicing with VMF-225, by simulating aircraft carrier operations. The VMF-225 squadron was often dubbed "two and a quarter." The squadron had twenty-four F4U-4 Corsairs. Our training involved Field Carrier Landing Practice (FCLP), using a MCAS, Cherry Point runway. The simulated carrier training included being waved off by the VMF-225 Landing Signal Officer (LSO), 1st Lieutenant Richard "Dick" Flanagan. The LSO gave close-in approach, and landing signals, to the pilot of the landing airplane. His last signal, before landing touchdown was a cut signal; given by slashing one of his two large colorful paddles across his throat. The pilot of the landing plane, now over the simulated ship's fantail, would immediately respond by reducing (cutting) his aircraft throttle, to its idle position. The aircraft would then touch down on the runway; and the pilot, leaving the arresting hook retracted, would add full engine power, and takeoff straight ahead; leaving the aircraft wheels and flaps down, taking interval on the airplane ahead; turning left to the downwind leg, paralleling the ship; but in the opposite direction.

When opposite of the moving ship, the pilot would start a left turn, and line up behind the carrier deck, for final approach for a carrier landing. The close-in term was "in the groove." At this point, the pilot would start responding to signals from the LSO, who stood on a special platform at flight deck edge, near the stern of the ship.

Wave-offs to the approaching aircraft pilot were signaled by the LSO, waving both brightly-colored paddles back and forth over his head. Wave off signals were understood to be mandatory. Any pilot who violated the wave-off, and attempted to land aboard ship, would likely lose his wings, and his military flying would be terminated.

Aircraft flight decks are very crowded, dangerous places, with simultaneous catapults, arrested landings, bomb and rocket loading, aircraft refueling, and elevators lifting aircraft from the hangar to the flight deck, and planes taxiing to exact spots for a catapult launch, or for a fly-away takeoff. The carrier flight deck, where all this is taking place, is only a few hundred feet long. Flight deck personnel were identified by the color of their shirts, which represented their duties; for instance: red for ordnance; yellow for plane handlers; purple "grapes" for refueling personnel; green for maintenance personnel; and blue for airplane captains, who assist pilots getting in and out of aircraft cockpits. During flight operations, crash and firefighting personnel - wearing protective clothing - were always positioned in the flight deck edge catwalks.

Chapter 10: USS Siboney - Caribbean Deployment

The aircraft carrier we were assigned to - the USS *Siboney* (CVE 112) - was an escort aircraft carrier; just over five hundred feet long. The carrier was built between April and November of 1944, and was launched on November 9, 1944 at the Vigor Shipyards in Seattle, Washington. The ship was designed to operate with up to thirty-four Aircraft. VMF-225, with our two additional photo Hellcats, had a total of twenty-six Aircraft. The *Siboney*'s turbine engines generated up to sixteen thousand HP. Shafted to it were two large bronze screws (propellers) that could drive the USS *Siboney* to its maximum (flank) speed of nineteen knots. The ship's crew numbered slightly over one thousand.

Bob Warren catapults off the USS *Siboney*, near Norfolk, VA

VMF-225, led by Major Charles Kunz, USMC, as planned, intercepted the *Siboney* off the Virginia Capes; about twenty-five miles southeast of Norfolk. Major Kunz kept the squadron in tight formation, until the standard "Your Signal Is Charlie" call was radioed from the ship, along with a steady green Aldis Lamp. Those signals meant that the ship was ready to start recovering aircraft. Receiving that call, six of the squadron aircraft broke from a tight Echelon formation, descended to five hundred feet into a long Trail formation, took interval between aircraft, and commenced carrier landing approaches. Until the ship was completely ready to recover aircraft, each approaching aircraft would be waved off while still in the groove.

My Barrier Crash

The pilot to land first, would be the one in the groove, when the ship was ready to start recovering aircraft. I was approaching the ship in the groove. I did not get the expected wave-off signal. Instead, the LSO held his paddles with arms straight out from his shoulders; indicating that my approach was normal. He signaled that I was slightly fast, by momentarily dropping one paddle down, and then returning the paddle to it former straight out position. He then gave me the cut signal. I responded by chopping the throttle back to idle.

After touchdown, I felt the Hellcat wheels bumping over eight or nine arresting cables. However, the Hellcat did not stop until crashing into the barrier (the fence), consisting of two heavy cables raised from their stowed position, one above the other, and stretched completely across the flight deck. When raised, one of the cables is about three feet high and the other is about seven feet. The propeller of my Hellcat hit both the high and low cables simultaneously and the struts above my Hellcat's wheels contacted the lower barrier cable.

When I realized that my airplane was not stopping, I must have followed my natural instinct to stop, by fully applying the brakes. Applying full wheel brakes would likely raise the aircraft tail, and then, when slamming into the barrier cables, the aircraft could flip upside down. I don't know who applied my Hellcat's brakes. I don't recall doing so, but there were two fresh, burned rubber, black streaks down the flight deck, that stopped where I hit the barrier.

My Hellcat did not flip over, but only seemed to bounce around on the flight deck. My tight shoulder straps kept my head from slamming against the cockpit instrument panel. Pieces of that spinning propeller pierced the wooden flight deck, and fell into the hangar deck below. The propeller blades remaining on my Hellcat appeared to be partially "feathered," having scraped the engine cowling. About a third of one of its propeller blades was gone.

Bob Warren's F6F following the barrier crash on the USS *Siboney*

Fortunately, no one was injured. When my Hellcat stopped bouncing around after hitting the barrier, the Ship Captain's voice from the bridge ordered, "Pilot of that plane report to the bridge." I unstrapped from the Hellcat cockpit, took my broken arresting tail hook from the LSO, who handed it to me. Carrying the broken tail hook, I climbed the ladder outside the ship's superstructure, up to the ship's bridge. Somehow, I sensed that I was not being summoned to join the Captain in his sea cabin. I expected some admonishment, because I had just torn up an area of his ship's flight deck. However, he was very nice to me, first smiling, then stating, "Welcome Aboard." He then asked, "You had a good pass, didn't you Lieutenant?" I responded by describing the LSO's brief fast signal before he signaled a cut. I think the Captain was checking on my mental condition, and attitude, after crashing into the ship's barrier cables on my first aircraft carrier landing. After noting that I was unhurt, and still rational, he casually stated that I would qualify later that afternoon, with the rest of VMF-225.

The Captain then turned his attention to the deck activity, where the VMF-225 Corsairs were now making arrested landings, folding their Corsair wings, taxiing across the flight deck onto the deck level elevators, and being lowered to the hangar deck. That afternoon, alternately using Rocky Opeka's remaining Hellcat, we both made the qualifying number of takeoffs and landings.

My seriously damaged Hellcat was later stricken from the inventory of U.S. Navy airplanes. My crash into the barrier was obviously caused by the Hellcat arresting tail hook breaking off, when it contacted the flight deck. Accordingly, a formal aircraft crash investigation board was not convened. Pilot error was never an issue. I felt that the VMO-354 Squadron Engineering Officer should have magnifluxed (metal X-ray) the arresting hook, before our carrier deployment.

I flew my aircraft carrier qualification flights that afternoon, by successfully making the required five takeoffs and landings. Prior to each takeoff, my Hellcat was pushed backwards until three hundred seventy-five feet of cleared flight deck space was straight ahead. Just before takeoff, I lowered the flaps, held the brakes, and added full engine power. The yellow-shirted launch officer would spin his signal flag over his head until he was satisfied that full power had been achieved. The launch officer would next point his flag forward, signaling me to release the brakes and takeoff straight down the flight deck. He would kneel, to allow the aircraft wing to pass safely over his head. The squadron F4U Corsair pilots all completed carrier qualification, by flying six aircraft at a time. Different than the FCLP, each aircraft landing approach was flown with the arresting hook down; enabling the landing aircraft to snag one of the arresting cables, and after a short run out, abruptly be stopped (arrested) on the deck. A replacement Hellcat, for my seriously damaged Hellcat, was flown to the USS *Siboney*.

During our deployment with VMF-225, aboard the *Siboney*, Rocky Opeka and I, flying the two photo Hellcats, were often launched, to locate and photograph some target, which the Corsair squadron would later attack. The exercise introduced realism, and purpose, for our training as the fighter squadron photo pilots. Some of the targets selected for training, were over one hundred miles from our launch position. Flying these assignments would require us to plot the ship's Speed of Advance (SOA), steaming direction, surface wind direction, and wind speed, on our cockpit plotting boards. Plotting was done in the Pilot's Ready Room, aboard ship. We carried our plotting board to our airplane, from the Pilot's Ready Room. Using the plotting board, we would accurately know where the ship would be when we returned.

I had learned how to use a plotting board to solve Moving Base problems while attending the U.S. Navy pre-flight school at the University of Iowa, several years earlier. On one of those photo missions, we were sent to photograph a village on the island of Cuba. Our ship carried the name, *Siboney*, the same name as that village. The village had some historical significance, as it was the first landing site of American Troops on the island of Cuba during the Spanish-American War in 1898.

Naval Station, Guantanamo Bay, Cuba

During our carrier deployment, we were granted liberty several times, at the Naval Station, Guantanamo Bay, Cuba. Long referred to as "Gitmo," the Naval Station provided protected deep water anchorages, and dockside services, for all types of domestic and foreign ships. Gitmo is located east of Santiago, on the south coast of Cuba. The Naval Station encompasses forty-five square miles of land and water area. In 1903 it was leased from Cuba, by the United States Government, for a coaling and refueling station for ships sailing from Europe, and from United States ports, most proceeding on to South America; and when completed, to the Panama Canal. The original cost of the lease was $2,000 a year; later renegotiated to $4,085, in 1934 - the year Gitmo was designated a U.S. Naval Station.

Gitmo had two operating airfields. One was McCalla Field; built along the east side of the Naval Station, at the edge of the water. The airfield had three runways with the longest being four thousand, two hundred feet. The other airfield was named Leeward Point Field; and was located directly across the bay entrance from McCalla Field. Having no buildings, Leeward Point initially served as an outlying airfield.

The USS *Siboney* entered Gitmo Bay, and anchored on most weekends. Shore liberty was granted to one half of the ship's crew, and to the VMF-225 pilots. During the ship's next Gitmo visit, the other half of the crew was granted liberty. The enlisted men enjoyed visiting the beautiful swimming beaches, or the active on-base Enlisted Club, which offered USO Shows, or other live entertainment. Officers enjoyed similar entertainment at the on-base Officer's Club. Liberty boats would shuttle back and forth between the ship and the host Naval base. Liberty always ended at midnight.

At first light each Monday morning, the *Siboney* weighed anchor, and commenced daily flight operations, as it exited the bay entrance. I vividly recall approaching the ship early one morning for a landing, and being waved off, because Rocky Opeka's Hellcat had flipped upside down after crashing into the same flight deck barrier I had hit, on my first aircraft carrier landing. Rocky's Hellcat snagged an arresting cable; then under tension, the cable broke. Ends of the broken cable snapped back, hitting a sailor who was watching aircraft landings from the catwalk, at the edge of the flight deck. The cable hit the sailor in the head, causing a very serious, if not fatal injury. Again, aircraft carrier flight decks are very dangerous places.

The *Siboney* immediately ceased all flight operations, and entered Gitmo Harbor at flank speed, in order to get the injured sailor to the Gitmo Naval Base hospital as quickly as possible. Meanwhile, Rocky Opeka was extracted from underneath his crashed Hellcat, shaken but uninjured. With several Corsairs, I diverted to nearby McCalla Field, and landed.

Our deployment route through the Caribbean Sea area included passing Haiti, the Dominican Republic, Puerto Rico, St. Thomas and French St. Martin, St. Croix, and the Dutch Island of Aruba. Our three-month deployment passed quickly, and we returned to MCAS, Cherry Point, with VMF-225; now confident, experienced, and qualified aircraft carrier pilots. After landing home at Cherry Point, Rocky Opeka and I returned to VMP-354; our photo squadron. After launching its Marine Corps squadron, the USS *Siboney* returned to the Norfolk, Virginia U.S. Naval Base.

Return from Caribbean Deployment

Being launched from the *Siboney,* for the last time, was wonderful. We flew home to Cherry Point, where we were reunited with our families. We had wonderful junior officer neighbors, who also lived in neat rows of Quonset huts. Like the Quonset hut apartments we had lived in at NAS, El Centro several years before, each Quonset apartment had two bedrooms, a single bathroom, a small kitchenette, and a living room. All rooms were well lighted by glass windows. The Quonset apartments were classified as "inadequate housing"; so we did not have to pay our entire housing allowance to live there. Instead, we paid a total of $30 per month for our apartment; just enough to meet the costs of utilities, maintenance, and yard upkeep. Each Quonset hut had two identical apartments; facing opposite directions from each other.

Bob, Bill & Millie Warren, Cherry Point, NC (Dec 1948)

Our "attached" neighbors were Lieutenant William T. "Bill" Witt, and his wife, Trudy. Bill Witt and I had been together on our recent deployment to the Caribbean Sea area, aboard the USS *Siboney*. One day, when Bill Witt was polishing his car, our little son Bill was asking a barrage of never-ending questions. Bill Witt told our son that if he did not quit asking questions, he would tie him to one of the many large pine trees in our neighborhood. After that, and for the next few mornings, our son would streak out of our Quonset hut door, looking for Bill Witt. If he saw him, our son would say, "Tie me to a tree, Bill Witt! Tie me to a tree!"

While I had been deployed to the Caribbean Sea area aboard the USS *Siboney*, our VMP-354 squadron had changed commanding officers. Major Harlen E. "Tex" Hood was relieved by another very capable squadron commanding officer, Major Toler Bryan. He was the proud owner of a 1937 Lincoln Zephyr coupe that had been restored to "mint" condition. Its long sloping downward trunk lid added to its beautiful design. Early one morning, he asked me to ride in his Lincoln Zephyr with him to New Bern; about 19 miles from Cherry Point. When we departed, he told me that first, he had to make a quick stop at our air group headquarters, located inside one of the large permanent hangars at Cherry Point. When he stopped and parked his Lincoln Zephyr and shut off its engine, I expected to wait in his car. But, he told me to accompany him, so I opened the passenger door, got out and walked with him into one of the hangar offices.

Meanwhile, at the open end of the hangar, several F4U (Corsairs) were parked side by side with wings folded, and wheels chocked. The mechanics were performing the Corsair engine warm-ups, from inside the cockpits. The checks included switching the dual magnetos "off" and "on," at high engine power, while the mechanic applied full pressure to both wheel brake pedals. For some reason, one of the Corsairs "jumped" its chocks, spun around, and the two adjacent propellers hit each other. Propeller sections broke off with "shrapnel" flying in all directions. Although there was extensive damage to several of the parked Corsairs, there were no injuries to personnel. One 15-inch section of a broken propeller flew past the hangar, across the automobile parking lot, and came down at a slant, slicing through the roof of Major Bryan's Lincoln Zephyr, and exited through the right passenger window where my head would have been, had I not gone into the hangar with Major Bryan. Surveying the scene, I gave thanks to God for His obvious Divine intervention, in preventing my demise. For the next year, I enjoyed flying our squadron F4U Corsairs, F6F Hellcats, and the very fast, twin-engine F7F Tigercats.

Bob Warren piloting a Grumman F7F Tiger Cat, Cherry Point, NC

    The Tigercat had a unique single hydraulic system. Other fighter aircraft had a separate hydraulic system for their wheel brakes; but the Tigercat did not. The Tigercat's single hydraulic system operated its brakes, wheel retracting, and wing flap and wing folding system. If the Tigercat hydraulic system failed, the pilot could isolate the failed part of the system from the cockpit. Most often, it was the landing gear lowering system that would fail. To be certain that I understood how the Tigercat hydraulic system worked, my Commanding officer had a Tigercat placed on supporting screw jacks, and lifted off its parking lot surface. I then had to unlock the wheels and use a hydraulic pump handle inside the cockpit to raise the wheels to the up and locked position. That required over seven hundred very tiring pumps to get the wheels up. Because of gravity, only about three hundred pumps were required to lower the wheels to the down and locked position.

The Tigercat , with its twin four thousand HP engines, was sleek, powerful, and fast. The plane was a joy to fly, in spite of its poorly designed hydraulic system. Unlike the Corsairs and the Hellcat "tail draggers," the F7F had a nose wheel that allowed it to track straight down the takeoff or the landing runway; with no tendency to swerve, even if landing with only one engine running. But, landing with only one of its two engines running made it impossible to taxi and maintain directional control. Therefore, if there was just one engine running, that engine was cut (stopped), and the Tigercat would have to be towed to its squadron parking spot.

Once, VMP-354, flying its Tigercats, participated in a joint service exercise at The Army Air Corps' Eglin Airfield located east of the Pensacola Naval Air Station. During that exercise, we flew our Tigercats from Baron Field; a small outlying airfield, located not far from NAS, Pensacola, in nearby Foley, Alabama. With several other squadron pilots, I was permitted to return to Cherry Point, and drive back to Foley with Millie and our active toddler son, Bill. Another photo squadron pilot named Bob Crone, his wife "Curlee," and their little daughter Sally, were following us from Cherry Point to Alabama. Driving behind us, they watched our son Bill continually throw his toys out of the rear window of our car. During the joint service exercise at Eglin Field, Millie and I stayed in a motel in Foley, Alabama, where we celebrated the second Birthday of our son, Bill.

Bill Warren and Sally Crone, Cherry Point, NC (1950)

The Fly Home Program

While pilots in VMP-354, we could submit a request to fly one of our squadron airplanes "home" to visit our families on Saturdays, remain overnight (RON), and then fly back to Cherry Point on Sunday. Of course, certain criteria were required, to ensure the safety of the aircraft and the squadron pilot; including planned refueling stops, weather restrictions, and security of the airplane at the home destination. The solo cross-country flights were accomplished on weekends, so as not to interfere with weekly training. These solo flights to our homes were encouraged, because it placed the entire responsibility for the aircraft on the pilot.

Many of the things that were routinely done by the ground crews had to be done by the pilot. On trips home, the pilot had total responsibility for refueling with the proper high-octane fuel, ensuring that the engine oil level was correct, confirming that aircraft tie downs were attached, draining accumulated water from the bottom of the aircraft fuel tanks, and locking the parked aircraft controls. We also had to submit a complete return cross-country flight plan back to Cherry Point. Prior to starting the engine, the propeller had to be manually pulled through, several times, to remove the accumulated oil from the lower engine cylinders. Turning the propeller prevented damage to the bottom cylinders due to liquid (oil) compression.

One weekend, I flew a Hellcat to Benton Harbor, Michigan. After my planned landing and refueling at NAS, Columbus, Ohio, I proceeded on to Benton Harbor. When I approached my Benton Harbor airport destination, the airport was experiencing a severe thunderstorm. I flew south, toward South Bend, Indiana to avoid the dangerous storm. That route took me over the Niles, Michigan airfield, where my brother, Bill Dean, had learned to fly. I decide to land there, as it was only a few miles from Benton Harbor, and the weather at Niles was CAVU (Ceiling and Visibility Unlimited).

The Niles airfield had a grass runway, causing me to land my Hellcat as gently as possible. I stayed at Niles for an hour; giving the thunderstorm time to move away from Benton Harbor. Some of the airport personnel were very nice; and they told me that the airport owner, Lee Roskay, had often bragged about my brother's flying accomplishments. Lee Roskay was my brother, Bill's first flying instructor. Bill had learned to fly, and soloed, at that same small Niles airfield several years before. My brother went on to become an accomplished and highly respected Northwest Orient Airlines Captain. I was happy that I landed at Niles, and was somewhat relieved that the grass runway supported the weight of my Hellcat during landing. An hour later, I took off for Benton Harbor.

After taking off from Niles, I hardly had time to raise the Hellcat wheels and flaps when it was time to lower them again, in preparation for landing at the Benton Harbor Airport. The airport had several hard surface runways. I was familiar with the fixed base operators at Benton Harbor, as I had flown there often while on Terminal Leave following WWII. Several of my family members were there to meet me; including Millie's dad, Rudy Weber; her mother, also named Millie ; my mother, Ruth Warren; Millie's aunt and uncle, Emma and Claude Mast; and several more family members and friends. They all seemed fascinated watching me attach the Hellcat wing tie downs, chock the wheels, and secure the Hellcat controls. Little did they know, I had never done those things alone before.

I showed Rudy Weber and Claude Mast how to climb up the side of the Hellcat from behind the wing, using the built-in spring-loaded grips and handles. They then climbed up the side of the Hellcat and stepped onto the wing, one on each side. The cockpit canopy was open so that when they looked into the open cockpit, they stared at the full panel of instruments, and the many cockpit controls. I think they were both somewhat in awe. Claude finally said to Rudy, "By God Rude, you have to know something to do all of this."

The next morning, they all watched, as I prepared the Hellcat for departure. I told them "goodbye," and started the Hellcat engine, taxied to the end of the takeoff runway, lined up on the runway, added full throttle to that two thousand HP engine, and took off. I climbed several thousand feet and then I dove down sharply toward the same runway, picking up air speed. I crossed the airport low at over three hundred fifty miles per hour. I then flew back over the airfield, wagged my wings, followed by a slow roll; not to show off of course, but only to say goodbye. I then set my course toward NAS, Columbus, Ohio, where I refueled, took off, and arrived back at Cherry Point by Sunday afternoon.

Several months later I made the same flight to Benton Harbor in a twin-engine F7F Tigercat. Several small children were photographed with me on top of the nearly level Tigercat wing. Again, after takeoff, I buzzed low over the airfield, going about four hundred miles per hour this time. I pulled up and executed an Immelmann Turn, which is started like a loop, but when inverted at the top of the loop, I rolled the Tigercat to level flight. I suspect the onlookers were somewhat impressed. Again, I was just saying goodbye; this time by using a different acrobatic flying maneuver.

Marine Air Group (MAG) Staff Assignment

I had flown with VMP-354 at Cherry Point for two years, when I was told that I had to leave the squadron for a staff job. I had several choices; one was to remain in Marine Aircraft Group 14; the other to be transferred to the parent Second Marine Air Wing Headquarters staff. I felt very fortunate to have been assigned to the Air Group S-3 (Operations) office as the Assistant S-3. My boss was Major Marion Carl. In my opinion, Major Carl was the best pilot in the Marine Corps. He was soon promoted to Lieutenant Colonel. I was still a First Lieutenant.

The senior non-commissioned officer assigned to the S-3 office was called the Operations Chief. He was Master Sergeant Bill Buskirk who was a very experienced pilot. Enlisted pilots were officially called Naval Aviation Pilots (NAPs). Like many senior enlisted men, Master Sergeant Buskirk taught his lieutenant a lot; while always maintaining a respectful attitude toward my officer's rank. I felt extremely fortunate to have both an outstanding Operations Chief, and Lieutenant Colonel Carl, a very skilled pilot, as my boss.

Lieutenant Colonel Marion Carl, USMC

Lieutenant Colonel Marion Carl had a brilliant career in Marine Corps Aviation. During his career, he set the World Speed Record of six hundred fifty-one miles per hour (25 Aug 1947) and the World Altitude Record of over eighty thousand feet (21 Aug 1953). While setting those records, he flew a small, red Douglas Skyrocket (D-558-II), which is now on permanent display at the National Museum of Naval Aviation in Pensacola, Florida. He flew other preliminary flights, leading to Chuck Yeager breaking the sound barrier for the first time, on 14 Oct 1947.

While assigned to the Naval Air Test Center at Patuxent River (PaxRiver), Maryland, Colonel Carl tested several high performance Navy fighter and attack aircraft. One was the McDonnell Douglas FH-1 Phantom; a twin jet engine fighter plane. Prior to his assignment as the MAG-14 Operations Officer, he had commanded the first Marine Corps jet fighter squadron. It was equipped with same McDonnell FH-1s that he had tested at PaxRiver. His brilliant record as a fighter pilot dated back to the South Pacific where he commanded a Marine Corps fighter squadron; first equipped with Grumman F4F Wildcats, and later with Chance Vought F4U Corsairs.

While flying in the South Pacific, he personally shot down eighteen enemy Japanese airplanes; for which he was awarded the Navy Cross. His flying skill was well-known, and admired in both the Navy and Marine Corps. He liked any machine that had a motor. He often borrowed my small Cushman motor scooter, and rode it around the Cherry Point Air Station, and sometimes to his on-base house for lunch.

When I was his Assistant Operations Officer, I often received calls from the Cherry Point aircraft control tower. The calls were to relay a call from Marion Carl asking me call his wife, Edna, and tell her that he would not be home for lunch or dinner because, he was flying to NAS, Jacksonville, Florida, or to some other destination. My duties were made much easier because everyone wanted to please Marion Carl. Accordingly, as his assistant, I probably received a lot of undue kindness. To maintain my required flight proficiency, I usually flew Hellcats, Corsairs, and the twin-engine Tigercats, with my former photo squadron, where I was always welcome to fly.

Reburial Detail in Chicago

During the years following WWII, troops from all of our U.S. Armed Services who had died in combat overseas, could be brought home for reburial. The next-of-kin of those deceased had several choices to make regarding burial. First, the remains could be left overseas where they had fallen. Second, survivors could choose to move the remains to an overseas National Cemetery, such as the National Memorial Cemetery of the Pacific (Punchbowl) in Hawaii. Another option was burial at sea, from a U.S. Navy ship. Another choice was to have the remains shipped home for reburial in an established cemetery; whether at Arlington National Cemetery, another Veterans cemetery, or a family cemetery near the home of the deceased serviceman. I was in the process of planning for a deployment to Puerto Rico, when I was notified by the MAG-14 Adjutant that I had been selected to be a body escort for deceased Marines, who were being returned home. I received Temporary Additional Duty (TDA) orders to proceed to Chicago, for reburial duty. The orders allowed travel days to and from Chicago.

With my wife, Millie, and our toddler son in our car, we left Cherry Point for temporary reburial duty in Chicago. I left Millie and our son Bill in southern Michigan with her parents. I then drove one hundred more miles, around the south end of Lake Michigan, to Chicago, where I reported to the Army Graves Registration facility on Chicago's south side. The facility resembled a large commercial warehouse. Entering the facility for the first time, I saw a large sign that read, "YOUR ONLY CONSIDERATION IS FOR THE NEXT-OF-KIN." The sign drove home the point that the next-of-kin were meant to be the primary consideration for all body escorts. I learned I would be escorting the bodies of Marine Corps officers who usually had the same military rank as mine. After attending a short briefing, I was told that there were no bodies of Marines for me to escort at that time. When I told them I was staying in nearby southern Michigan where I could easily be reached by telephone, I was given permission to return to Michigan. Going forward, I was always notified at least forty eight hours before I was required to be back in Chicago.

 While carrying out my orders, I escorted five deceased Marines; two to the Fort Snelling National Cemetery near Minneapolis. In both cases, I escorted the body on the streamlined train called the Hiawatha, which went from Chicago to Minneapolis. I was met each time by a designated funeral home director, who loaded the body in a hearse, and drove to the funeral location. Each funeral was slightly different, as the wishes of the next-of-kin varied. On one of those trips to Minneapolis, burial could not be completed, as the ground at the Fort Snelling cemetery was solidly frozen. The other service was held in the large chapel at DePaul University, in Chicago. Two more of the services where I served as military escort, were in cemeteries and churches, located in rural Indiana and Illinois.

 In those trips, I rode in a hearse with the deceased Marine's flag-draped casket. At DePaul University I told the parents of their deceased son that I was sorry that an escort of their faith had not been assigned. The parents responded by telling me how pleased they were, to have me as their son's body escort. They were truly very kind and considerate people, who later wrote a letter to the

Commandant of the Marine Corps expressing thanks for my participation in their son's funeral. Following my fifth and last body escort funeral, I received a written endorsement that my duties had been completed and that I could return to my permanent MAG-14 command at MCAS, Cherry Point.

With my temporary reburial assignment over, I caught up with my air group (MAG-14) at Ponce, Puerto Rico, where it was still deployed. I flew a F7F Tigercat back to Cherry Point. The plane had been slightly damaged, when a pilot had taken off and raised the wheels too soon, resulting in damage to both propellers. I had to wait for new propellers to arrive, and be installed, before returning home to Cherry Point. I refueled on my way home, at Guantanamo Bay and again, at NAS, Miami.

Chapter 11: Transition to Helicopters

Lieutenant Colonel Marion Carl had learned to fly helicopters while a test pilot at the Naval Aviation Test Center, Patuxent River, Maryland. When the first HO3S helicopter was received at MCAS, Cherry Point its use was restricted to Air/Sea Rescue operations. The helicopter had been received from the first Marine Helicopter Squadron One (HMX-1) at Quantico, Virginia, along with two helicopter pilots, and several maintenance men.

With the advent of the atom bomb, HMX-1 had been established at Quantico in 1947, to study a way the Marine Corps could avoid the crowded WWII-type landing beaches. The Sikorsky HO3S had a single-pilot cockpit, and three passenger seats immediately behind the pilot. Maintaining weight and balance in the HO3S—called Allowable Center of Gravity—was critical. If more than two rode in the passenger seats behind the pilot, about sixty pounds of ballast had to be placed in front of the pilot. A large rock was usually the ballast of choice.

The HO3S had a single (lifting) rotor configuration. At the end of a long tail cone, small tail rotor blades, driven by a shaft from the helicopter's main transmission, rotated in a vertical plane. The tail rotor blades were hinged, and controlled by the pilot's rudder pedals; which provided anti-torque, and directional control. The HO3S was powered by a Pratt & Whitney four hundred fifty HP radial engine.

When Colonel Carl asked to fly the Search and Rescue HO3S helicopter at Cherry Point, he was told that he was no longer current; meaning that it had been too long since he had flown that aircraft. That afternoon, he flew a F4U Corsair to NAS, Patuxent River, where he had served as a test pilot, and he "got current" in the HO3S helicopter. He then flew the Corsair back to MCAS, Cherry Point. Being "now current," the next day Colonel Carl took me with him in the HO3S on a local flight. This flight was my first helicopter ride.

When the Korean War started in June of 1950, a detachment of HO3S helicopters was deployed from Quantico. The helicopters were assigned to Marine Observation Squadron 6 (VMO-6), and were sent to Korea, along with several smaller Bell HTL (bubble canopy) helicopters. They landed with the Marine Brigade that had been rushed to the Korean Pusan Perimeter. For the first time, helicopters were used in combat, by the United States military.

All of that sparked my interest in flying helicopters. So, I requested a transfer to HMX-1 at Quantico. My tour at Cherry Point was nearing the end, and I received orders to Quantico quickly. Only one problem complicated my transfer. Millie was due to have our second child, and was already a month late in giving birth. I requested and received a thirty-day delay in my transfer. On 3 July 1950, our healthy new baby daughter finally arrived at the Cherry Point base hospital. We named her Jeanne Kay. The total hospital bill was $7.50; representing the cost of Millie's food. Millie's mother had flown to Cherry Point to be with Millie when her baby was born. When Jeanne was two weeks old, Millie's mom flew back to Michigan, and we loaded our car, departed Cherry Point, and drove north to Quantico.

During my thirty-day delay, I had flown to Quantico and rented a new house located near the main entrance to the base, in Triangle, Virginia. As some sort of a military or Korean War "expedient," I was permitted to fly the Marine Corps R4D transport aircraft on a "training flight" to Winston Salem, North Carolina. There I purchased new furniture for our house. After loading the new furniture in the R4D, the training flight continued to MCAS, Quantico where I was provided a military truck to move the furniture to our rented house in Triangle.

I then flew the R4D transport back to Cherry Point, and waited for our baby to be born. A week after arriving at HMX-1 in Quantico, I received Temporary Additional Duty (TAD) orders to the Naval Air Station at Lakehurst, New Jersey, for helicopter flight training. We purchased commercial airline tickets for Millie to fly with our two children, Bill and Jeanne, to her parents' home in Michigan, where they stayed while I was learning to fly helicopters at Lakehurst. After their departure for Michigan, I drove our car to Lakehurst and reported for flight instruction in the Navy's Helicopter Training Squadron 2 (HU-2).[i]

Bill and Jeanne Warren (1950)

Unlike a fixed-wing airplane, the helicopter has no inherent stability. But, almost like a fixed-wing airplane, the helicopter has a centered cockpit control stick and two rudder pedals. The helicopter has an additional control long lever called the collective pitch. The control is hinged on its lower end, on the left side of the cockpit. A twisting motorcycle-type throttle is mounted on the top end of that collective pitch control. Raising the hinged collective pitch lever causes the helicopter to rise. Lowering it, settles the helicopter. The centered control, called the azimuth stick, causes the helicopter to remain in place when hovering, or to fly forward, sideways, and even backward, when the azimuth stick is moved in the desired direction.

The two rudder pedals, controlled by the pilot's feet, maintain directional control, and keep the helicopter from spinning around, due to the torque created by the main lifting rotor. When pushed, the rudder pedals cause the vertical tail rotor blades to increase or to decrease their pitch (bite), and accordingly, maintain the helicopter pointed and moving in the desired flight direction. The controls I've described are basic for a helicopter having a single large lifting rotor with a tail rotor to maintain directional control.

The two helicopters used for helicopter flight training at Lakehurst were the small, bubble canopy, Bell HTL, and the Sikorsky HO3S. Both were single-rotor helicopters. The first helicopter I flew as a pilot at Lakehurst in 1950 was the Bell HTL. The helicopter was powered by a two hundred HP Franklin engine, and had a two-blade main rotor that was thirty-five feet in diameter. The helicopter flew at sixty miles per hour, and could lift two individuals. Its range was one hundred fifty miles.

The last helicopter I flew at MCAS Tustin, California before my retirement in 1969, was a Sikorsky CH-53, powered by two General Electric T-64 turbo-shaft jet engines; each generating three thousand eight hundred twenty-five HP. This helicopter lifted thirty-five combat Marines, or twenty-four stretcher patients with four attendants, or over four tons of cargo, carried internally, or in cargo nets suspended below the CH-53 cabin. The five main rotor blades were seventy-two feet in diameter; and the tail rotor was seventeen feet in diameter. It flew at one hundred eighty-five miles per hour; and its range was five hundred seventy-eight miles. What an evolution I was privileged to witness!

My first helicopter training flight - in the small bubble canopy Bell HTL - was at Lakehurst, on 2 August 1950. The helicopter was equipped with wheels; instead of the Marine version of the HTL, which lands on two skids. After ten training flights, each lasting about an hour, I soloed on 9 August, with less than seven helicopter flying hours. My instruction continued while flying the little Bell HTL until 16 August when I had my first instructional flight in the Sikorsky HO3S. I completed the prescribed helicopter training syllabus, and on 24 August - only twenty-two days after my first flight at Lakehurst - I was officially designated a qualified helicopter pilot.

My instructors were all U.S. Navy helicopter pilots. During my training, many of them would suddenly disappear, when they received orders to report to a battleship, or other ships off Korea for duty, flying helicopters, as Naval Gunfire Spotters. I had twenty-seven different instructors in the twenty-two days I was at Lakehurst. The Korean War had begun in earnest and helicopter flight training was accelerated. Most of the students at Lakehurst were Marine Corps pilots, who would soon return to Quantico, and teach other fixed-wing pilots to fly helicopters.

One Marine pilot who completed helicopter transitional training at Lakehurst was Lieutenant Colonel Keith B. McCutcheon. After Helicopter training at Lakehurst, he returned to Quantico, and became the Commanding Officer of HMX-1. The Chief of Naval Operations authorized HMX-1 to train and designate qualified helicopter pilots at Quantico. This circumstance was soon to dictate my role, when I returned to Quantico.

Free Ballooning at Lakehurst

My temporary orders to NAS, Lakehurst were for a thirty-day training period. After completing the helicopter training syllabus, I still had six days remaining, before I had to officially check out, and drive back to HMX-1 at Quantico. While in helicopter training, I noticed that about once a week, several trucks would drive out of one of Lakehurst's massive hangars that had been built years earlier to house the Navy's semi-rigid dirigibles (airships) like the USS *Akron* and the USS *Macon*. These semi-rigid dirigibles were part of the U.S. Navy's ongoing Lighter Than Air (LTA) Program. Now they were also being used to hangar several non-rigid blimps that patrol our coastlines.

  Each truck carried a large helium-inflated balloon, which was fastened to a square wicker basket, which carried a crew of four. Watching each balloon slowly rise, and drift away from its truck, was fascinating. Each balloon rose to a different altitude; up to several thousand feet, and each drifted over farmlands in a westerly direction from Lakehurst.

  I thought that this was likely to be the only opportunity I would have in my career to go free ballooning; so, I decided to try and hitch a ride in a balloon. I drove to that big hangar, went inside, and inquired about hitching a ride. I was directed to the Commanding Officer, Navy Commander Charles Bolan's office. I approached, and made my request to fly in a free balloon. He responded by saying, "The Navy doctors want to go; and the Navy nurses want to go; and now, the goddamn Marines want to go." He told me to return the next morning, and he would consider my request.

  I returned the next morning; wearing my flight suit, and my fore and aft Marine Corps cover (cap). I was told to climb into one of the trucks beds, and then further climb into the wicker basket that the truck was carrying. I noted numerous filled sandbags hanging on the outside of the wicker basket; and I was standing on a coiled thick rope on the bottom of the basket. Commander Bolan, and two additional Navy officers, climbed into the basket with me. As we drove out, I watched as two instruments - a compass and an altimeter - were attached to the tethering ropes, just above the wicker basket.

I was handed a folded AAA road map and told I would be the balloon navigator on the flight; whatever that meant in a non-steerable free balloon. Next, some additional sandbags were removed from skids protruding from each end of the basket. The balloon and our wicker basket, with twenty-one sandbags still hanging on its outside, slowly started to rise, drift away from its truck, and rose over the base. We then drifted across the New Jersey farmland, west of the base. When I looked back, I saw six more balloons rising. Each was followed by the truck that carried their balloon from the hangar. Looking down, I saw our truck also following our balloon. I unfolded the map to pretend that I really was navigating.

When our altimeter showed that we had climbed to five hundred feet, the heavy coiled rope on which we had been standing was tossed over the side of the basket. Attached to a basket skid, the rope hung down about two hundred feet. The purpose of the rope was to become automatic ballast, slowing the balloon's rate of descent as the weight of the rope transferred from balloon to ground.

Except for our conversations, it was quiet, because all the noises associated with aircraft flying were absent. We were floating with the wind, and had no engine noise. We could hear conversations in other balloons flying nearby, and occasionally, we heard dogs barking at us.

We made several landings. When our basket contacted the ground, the skids dug into the soil because the rope had been tied, in error, to the side of the basket skids, instead of at end of the skids. The error caused the basket to tilt sharply, and we had to hang on, to keep from being catapulted headfirst out of our wicker basket. Repeated takeoffs were accomplished, by emptying sand to lighten the load.

When the balloon floated under a cloud, the balloon would descend sharply. Once when that happened, we were flying over a wooded area, and the basket bounced off tree tops. The more experienced balloonists would duck down inside the basket. I did not; and I lost my Marine Corps cover, when it was brushed off by the top limbs of a tree. I completed the remainder of the three-hour flight bareheaded.

Some landings were made in fields where crops were growing; and our landings would wipe out rows of tomatoes, corn, or other farm crops. We made our final landing after three hours. When we had no more sand to drop, a special line was pulled that opened a rip panel at the top of the balloon, allowing the helium gas to escape. After the deflated balloon collapsed, the balloon was folded, and loaded on our truck for the ride back to Lakehurst.

The balloon I "navigated" for three hours was officially designated a ZTF, No. 818. The condition of the flight was "Daylight Visual." My Aviator's Flight Log Book shows that the flight was at NAS, Lakehurst on 23 August 1950.

Two days after my balloon flight, I stopped by Commander Bolan's office to thank him for taking me in his balloon. He was busy verifying claims from farmers who had some of their crops damaged or destroyed, by the balloons that landed in their fields. He said that it was amazing how a balloon could select and land only on special types of vegetables; prize tomatoes, and hybrid seed corn. Those New Jersey farmers obviously knew very well the drill, to submit damage claims.

In the thirty days I spent at Lakehurst, I logged thirty-one helicopter hours, on thirty-nine flights, and three free balloon flying hours on one flight. On 30 Aug 1950 I had my temporary orders endorsed at Lakehurst, and drove back to Quantico. Millie and our two small children returned from Michigan, and joined me. We were all happy to return to our newly rented home.

Pooling Ignorance

When I returned to Quantico from Lakehurst, HMX-1 was now commanded by Lieutenant Colonel McCutcheon, who had completed helicopter training at Lakehurst about two weeks ahead of me. When I reported to HMX-1, he told me that HMX-1 had two main missions; the first being transitioning Marine Corps pilots from flying fixed-wing airplanes to flying helicopters, and to participating in local vertical development flight demonstrations.

HMX-1 had just sent a contingent, which included most of its experienced helicopter pilots, and maintenance men, to Korea. The Chief of Naval Operations had then authorized helicopter training at HMX-1 at Quantico, and officially designated Marine Corps pilots as helicopter pilots. With the deployment of the experienced pilots from HMX-1 to Korea, I suddenly became one of the "experienced" helicopter instructors left at Quantico. With only twenty-two days, and thirty-one helicopter flying hours at Lakehurst, I felt that I would almost be pooling ignorance with my transitioning students.

The second mission given to HMX-1 was to develop vertical assault (helicopter) tactics. To support the vertical assault mission, the Navy purchased twenty Piasecki HRP-1, tandem-rotor configured helicopters. Twelve were delivered to HMX-1 at Quantico, directly from the Piasecki Aircraft Corporation in Morton, Pennsylvania.

With its long fuselage, and with its same size lifting rotors mounted on each end, the HRP-1 was referred to as the HARP or sometimes by its nickname, the "flying banana." The rotors were each forty-one feet in diameter, and they turned in opposite directions. The aft rotor was mounted high above the fuselage; providing blade clearance above the forward rotor.

By turning in opposite directions, each rotor canceled the torque of its opposite. Therefore, the HRP-1 did not need an anti-torque tail rotor. Further, all power, except for a small amount of friction, was available for main rotor, useful load lifting. The HRP-1 was powered by a Pratt & Whitney, six hundred HP, radial engine, mounted inside the fuselage, over the main landing wheels, and behind the ten troop-carrying seats. Two tandem pilot seats were mounted in the nose of the helicopter. The HRP-1 could be flown safely with only one pilot flying from the forward cockpit.

The HRP-1 fuselage was covered by a treated fabric, which lessened the helicopter's weight considerably. However, vibration easily tore the fabric, and the fabric would have holes punched through it when landing in the rough terrain of the Quantico artillery impact area. Seeing a large portion of fabric fly off the helicopter fuselage, was disconcerting to HRP-1 pilots; and probably even more so to the Marine troops, being carried.

The HRP-1 developer, Frank Piasecki, became a very familiar figure at HMX-1, where he worked closely with Colonel McCutcheon in planning vertical assault exercises. Other HRP-1s were delivered to the Coast Guard for air/sea rescue development. Some HRP-1s were assigned to ships, to develop mine sweeping and anti-submarine warfare exercises and tactics. Many of those pioneering applications were found to be practical, and now have become standard military practices.

Colonel McCutcheon said that one of my first flying duties at HMX-1 would be to learn to fly the tandem rotor HRP-1. My first HRP-1 flight was on 12 September 1950, and the last on the following 13 December. I had flown the HRP-1 for fifty-five flight hours, on fifty-six flights, while participating in several helicopter vertical development exercises.

HRP-1 Demonstration; Quantico, VA (Nov 1950)

In November, HMX-1 started receiving the upgraded HRP-2s from the Piasecki helicopter factory. The main difference between HRP-1 and HRP-2 was that the fabric that covered the fuselage, had been replaced with thin metal; which at least made the helicopter more sturdy, and safer than its HRP-1 predecessor. During that same period, I had instructed fixed-wing Marine pilots transitioning to helicopter flying in Bell HTLs, logging fifty hours, on forty-seven flights, and four hours on three flights, in the Sikorsky HO3S.

During the first two weeks of December 1950, nearly all of the flights at Quantico were training flights; flown in the small, bubble canopy Bell HTLs. I instructed transitioning pilots on four flights in a single December day, and two flights on December 10, my twenty-seventh Birthday.

My last flight at HMX-1 was on 14 December, as I had received PCS orders, transferring me to MCAS, El Toro, California to join the nucleus of HMR-161, to train for combat in the world's first all-helicopter troop carrying squadron. I had a total of one hundred thirty helicopter flying hours, logged at Lakehurst during August, and at Quantico over four months. I felt very confident that I could handle almost any emergency helicopter situation.

Chapter 12: Santa Ana - Camp Pendleton - San Diego

Transfer to California

On 15 December 1950, Millie and I departed Quantico, and started our driving trek to California with our two children, toddler Bill and baby Jeanne. We stopped in Michigan and celebrated Christmas and the New Year with our parents. We left Michigan, and drove to St. Louis, Missouri, where we had planned to meet our friends, Lieutenant Lewis and Ann Street, who convoyed with us to California with their two small children, John and Cathy. Lieutenant Street was also on PCS orders from Quantico, to California.

After rendezvousing with the Streets in St. Louis, we continued our trip to California. Crossing the open spaces of Texas, our two-car convoy found it difficult to maintain the speed limits. Ann, driving the Street's car, led the convoy, and at times, she greatly exceeded the speed limits. At one stop, we asked Ann why she was driving so fast, and she answered, "I don't know, we were just talking." Millie rode with Ann most of the way.

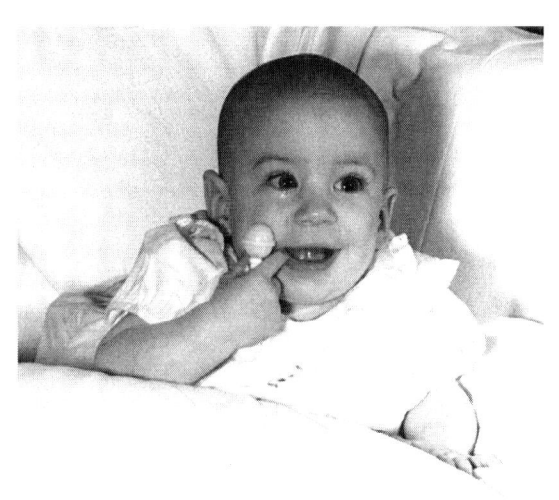

Jeanne Kay Warren, 6 months old

At one cafe stop in Texas, a waitress spotted Jeanne in her baby basket. She grabbed the basket handle and swooped into the restaurant kitchen to show Jeanne off to the restaurant cooks, telling them, "Look at this cute little thing." The waitress' description of our little six-month old baby girl was exactly right.

When Lew Street and I reported to the Marine Aircraft Wing at MCAS, El Toro, California, we were assigned to temporary quarters. The quarters were the very familiar Quonset huts. We stayed in them for a few weeks until we purchased our first home at 2235 Magnolia Avenue, Santa Ana, California. Lew and Ann Street bought a house on the same street.

We knew we were to be assigned to the world's first all helicopter squadron, when it would be commissioned on 14 January 1951. The squadron, HMR-161, would open the old closed U.S. Navy Lighter Than Air (LTA) base at Santa Ana; only about three miles from where we had purchased our house.

Incidentally, the cost of our new three-bedroom house, including a one-car garage, was five thousand six hundred dollars. At the end of our street, development stopped; leaving open farmland that reached several miles to the city of Costa Mesa. Millie and our children stayed in that house while I was flying helicopters in Korea, and when I was stationed at MCAF, Santa Ana (later called MCAS, Tustin), or at MCAS, El Toro. Whenever I received orders transferring me elsewhere, we rented our house to the same couple. They were excellent renters, who always took care of our house. The rent we charged was sixty-three dollars per month; the exact amount of our monthly mortgage payment.

The El Toro and Santa Ana air fields are ideally located for fixed-wing and helicopter flying, as they are three miles apart. Accordingly, each has its own traffic pattern; the faster fixed-wing traffic at El Toro, and the slower helicopter traffic at Santa Ana. Both airfields were only forty miles from Camp Pendleton; the home of the Third Marine Division. That close proximity made air support and vertical assault training, involving landings from amphibious ships from the nearby Naval Base in San Diego, or simulated at Camp Pendleton, very easy. Exercises by Marine helicopters from MCAF, Santa Ana, receiving close support from fixed-wing aircraft based at MCAS, El Toro, were easy to plan and practice.

First, it was necessary to train the helicopter crews to operate in unprepared rough terrain, and from aircraft carriers, so a flat open field at the northern end of Camp Pendleton was selected, and prominently marked to simulate an aircraft carrier flight deck. It was marked with exactly the dimensions (size and shape) of an Escort (CVE) Aircraft Carrier flight deck. In addition, six helicopter landing spots were marked and spaced on the "carrier" flight deck. We flew several of our HRS-1 helicopters to the Camp Pendleton "carrier," and landed on the marked spots, from which we could also load troops and safely take-off. After landing, the helicopter's rotors and engines were stopped, and infantry Marines from Camp Pendleton practiced loading and unloading, with full packs and weapons, as if they had to quickly leave the helicopter, under various combat landing situations. The use of that simulated aircraft carrier proved valuable training for both our helicopter crews, and the troops.

Marine Corps Air Facility (MCAF), Santa Ana, California

During WW II, MCAF, Santa Ana was known as a U. S. Navy Lighter Than Air (LTA) blimp base. Two very large hangars had been built; each a thousand feet long, and over one hundred eighty feet high, and numbered Hangars #1 and #2. They were separated by a large, circular, asphalt dirigible and blimp landing mat, with a short protruding runway. Additionally, smaller blimp landing mats; each circular, and five hundred feet in diameter, were constructed near the outward end of each hangar. The hangars were constructed entirely of wood; except for the three massive, concrete-framed metal doors that opened from the middle, outward to the hangar sides. Each hangar had identical telescoping doors at each end. The doors rested on large railroad train wheels, which carried the tremendous weight of the doors, guided, and kept into place vertically, by matching top and bottom railroad tracks. Hangar door opening and closing power was provided by identical, large electric motors mounted on each door.

    The LTA hangars were originally designed and built large enough to house the pre WW II rigid dirigibles such as the USS *Akron* and the USS *Los Angeles*, which were each almost as long as the hangars. After landing, those large airships were moored to a mobile mast, and when so attached, the airship would be towed into one of the two LTA hangars by a large mast, that moved along railroad tracks, into the center of each hanger. The railroad tracks ran through the center of one hangar, then curved across the large, asphalt landing mat, and into the open door center of the other.

    The U.S. Navy had constructed a helium (gas) generating plant alongside Hangar #1. Its purpose was to provide the gas needed for lifting both dirigibles, and later in WW II, for blimps used to patrol U.S. coastlines, extending from Newfoundland to Texas, then around the Gulf of Mexico coastline to the Panama Canal, and along our Nation's west coast, from California to Oregon and Washington. During WW II, U.S. Navy blimps also patrolled the Mediterranean Sea Area, from bases in ten friendly foreign countries.

    The Hangar #1 helium-generating plant was the only such helium gas-generating plant in the U.S., west of the Rocky Mountains. Accordingly, extra helium gas that was produced was sold to civilian companies; for instance, those companies that used helium gas for welding. Full helium-loaded railroad tank cars were moved to and from the generating plant, on a railroad spur, through a special perimeter train gate, where it joined the main railroad line leading south to San Diego, or north to Los Angeles, and beyond.

MCAF, Santa Ana (LTA) was only a ten-minute flight from the Santa Ana Mountains; rising to an altitude of over four thousand feet. From the highest mountain peak, named Saddleback Mountain, to lower elevations, numerous excellent rough-area landing training sites were readily available. Inexperienced pilots were limited to the lower-elevation landing sites. As they gained experience, they were permitted to "move up the mountain" to higher elevations, and to smaller landing sites. Increasing helicopter pilot flying hours, in order to become familiar with the helicopter lift flight range, was a very important part of our squadron training. I learned that important detail, by flying one of our new Sikorsky HRS-1 helicopters from Quantico, Virginia to Santa Ana, California. Overall, the rough-area training received at LTA proved very valuable for combat operations, just a few months later in the rugged mountains of northeastern Korea, flying in support of the 1st Marine Division.

The first HMR-161 squadron helicopter was flown from Quantico to Santa Ana, in early April 1951,by Major William P. "Mitch" Mitchell and Major Robert E."Tex" Kelly. I was not there to witness their arrival, as I had returned to Quantico, to fly the second squadron HRS-1 from Quantico to Santa Ana.

At Quantico, I flew four short, familiarization flights on 10 and 11 April. On 12 April, 1951, I started my flight from Quantico to California. To measure the HRS-1 gas consumption in gallons per hour, my first leg was flown from Quantico to Richmond, Virginia. The second leg was from Richmond to Greensboro, North Carolina. Those two legs required 4.2 flying hours. On 13 April, I flew three more flights from Greensboro to Spartanburg, South Carolina; to Atlanta, Georgia; then on to Birmingham, Alabama. Those three flights added 8.1 flight hours to my HRS-1 cross country flying experience. On 14 April, I added an additional 8.2 flight hours, stopping at Jackson, Mississippi; Monroe and Shreveport, Louisiana; and Dallas, Texas. Those flights on 14 April were flown on Millie and my 6th wedding anniversary.

      Leaving Dallas on 15 April, I flew to El Paso, Texas; with refueling stops at Abilene and Wink, Texas. Between Wink and El Paso I had my first experience in flying several thousand feet above the ground, when I crossed Guadalupe Pass in west Texas, My ground speed was slow, because I flew against very strong headwinds. I crossed the pass, flying a few feet above the rocks at the five thousand, four hundred, thirteen foot pass summit. The terrain dropped away sharply, and I was suddenly flying at about thirty eight hundred feet above the town of Salt Flat, Texas. Without fixed wings, or the ground for reference, the HRS-1 seemed to be dangling on a string. Also, I experienced a strong tendency to dive to a lower altitude, and to possibly exceed the allowable helicopter rotor and air speeds. The flights from Dallas to El Paso netted another eight helicopter pilot hours for me.

      The next morning, when preparing for takeoff, I called The El Paso aircraft control tower, and requested clearance to taxi. I did this to avoid blowing dust and dirt over several parked civilian General Aviation aircraft. The HRS-1 had four rubber-tired wheels; so it could be taxied away from those civilian aircraft before lifting off. I radioed the control tower and requested, "Clearance to taxi". There was a long pause from the tower operator who questioned me over the radio, "How do you taxi one of those things?" I radioed back, "I'm no aeronautical engineer, I just push some levers and it goes." With that, the control tower radioed, "Cleared to taxi". It was easy to taxi the HRS-1. The pilot first had to release the parking brakes; then slightly raise the collective pitch lever, to reduce the helicopter weight. Then, pushing the azimuth stick forward, the helicopter rolled forward, away from the parked civilian airplanes at

El Paso. Steering was done by use of the foot-operated rudder pedals, using individual wheel braking, in combination with tail rotor blade pitch changes, to taxi in the desired direction.

On 16 April 1951, I successfully completed my helicopter flight across the United States. After taxiing away from the civilian airplanes at El Paso, I took off for Lordsburg, New Mexico, where I refueled the helicopter and flew on to Yuma, Arizona. Then, I flew home to MCAF, Santa Ana. Those three flight legs required a total of 9.4 flying hours. My flights across the country from Quantico, Virginia to Santa Ana, California took five days, averaging 7.6 flying hours per day in the helicopter cockpit, with fifteen refueling stops in ten different states.

During a day of rest on 17 April, Millie and I celebrated our belated sixth wedding anniversary at dinner with our two small children. On April 18th, I flew two instructional flights into the nearby Santa Ana Mountains. Our HMR-161 squadron received its fifteenth helicopter on 30 June 1951. With our full complement of helicopters, pilot, aircrew and helicopter mechanic training was intensified. Training was expanded to include troops from the Marine Division at nearby Camp Pendleton, California.

Marine Corps Base Camp Pendleton

One of the largest Marine Corps bases in the world, Camp Pendleton has an intriguing past; filled with the charm of Spanish explorers, herds of thundering cattle, skilled vaqueros, and tough Marines; all contributing to its rich history. In 1821, marking Mexico's independence from Spain, the Californios became the new ruling class of California. The new Mexican Governor awarded land grants and ranchos to those business leaders. The area that would become Camp Pendleton, was called Rancho Santa Margarita y Las Flores; and it supported a thriving cattle industry. That name stayed with the ranch until it was acquired by the Marine Corps in 1942, for the purchase price of $4,239,062.

The Base was dedicated on September 25, 1942, at a ceremony attended by President Franklin D. Roosevelt It was named in honor of World War I Marine Major General Joseph H. Pendleton, who had long advocated for the establishment of a Marine Corps west coast training base. After only five months of construction, the first Marine troop unit to arrive at Camp Pendleton, following a four day march from Camp Elliott near San Diego, was the 9th Marine Regiment; commanded by Colonel Lemuel Shepherd. Colonel Shepherd graduated from the Virginia Military Institute (VMI), and fought in WW I, WW II, and in Korea. He later rose in rank to become a four star general, and was selected for assignment as Commandant of the Marine Corps.

Camp Pendleton is located in San Diego County and, covering one hundred, twenty-six thousand acres, it reaches Orange and Riverside Counties to the north, the city of Fallbrook to the east, and the city of Oceanside to the south. Its area includes three mountain ranges; and includes over twenty miles of wide Pacific Ocean beaches; ideal for Navy/Marine Corps ship-to-shore amphibious training. The original Rancho had two hundred fifty miles of roads, and that has since been greatly increased to five hundred thirty miles. The two most prominent roads are named after two WW II Marine Corps heroes, who both were awarded the Medal of Honor. The main road through the southern part of the base is named Vandegrift Boulevard, after four-star General Alexander Archer Vandegrift, who won the Medal Of Honor for turning the Japanese back for the first time in World War II, at Guadalcanal. Basilone Road is the main road across the north end of the base, and is named for Gunnery Sergeant John Basilone who was killed on Iwo Jima, and is the recipient of both the Medal Of Honor, for his courageous actions at the Battle of Guadalcanal and, posthumously, the Navy Cross, for his courageous heroism during the Battle of Iwo Jima.

Permanent camps have been built along both of these roads. Each camp is large enough to house and train Marine Corps units up to regimental size. All have been named to reflect a rich Spanish heritage; for example, Las Pulgas, San Onofre, Del Mar and Margarita. Live firing areas have been established, including several rifle ranges, and safe impact areas for mortar, tank and artillery firing. Camp Pendleton has a single-runway airfield, and is home to various small, fixed-wing naval gunfire-spotting aircraft, and a helicopter observation squadron.

Our helicopter training with troops from Camp Pendleton, simulating combat operations, ended in July, 1951. Our helicopter flight operations at LTA were limited to test flights, in preparation for overseas deployment. As July passed, the din of helicopter engine noise, and whirling rotor blades at MCAF, Santa Ana, gave way to the racket of crating and packing squadron equipment and supplies. During late July and early August, 1951, I attended a four-week U.S. Navy Air Intelligence School at the Alameda Naval Air Station, located in the upper San Francisco Bay area. I would fly as a passenger on a weekly mail flight to Moffett Field, located in the lower end of the San Francisco Bay area. I would then call the Navy motor pool in San Francisco and request staff car (a sedan) for transportation to NAS, Alameda; a drive from Moffett Field of over an hour.

I did not tell the motor pool dispatcher that I was a Marine Corps Captain, rather than a U.S. Navy Captain; the rank equivalent of a Marine Corps full Colonel. It worked for me every week that I attended the Air Intelligence School. By the time I finished the Intelligence School, my helicopter squadron was making final preparations to depart for Korea. Tons of squadron equipment was trucked to the Naval Air Station, dockside in San Diego, and loaded aboard an amphibious cargo ship, the SS *Great Falls Victory*, for transport to Korea.

On 14 August, 1951, I said Goodbye to my wife Millie, and our two small children, Bill and Jeanne; leaving them at our home on South Magnolia Avenue in Santa Ana. They would live there during my combat tour in Korea.

Bill and Jeanne Warren, Santa Ana (1951)

I did not see them again for nine months, when my tour in Korea ended. That same day, all fifteen of our squadron helicopters were towed from their massive LTA hangar, for the last time. The helicopter engines were started, the rotors engaged, and the entire helicopter covey took off for NAS, San Diego. Only four helicopters could be landed safely on the USS *Sitkoh Bay,* because its flight deck was nearly filled with U.S. Air Force F-86 fighter aircraft, also being transported to Korea. The other eleven squadron helicopters landed at NAS, North Island, and were towed to the nearby dock, where they were lifted by dockside cranes up to the *Sitkoh Bay* flight deck.

The remaining personnel from our squadron spent their last night in their barracks at MCAF, Santa Ana. After an early morning reveille followed by morning chow, they were transported by trucks to MCAS, El Toro, and flown to NAS, North Island by Marine transport aircraft. From there, they were bused to the ship's gangplank, and boarded the *Sitkoh Bay*. After being escorted to their troop compartment, where they stowed their packs and rifles, our squadron spent its last night in the United States aboard ship; the same ship that had carried my Night-Fighter squadron VMF(N)-543, to Okinawa in April of 1945.

Chapter 13: Arrival in Korea

Early on 16 August 1951, the USS *Sitkoh Bay* sailed from San Diego with one hundred, thirty-four enlisted men, forty officers, and fifteen Sikorsky HRS-1 helicopters aboard. The USS *Sitkoh Bay* was built during WWII and was designated an escort aircraft carrier (CVE). The ship was relatively small, at just over five hundred feet long. I became familiar with the *Sitkoh Bay* in WWII when it transported my Hellcat night-fighter squadron to Okinawa. Major William P. Mitchell was the senior officer in charge of our helicopter squadron while aboard the *Sitkoh Bay*.

Our permanent squadron commanding officer, Lieutenant Colonel George Herring remained at MCAF, Santa Ana, with one additional officer, and ten enlisted men, to perform the last cleanup and administrative duties required of a departing squadron. Colonel Herring and the others who had remained, then departed for Japan on military aircraft. From Japan, they flew on to Korea; arriving ahead of the *Sitkoh Bay*.

After sailing across the Pacific Ocean, we finally sighted land from the *Sitkoh Bay,* while passing the southern Japanese Islands. We then sailed across the Sea of Japan, to Korea; completing the last leg of the long non-stop sea voyage from San Diego. At the Pohang, South Korea harbor, the *Sitkoh Bay* dropped anchor on 31 August 1951.

Squadron Positioning for Combat

Shortly after the squadron flight deck morning muster on 1 September, Colonel Herring caught up with his squadron; landing aboard the anchored *Sitkoh Bay,* in a small bubble canopy Bell HTL helicopter, bringing with him welcome mail from home. He reassumed command of the squadron. With thirty-five officers and twenty-two enlisted crew chiefs aboard, he led his fifteen HRS-1 helicopters ashore in Korea; landing at the Pohang K-3 airfield, where he reported to Major General Christian Schilt, at the General's 1st Marine Aircraft Wing (1st MAW) headquarters. At that time, I had no idea that about two years later, I would become General Schilt's Aide-de-Camp; and would remain in that assignment for five years.

For now, however, someone had to fly that little Bell HTL ashore. I was selected; although it had been over nine months since I had flown the Bell HTL; while instructing at Quantico. So, my first helicopter flight in Korea was not in an HRS-1 helicopter, as I had anticipated; but rather in a small bubble canopy HTL.

Surprise orders were not usual; but sometimes flexibility was necessary. With the final departure of the fifteen HRS-1 helicopters, and my small bubble canopy Bell HTL, the *Sitkoh Bay* weighed anchor at Pohang, and sailed south to the harbor at Pusan. The remaining squadron personnel crated, and otherwise prepared, the remaining equipment and supplies for transfer at Pusan from the *Sitkoh Bay,* to a Japanese-owned LST. The LST had already received the squadron cargo and supplies shipped from San Diego aboard the transport ship, SS *Great Falls Victory*. The fifteen squadron helicopters that had departed Pohang were flown south to the K-1 airfield near Pusan.

Squadron Rear Echelon Location

Our squadron was now together for the first time since leaving MCAF, Santa Ana. We were well trained, positioned, supplied, and organized to move north, and provide vertical lift combat support to the 1st Marine Division, located several hundred miles north in the steep rugged mountains of eastern Korea.

Planning for the squadron move included having the Japanese LST sail north, stop, and off-load the personnel and supplies, and helicopter repair and servicing equipment, to establish a permanent squadron rear echelon support installation at K-18 (Kang Nung) airfield. Shelter tents were erected for aircraft maintenance, and living tents for the squadron's rear echelon personnel.

Lumber was scarce; and large amounts were required to reinforce the tents, and to otherwise prepare for the frigid winter months ahead. At the rear echelon, mandated helicopter checks and inspections would be required. Helicopter engines, transmissions, rotor heads, and rotor blades would often require changing or repair. Messing facilities were required, and canvas personnel tents were reinforced using that scarce lumber. Additionally, we also experienced a shortage of nails. As a result, each four-man personnel tent was allocated only nine nails to hang freshly washed utility uniforms to dry. Our squadron's rear echelon was quickly referred to as "Camp Nine Nails".

Forward Echelon Location

After unloading the cargo needed to build and operate the squadron K-18 rear echelon, the Japanese LST sailed a few more miles north from K-18, to a beach near the small coastal fishing village of Chumunjim. The last of the squadron supplies, personnel, and equipment were moved ashore, loaded onto large trucks, and positioned to form a convoy.

After loading, the truck convoy headed north a few miles to the seaside village of Yang Yang; then turned northwest, climbing on a twisting narrow mountain road, up and over the five-thousand-foot Yang Yang Pass. After crossing that pass, the truck convoy now wound downhill, until it intercepted a north/south road that led to and from the 1st Marine Division area of combat operations. That road was the Main Supply Route (MSR), used by trucks and other ground vehicles to haul ammunition, food, water, motor transport fuel, rolls of barbed wire, lubricants, and a myriad of supplies to the subordinate regiments, battalions, companies, and platoons of the 1st Marine Division. In addition, the MSR was used to supply some specialty units, such as the Division Reconnaissance Company, the Division Shore Party Platoon, and the Division Medical Companies.

      Our squadron personnel who rode in the truck convoy that started at the village of Chumunjim, carried equipment and supplies needed to quickly select and set up a squadron forward echelon in a large valley between the 1st Marine Division headquarters and its frontlines. The rice paddies in the valley were green, when the construction of the squadron forward echelon was started. A small dirt runway airfield had been built between the 1st Marine Division headquarters and our squadron forward echelon. The runway was designated X-83 and was the home of Marine Observations Six (VMO-6). That squadron's helicopters departed Quantico over a year before HMR-161 helicopters existed. The squadron had landed in the Pusan Perimeter, with the Marine Corps ground troops that had stopped the advance of the North Korean Army. The squadron also operated small Bell HTL bubble canopy helicopters, a few Sikorsky HO3S-1, and VMO-6 helicopters, which were all used for casualty evacuations, liaison missions, and occasional downed-pilot rescue missions.

      The HO3S-1 helicopters were underpowered, and could carry only three Marines; including the pilot. The Bell HTLs were fitted with stretchers on the helicopter landing skids. VMO-6 had done a magnificent job while supporting the 1st Marine Division from the Pusan Perimeter to where the division was deployed in Korea; now at the dirt runway X-83 airfield, where our two squadrons co-located. VMO-6 had been busy supporting the 1st Marine Division units when the first elements of HMR-161 arrived and began to set up operations at the north end of X-83; the temporary dirt runway airstrip. VMO-6 also flew small high-wing OY-1 gunfire spotter airplanes.

Our much larger HRS-1 transport helicopters were capable, for the first time, of lifting and supplying entire 1st Marine Division battalions. VMO-6 helicopters continued to provide many critical casualty evacuations. Two of our HRS-1 helicopters arrived at the new squadron forward echelon on 3 September 1951. The following morning, ten more arrived; and the squadron's forward echelon area quickly began taking shape; with landing spots numbered and marked. Messing areas were selected. In addition, under the supervision of the squadron Flight Surgeon, Lieutenant Donald D. Hillan, USNR, medical and dental tent locations were selected, and equipped quickly. Field sanitation areas, to include latrines and pee tubes, were built as far away as possible from messing facilities. Sheltered aircraft maintenance areas were laid out, constructed, and equipped.

The Division Shore Party Platoon Marines were taught, and practiced fastening cargo nets to hooks hanging several feet under hovering helicopters. Troop loading sites were selected carefully. The sites had to be free of obstacles that could damage a helicopter because of the down wash from a hovering helicopter. Standard hand signals that would be recognized by the pilots, were taught to the Shore Party Platoon members, so helicopters pilots could be guided to safely hover above the cargo nets, while the nets were attached to the hooks. Troops waiting to be transported were briefed to always approach the helicopter away from its rapidly spinning tail rotor. When arriving at a landing zone and unloading, the troops were briefed to crouch, and wait on the ground just outside of the helicopter cabin door, and to not charge uphill into the dangerous main rotor plane, while other Marines were still unloading. Quickly clearing cargo from landing zones was necessary, to make room for the next load to arrive; thus establishing and maintaining proper shuttle intervals.

South Korean Laborers

When the MSR could no longer accommodate forward vehicular travel, South Korean laborers were used to carry the required ammunition and supplies on to the forward 1st Marine Division combat units. Seeing those long lines of small South Koreans, called "Chugie Bears," was pitiful. Loads, weighing at least one hundred pounds, were strapped to their backs. They struggled along the steep mountain trails, with their heavy loads of ammunition, water, rations, and rolls of barbed wire. A rope tied a long line of twenty or more laborers together. The purpose of the rope was to rescue a laborer who stumbled, slipped, and fell off the narrow trail. He, and his valuable pack of supplies, could then be retrieved, by pulling him back up to the trail.

Within a few days after the arrival of our helicopter squadron, the Chugie Bears would be relieved of their formidable load-carrying burdens. They could now perform less physically demanding work, such as properly loading and positioning cargo nets, to carry two full fifty-five gallon fuel drums, ammunition cans, boxed rations, fresh water containers, mail bags, empty sand bags, rolls of barbed wire, and many other supplies required by frontline troops.

The forward echelon soon became a beehive of activity, and was organized enough that the first squadron mission could be planned. Our squadron sent reconnaissance flights to search the hills for suitable landing sites, and to plot routes to and from our forward echelon loading sites.

First Combat Mission

By September 13th, our squadron was well-prepared for its first combat mission, named Operation Windmill I. The mission was to determine if a frontline battalion, under enemy fire, could be supplied completely by helicopter. Thousands of pounds of ammunition and supplies were carried in cargo nets to a draw (small valley) approximately a hundred yards behind the forward units of a Marine battalion attacking northward. Before departing to get the next load, the helicopters had to wait in a semi-hover, with the left side wheels jammed against the hillside, to provide a level cabin surface. The wheels on the right side of the helicopter were flying several feet above the ground. Wounded Marines, some on stretchers, could then be loaded through the level helicopter cabin open door. Although we had not specifically trained to conduct casualty evacuation, we quickly learned that our wounded Marines would never be left behind untreated. On our return trips, the wounded Marines were taken to one of the 1st Marine Division medical companies located just south of our X-83 airfield. These evacuation flights were less than ten minutes from the frontlines where the Marines had been wounded. No doubt, fast emergency medical treatment saved the lives of many of those seriously wounded Marines.

U.S. Navy Hospital Ships

Our helicopter squadron also evacuated, day or night, the more seriously wounded from a 1st Marine Division medical company, to Navy hospital ships anchored off shore. Those hospital ships were painted White, and had several large Red Crosses painted on each side, and on the ship's helicopter aft landing platform. Those hospital ships were brightly illuminated at night, when receiving casualties. The hospital ship had a helicopter landing platform built on the stern (back) of the ship. Each hospital ship had two U.S. Navy Captains. One Captain was a surgeon who directed the hospital medical treatment and activities, while the other Captain, as with any Navy ship, directed all of the normal ship activities. The ship's Captain was always the senior, and could, if necessary, overrule the surgeon, if he felt the safety of his ship was endangered.

When one of our casualty evacuation helicopters approached a hospital ship, medical personnel would crouch at the edge of the helicopter landing platform. Immediately upon helicopter touchdown, the medical personnel would unload the stretchers, and the wounded Marines would quickly be carried to one of the hospital ship operating rooms. Hanging IV bags and tubes were always evident. When possible, the wounded Marine's soiled uniform had been cut away and discarded at the medical company, while the patient was being readied for transport to the hospital ship, where absolute cleanliness was essential.

On my first casualty evacuation flight to a hospital ship, First Lieutenant Art Rawlings was my co-pilot. The hospital ship may have been the USS *Haven* (AH-12), the USS *Consolation* (AH-15) or the USS ' (AH-16), anchored off the Korean East Coast. Each hospital ship was over five hundred feet long, with a seventy-foot beam width. Hospital ships each had seven to eight hundred patient beds for the wounded.

We approached the ship for landing from its stern, thinking that ships at anchor always swung into the prevailing wind. I soon learned that was not always correct. In Korea, the strong tides often caused the anchored ships to swing into the prevailing tide, not into the prevailing wind. We slowly approached the ship's helicopter landing platform from its stern, expecting a landing into the wind. Our helicopter was shaking because, yet unknown to me, we were approaching the ship's crosswind. Accordingly, our helicopter was not maintaining maximum lift.

Helicopters, like fixed-wing aircraft, gain lift by taking off and landing into the prevailing wind. When Art Rawlings noticed the ship's flag flying straight out toward the side of the ship, and not toward the stern, we waved off. We altered the direction of our approach to the helicopter landing platform from the side of the ship, this time into the prevailing wind, and we landed safely. The only known area of the world with stronger tides than Korea is the Bay of Fundy in Canada's Maritime Provinces, where recorded daily tides rise and fall over fifty feet. With the start of our historic resupply and casualty evacuation missions on 13 September 1951, our HMR-161 enlisted men and pilots began to realize what lay ahead in the forthcoming days, weeks, and months.

HMR-161, Korea, 1951

(Bob Warren is 5th from the left in the 2nd row from the back)

One week later (on September 19th) our squadron flew its second resupply mission (Operation Windmill II), which was a repetition of the first, but into a different area, and on a smaller scale. However, on the next day, a new type of mission was undertaken.

The Experimental Mission

Our new mission was to transport the 1st Marine Reconnaissance Company to the razorback ridges, simply called "The Hill," to relieve a South Korean Army Regiment, which held positions overlooking enemy frontlines. Since no suitable landing sites were available on "The Hill," members of the division shore party platoon, now attached to our squadron, were flown to selected landing zone sites. Equipped with axes, shovels, and demolitions, they were lowered on knotted ropes from a helicopter hovering over the still unprepared landing sites. The shore party then quickly cleared two large landing sites. Less than an hour after the shore party had departed, the troop shuttle began.

The reconnaissance Marines were taken quickly to their positions; and afterward, heavy equipment, ammunition, food, barbed wire, and other support items were flown in by helicopter. Some loads were carried inside the helicopter cabin, while others were slung in cargo nets that were released from the helicopters, while hovering over the landing sites.

Picking up and releasing cargo from a hover eliminated landings, and saved valuable time, and increased the volume of cargo that could be moved in any given length of time. For the first time in military history, the Marines airlifted troops, supplies, and equipment into the frontlines within range of the enemy's small arms. The era of vertical deployment had begun, and was ready to grow and mature.

Just as the Marine Corps had pioneered in developing the strategic and tactical doctrines for ship-to-shore by boat amphibious warfare, the Corps now proved the practicality of using helicopters to provide further flexibility to amphibious landings. After this operation, congratulatory messages were received from General Clifton B. Cates, Commandant of The Marine Corps, and from Major General Gerald C. Thomas, Commanding General of the 1st Marine Division. The following dispatch was also received from Major General Clovis Byers, U.S. Army, who commanded the adjacent Tenth Corps, located to the west, which included the 1st Marine Division:

"Hearty congratulations to you, and those organic and attached units of the First Marine Division that participated in the first combat use of helicopters in the relief of units in the battle position. Your imaginative experimentation with this means of transport is certain to be of lasting value to all of the services."

Subsequent Missions

Our first wire-laying mission was flown on 22 September, when our HRS-1 helicopters strung more than twenty miles of telephone wire, over rugged mountains, in less than one-half hour.

Operation Blackbird took place on 27 September. A re-enforced rifle company (two hundred forty-five Marines) with their equipment, was lifted under the cover of darkness, to a forward position into a large, five-mile by five-mile depression in the rugged Korean mountains called the Punch Bowl. To get into, and out, of the Punch Bowl, helicopters had to use the same pass when entering or departing. Before entering the pass, navigation lights were turned off, and not turned on again until the helicopters exited the pass. The helicopters obviously had to enter and depart the lone pass at different altitudes.

After entering the pass without lights, precise times on headings and letdown air speeds had to be followed exactly, allowing helicopters to maintain the necessary two-minute intervals between helicopters. The landing site inside the Punch Bowl was very dimly lit, with hooded flashing lights we had borrowed from road construction sites back at MCAF, Santa Ana the night before departing for Korea. The term used for such borrowing is sometimes called "midnight requisition." Ignoring how we obtained the lights, those lights served our purposes very well in Korea.

After quick unloading at the landing site, helicopters had to takeoff and climb, again with precise timing, and at specific altitudes, in order to avoid mid-air collisions with other unlighted helicopters landing or retiring at the same time. Only six helicopters were used. The most experienced participating pilots agreed that, thus far, it was the most dangerous combat mission flown. For participation in that mission, all pilots, including me, received a Distinguished Flying Cross (DFC) medal.

The next night, we lost our first helicopter since arriving in Korea. On a night training flight near the forward echelon, one of our helicopters crashed and burst into flames. All crew and other occupants escaped from the wreckage, uninjured. One lucky Marine who escaped was the nephew of President Harry S. Truman. We also counted ourselves lucky that he escaped.

When hospital ships were not available, we evacuated the seriously wounded Marines to a Mobile Army Surgical Hospital (MASH) located at an airfield on the East Coast of the Korean Peninsula. From that location, medically equipped cargo airplanes could fly the seriously wounded to hospitals in Japan.

Summing up September 1951

By the end of September 1951, our first three weeks in combat in Korea, HMR-161 pilots had flown five hundred sixty pilot hours, on two hundred fifty-eight missions. Our helicopters transported over one thousand one hundred Marines, and hundreds of South Korean Army soldiers. One hundred fifty wounded Marines were evacuated from the frontlines. Additionally, we had transported sixty-two tons of supplies and equipment to frontline combat units of the 1st Marine Division. We were all proud of those accomplishments; all completed during the last eighteen days of September 1951.

The Construction of Revetments

During September, Captain Keith W. "Cos" Costello, one of our enterprising squadron pilots, thought that our helicopters were sitting ducks; vulnerable to enemy aircraft strafing. Our squadron operating area was only a mile from the frontlines. In addition, the possibility of damage to our helicopters by infiltrators existed. Accordingly, Captain Costello was granted authority to supervise the construction of a below-ground revetment for each of our fifteen helicopters.

First, he somehow procured a small bulldozer. The source of such procurement remains a mystery that has never been solved; probably because it was never investigated. We did note however, that the letters U.S. Army and the bulldozer serial numbers had been painted over, when it had arrived in our squadron area. At each revetment site, the bulldozer scooped out enough dirt to make a large revetment hole. A short ramp leading down into each revetment hole was graded and covered with Pierced Steel Planking (PSP) as was the bottom surface of each revetment. Each helicopter was easily rolled on its wheels, down into its revetment, and with the rotor blades folded along the back of the helicopter cabin, it was completely underground.

The revetment design and construction were a great success, until the October rains came. The revetments, having no drainage, quickly filled with water. The squadron now had fifteen new swimming pools. To avoid accidentally falling into one of these fifteen water-filled revetments pools, they were covered with crude wooden pallets and clearly marked with "No Swimming," and other warning signs.

October 1951

Curious visiting VIPS to our squadron who wanted to view our somewhat unique combat operations included: Assistant Secretary of Defense, Anna Rosenberg; Chairman of the Joint Chiefs of Staff, Army General Omar Bradley; the newly appointed Commandant of the Marine Corps, General Clifton B. Cates; Army Generals Matthew B. Ridgeway and James A. Van Fleet; Army Lieutenant General McLean; 10th Corps Commander, Army Major General Clovis Byers; Commanding General of the 5th U.S. Air Force in Korea, Major General Everest; U.S. Navy Admiral, Arthur W. Radford; and Major General Christian Schilt, Commanding General of the 1st Marine Air Wing in Korea, the command to which we were attached. General Schilt's Air Wing command provided our vital aviation personnel, and a myriad of aviation repair parts and supplies, including high octane aviation gasoline. Brigadier General Clayton C. Jerome, a Marine Corps aviator, accompanied General Cates from Headquarters, U.S. Marine Corps, in Washington. D.C.

At times there were so many stars in the area that Lieutenant Art Rawlings dubbed the squadron "An Astronomer's Paradise." Several of those VIP dignitaries who visited our squadron expressed a desire to ride along on flights to the frontlines. We discouraged such outings, citing interference with planned and ongoing missions, interruption of frontline actions, and exceeding the weight- carrying and seating limitations of our transport helicopters. We knew of course, ride-alongs meant that others in their staffs would be included as ride-along passengers, and our badly needed combat support flights would be reduced, and replaced by such non-productive, and very dangerous VIP helicopter tour services.

Marine Major General Gerald C. Thomas, who commanded the 1st Marine Division, and thus approved most of our helicopter operations, was able to intervene, and provided the buffer the squadron badly needed. He assumed the role of unofficial host for those VIP visits. His influence was a great help to prevent dangerous frontline combat exposure of those high-ranking dignitaries.

For the most part, the VIPS understood, and were satisfied to just observe our day-to-day helicopter operations, which they had never witnessed before. No doubt, they all envisioned just how future helicopter operations might affect their service. Army Major General Clovis Byers was correct when, in his earlier congratulatory message, he ended with the following sentence, "Your imaginative experimentation with this means of transport is certain to be of lasting value to all the services."

We felt pride in all the attention we were receiving. Squadron morale remained very high with all those flag officers present and watching, while our squadron was resupplying frontline units, transporting troops, laying communication wire, completing reconnaissance flights, doing casualty evacuations, and hunting guerrillas. We enjoyed showing our many helicopter capabilities to those distinguished visitors, away from the 1st Marine Division frontlines.

Operation Bumblebee

On 11 October, Operation Bumblebee took place, when HMR-161 effected the relief of a Marine frontline assault battalion, by lifting one thousand Marines to Hill 844. This airlift was the first of an entire battalion by helicopter, in history. Marines who were being relieved, had occupied that hill for over six weeks, and came out looking like part of the landscape. The first flights carrying fresh troops forward, returned empty, because the troops being relieved, still had to occupy their positions, until the relieving fresh troops arrived.

Later in the operation, when there we no more fresh troops to carry forward, the lift requirements reversed, and only the relieved troops were transported on the return flights. Operation Bumblebee proved that helicopters could airlift large numbers of troops, by using a fast shuttle system. In the future, using squadrons with larger helicopters, the Marine Corps would be capable of making amphibious landings from ships dispersed at sea; bypassing strongly fortified positions. The era of vertical envelopment was rapidly maturing, and spreading.

Support for a Republic of Korea Company

On 15 October, an urgent request was received from the adjacent 10th Corps, Commanded by Major General Byers, U.S. Army. Units requiring emergency support were elements of the 6th Republic of Korea (ROK) Division. One of its Companies, then on the attack in their Operation Wedge, had over- extended its supply line to such extent that logistical support by road was inadequate. The regiment's subordinate South Korean company was in dire need of mortar ammunition, recoilless rifle ammunition, rations, water, and medical supplies. A typhoon in the Sea of Japan prevented the normal air drops of cargo planes flying from Japan.

When our six helicopters landed at the site of the over-extended unit, we found several wounded South Korean Army troops, who needed to be evacuated immediately. Forty-one seriously wounded, South Korean soldiers received onsite emergency treatment, directed by our squadron Doctor, Navy Lieutenant Don "Doc" Hillan, and provided by two Navy Hospital

Corpsmen. They were then evacuated to Army medical facilities, located in the Army 10th Corp's rear area.

Loads of required ammunition and supplies were assembled, and flown forward to the over-extended Korean Army Company in cargo nets, which were loaded by our trained Division Shore Party Marines. One U.S. Army logistics Colonel, watching the Marine helicopter lift in progress was heard to say, "We are going to get a thousand of those things (helicopters)."

The U.S. Army often deals realistically in big numbers. By comparison to Marine Corps units, Army units are truly big, sometimes unwieldy, but always huge to Marines. In addition to flights to and from the 10th Corps, I flew five emergency evacuation and resupply flights, in support of the over-extended South Korean Army Company on 15 October. We then flew back to our X-83 squadron area. The 1st Marine Division denied a 10th Corps non-emergency request to use our HMR-161 helicopters again the next day.

Operation Bushbeater

Operation Bushbeater commenced on 19 October; the purpose of which was to move patrols of the 1st Marine Division Reconnaissance Company into positions along both rear flanks of the division sector, by helicopter. From those positions, the Marine reconnaissance patrols converged toward the division's MSR, while beating the bushes for infiltrators. Since no landing sites were available along the razorback mountain ridges, the helicopters had to hover while the patrol members, some carrying demolitions to blow up huts being used by the infiltrators, jumped to the ground. The huts were destroyed by grenades, flame throwers, and demolition charges.

During this operation, which lasted two days, the squadron had two of its helicopters severely damaged. Helicopter HR-6 lost power, and limped along a ridge for a few seconds, and balancing precariously, chewed into a grove of trees; and the main rotor chopped the helicopter tail cone off. The other, HR-9, crashed, and was severely damaged. However, by building a temporary landing zone nearby the crash sites, our maintenance personnel were able to remove major components of the two severely damaged helicopters. Those salvaged parts, and major helicopter components, were lifted out by helicopter, and flown to our squadron rear echelon facility (Camp Nine Nails) at the Kang Nung K-18 airfield. The components from the two crashed helicopters were used to assemble a single HRS-1. To honor the squadron numbers of the two crashed helicopters, the new helicopter was renumbered HR-69. The Navy's Bureau of Aeronautics number 128889 was selected, and assigned to the new cobbled together HRS-1 helicopter.[ii]

Disassembling the components and parts salvaged from two crashed helicopters, then re-assembling it into one helicopter, deserves a well-earned tribute to the ingenuity, skill, and bravery of our enlisted squadron helicopter mechanics, and to their non-pilot maintenance officers as well. Also, the Sikorsky Helicopter Company had assigned one of its civilian experts to accompany our squadron to Korea. His name was Mr. Lou Plotkin; and he was most helpful with detailed and technical helicopter maintenance knowledge. In each war a number was assigned to things that were unpleasant or otherwise bad; in Korea that number just happened to be "Numba-69."

Operation Rabbit Hunt

During the last three days of October, the squadron conducted Operation Rabbit Hunt. The mission involved combing the ridge lines and valleys forward of the 1st Marine Division headquarters, in search of enemy infiltrators, and the destruction of small mud-walled, thatch-roofed Korean houses, which provided shelter and cover for enemy infiltrators. On this mission, our helicopters carried Marines armed with thermite grenades, flame throwers, and Browning Automatic Rifles (BARs), while scouring the mountainous terrain. In all, several hundred dwellings were burned.

When non-combatant civilians were found, they were terrified to be loaded onto one of our helicopters, to be flown to a safe refugee site. I was saddened to view a South Korean mother, with two small boys, view the destruction of their home, before they were evacuated aboard my helicopter. One small Korean orphan boy named Ejungee, who arrived and stayed in our squadron area, was adopted by our enlisted Marines. At first, the little boy was a pitiful sight. He wore the smallest size Marine Utility Uniform available, but it was still many sizes too big for him. No one knew how he got to our squadron. He was fed, and 'Doc' Hillan checked his general physical condition. Other than being undernourished, he was pronounced quite healthy.

We estimated that he was about eight years old. He was provided his own metal mess kit, and was taught how to sterilize it, by dipping it into a large trash can filled with boiling water, (as all Marines are taught to do in the field), before getting into the mess line to receive food. Ejungee was provided an official medical record, and an official Marine Corps Service Record Book. He was given the standard inoculations by 'Doc' Hillan, and his medical condition was recorded in the little Korean boy's official medical record; which he always proudly carried with him. One of our pilots, while on R&R in Japan, purchased a complete cowboy outfit for Ejungee, at an Army Post Exchange in Japan. The outfit included a cowboy hat, two pearl handled six guns, and cowboy boots; plus a winter jacket and mittens. He was so proud of his new cowboy outfit.[iii]

Ejungee with John Irwin and Major Bill Mitchell

During October, our second month in Korea, two hundred and fifty-eight missions were flown. More than eighty-eight tons of cargo, and one-thousand five hundred 1st Marine Division troops were moved into combat. The squadron pilots logged three hundred eighty hours of combat flight time. Of course, those accomplishments were largely attributable to the skill and hard work of our helicopter maintenance Marines.

November 1951

During the early morning hours of November 1, it snowed. The snowflakes fell, and the Marines walking their posts inside the barbed wire barricade felt the snowflakes hit their faces like wet feathers. The captain of the Japanese LST that carried our squadron Marines up the East Coast of Korea from Pusan to Chumunjim didn't realize how accurate his prediction would be, when he said, "It will snow about November 1st." By mid-morning, the helicopter main rotors were cleared of snow by pulling ropes along the rotor blade tops. Reconnaissance, wire laying, and other support flights, could then be scheduled and flown. During the following eight days, preparations were made for a huge lift of troops, as other operations continued, including Operation Rabbit Hunt.

On November 10th, the squadron celebrated the 167th Anniversary of the Marine Corps. A three hundred fifty-pound Birthday cake was baked, and by tradition, the first piece of cake was cut by Major General John T. Selden, who had replaced Major General Thomas, as Commanding General of the 1st Marine Division. Celebration of the annual Marine Corps Birthday is a time-honored tradition, dating back to 1921. The size of the celebration does not really matter. Even the lone Marine recruiting sergeant in Alaska, has been known to organize a USMC Birthday party. At larger installations and bases, lavish annual Birthday balls are held, to include recognitions of both the oldest and the youngest Marines present. They are served the first and second pieces of Birthday cake. The annual U.S. Marine Corps message from the Commandant of the Marine Corps is read, regardless of the celebration size

After delivering special dinners and Birthday cakes, by helicopter, to the accessible frontline units, our squadron officers and enlisted men mixed, and enjoyed a delicious sit-down dinner in the same mess tent. The annual USMC Birthday celebration did wonders for morale in our squadron, and it provided a welcome break in our demanding combat support operations.

Operation Switch

The annual USMC Birthday party served as a short breather before the largest mission undertaken by our squadron, up to that time in Korea. Operation Switch began as soon as the cold early morning fog burned off enough for the helicopter pilots to see well enough to fly. Operation Switch was the largest helicopter troop lift, thus far. The operation had another important feature, in that the fresh troops were moved into battle positions, and the troops being relieved were flown back to the rear area, which inspired the name Operation Switch. The Marines being relieved from their frontline positions looked like part of the earth. Only their weapons appeared clean.

Delivering a load of weary Marines back to the rear area took about fifteen minutes for each helicopter. When the Marines arrived, they were fed hot chow, showered, and issued new uniforms, including clean socks and boots. Without helicopters, the walk to the rear area would have taken about fourteen hours, down slippery mountain trails.

Thanksgiving Day Celebration

Thanksgiving Day was celebrated in grand style, by our helicopter squadron. Our helicopters delivered turkey dinners, in large thermos containers. The containers, filled with over a thousand pounds of Thanksgiving dinners, were delivered to frontline positions, where chow lines were quickly set up, behind protective sand bag barriers. The troops patiently waited in line; each with his mess kit, to get a complete steaming hot Thanksgiving dinner. The dinner included hot turkey and dressing, mashed potatoes and gravy, pumpkin pie, cranberries, and steaming hot coffee.

On the day following Thanksgiving, members of the Division Reconnaissance Company were landed at frontline sites, where their patrols began. On return flights, their captured prisoners-of-war were flown to the 1st Marine Division command post. Those enemy soldiers had infiltrated through the Marine frontlines at night, to surrender themselves. During the month of November 1951, our squadron had flown over seven hundred hours, on three hundred eighty missions, carrying over two hundred sixty-six thousand pounds of cargo and supplies. More than three thousand Marines, including forty wounded Marines, were evacuated from frontline positions.

Operation Foxhole Relief
Lifted 1,950 Marines from 1st Marine Division, Korea (1951)

December 1951

Blasts of cold air from Manchuria arrived, and temperatures often dropped to below freezing. Our helicopters had no heating system. Some genius at the headquarters of the Marine Corps had determined that to save weight, heaters in our helicopters would not be installed. The HRS-1 cockpit provided only a small space between the motorcycle-type throttle, and the sliding cockpit glass window. This left the pilot only enough room to wear a very thin glove; as he had to add or reduce engine power, by constantly twisting the motorcycle-type throttle. At the end of the flight, the pilot in the left cockpit had to pry his cold hand and fingers from around the throttle. Except for our hands, our warm winter down-filled uniforms kept us reasonably warm when flying.

The bitter cold slowed most of our squadron operations. For instance, when attempting to start our helicopter engines, the engine starter shafts often broke, causing damage that required removal of the engine, in order to replace the broken starter shafts. To ensure that the engines were properly warmed before starting, canvas-shrouded engine heaters were used. Following each engine heater use, a pilot would then start the engine of each helicopter scheduled to fly that morning; running it until the cylinder head temperature gauge rose to normal running temperature. That quickly became the job of the daily assigned Squadron Duty Officer (SDO).

Aircraft Maintenance Tent, Korea (1951)

The SDO job was rotated among the junior officers, whose name would be announced at the evening troop muster. We all knew that the SDO would be required to start the engines of several helicopters, during the frigid early morning hours. This usually triggered the following loud speaker announcement: "Congratulations, Lieutenant (last name), you just joined the Warm-Up Team; so stay cool."

The SDO had many other duties. The officer was expected to visit and inspect the squadron perimeter sentries, with the Sergeant of the Guard, throughout the night, and maintain the facility fire watch. In addition, the officer also ate all three meals with the enlisted men in their tent chow hall, and provided a report, relative to food quality and quantity, to the squadron Executive Officer each morning.

The food we received came from U.S. Army supply sources, and the amount of food received was based upon daily head counts. Their always seemed to be a shortage of meat. Therefore, daily head counts were strangely increased to solve the meat shortages. The SDO also reported any usual events that occurred during his watch, to the squadron Executive Officer. In addition, the SDO provided a list of our squadron helicopters that were in an "up" status, which meant they were ready to fly. Serving as unit duty officers, young Marine Lieutenants learned to accept responsibility, and if necessary, take immediate action.

The change in the cool fall, to frigid winter weather, caused many other significant changes in our attempts to stay warm. For instance, in the fall we had heated our four-man tents with crude makeshift heaters. The heaters were made by cutting a standard, empty, khaki-painted fifty-five-gallon metal fuel drum, in half. From each metal drum, two crude tent stoves could be made. First, the open end of the fuel drum was placed on the dirt tent surface, in the middle of the tent, with the closed end of the drum faced up. Then, a six-inch hole was cut in the closed top of the drum. The hole accommodated a long stove chimney; made by welding empty artillery shell cases together, until the chimney was long enough to protrude through the top of the tent. The chimney was welded securely to the drum. At this point in the construction, all that was now required to use the makeshift tent stove, was another hole in the drum, large enough for wooden fuel to be poked inside the open stove.

We made sure to orient the open hole of the heater toward the tent door for a good reason. Early in the morning, we poured gasoline over the wood fuel, stood outside the framed tent door, and threw lighted matches at the stove fuel hole. When a lighted match landed on or near the stove fuel hole, a sheet of flame flew through the open tent door, and a fireball shot up the chimney, leaving the stove wood below burning. The heater took the chill out of the early morning air inside our tents, and burned long enough to permit moving from our warm sleeping bags on folding cots, to quickly getting dressed in our warm clothes. Having accomplished its temporary purposes, the fire-in-tent stove heater soon burned out.

Bob Warren in squadron area, Korea (1951)

As the December weather became much colder, our crude home-built tent stoves were replaced with standard oil heaters. Each heater included a long, four-inch diameter chimney, which was easily attached to its heater. These heaters were used, throughout the squadron, to provide warmth in troop tents, aircraft maintenance tents, and other work areas. However, heaters were not placed inside the sheltered latrines. That guaranteed quick cold-latrine occupant turn-around times. Our favorite tent contained the mess hall, because it was always warmed by the cooking fires, and it was where hot coffee was available, around the clock.

The heater fuel was a low-grade diesel-like fuel, that had an unpleasant petroleum odor, whether being burned in the heaters or not. The bitter cold made it necessary to bring small containers of fuel into the tent, or other heated spaces. If the fuel containers were located outside the tent, the liquid fuel would not flow freely, and the fuel-starved heaters would then sputter and stop burning. However, even when burning properly, the air/fuel combustion was far less than ideal. At times this caused oily soot to cling inside the chimneys, and sometimes the heater would catch fire. The result was a small volcano-like eruption of burning soot, spewing out the top of the tent four-inch stovepipe, and still on fire, the burning soot would burn holes in the tent. When these fires happened, the tent occupants would pound on the tent roof from the inside, hopefully causing the burning chunks of oily soot to roll down and off the canvas tent roof, before holes burned entirely through their tent canvas roof.

We removed the protective pallets covering the fifteen former revetments; as the water in Captain Costello's swimming pools had now frozen solid. Each was now given a skating rink number, matching the squadron number assigned to each of our squadron helicopters. However, there was no Rink 6, nor a Rink 9, as parts from those to two numbered squadron helicopters had been cobbled together to make a single complete HRS-1 helicopter; now Numba-69.

When Numba-69 flew initially, the helicopter still lacked front wheels. Instead, two flat, spade-like feet were welded to the helicopter, as substitute front wheels. The hybrid helicopter was primarily used on the daily mail flights between our squadron K-18 Rear echelon, and our X-83 Forward echelon squadron facilities. In the air, HR-69 appeared like any of our squadron helicopters. However, when it landed, having no front wheel strut assembly with shock absorbers, it sat markedly nose low. At the other end, about fifty feet distant, the HR-69 tail cone pointed sharply skyward. Eventually, two nose wheel assemblies arrived, and were installed; making it just another squadron HRS-1 helicopter. However, its unique HR-69 numba was never changed.

Numba-69 was flown to and from our forward and rear echelons to deliver mail - outgoing and arriving, including Christmas packages from home. The number of Christmas mail delivery flights, to and from the 1st Marine Division Headquarters, and the forward positioned combat units, increased sharply in December; often requiring that the Christmas mail be carried in cargo nets, slung under our helicopters.

A large number of flights were also made to numbered frontline landing sites, with fifty-five-gallon drums of fuel oil carried in their cargo nets. The drummed fuel was used to heat bunkers, where returning patrols, and other frontline Marines, could find warmth and sleep.

Based on the myriad of our squadron helicopter missions, a poem titled *An Angel with a Rotary Wing* was written. Captain Bert Herrin, the principal author of the poem, was a HMR-161 pilot. Here is the text of the poem:

If you listen, you can hear

Whirling rotors slap the air,

In a minute she'll come stealing

Through that valley over there.

   'Neath the ridge line, down the gully,

   Fanning treetops in her wake,

   Like a horse that's gone a flyin'

   To run down Medusa's fake.

     At her bosom, she grips firmly

     To the cargo net below,

     Filled with items necessary

     To our warriors, they will go.

       Gifts of food and ammunition,

       Wine, and guns, and mail from home.

       Brought up to the foremost outpost

       That no man may feel alone.

         Now she's slower, now she hovers.

         Gently lets her cargo down,

         Then flies sideways to a clearing

         Lets herself upon the ground.

From the hillsides' winding trails,

Down the paths they trudge and slide,

Come the men who've earned their passage

For a helicopter ride.

Some on stretchers, lowered gently,

Others manage on their own.

Bleeding, shattered, broken figures,

With their courage freedom's sown.

Then they're lifted up inside her,

All ready – up she'll climb!

Off the clearing, down the gully,

Save a life by racing time!

Now she lands back down the valley,

Crossed red banners hail her in.

Medics scurry 'neath her rotors

To unload the wounded men.

As they leave, they smile upon her

Heartfelt thanks in silence sing,

She was sent to them from Heaven,

An angel with a rotary wing.

Christmas Card from Old Korea

On 21 December 1951, we received a call from the 1st Marine Division Surgeon stating that a badly wounded Marine required treatment on a hospital ship. The wounded Marine had been stabilized locally. However, hospital care was now considered critical. I was on duty that night, as the assigned squadron standby evacuation pilot. My co-pilot was my longtime friend Captain Lewis Street. After receiving the hospital ship location off the east coast of South Korea, and its radio call sign, we flew a short distance to the medical Company where the critically wounded Marine was located. After he was loaded aboard our helicopter on a stretcher, accompanied on the flight by two hospital corpsmen, we took off.

Our night flight to the hospital ship required flying south above the MSR, which was easy to see because of the many vehicles driving north with their headlights on. By keeping those surface lights in view, we were able to navigate through the very mountainous terrain below. Suddenly the lights disappeared, as I had flown into a cloud, and without any visual or radio navigational aids, I was suddenly flying on instruments. To continue would only result in the crash of our helicopter into a cloud full of rocks. I quickly decided that my only option was to make a one hundred eighty-degree turn. Now flying on instruments, we flew back north for several minutes, and eventually we flew into clear air. We continued to fly north, until we spotted a non-moving light.

I told Lew Street that was where we would be landing, and spending the rest of the night. Spirally down steeply around that prominent light, I saw there was nothing between my helicopter and the light; so we would not fly into anything. After cautiously reducing our altitude, and slowing the helicopter airspeed, I turned on the helicopter landing light, selected an open field, and landed.

Immediately, several vehicles painted with large red crosses appeared. I felt extremely fortunate that I had landed at a 1st Marine Division medical Company; which had not leap-frogged forward, with the attacking Marines, only because a fire had destroyed part of their medical facility. Our seriously wounded Marine was taken away in a medical ambulance. I never learned whether he lived. I prayed that he did, because we had not been able to get him to a hospital ship. We ate some food, and enjoyed some medicinal brandy, provided by the medical Company doctors. Our entire helicopter crew then slept soundly all night, in our flight suits, on folding cots.

The next morning, we ate breakfast, and realized for the first time how fortunate we had been, while spiraling down the previous evening in the dark. I had landed adjacent to a sheer five-hundred-foot-high cliff. Before we departed, the medical Company doctors showed us a Christmas card they had designed. The card was intended to be mailed to some person who had not yet enjoyed the experience of a Christmas combat tour in Korea. The card displayed a pretty Christmas scene, viewed from inside a house, through a window. It showed Santa Claus, his sleigh, and a team of reindeer outside in a snow-covered yard. The Christmas card included the following verse:

> "Christmas greetings, from old Korea
>
> Land of lice and diarrhea.
>
> From these shores we've half-mastered
>
> Merry Christmas, you lucky bastard."

Chapter 14: Korea Winter and Spring Operations

During December, we learned that our very capable, highly respected, and popular squadron commanding officer, Lieutenant Colonel George Herring had received orders to Headquarters, U.S. Marine Corps, in Washington, D.C. He would be serving as Aide-de-Camp to the Commandant of the Marine Corps, General Lemuel C. Shepherd. Colonel Herring was relieved as our squadron commander, by Colonel Keith B. McCutcheon. We all knew the Colonel well from Quantico; where most of our pilots learned to fly helicopters.

Colonel McCutcheon was highly respected, and a forward-thinking Marine officer, who had a vision for use of helicopters in Marine Corps amphibious operations. His assignment, to command a helicopter squadron in combat, proved the plans of Marine Corps leadership, regarding future amphibious operation innovations. Colonel McCutcheon was a brilliant Marine officer who, before receiving a commission as a Marine Corps officer, had graduated from the Massachusetts Institute of Technology. Years later, he was the first Naval Aviator to wear the four stars of a Marine Corps General Officer; albeit only for one day.

To get promoted, the Colonel was required to pass a physical examination. He had cancer, and thus could not pass the required physical. A special Act of Congress waived his physical examination requirement. He retired a four-star General Officer the next day. I knew him very well, as we had attended the helicopter transition training program together at NAS, Lakehurst, New Jersey. Later at Quantico, he was the Commanding Officer of HMX-1; to which I was assigned as a helicopter flight instructor. Now at HMR-161 in Korea, I flew with him almost every day.

USO Show

December flights accomplished by our squadron intensified, mainly to deliver Christmas presents to the frontline Marines. The bitter cold weather demanded daily troop and cargo flights. I flew forty combat flights during December. On Christmas Day, I flew actress Jan Sterling, and actor Paul Douglas, to frontline positions, where they put on a USO-type show. Their modified show was limited to one stop, as blinding snow prevented our flying to other areas. I know those Marines were disappointed. I will never forget the pleasant perfume fragrance that wafted into the helicopter cockpit. Otherwise, those talented entertainers were heavily bundled in warm clothing, and therefore, almost nondescript. During December 1951, I flew a total of thirty-two combat flights, and another ten hours of courier, test, and visiting VIP flights.

January 1952

On 16 January 1951 I flew the 1st Marine Division Operations Officer (the G-3) from the Division Headquarters, to the Battleship USS *Wisconsin*. That ship, operating off the East Coast of South Korea, was providing Naval gunfire support to the 1st Marine Division, by firing its sixteen-inch guns, which could reach targets at distances up to twenty miles. Each sixteen-inch projectile weighed a ton.

The Division G-3, who was a Full Colonel, was waiting at the division helicopter pad, when I landed. His actions clearly indicated that he really did not want to go. We normally didn't leave the helicopter cockpit, to pick up personnel with less than flag rank (Generals and Admirals). But, when the waiting Colonel did not get aboard, I asked my co-pilot, Captain Cal Austin, to hold the helicopter controls, while I climbed out of the cockpit and down the side of the helicopter.

I was annoyed, so I took the offensive. First, I saluted him; and then firmly, I told him that it would be necessary to wear a life jacket on this mission. Colonels don't like to be put on defense by Captains; as I was clearly doing. Also, he was obviously unfamiliar with Naval Aviators life jackets. I purposely waited for him to try to put it on properly. Finally, I asked my helicopter crew chief to show him the proper way to wear, and use it.

He was fuming as he was now taking instructions from an enlisted man. He then vented his anger by asking me, "Do you know you are late?" I informed him that our mission was to meet him at 0800, and that was exactly when we arrived. Next, he asked, "Where are we going?" I responded that we were to take him to the USS *Wisconsin* for a naval gunfire conference. He next asked, "What's its position?" I told him that it was off the East Coast of Korea, sailing along the fifty gridline but that I did not know how far to sea it would be, "Because Colonel, warships do move." He then wanted to know what the ship's call sign was. When I told him, he asked, "Is that Channel Red?" When I assured him that it was, he finally got aboard, after wasting about fifteen minutes asking his dumb, bullying questions. I was disgusted, and concerned that this fifteen-minute delay could somehow affect the ship's schedule, or its plans for our arrival.

The Battleship USS *Wisconsin*

When we crossed the coastline, and headed East to find the *Wisconsin*, the winter weather was terrible. The sea surface was solid foam, with the high wind and whitecaps churning the water seemingly in all directions. The sea temperature was near freezing, and had our helicopter engine failed, it would have been necessary to land in the open sea. Our survival time would have been only a few minutes, even if we had been able to inflate our life jackets. We were not wearing the aviator's immersion (poopy) suits, as our squadron had none. They were very bulky, and difficult to put on and take off. I called the ship (on Channel Red) and reported "feet wet" when we headed out to sea. About twenty minutes later, we sighted the massive battleship. The battleship turned, so we could land across the ship's small fantail into the strong wind, and therefore, avoid any rough air burble, created by the ship's superstructure.

Over the intercom, I told our crew chief to give his radio earphones to our passenger. I wanted to ensure that the Colonel would be fully concerned about the hazards of landing my helicopter on the ship's small fantail. I guess I really wanted to scare the hell out of him; which turned out to be easy. With all those hazard warnings received by radio while landing aboard, I was probably somewhat scared myself. For instance, the three sixteen-inch gun barrels were lowered, to provide a four-foot clearance under our helicopter main rotor. At the stern of the ship, a loading crane further used the deck space, forcing us to squeeze in to land. As soon as we touched down on the ship's fantail, our pompous grunt Colonel was out of the helicopter immediately; walking away with no expression, or gesture, of thanks. Also, our crew chief had to run and catch up with him, to retrieve the squadron life jacket, which he had forgotten to take off after we landed.

After landing, my co-pilot and I went to the officer's wardroom, and our crew chief was taken to the ship's Petty Officer's Mess for a hot breakfast. We also wanted to remain long enough to take a badly needed, hot shower. However, we were told to depart immediately, because the ship would be firing those three aft sixteen-inch guns. The concussion would cave in the side of our helicopter, or worse. At the ship's order, we took off in a hurry, without our pompous passenger. Good riddance! I don't know how he returned to the 1st Marine Division headquarters. I never asked, and I really didn't care. Experiences like mine might have been what partially prompted the unusual assignment of a full Colonel (McCutcheon) as our squadron commanding officer, which would automatically protect us from similar bullying attempts by any senior 1st Marine Division staff officers. In addition to the flight to the *Wisconsin,* and a few post-maintenance test flights, I logged a total of thirty-one combat flights during January 1951.

Operation Ripple

The tempo of 1st Marine Division operations slowed somewhat during January and February, as fights to gain ground, and positions, had almost ceased. The 1st Marine Division had set up for defense. Our squadron took advantage of the pause, to try something new.

A scheme was concocted, to fire rockets into enemy positions, from rocket launchers carried by helicopters, positioned close in to the enemy frontlines. After firing, the rocket launchers and the crews had to relocate quickly, to avoid enemy counter-battery fire, which could be expected within a few minutes after the rockets were fired. The maneuver took three of our squadron helicopters to accomplish this mission.

- The first helicopter carried the empty rocket launcher, slung beneath the helicopter.
- The second helicopter carried the rockets, also slung beneath the helicopter in cargo nets.
- The third helicopter carried the rocket launcher loading and firing crew.

After firing, the rocket launcher had to quickly be re-attached below the first hovering helicopter. The unused rockets in cargo nets were attached beneath a second helicopter, rapidly. The third helicopter was used to fly the scrambling rocket launcher loading and firing crew away from the firing site, to safety. Then, we set up again, and fired rockets from a second rocket firing site. The whole process was repeated at two more locations.

This rocket launching effort was dubbed Operation Ripple because of the ripple sequence of the rapid firing of twenty-four rockets. Operation Ripple was the brainchild of HMR-161, the 1st and 11th Marine Division staffs, and the 1st Marine Division's artillery regiment. At that time, the 1st Marine Division troops, supported by our helicopters, had driven farther into North Korea than had any other allied fighting unit.

Armistice Meetings at Panmunjom

Armistice talks between the United Nations (U.N.) and the North Korean/Chinese negotiators, were being held daily at the Armistice site at Panmunjom, which is located about thirty miles North of the South Korean capital city of Seoul. The chief U.N. negotiator was Vice Admiral C. Turner Joy, U.S. Navy; who was also Commander, U.S. Naval Forces Far East. His headquarters was in Tokyo, Japan, co-located with the headquarters of General Douglas MacArthur, Supreme Commander for the Allied Powers, in the Far East. The on-site U.N. negotiators lived in a heated train at Munsan, just south of the frozen Imjin River. To reach Panmunjom, the U.N. negotiators had to cross the Imjin River, in military vehicles, over a temporary, hastily engineer-constructed, pontoon bridge. Floating river ice, released during a sudden weather thaw, destroyed the pontoon bridge, and accordingly, the U.N. negotiators could not attend the daily armistice meetings.

HMR-161 was quickly assigned to provide two helicopters daily, to transport the U.N. negotiators from Munsan to Panmunjom for their daily 11 a.m. meetings. Immediately, two squadron helicopters flew across Korea to Munsan; ready to fly the U.N. negotiators back and forth to Panmunjom. The two helicopters stayed three days, and were relieved by another two, until the pontoon bridge was replaced.

Bob Warren, Pilot; Peace Delegates, Panmunjom, Korea (1952)

Downed Pilot Rescue Mission

Major Bill Mitchell and I were sent forty miles behind enemy lines, to attempt the rescue of a Navy helicopter pilot who had been shot down. Rescue missions like this one were normally assigned to small HO3S-1 helicopters, flying from LSTs. Those small LST rescue ships would take position near the east coast of North Korea, when significant U.S. Navy/USAF air strikes were being conducted. If an air strike plane was shot down in enemy territory, the LST would launch its helicopter, and attempt the rescue.

However, our rescue attempt was different; in that we were attempting to rescue the crew of one of the rescue helicopters, which had also been shot down earlier that day, near the city of Wonsan. An earlier rescue attempt was made by the USS *Manchester*'s naval gunfire HO3S -1 spotter helicopter, but enemy

231

ground fire had driven away that helicopter, and it returned to the *Manchester* severely damaged.

In order to get the latest information, concerning the latest rescue attempt situation, and to select and plan our route to the rescue site, we landed aboard the *Manchester,* where we viewed the severely damaged helicopter. After landing, the blades of the helicopter were folded, and the helicopter moved forward against the ship's superstructure, where it was tied down. Because of the visible enemy fire damage to the helicopter, it was doubtful that the helicopter would ever fly again. After a quick briefing, we took off, and proceeded to the rescue site. We experienced no enemy ground fire, as we were covered (protected) by a squadron of Navy Corsairs.

As we approached the rescue site, those Navy Corsairs were actively strafing multiple enemy sand-bagged gun emplacements. Accordingly, and as far as we knew, we did not receive enemy fire from the ground. We quickly located the downed helicopter, but could see no movement near it. However, our crew chief spotted some enemy troops. Using his Thompson machine gun, he opened fire on them. The gun fire startled Major Mitchell and me; as neither of us knew that our crew chief, Technical Sergeant Walt Mortimer, had brought a machine gun along. Not knowing this, we thought the firing was directed at us. After hovering over and around the shot down helicopter, we saw no activity, and reported that to the Navy F4U squadron leader[iv] who radioed back, "Well, you couldn't have tried any harder." Our flight back to our squadron was about forty miles south, and again, mostly off-shore and uneventful. Based on that rescue attempt, our helicopter crew of three were recommended to receive a Distinguished Flying Cross by our HMR-161 commanding officer.

The pilot of the helicopter we tried to rescue was Duane Thorin, a Navy enlisted chief petty officer. I met him later in

Washington, D.C. He told me that he heard and saw our HRS-1 rescue helicopter. However, his North Korean/Chinese captors had pointed their rifles at him; thus not letting him, or his crew, move from their small cave hiding place. After he had been interred at a POW camp, he returned through the Prisoner of War exchange site at Panmunjom. It was called Operation Switch where the POWs from each side were exchanged.

Thorin later authored a book, titled *A Ride to Panmunjom*. He autographed a copy for me; inscribing the book as follows, "To Captain Bob Warren, the Marine pilot who tried to prevent me from writing this book." After his release from a POW Camp, Duane Thorin had been commissioned to the rank of Ensign. Seeing his single Ensign's gold bar—denoting a very junior Navy officer rank—was odd on his Navy Officer's uniform, because that same uniform displayed several rows of combat ribbons, which he received for service and bravery.

Move Across Korea

To protect the Korean capital city of Seoul from an invasion by the North Korean Army, the U.N. Force Commander, General James Van Fleet, issued a warning order to the 1st Marine Division to prepare for a move southwest across the entire Korean Peninsula, to establish blocking positions thirty miles North of Seoul. Our helicopter squadron HMR-161, was to move simultaneously with the 1st Marine Division, to the new operating site.

Within the assigned division boundary, we had to stake a claim to our new forward operating site, as well as a new operating site for our squadron rear echelon; which was moving from its original location at the K-18 (Kang Nung) airfield. The site selected for the rear echelon was near Ascom City; which was northeast of Seoul, where several warehouse buildings could be used for rear echelon helicopter repairs, beyond what could be accomplished at the newly selected forward echelon site.

I flew with Colonel McCutcheon across the Korean peninsula, to select and stake our claim to our squadron's new forward operating site. After selection, and sketching the new forward echelon operating site on maps, we flew to the 1st Marine Division command post, where Colonel McCutcheon received approval for our new operating site claim from the Division commander. We then flew back to our squadron location. The new site was duly marked on the 1st Marine Division maps. When Colonel McCutcheon told a few members of his squadron about the forthcoming move, he asked me to "Tell 'Cos' (Captain Costello) to get rid of his small bulldozer."

With the new site selected and approved, our squadron commenced making plans to strike our camp, and travel in a long vehicle convoy with the 1st Marine Division, across the Korean Peninsula, to our new location. Many of our flights were to transport various 1st Marine Division staff members to the new operating area, and return. Of note, the maps being used by subordinate units of the 1st Marine Division now all included the location of their helicopter landing sites.

Back at our original forward operating area, our troop lifts were now one-way; principally to move Marine units from their frontline positions, back to staging areas, for their convoy truck transport to their new locations. Flights transporting members of the 1st Marine Division staff to the new 1st Marine Division command post were flown on 21 April.

On 23 April 1952, I left our original forward echelon area for the last time, and flew a helicopter to our new location, north of the city of Seoul. I was nursing a bad cold, and accordingly did not transport any troops from our squadron. My helicopter load consisted of rations, including a carton of precious fresh eggs, and our little Korean boy Ejungee. The flight took over two hours. At Seoul, Ejungee was turned over to a South Korean orphanage. We all missed the little guy.

On 27 and 28 April 1952, I flew the Secretary of the Navy, Dan Kimball, on a tour of the new 1st Marine Division areas, including a tour of the Division's frontlines. The new terrain was almost flat, compared to the mountainous terrain areas recently vacated. Accordingly, it offered almost no opportunity for our squadron flights to fly behind the hills in defilade[v]. However, due to the progress at Panmunjom toward reaching an armistice, both opposing forces largely stood their ground, by limiting their efforts to small unit patrol activities.

The Panmunjom Armistice Site

Our new squadron location made it much easier to provide helicopter flights for the U.N. negotiators' base site at Munsan. Although only a few minutes flying time away, those helicopters and crews stayed at Munsan. On 29 March 1952, I made my first flight to transport U.N. negotiators from Munsan, to the armistice site, for their daily 11:00 a.m. meetings. Some of those meetings lasted several hours; while others took less than thirty minutes.

The meetings between the U.N./South Korean, and the North Korean/Chinese negotiators took place in a large tent, across the street from some tiny mud-hut houses near Panmunjom. All Panmunjom residents had been evacuated from those mud huts. Two smaller warm-up tents were used, to allow negotiators to meet privately, prior to the daily meetings at 11:00 a.m. A two-and one-half-mile circle marked the site area where no one from either side could carry a weapon of any kind. Nor were any troops permitted, except two armed sentries from each side, who stood on duty, day and night, on each side of the meeting tent. The site was marked by large, brightly colored balloons, flying from around the site perimeter. The balloons served to prevent air strikes on the armistice meeting site. Artillery firing had to be outside of the armistice site circle; and artillery firing over the site was forbidden.

The Armistice Negotiators

Each morning the North Korean/Chinese negotiators, headed by their chief negotiator Nam II, and several more Korean and Chinese officers arrived, riding in old open Russian jeeps; or occasionally in a captured U.S. Chrysler sedan. The sedan no longer had shock absorbers, and the sedan body was suspended only by low, worn out vehicle springs. They arrived daily, after their long and bumpy ride over dirt roads, from the North Korean city of Kaesong. Initially, the U.N. negotiators arrived in well-maintained staff cars, after crossing the pontoon bridge over the Imjin River.

When the thawing ice destroyed that pontoon bridge, HMR-161 was immediately tasked to provide helicopters to transport the U.N./South Korean delegates. From our original location, two helicopters were sent. The second helicopter provided a backup, if needed. After the squadron moved to the new location, a single helicopter was sent to the nearby Munsan site.

From 29 March through 8 April 1952, I flew the U.N./South Korean delegates from Munsan to Panmunjom, and returned them after their meetings. After one of the daily meetings, I flew the senior U.N. Armistice negotiator Vice Admiral C. Turner Joy from Munsan to Yungdun-po airfield, located across the Han River from Seoul. His headquarters was in Tokyo, Japan.

On the day I flew him to Yungdun-po, the weather was terrible; with driving rain, fog, and very poor visibility. Pilots called it bird-walking weather. He was concerned whether the bad weather would prevent me from flying back to Munsan, to be available to fly the delegates to their meeting the next day. I assured him that if I could not return, I would notify my squadron, in time to provide another helicopter for the mission to Panmunjom the next day. The backup plan was not necessary, because I returned to Munsan safely, after he departed for Tokyo in his Navy patrol bomber. At breakfast the next day, I was surprised to meet several other high-ranking U.S Military officers. In addition to Vice Admiral Joy, I met Army General Matthew B. Ridgeway who had succeeded General MacArthur as Supreme Commander for the Allied Powers in the Far East; and Army General James Van Fleet who commanded all U.N. Forces in Korea. They seemed curious, as to why relatively low-ranking Marine officers were present; until they learned that we were the helicopter pilots who flew the delegates to and from Panmunjom. They were all very kind and considerate officers, who expressed their appreciation to us. I flew my last flight to Panmunjom on 8 April 1952. The armistice issues still being negotiated were: first, Prison of War (POW) Exchange; and second, The Ports of Entry.

From 9 to 24 April 1952, I flew ten administrative flights; mainly to and from Ascom City, which was our newly selected rear echelon area. My last HMR-161 helicopter flight in Korea was on 24 April 1952. I had flown in Korea for eight months. I departed Korea on 26 April, to enjoy my accumulated leave in the United States, and then to report to MCAS, Tustin, California, for the ambiguous assignment of "duty involving flying." I had been promoted to the rank of Captain; and had received two Distinguished Flying Crosses; one for my flight on 8 February 1952, on a downed-pilot rescue mission.

Since my arrival in Korea on 4 September 1951, until I departed HMR-161 on 24 April 1952, I had flown two hundred combat hours on two hundred thirty-one flights, in eight months. I was very proud of what our helicopter squadron had accomplished while supporting the 1st Marine Division in combat. Further, I realized that we had initiated a new chapter of Marine Corps Amphibious development. While proud of my contributions, I was getting weary, and was ready to return home to my family in Santa Ana, California.

Chapter 15: 1952 Return From Korea

Joyful Family Reunion

My flight home from Korea, was aboard a military transport airplane to Tokyo, and then on a TWA airliner to Los Angeles International Airport (LAX), after a couple of mid-Pacific stops for fuel. Millie and our two small children, Bill and Jeanne, plus our dachshund Ginger, met me at the LAX terminal. Our wonderful little family was delighted to be together again. I was amazed to see how much our children had grown during the nine months I was in Korea. I had earned a long leave.

Jeanne, Millie and Bill Warren, Santa Ana, CA (1952)

After getting settled into our South Magnolia Street bungalow in Santa Ana, we started a long driving trip to Michigan to visit our families for a couple of weeks. On our drive back to California, we stopped to see my brother Bill Dean. Bill was a captain with Northwest Orient Airlines. Bill, his wife Margaret, and their daughter Gretchen lived in their home in Bloomington.

After our visit, we drove West, through the Badlands of South Dakota to Wyoming; and entered the East Gate of the famous Yellowstone National Park. We stopped there, and viewed Old Faithful Geyser, as it put on its hourly show of water and steam, shooting several hundred feet into the air. We departed Yellowstone Park at its West Gate, and headed to our next planned stop in Dillon, Montana. One of our night-fighter pilots, Carl Davis, with whom I flew at Okinawa and Saipan, lived there with his wife Martha. Carl had completed law school, established his law practice in Dillon, and purchased a new home there.

In addition, Roy Forrester had also returned from Saipan, was discharged from the Army, and took over his father's ranch outside of Dillon. He had married Carl's sister, Annie Davis who had served with the Red Cross during WWII in Europe. We had a wonderful time in Dillon. Roy raised foxes, and our son Bill was fascinated to see Roy Forrester open a box from the top, reach down, and with his gloved hand, quickly grab one of the foxes, and pull it out of the box. Roy also taught Bill to catch rainbow trout by snagging a fish, handing the fishing rod to Bill, who would catch the fish by himself, and pull it out of the water. In the evening, we would journey into the nearby foothills, and have a very enjoyable fish fry picnic around a campfire.

Our stays in Montana, including many during the years to come, were always exciting, and always fun-filled, visiting Carl Davis, Roy Forrester, and their gracious families.

From Dillon, we drove South through Twin Falls, Idaho, and Salt Lake City, Utah. We stopped, and swam in Great Salt Lake, where the high salt content in the lake water made it impossible to sink. After driving away from Salt Lake City, we drove to St. George, Utah where we stopped and rested in the afternoon, in preparation for crossing into Nevada, and driving across the vast desert at night. Automobiles did not yet have air conditioners. Therefore, the only way to avoid driving on very hot days was simply to cross the desert at night. We stopped in Las Vegas, and spent some time resting, and visiting the fascinating Hoover Dam. From Las Vegas, we drove into California, and on to our home in Santa Ana.

Bob and Millie dressed for the USMC Birthday Ball
El Toro, CA (1952)

Headquarters and Maintenance Squadron

My leave was over. As ordered, I reported to the Aircraft, Fleet Marine Force Pacific (AirFMFPac) headquarters at MCAS, El Toro, California. From there, I was ordered back to the very familiar, nearby MCAF, Santa Ana, where I trained prior to my combat tour in Korea. With orders in hand, I felt very much at home, as I returned to the familiar old LTA Blimp Hangar #1. The surroundings were familiar, but the organization had greatly expanded from our previous single squadron, to a newly full Helicopter Aircraft Group [MAG(HR)-16]. Regardless of the types of aircraft being flown, a MAG consists of a Headquarters and Maintenance Squadron (H&MS), a Marine Air Base Squadron (MABS), and several numbered flying squadrons. MAG-16 now occupied both LTA Hangars #1 and #2.

The H&MS is staffed with MAG Headquarters personnel, including the MAG Commanding Officer. The H&MS provides maintenance capability for the flying squadrons, that is above their level of minor aircraft maintenance capability. For instance, it has equipment required to change engines on the flying squadron's airplanes.

Marine Air Base Squadron (MABS)

The MABS provides all personnel and equipment to operate an airfield, for thirty days in combat. The airfield setup includes:

- A supply of consumables, to include motor vehicle fuel, high octane aviation fuel, food, and water.
- A portable aircraft control tower, and trained tower operators.
- The truck transportation to move supplies and equipment for the MAG squadrons.

- A complement of ambulances, radio jeeps, fuel and fire trucks, and other specialized vehicular equipment.
- The supplies necessary to provide repairs for the MAG motor transport vehicles.
- A galley, and messing equipment, required to feed the entire MAG during combat operations.
- A complement that maintains internal and external security for the entire MAG.
- A zealously guarded armory, that issues individual, and aircraft mounted weapons.

The armory issues a rifle, and ammunition, to members of participating MAG units, for annual qualifications. Qualifications support the philosophy that "Every Marine Is First, A Rifleman."

My orders specified assignment to the H&MS, where I was assigned to the MAG as the S-3 (Operations Officer). My specific duties involved scheduling and testing helicopters, before each was returned to its flying squadron. The H&MS had ten helicopters assigned to it; meaning that MAG staff pilots did not have to interrupt training schedules of the numbered squadrons, to access helicopters. The H&MS pilots were required to participate in all training, as though they were flying in a numbered squadron.

One of my first requirements was to conduct day and night field carrier landing practice (FCLP). On 10 June 1952, I landed aboard the USS *Badoeng Strait*, an escort aircraft carrier that was operating off the Southern California coast. I completed the qualifying number of day and night aircraft landings, thereby updating my aircraft carrier qualification before flying back to MCAF, Santa Ana.

Bob and Bill Warren in HRS-1, MCAF Santa Ana, CA (1952)

Second Flight Across the United States

On 7 August 1952, I was ordered to Quantico, Virginia, to ferry a newly manufactured HRS-2 to California. The HRS-2 looked and flew just like its HRS-1 predecessor. The newer aircraft was strengthened; particularly the long tail cone, which had failed several times during combat operations in Korea.

On 12 August I commenced my second helicopter flight across the United States. Departing from Quantico, Virginia, I generally followed the same route that I had in my first helicopter flight; with only a few different refueling stop changes. On this second flight, I made refueling stops in North Carolina and Alabama. My route was also changed slightly as I did not fly to Yuma, Arizona. Instead, after leaving Lordsburg, New Mexico, I made refueling stops at Douglas and Phoenix, Arizona. At the California/Arizona border, I refueled at Blythe, California before flying home to MCAF, Santa Ana.

I completed my second helicopter flight across the United States; refueling in eleven states in five days, and logging forty more pilot hours. My flights averaged nine hours per day. Again, a cross country flight in a low flying helicopter proved the best way to view our beautiful country from the air. My helicopter flying time during August 1952 totaled sixty-five hours.

In September, I flew aboard the aircraft carrier USS *Valley Forge* (CV-45), for additional day and night qualification. The ship was operating in its assigned area; just off the west coast of California.

After completing my required night landing, I stopped at Pri-Fly to observe further night takeoffs and landings. Pri-fly is located above the aircraft carrier flight deck, about midway between the ship's bow and stern. From there, the Carrier Air Group Commander (CAG) directs all the ship's flight operations. The ship's captain is directing all other ship operations from the ship's bridge.

Of course, during flight operations, the ship, like all aircraft carriers, steams into the wind, in order in order to provide maximum wind speed down the flight deck. While I was observing flight operations from Pri-fly, the ship's captain called the CAG on the ship's intercom system and asked, "When are you going to let me turn? I've gone through my assigned area, another ship's area; and if you don't let me turn soon, I'll be in downtown Los Angeles." After renewing my Carrier Qualifications (CARQUALS), I flew back to MCAF, Santa Ana.

Non-Commissioned Officer (NCO) Leadership School

In September 1952, I received Temporary Additional Duty (TAD) orders to the NCO Leadership School at MCAS, El Toro; where I was assigned as an instructor. Because El Toro was only three miles away, I remained administrative on the roles of my helicopter squadron at MCAF, Santa Ana. Accordingly, my orders to the school were temporary; meanwhile I was assigned to the school as full-time instructor for the next ten months. Twenty-five Staff NCO students were assigned to each numbered class. Classes lasted three weeks, and attendance was purposely limited, in order to make close associations between NCO students and the six instructors possible.

Classes convened five days a week, Mondays through Fridays from 8:00 a.m. (0800) to 5:00 p.m. (1700), with a one-hour lunch break. Each school day started with a personal inspection of students, standing in ranks. The uniform to be worn the next day was announced at the close of each school day. The announcement ensured that each NCO had a complete uniform; whether it be standard khaki, utility, or dress blue; and that the uniform fit properly. This practice was intended to teach the lower ranking Marines that their NCOs were setting the example of excellence for all their Marines to emulate.

The real purpose of the leadership school, however, was to teach the highly qualified NCOs to more easily impart their vast aviation technical knowledge and maintenance skills, to Marines of lesser ranks. Our object was to teach the NCOs proper classroom techniques, and other teaching methods. In other words, we were teaching teachers.

We taught skills, such as the proper use of a simple pointer in the classroom, to teach the NCOs the importance of maintaining eye contact with members of a class. The same was necessary when teaching outdoors; along with always making sure that those being taught, never had to face the sun.

The student NCOs were required to eat three meals each week with lower ranking Marines in their mess halls; including one breakfast, one lunch, and one dinner. The next day, the NCOs were required to submit a one-page written report describing the overall mess hall cleanliness, as well as the food quality and quantity. This exercise taught the NCO to always be concerned about the welfare of their Marines; at the same time, it improved their own writing skills.

All classes could best be described as student-friendly. Too, as a school made up entirely of senior NCOs, disciplinary problems did not exist. Teaching at the NCO Leadership School was a real joy, and an honor. The school was the brainchild of Major General Vernon Megee; who at that time commanded the Third Marine Aircraft Wing at El Toro. Touring the school soon became included in the schedule of other visiting Marine Corps Flag Officers; including a visit to the school by General Lemuel Shepherd, Commandant of The Marine Corps.

Soon thereafter, NCO Leadership Schools were started at several major aviation and ground commands, throughout the Marine Corps. Major General Megee also directed that successful completion of the NCO Leadership School would always be noted on the next fitness (efficiency) report of each school graduate. Accordingly, interest in attending the school rose markedly. The school had a humorous sign that read, "You can no more teach what you 'aint' learned, than you can go back to where you 'aint' been."

The officer in charge of the school was Captain Robert "Terry" Lynch, with whom I had served years earlier at MCAS, Cherry Point in VMP-354, our photo squadron. As always, Terry Lynch did a superb job, and I was honored that he requested my assignment to the school. I always learned from him.

While instructing at the school, I rode in a jet airplane for the first time. It was a Douglas F3D twin jet fighter, which had the first side-by-side pilot cockpits. The jet was piloted by Captain John Fisher who was also one of our NCO Leadership school instructors. In June 1953, my ten-month temporary assignment to the NCO

Leadership School ended. The NCO Leadership School was closed, because there were no more eligible NCOs at MCAS, El Toro to attend. I was ordered back to my helicopter squadron at MCAF, Santa Ana, where I again regularly flew helicopter test, administrative, and training flights.

Chapter 16: Aide to General Schilt

Interview and Selection

During June 1953, I received a telephone call from my friend, Captain Richard J. "Jake" Schriver, who had served in Korea, Hawaii, and now for two years at MCAS, El Toro, California as Aide-de-Camp (Aide) to Major General Christian "Frank" Schilt. Jake Schriver was due for relief, and anxious to return to flying jet fighter aircraft. He told me that General Schilt was interviewing several Captains as his prospective Aide, and that he wanted to talk to me the next day.

The next morning, I arrived at the General's office at El Toro wearing a summer khaki uniform; crisp and neatly pressed. My cordovan shoes were highly polished. While waiting for my interview, I asked Jake why General Schilt wanted to interview me. He was very non-committal, except that he mentioned that I had one thing different from all the others being interviewed.

After standing at attention in front of General Schilt's office desk, I reported "Captain Warren reporting as ordered, sir." He quietly said, "At ease." He then rose from his desk, approached me, and shook my hand. He thanked me for coming to his office. He had that wonderful quality of making those of lesser rank quickly relaxed. He guided me to comfortable office chairs, away from his desk. We had a friendly hour-long uninterrupted conversation. He asked about my previous Marine Corps assignments, and about my wife, Millie, and our two children. He asked where they had lived while I flew helicopters in Korea, and whether I had ever had an aircraft accident. I told him that my family stayed in the bungalow we had purchased in nearby Santa Ana, and that we were still living there. Then I briefly described my accident aboard the USS *Siboney* when my F6F Hellcat's arresting hook broke off, and I crashed into the ship's barrier.

He recalled flying in a helicopter that I was piloting several times in Korea. He also wanted to know how long I had known Captain Schriver. I told him that we had flown twin-engine F7F Tigercats, F4U Corsairs, and F6F Hellcats in the same photo squadron at MCAS, Cherry Point from 1946 to 1950.

General Schilt then told me that he was still responsible for the Marine Corps squadrons in Korea, Hawaii, and of course, El Toro, as well as the helicopter squadrons at nearby MCAF, Santa Ana. Accordingly, he told me that considerable travel would be involved, and that his aide would be required to accompany him on those, and other trips. I had the feeling that he was spending an inordinate length of time with me. I was also concerned, because my eyes were almost riveted on the blue Medal of Honor ribbon that he wore on his uniform shirt, above his Naval Aviator Wings. I knew our conversation was ended, when he rose, shook my hand again, and thanked me. He told me that his selection would be announced within a week.

Aide Selection Announcement

Two days later, Jake Schriver called to tell me, that I had been selected, and was to report to General Schilt's office the following morning, and commence my duties as General Schilt's new Aide. Jake then revealed to me that one thing that I had different than the others who were being considered, was that I was an experienced helicopter pilot. Within about two weeks, I realized that probably the main reason I had been selected as General Schilt's Aide, was that he wanted to learn to fly helicopters. What better way to learn to fly a helicopter, than to have your Aide always available as your flight instructor?

The next week, I was told to arrange for a helicopter to fly for about an hour at nearby MCAF, Santa Ana. Further, I was told that General Schilt would fly in the cockpit with me. He revealed that he had been studying the HRS Helicopter Handbook, to become familiar with the HRS operating systems. That is how I became the flight instructor for a legendary Marine Corps hero who, incidentally, was five pay grades (a Captain O–3 to Major General O–8) above me in rank. At first, the difference in rank and pay grade was somewhat intimidating.

General Schilt's First Helicopter Instruction Flight

On his first helicopter instruction flight, General Schilt took his driver Sergeant Priestly, and George (the Schilt family dog), to ride as passengers in the HRS helicopter troop cabin. George was a small brown and white dog, of questionable lineage. All went well, until I started the helicopter engine, and George, frightened by the loud noise, leaped out of Sergeant Priestley's arms, and bounded out through the helicopter open door, with Sergeant Priestley running in hot pursuit after him. When last seen, George was streaking toward the General's staff car, which was parked near LTA Hangar #2, being chased by a tall Marine Corps Sergeant. By then the helicopter engine had started, and was running smoothly. I did not know whether I should stop the engine and help rescue George, or continue the flight by engaging the helicopter rotors. Watching, General Schilt just grinned, and gestured that we should continue.

So, I released the rotor brake, and explained that I was engaging the helicopter rotors. We spent most of the hour on the hard surface mat, learning to set, and then unlock the parking brakes; taxiing the helicopter, by steering it around the large asphalt mat, with the right and left rudder pedals linked to the tail rotor, and slight use of the individual, toe-operated brakes; and stopping it, by depressing the brake pedals at the top of each pedal. I then called the airfield control tower, and requested takeoff clearance.

When safely airborne, I turned control over to General Schilt. My objective was to demonstrate the effects of the collective pitch; a control that when raised or lowered, simultaneously changes the pitch of all the main rotor blades. The helicopter also had a motorcycle-type throttle; which when twisted by the pilot, added or reduced engine power. A fixed-wing aircraft does not have a collective pitch control.

After flying thirty minutes, I took control again, called the airfield control tower, and landed. I then directed (more like asked) him to taxi the helicopter back to its original parking spot; but this time I told him to raise the collective pitch slightly, to make it much easier to taxi. He did, and he commented on the intercom that he noticed the difference. Except for George escaping, the flight was a normal, first instructional flight experience, which I had learned and followed, when instructing fixed-wing pilots, during transition to flying helicopters at Quantico years earlier.

After exiting the helicopter cockpit, I signed the Aircraft Yellow Sheet, while General Schilt, as always, shook hands with the helicopter crew chief, while expressing his thanks. By then Sergeant Priestley had successfully captured George, and we rode back to General Schilt's El Toro headquarters.

While in the rear seat of his staff car, I reviewed his first helicopter instructional flight. He asked several pertinent questions; reflecting that he anticipated learning fast. I also briefly told him what to expect during his next instructional flight. Upon return, I made sure that the flight was properly entered in his flight log book, and in my log book as well. Unless General Schilt was on a trip with his Aide/instructor, he flew the helicopter several times every week.

Serving at El Toro

General Schilt's Chief of Staff was Colonel Paul A. Putnam who had commanded VMF-211, the fighter squadron on Wake Island that had flown until it had no more airplanes. Wake Island was overrun and captured by the Japanese. Colonel Putnam spent the remainder of WWII (from December, 1941 to September, 1945) in a Japanese prison camp.

I always felt that, in addition to my normal duties, I was also the unofficial Aide to the Chief of Staff. Mainly, I kept him informed regarding what General Schilt was doing, or what he planned to do. I know that he always appreciated the information.

His office was directly across the hall from General Schilt's office. I recall one incident, when two Marine Lieutenant Colonel fighter pilots came to General Schilt's office to respectfully protest their orders to helicopter flight training. I was instructed to take them to Colonel Putnam's office first. After entering, they stood until Colonel Putnam finally raised his head, looked at them over his half-glasses, and asked, "Gentlemen, have you read your orders?" When they both acknowledged that they had done so, he told them, "Fine; you're excused." He was very adept at deflecting similar problems or situations, away from General Schilt

My office was adjacent to General Schilt's, with a door between. On my desk was a very old intercommunications control box; about eight inches long and six inches high. The intercom had multiple stations accessed (opened) by pushing a small station switch up, to answer a call, or to call another office in the headquarters administration building. The device was always referred to as the "squawk box." To cease communications, and shut it off, it was necessary to center the open switch. Each major office in the headquarters office building had one of those squawk boxes, including General Schilt's office, and Colonel Putnam's office.

Forgetting to shut off the squawk box was easy. I received several verbal warnings about its use, and accordingly when called, I was cautioned to center the switches immediately. An often-repeated story about a previous commanding general, had him beckoning his aide using the squawk box saying, "Come into my office this minute." His aide responded with a quick, "Yes, sir," and hurried into the General's Office. It was late on a Friday afternoon, and the aide forgot to center the squawk box switch, thus leaving communications to the General's office open. The General instructed his aide to do several things that afternoon. The aide departed, and after closing the General's office door murmured, "Damnit, come the revolution, I'll be in there, and he'll be out here." A firm voice message, transmitted through the open squawk box, immediately said, "There isn't going to be any revolution, Captain. So, I suggest that you now get to work." Ouch!

Major General Christian Schilt promoting Bob Warren
to the rank of Major, El Toro, CA (1956)

Millie, Bob, Jeanne and Bill Warren, Santa Ana, CA (1955)

General Schilt's Career, and My History with Him

I served as General Schilt's Aide for two years, at El Toro. During that time, I learned that during WWI, he had deployed to Ponta Delgada in the Azores, with the 1st Marine Aeronautical Company. That company was the first American flying unit of any service during WWI to deploy overseas, completely equipped and trained. The unit departed Philadelphia on 8 January 1918. Its mission was to prevent attempts by German submarines to establish refueling bases in the Azores. That aeronautical company had a mixture of eighteen float airplanes, with two long pontoons, and flying boats. The Marine pilots maintained a full schedule for nearly a year; flying seventy miles, with a two-hour supply of gasoline; often in inclement weather "without radios, signaling pistols, or homing pigeons." General Schilt was then an enlisted man, who oversaw aircraft maintenance. He later earned his Naval Aviator Wings, and commission at Marine Flying Field, Miami, Florida.

General Schilt's Medal of Honor

For his courageous flights on 6, 7, and 8 January 1928, then Lieutenant Schilt evacuated ten wounded Marines, on ten flights, in Quilali, Nicaragua. He landed on the Quilali main street, and then took off ten times under enemy fire; each time with a wounded Marine riding in the second open cockpit. Also, his bi-wing airplane had no brakes. So, to shorten his landing rollout distance, Marines would run into the street, and grab the wingtips on both sides, to further slow the landing airplane. For those brave, lifesaving actions and extraordinary flying skills, Lieutenant Schilt received the Medal of Honor from President of The United States, Calvin Coolidge, on the White House lawn, with Commandant of the Marine Corps, John A. Lejeune proudly observing. Lesser known, was that Lieutenant Schilt was granted a leave, for the purpose of surveying potential landing sites for the expanding Pan American Airways Service, in Central and South America.

Marine Air Reserve Training Command

Following various combat assignment in WWII, General Schilt became Commander of the Marine Corps Air Reserve Training Command (MARTCOM), which was headquartered near Chicago, at NAS, Glenview, Illinois. He believed that the combat experience gained during WWII by the Marine Corps' combat- experienced pilots, and very skilled, enlisted aviation mechanics should be retained.

Marine Air Reserve squadrons were organized near twelve major cities throughout the United States. For instance, a squadron flying F4U Corsairs, and later flying Douglas AD Skyraiders, was organized at NAS, Grosse Ile, Michigan near Detroit. My close friend, Lieutenant Allen Schutter, with whom I flew in combat at both Okinawa and Saipan, was a member of the Grosse Ile Reserve

Squadron. Just five years after WWII ended, those reserve squadrons were recalled to active duty; being already organized, and ready to fight in Korea. Often, during peacetime deployments to Cherry Point or to El Toro, General Schilt would visit stating, "I just wanted to stop, and say hello to the reserves."

During his tour at MARTCOM, General Schilt also visited the McDonnell Aircraft plant in St. Louis, Missouri, where it was building jet-powered fighter aircraft for Marine Corps squadrons. The jet was called the FH-1 Phantom. The Phantom was a single-seat, twin jet engine aircraft. General Schilt flew the Phantom-1 at the McDonnell plant; making him the first Marine Corps general officer to pilot a jet-powered fighter airplane. Later, the Marine Corps stood up its first jet fighter squadron (VMF-122) at MCAS, Cherry Point, North Carolina. The squadron commanding officer was my former boss, Lieutenant Colonel Marion Carl.

Marine Corps squadrons were deployed to Korea, soon after the initial invasion into South Korea, by the armies of North Korea. Those squadrons provided close air support for the U.S. Army and the Marine Brigade that were sent to Korea. General Douglas MacArthur requested that "a Marine Division" be sent to Korea, to prevent South Korea from being completely overrun by invading North Koreans.

The problem was that President Harry S. Truman and his WWI "cannon cocker" (artillery) buddy Louis A. Johnson—now the Secretary of Defense—were trying to reduce the Marine Corps to a ceremonial regiment (whatever that was). They suddenly realized that the Marines were the only troops trained and available to deploy from the United States to help save the small Pusan Perimeter from being completely overrun by North Korean Army troops. Marines from both Camp Pendleton and Camp Lejeune were joined, and organized into a brigade. The aviation squadrons were largely from MCAS, Cherry Point, and MCAS, El Toro. Both Marine

Air and ground Marines units had been sharply reduced; some near the point of non-existence. However, they were now cobbled together on the west coast, and organized into fighting units to form one Marine Brigade of ground marines, and one Marine Aircraft Group. In addition, a small number of helicopters with HMX-1 squadron pilots in Quantico, Virginia were attached to a Marine Observation Squadron, and deployed to Korea.

Following the Brigade landing in Korea, the Marine air group operated and flew support missions from airfields in Japan, and from the small aircraft carrier USS *Badoeng Strait*, flying F4U Corsairs. The observation squadron landed, with its small high-wing spotter airplanes. The helicopters from HMX-1 in Quantico, led by Major Victor A. "Vic" Armstrong, began air operations immediately. The brigade was expanded to full Marine Division, with Brigadier General Oliver P. Smith in command, and the air group was expanded into a full Marine Aircraft Wing under the command of Major General Field Harris. After the 1st Marine Division made the now famous Inchon landing, followed by bitter cold winter operations at the Chosin Reservoir, Major General Field Harris was relieved by Major General Christian Schilt, in July 1951.

On the Marine Corps Birthday, celebrated on 10 November 1951, the North Koreans, facing the 1st Marine Division, were given a wake-up call when eighty-five Marine Corps fighter and attack aircraft, led by Major General Schilt, attacked their frontline positions. The attacking aircraft squadrons were all armed with bombs and rockets. General Schilt was then in his mid-fifties; and was flying a twin-engine Grumman F7F (Tigercat). His wingman was his aide, Captain "Jake" Schriver.

From our HMR-161 position near the frontlines, we could easily view the Marine Corps Birthday air strike. Our Helicopter squadron, HMR-161 also celebrated the Marine Corps Birthday by baking a very large, multi-tiered Birthday cake, several feet high, which was ceremoniously cut by Major General Gerald C. Thomas, Commanding General of the 1st Marine Division.

General Schilt was a true leader, who maintained his wonderful sense of humor. On one occasion, he flew with his aide, Captain Schriver, to a remote Korean airstrip located near the 1st Marine Division headquarters. From there, General Schilt could easily visit the 1st Marine Division, VMO-6 and HMR-161, the two squadrons that were under his command, and co-located at a dirt landing strip called X-83. After one such visit, General Schilt flew back alone to his K-3 (Pohang) headquarters, purposely leaving his aide Captain Schriver behind. The worried Jake Schriver stayed in my tent at HMR-161 all night.

The next day, he rode on our helicopter daily mail flight, to our rear echelon at K-18. From there Jake Schriver caught another flight, back to General Schilt's headquarters at K-3. The entire air wing staff knew that Jake Schriver was purposely left behind, when General Schilt flew back to K-3. General Schilt's Chief of Staff seriously warned the waiting Jake that he was probably in deep yogurt.

When Jake mustered enough courage to try and explain his overnight absence to General Schilt, he entered the General's office and was surprised-and very relieved-to see the wing staff assembled, and as one, they cheered his safe return. The general grinned and said to Jake, "I wondered if you would ever get back to work."

General Schilt truly liked Jake, and kept him as his aide when he was transferred to Hawaii. Jake, still a bachelor, enjoyed a thirty-day leave in the United States, and while in California, purchased a new Cadillac convertible. He arranged to have it shipped to Hawaii. General Schilt had a bogus message delivered to Jake, telling him that while being loaded on a ship, his new automobile had unfortunately been dropped on the dock at Long

Beach; but that it was still being shipped to Hawaii in its damaged condition. Of course, Jake met the ship when it docked in Hawaii, and was very relieved to see his new car, which had never been dropped, or otherwise damaged. He quickly realized that General Schilt had pulled another "Gotcha" on him.

After his tour in Hawaii, General Schilt received orders to MCAS, El Toro, and to assume command of Aircraft, Fleet Marine Force, Pacific. Captain Jake returned to California with General Schilt, and remained as his aide until I relieved him in July 1953.

Staff Pilot, Captain Kelvin Bailey

At El Toro, General Schilt had selected Captain Kelvin "Kel" Bailey to be his staff pilot. In that assignment, "Kel" Bailey and I planned General Schilt's flight trips from El Toro. I had to work closely with Kel, to let him know when and where General Schilt planned to go. Most of the flights were in the United States, and flown in a Douglas R4D-8, a twin-engine Super DC-3 transport aircraft. However, on the longer flights from El Toro to Hawaii, and on flights to the Far East, a four-engine C-54 Skymaster was used. In Hawaii, General Schilt would visit a Marine aircraft group based at MCAS, Kaneohe Bay and Marine Transport Squadron VMGR-252, which operated from NAS, Barber's Point. Both locations were on the island of Oahu.

Flights to the Far East would then continue to Wake Island; landing at that mid-Pacific Ocean island for fuel, then proceeding to the first planned Far East destinations; either Korean or Japanese military airfields. Simple hot meals were prepared on those long flights by a multi-talented crew, whose only stove was a two-burner electric hot plate located in the rear of the C-54 passenger cabin.

I accompanied General Schilt from El Toro to the Far East during November 1953, January 1954, and May 1955. General Schilt's return flights to El Toro left from NAS, Atsugi located near

Tokyo, then flew over the northernmost Japanese Island of Hokkaido. Staying east, and well clear of the Russian-held Sakhalin Island, we flew Northeast to Attu Island, the westernmost of the U.S. owned Aleutian Islands in the State of Alaska. From Attu, our return flight route followed the Aleutian Chain of Islands, landing at Adak for fuel. During WWII, some U.S. troops had been stationed on Adak. The troops planted thirty-nine evergreen trees. While the trees lived, they never grew higher than three to four feet because of the harsh climate. A sign had been painted at the edge of those little evergreen trees that read, "You Are Now Entering Adak National Forest."

From Adak, the flights proceeded to Anchorage; landing at Elmendorf AFB, and we stayed overnight at Fort Richardson, a nearby U.S. Army base. From Anchorage we flew non-stop back to California, passing over Juneau, Alaska; Vancouver, Canada; Seattle, Washington; Portland, Oregon; San Francisco, California; and lowering altitude over Los Angeles, before finally landing back at MCAS, El Toro, where the flight had started.

The major difference on those flights was the length of daylight and darkness in the northern latitudes. On the November 1953 winter flight, the days were very short. While flying along the Aleutian Islands toward Anchorage in darkness for only a few hours, we noted a strange lighted sky ahead. The light was dawn of a short day, which lasted only about five hours, before darkness again. By contrast, on the May 1955 summer flight, the days were very long, and much of the flight over the Aleutian Islands was during daylight hours. In those Northern latitudes, the length of days and nights during winter and summer months was quite significant.

Repeated Flights to Indian Springs

Between those long trips to the Far East, many other shorter flights with General Schilt were scheduled. Several flights were to Indian Spring, Nevada, to witness the explosion of a ten-thousand-kiloton atomic bomb. We had flown there from El Toro several times; only to have the atomic bomb explosion delayed. Each flight left MCAS, El Toro after midnight; arriving in time for the planned dawn explosion.

Finally, after several delays, on 22 March 1955, the bomb was detonated. Returning home, I went back to bed and about an hour later I was awakened by my excited wife who, after several previous delays awakened and exclaimed, "Bob, you were supposed to fly to Nevada today." I sleepily informed her that I had already been to Nevada that morning, that the bomb had been detonated, and that I had returned safely and went back to bed, all while she slept soundly. I told her that I had been exposed to radiation and that some radiation glow was possible. I took a flashlight to bed, and when I turned the flashlight on, sure enough the radiation glow could plainly be seen.

The Atomic Bomb Explosion Experience

Indian Springs is located about one hundred miles north of Las Vegas, Nevada. The bomb rested atop a two-hundred-foot tower, constructed mostly with aluminum platforms, and supporting beams. Various items of military equipment and vehicles had been placed at precise intervals from the tower outward, to see and measure the effects of the explosion. About two miles from the tower, personnel trenches had been dug to a depth of eight feet. Several rows of sandbags were placed along the top of each trench. Those of us who witnessed the explosion were required to wear steel military helmets.

It was still dark, when the bomb was detonated. We were briefed to face down toward the bottom of the trench and to close our eyes so we wouldn't be blinded. However, when the bomb detonated, the whole trench was instantly illuminated with a very intense white light. Next, the whole trench shook like we were having a major earthquake. Some of the sandbags that had been placed above broke open, and sand rained down on us. The sand shower was followed immediately by a thunderous noise from the exploding bomb.

After about an hour, we were permitted to climb out of the trench and view the damage done to the military equipment. Trucks of various sizes near the tower were demolished completely. In addition, slivers of the aluminum tower beams were scattered over the landscape, and appeared as if a giant knife had sliced through them. We were all exposed to radiation, which was recorded in our medical records.

MCAS, Yuma, Arizona

Other memorable trips on which I accompanied General Schilt from El Toro, included a flight to Yuma, Arizona, to officially take possession of a former U.S. Air Force airfield near the city of Yuma. It now officially became, MCAS, Yuma, Arizona. The airfield was a joint-usage airfield, built on three thousand acres, and used by Yuma for civilian aircraft. The airfield was located in the southwest corner of Arizona, bordering Mexico and California. This airfield had long been the home base for the Marine Corps vertical-rising jet squadrons. That aircraft, designed by British Aerospace, and designated the AV8-B Harrier by the Marine Corps, is commonly called a "jump jet."

Over the years, the Harrier has proven to be a very reliable close-air support aircraft for the Marine Corps, because it can be operated much nearer to the troops being supported, than can other fixed-wing aircraft that require airfields with long runways, or launches from aircraft carriers.

Marine Corps Harriers continually demonstrated excellent close-air support capability during the various Gulf Wars, where it operated from both aircraft carriers, and from unprepared locations ashore. The British Royal Navy had used the Sea Harrier against the Armed Forces of Argentina in the 2 April to 14 June 1982 war for repossession of the Falkland Islands, which had recently been invaded, and lost to Argentina.

The Gadsden Land Purchase

The location of the airbase at Yuma was on land bought by the United States in what is known as the Gadsden Purchase, which was negotiated between 1882 and 1885, and defines the present U.S. southern border in Arizona and part of New Mexico. The purchase included twenty-nine thousand, six hundred seventy square miles of property. That purchase was important, because it provided the land for the route on which a second Transcontinental Railroad across the southern United States could be built. The U.S. Envoy who negotiated with Mexican President Santa Ana, the purchase price of ten million dollars was James Gadsden, the United States Ambassador to Mexico. The Mexican government was in dire need for funds to support its Army; mainly for protection against marauding Indian tribes.

St. Paul Winter Carnival

Another of the memorable flights I made with General Schilt was to Minneapolis, Minnesota, on 6 March 1954, after General Schilt had accepted an invitation to be the grand marshal of the nearby St. Paul Winter Carnival. Being a grand marshal included riding in a long parade, in a Cadillac convertible with its top down, so the people along the parade route could plainly see the parade grand marshal. I rode in the front seat, where it was warmer, with the automobile car heater on MAXUMUM, and my legs wrapped in a blanket. The outside air temperature was about fifteen degrees. My best St. Paul Winter Carnival memories are....Brrrrrr!

Another Interesting Far East Trip

During May 1955, General Schilt made another flight to the Far East. After visits to the Marine Corps Air Units in Hawaii, our flight made the usual refueling stop on Wake Island; and then the flight proceeded to Guam. Next, we went to Peleliu Island, where General Schilt had been the Island Commander during WWII. From Peleliu, the flight overflew the abandoned airfield on nearby Angaur Island, where several old B-24 Liberator hulks were still recognizable. Those bombers had not been moved for ten years. From Peleliu our flight proceeded to NAS, Sangley Point, located near the Philippine capital city of Manila. From NAS, Sangley Point, we flew to Hong Kong; landing at the Kai Tak single-runway airport which extended from the city of Kowloon into Kowloon Bay.

Hong Kong had been under British rule for one hundred ninety-six years. Following the first opium war in 1842, it was ceded to the British. Britain's new colony flourished as an East-West trading center, and as the commercial gateway and distribution center for southern China. In 1898 the Hong Kong British Crown Colony was granted an additional ninety-nine-year lease extension to rule Hong Kong, and its two hundred adjacent islands, located nearby in the South China Sea. The colony was so ruled, except for 1941-45, when in WWII, the Japanese captured and ruled Hong Kong. The ninety-nine-year lease was to end on 1 July 1997, when sovereignty of Hong Kong would revert to China.

While in Hong Kong, General Schilt made a planned visit to the United States Embassy, concluding his three-day stay in Hong Kong. From Hong Kong, our flight proceeded to Tainan airfield, near the southwest end of Taiwan, facing mainland China. The next stop on General Schilt's flight was to Naha; now the Capital of the Okinawa Prefecture. From Naha, our flight proceeded to Pohang, Korea (K-3 Airfield), where General Schilt had previously commanded an air wing, which included all Marine Corps Aviation activity in Korea, including the helicopter squadron (HMR-161) in which I had been a pilot.

President Syngman Rhee

After visiting K-3, General Schilt's flight proceeded to Kimpo Airfield (K-14), near the South Korean capital of Seoul. From K-14, I accompanied General Schilt to the office of Syngman Rhee, the President of South Korea. President Rhee was a staunch anti-communist, who was solidly backed by the United States. When General Schilt introduced me to President Rhee, he told him that I was a helicopter pilot who flew the U.N. negotiators to and from the armistice site at Panmunjom. President Rhee had previously met General Schilt, when the General had commanded the 1st Marine Air Wing from his Pohang (K-3) headquarters. Listening to the conversation between these two old friends was a pleasure for me. They obviously respected each other. President Rhee spoke near perfect English.

Although nearing eighty years of age, President Rhee was alert, and aware of the post-Korean War world events. He had received a PhD in International Law at Princeton University. At one point, President Rhee became serious, and said to General Schilt, "I hope when they come down again, that I do not have to see American boys again be wounded and killed." Of course, he meant that "they" were North Koreans invading South Korea, as they had done in1950. By that crafty statement, President Rhee implied that if the South Korean Armed Forces could be provided with an adequate number of modern military weapons and equipment, South Korea by itself, could successfully repel any future invasion by North Korea. President Rhee served as South Korean President from 1950–1960. He died at age ninety, in Hawaii, and his body was returned to South Korea, where it is buried in the Seoul National Cemetery.

After leaving K-14, General Schilt's flight proceeded to Atsugi, Japan, where it commenced the return flight to the United States. Our route then followed the usual route to Alaska; and home to El Toro, California with an additional stop at NAS, Whidbey Island, Washington, where a U.S. Navy squadron of anti-submarine aircraft was based. During this trip, the General's schedule was altered, for reasons to which I was not privy. I could only surmise that General Schilt may have been ordered to include visits to some new and unusual places; thus altering his usual route to gain more information, and updated conditions, related to a possible future role to be played by the Marine Corps in Asia. The trip included visits to places such as Hong Kong and Taiwan.

As a result of all this, I surmised that General Schilt would soon be assigned greater responsibilities. Without any specific knowledge, or the ability to predict the future, an expanded role for the General was only speculation on my part. His trip to the Far East began in El Toro on 5 May, and ended back at El Toro on 23 May 1955. Again, the aircraft used was the four-engine C-54 Skymaster, and again the aircraft was flown by General Schilt's staff pilot, Captain Kelvin Bailey.

Chapter 17: Transfer to Washington, D.C.

Later in May 1955, on a day when things were relatively quiet, and General Schilt was out of his office, my wife Millie stopped at my office, after visiting the El Toro Post Exchange. I asked her to stay in the office, and answer the telephone, while I briefly went to another office in the administration building. Only two telephones' numbers could possibly ring in my office. One was General Schilt's, and the other was mine. Since it was noontime, I didn't really expect that the telephone would ring while I was away briefly. I was wrong!

General Schilt's number rang, and Millie answered it. The caller was Lieutenant General W. Oscar Brice, calling from the Marine Corps Headquarters in Washington, D. C., to inform General Schilt that he was going to be transferred to Washington, to assume his new duties as Director of Marine Aviation. Millie and Lieutenant General Brice had a short, but very pleasant conversation. He asked to have General Schilt call him. She relayed this information to me, when I returned to my office. I told her that she (hopefully) would get a pay raise for handling that important call. I recall that she only glared at me, and I also heard her say firmly, "Don't ever leave me in your office alone again."

I informed General Schilt of the call from Washington. I'm certain that when he returned the call, General Brice informed him of his pending transfer to Marine Corps Headquarters in Washington, D.C., where he would be promoted to Lieutenant General (three stars) and assume the duties of the Director of Marine Corps Aviation. General Brice was retiring, and wanted to know if General Schilt wanted to inherit his personal staff. General Schilt declined the offer, stating "Thanks, Oscar. I know you have a fine personal staff, but my people know me very well; and not only that, they let me fly." We sure did; including of course, continuing his helicopter training on weekends at nearby MCAS, Quantico.

When I returned home to our home in Santa Ana that evening, I told my wife that we had to start packing, as we were being transferred to Headquarters Marine Corps, where I would continue my duties as General Schilt's aide. General Schilt took other members of his personal staff, including his staff pilot, Captain Kelvin Bailey, his aircraft crew chief, Staff Sergeant Stephens, his staff car driver Sergeant Priestly, and one of his personal stewards. Remaining at Marine Corps Headquarters, to continue working as secretary to the Directors of Marine Aviation was a civil servant employee named Lillian Mainhart. She was a talented, and very capable lady, with whom I was privileged to share an office, and with whom I worked closely for the next two years.

After receiving orders transferring him to Headquarters, U.S. Marine Corps in Washington, D.C., General Schilt told me that he did not need me to help him at El Toro, beyond the normal working hours. Allowing me to work regular hours was very considerate, as he knew that I needed time to arrange moving my family to Washington. First, we had to find a renter for our house in Santa Ana, which was really no problem, as the same couple moved into our house each time we departed.

Next, I had to decide what to do with the 1941 blue, six-cylinder Packard coupe which I had purchased for $125, and used as a second car to drive to and from work, for a total distance of seven miles round-trip. General Schilt's staff pilot, Captain Kelvin Bailey who lived in Laguna Beach, California, told me that he had purchased a new Plymouth, and would take delivery at the factory in Michigan, on his way to Washington. He told me that he would be willing to drive my Packard coupe to Michigan, with his wife Gwen. Kelvin Bailey related later that they almost abandoned my Packard coupe in the desert, when it overheated. But he made it to

Michigan, and no doubt, was glad that he was now driving his much more dependable new Plymouth. I drove our family car to Michigan, where we stayed with my wife's parents. We then convoyed to Washington, driving both cars, so that we remained a two-car family.

Jeanne and Bill Warren at Weber farm, Covert, MI (1955)

After arriving, we purchased a newly constructed home in Springfield, Virginia. Once again, I drove the old Packard coupe to and from work. Our son Bill attended school there, and completed fourth and fifth grades in a temporary modular schoolhouse, and Jeanne started kindergarten.

Jeanne and Bill Warren, Springfield, VA (1956)

Bill's fifth grade teacher was Miss Kay McCausley, who was from New Bern, North Carolina. New Bern is only twenty miles from MCAS, Cherry Point; both along the Neuse River. New Bern is named after Bern, Switzerland, which is its capital city. Kay McCausley was one of the talented Ray Charles singers. We attended one of his concerts at the Uline Arena in Washington, D.C. When Kay spotted us in the audience, she quietly mouthed, "Where is Bill?" and then "Where is Jeanne?" They were home with their baby sitter. Sometime later, Kay married a Marine pilot, who rose in rank to Colonel.

The Navy Annex

General Schilt's two adjacent offices were on the second floor of the Navy Annex. In addition to housing Headquarters, U.S. Marine Corps for fifty-six years, the annex also housed the U.S. Navy's Bureau of Supplies and Accounts (BUSANDA), and the Navy's Bureau of Personnel (BUPERS). Directly below our second-floor office window, was the entrance to Headquarters, Marine Corps. From our overview position, we could see The Commandant of the Marine Corps, General Clifton B. Cates (four stars), and many other lesser ranked deputies, including General Schilt, arriving almost every morning. General Schilt's official title was Deputy Chief of Staff, Marine Aviation, more commonly he was referred to as The Director of Marine Aviation. His second-floor offices were just down the hall from the Commandant's office; a two-minute walk away. After parking General Schilt's staff car, Sergeant Priestley would join Lillian Mainhart and me, in General Schilt's adjacent outer office.

Lillian Mainhart, Bob Warren and Sergeant Priestly (1956)

The Navy Annex was a four-story, eight wing structure, overlooking Arlington National Cemetery on one side, and the Pentagon at another end. Eventually Headquarters, U.S. Marine Corps was transferred to the Pentagon. The eighth wing of the annex was later torn down, to make room for the beautiful new Air Force Memorial; which was built in 2006. The one million square foot Navy Annex, built in 1941, and once housing six thousand federal employees, was demolished in 2013, after seventy years of use. The land on which it had been built was transferred to the U.S. Army, potentially to be used for expansion of Arlington National Cemetery.

Aide Duties in Washington

General Schilt's Aviation staff was located on the first floor, in wing five of the Navy Annex. After the staff's initial briefings on the present overall status of Marine Aviation, there was an almost endless stream of his staff arriving in his outer office, to present projects on which they were working, and hopefully to gain his approval. When the General was busy, those members of his staff had to wait in his outer office - my office.

They usually related what they wanted to talk to the General about, or what their response might be to some current or looming crisis affecting Marine Aviation. Consequently, I quickly got to know the members of his staff quite well, and always tried to develop a very harmonious relationship with each of them. All Marines who knew General Schilt admired him, and held him in high regard; which made my duties much easier. I earned my own bit of regard, after staff members learned that that they could trust me to not reveal any of their casual remarks to anyone, including to General Schilt

I always remembered that he, not I, was in charge. Aides sometimes mistakenly say "We" when referring to their general.

Sometimes he asked me about my views of certain projects on which his staff was working; especially anything concerning helicopters. I always knew that what I said to him would remain between us, in confidence.

The Marine Aviation concerns were seemingly endless; ranging from new aircraft procurement, to the administration of Marine Corps Air Stations and facilities, and the spare parts requirements for all airplanes in the Marine Aviation inventory. The Marine Aviation Safety Program was always on the front burner, and a close relationship with the Navy's Aviation Safety Center was crucial.

During his first few months as Director of Marine Aviation, General Schilt made many trips to the east coast Marine Air Stations. The first was to find out firsthand, the organization, dispositions, and combat readiness of the entire 2nd Marine Aircraft Wing, (2nd MAW) headquartered at MCAS, Cherry Point, North Carolina. Units of the 2nd MAW were also stationed at MCAS, New River. Many flying squadrons were continually deployed on aircraft carriers, participating in U.S. Navy 6th Fleet operations in the Mediterranean Sea and the Caribbean Sea areas. Other squadrons were deployed for training at the Naval Station, Roosevelt Roads, located on the eastern end of Puerto Rico. The Naval Station at Roosevelt Roads also included a Naval Air Station.

The flights from Washington, D.C. to Puerto Rico and return, would include stops at Miami, FL; San Juan, and NAS, Roosevelt Roads, Puerto Rico; St. Thomas Island, where General and Mrs. Schilt were previously stationed; and NAS, Guantanamo Bay, Cuba. Major Kelvin Bailey was always the staff pilot on those flights. At times, General Schilt would share the cockpit with his staff pilot. Sometimes when General Schilt was working in the airplane cabin, or if he was resting, I would share the pilot duties with my good friend Kel Bailey. The transport aircraft used by high ranking Marine

Corps officers were based at NAS, Anacostia, D.C., and included a twin engine Convair C-131 Samaritans (Navy designation was R4Y), several R4D-8 (super DC-3s), and four-engine C-54 Skymasters. Occasionally a Navy DC-6 would be provided to the Commandant of the Marine Corps for very long overseas trips. However, General Schilt normally used the pressurized Convair R4Y for shorter, stateside trips.

The Presidential yacht *Sequoia*, which was used by all Presidents from Hoover through Carter, was docked on the Anacostia River close to NAS, Anacostia. Kelvin Bailey struck up a friendship with the Sequoia captain, who arranged for my wife Millie, Kel's wife Gwen, and our two small children, Bill and Jeanne, to board and sail on the Sequoia, on short Anacostia and Potomac River trips.

Gwen Bailey with Millie, Bob, Bill and Jeanne Warren
aboard the Presidential yacht *Sequoia* (1956)

Naval War College

While in Washington, General Schilt was invited to participate in a symposium at the Naval War College (NWC), in Newport, Rhode Island. Established in 1884, NWC is the staff college and the "Home of Thought" of the U.S. Navy. NWC graduates approximately six hundred students each year. On 4 June 1956, General Schilt flew to NAS, Quonset Point, Rhode Island, where he spent time interacting with NWC students.

Kel Bailey and I flew back to Washington; but before returning to Washington, General Schilt told me to request a fifteen day leave for him, starting with his return from the NWC on 5 June. To be granted annual leave (thirty days per year), a standard leave request form must be completed, signed, and submitted to the next higher authority for approval. The next higher authority for General Schilt, was the Commandant of the Marine Corps, General Randolph M. Pate; whose Military Secretary was Colonel Ormond R. Simpson.[vi]

As soon as I returned in Washington, I filled out General Schilt's leave request form; except that I could not forge his signature. Therefore, I decided to use his facsimile stamp to sign the request. I took it to Colonel Simpson, and explained the reason for using the facsimile stamp. He looked at it and calmly said, "That's alright, Bob. I'll approve it for the Commandant, using his signature machine." That little experience taught me how things are done sometimes, at higher rank levels.

Lunch with Igor Sikorsky

On 28 July 1955, General Schilt visited the Sikorsky helicopter plant at Bridgeport, Connecticut. The general was hosted at lunch by Igor Sikorsky, who was attempting to sell new Sikorsky heavy-lift helicopters, for Marine Corps operations. During the luncheon conversation, Igor Sikorsky asked General Schilt if he had ever flown a Sikorsky amphibian (a multi-engine Sikorsky flying boat). General Schilt said that he had, and then held up his left hand that had the index finger missing. He told Igor Sikorsky that after he had landed the amphibian, he opened the cockpit window to gesture at a ground crewman, and the amphibian propeller had struck his hand and severed the index finger. General Schilt told Igor Sikorsky that I had flown Sikorsky HRS helicopters in combat in Korea. He also told Igor Sikorsky that he was learning to fly the HRS helicopter, and that I was his instructor, first at Santa Ana, and now at Quantico. I really felt honored to have met, and had lunch with the renowned Igor Sikorsky; the man who invented the helicopter.[vii]

Heavy Lift Helicopter Shopping

Igor Sikorsky then described a very large helicopter, capable of meeting the Marine Corp's heavy-lift ship-to-shore requirements. It was designated the CH-53. The CH-53 helicopter would be powered by twin turbo-shaft jet engines; each engine, mounted above the troop-carrying cabin, could deliver over three thousand shaft horsepower. The turbo-shaft engines provided power to drive the main rotor blades and a seventeen-foot diameter, anti-torque tail rotor. The CH-53 had thirty-five troop seats in its cabin. The Sikorsky company had a unique way of insuring that the users would be satisfied with the design, by inviting on-the-spot inputs from pilots, and rotor head and engine maintenance personnel. Sikorsky paid careful attention to details, such as troop entrance and exit techniques; ground and shipboard taxiing, and deck-spotting; external cargo and military equipment lifts; and the safety and ease of refueling. Each was given careful scrutiny.

First, a balsa wood, full size CH-53 was constructed. Users were then invited to inspect, and state their views to Sikorsky engineers. The CH-53 was a massive, single-lifting rotor helicopter;

capable, as mentioned earlier, of lifting thirty-five combat troops or twenty-four stretchers. The helicopter featured retractable landing and nose wheels, a retractable tail skid, and semi-automatic main and tail rotor folding. From its huge size, the CH-53 design required size-reducing features, so that it would still fit on an aircraft carrier elevator.[viii]

Assessing Readiness

When planning his many flights in the U.S., General Schilt would try to visit the Marine Corps Reserve Squadrons that were located near twelve large cities. He would receive briefings, to learn about each squadron's readiness to be recalled to active duty. Each Reserve Squadron would deploy to a large Marine Corps airfield, for two weeks each year. During August 1956, General Schilt was invited to participate in a Hoover Institution forum, at its Stanford University location. He flew to the nearby NAS, Alameda, located across San Francisco Bay, near Oakland, California; the closest NAS to Stanford. General Schilt knew that a Reserve Squadron had deployed to MCAS, El Toro for their two-week deployment. Instead of flying directly back to Washington, General Schilt flew to El Toro to visit that Reserve Squadron. Having the Director of Marine Aviation visit personally, always gave each Aviation Reserve Squadron a real shot in the arm, especially during their two-week deployments.

Helicopter Flying at MCAS, Quantico

Despite his demanding schedule, General Schilt still continued his helicopter pilot training, by driving to Quantico on Saturdays. He would ask me to call HMX-1, the helicopter squadron at MCAS, Quantico, and to specify the time he would be there to fly, and to tell them that he did not want all the fanfare normally associated with the visit of a three-star general. No honor guard, no music, no transportation, and no side visits to any other Marine Corps School units or facilities. He simply did not want to interfere with any Marine's day off. All he wanted was a fueled helicopter, with one crew chief ready to fly locally, for up to two hours. There was usually a lot of activity at MCAS, Quantico on weekends, as that is when most of the Marine pilots who were attending school classes all week, would fly, to maintain their required monthly flying hours. While changing from our uniforms into flight suits in the HMX-1 ready room, General Schilt always enjoyed chatting with other pilots; usually school students. On the weekends we were scheduled to fly at Quantico, General Schilt would have his staff car driver drive him from his quarters at the 8th & I Marine Barracks in Washington, D.C. to his office in the Navy Annex; where I would be waiting. From there, we rode together in his staff car to Quantico and back, which is about thirty miles each way.

It was a real joy to fly in the helicopter at Quantico with General Schilt. When airborne, he would often point out areas or fields where in the old days -pre-World War II days - many Marine Corps pilots stationed at Brown Field in Quantico, had made emergency landings. He would relate many of those situations, which were serious then, but now seemed quite humorous.

For instance, one pilot who was attending classes during the week, and had to fly on weekends, had made an emergency landing near Richmond, Virginia. He thought it was more important to get back to Quantico in time for his Monday morning school class, than to report that he had left his Marine aircraft unattended in a Virginia farmer's field. Apparently, the squadron commanding officer at Quantico's Brown Field, Major Roy Geiger, didn't agree. He removed that pilot from his class, ordered him to drive with the mechanics to the abandoned aircraft, to wait for it to be repaired, and then to fly it back to Quantico. In addition, he ordered the pilot personally, to pay for the mechanics' meals.

After meeting all of the flying requirements, General Schilt received his official Helicopter Pilot Designation; signed by the Chief of Naval Operations. I was pleased and honored, when asked to present that designation to him. As his instructor, I knew that he really had earned it.

Chapter 18: Trip to Europe

In August 1956, General Schilt directed his staff to plan a trip to London, England, where he would attend the Royal Air Force Airshow at Radlett. In addition, the general wanted to include the following stops: The Hague in the Netherlands; Rome; Naples; Madrid; and Port Lyautey in French Morocco, North Africa. The return flight would include a refueling stop at Lajes, the U.S. Air Force base built on the Portugese Island of Terceira, and then returning to the United States through Argentia, Newfoundland, Canada. Major Kelvin Bailey was to fly the four-engine C-54 on General Schilt's entire trip; starting at Anacostia, D.C. on 31 August 1956, refueling at NAS, Argentia, Newfoundland, and then proceeding directly to London.

The Royal Air Force Air Show featured the very large Royal Air Force Avro Vulcan bomber. The bat-shaped Vulcan bomber was used later by the British in its April-June 1982 war with Argentina, to recapture the British colony in the Falkland Islands. After ten weeks of bitter ground, air, and sea fighting, the British regained sovereignty over its remote Falkland Islands Colony in the South Atlantic Ocean.

Lord Louis Mountbatten

While in London, General Schilt took me with him to attend a military reception that was also attended by Lord Louis Mountbatten. General Schilt wore his uniform, as he felt that he was representing the Commandant of the Marine Corps. Lord Mountbatten was a tall, handsome, and imposing man who, resplendent in his Royal Navy Vice Admiral Uniform, presented a very commanding aura. When he spotted General Schilt, who was wearing his Medal of Honor, he approached and introduced himself to General Schilt who, in turn introduced his aide (me) to Lord

Mountbatten. After Lord Mountbatten and General Schilt chatted for a few minutes, two civilians approached, and suggested to Lord Mountbatten that he should move along to meet other reception attendees. Lord Mountbatten promptly dismissed them with the curt expression, "Pardon me gentlemen, but I wish to speak further with General Schilt"

His official title was First Earl Mountbatten of Burma; then later, he was the last Viceroy of British India. When India gained its independence, Lord Mountbatten served as governor-general of Independent India; as an advisor to India's newly elected President Nehru during India's transition from British rule to independence. Lord Mountbatten was murdered on 27 August 1979, while on his fishing boat in the Republic of Ireland. A large bomb, planted aboard his boat by the hostile Irish Republican Army, was remotely exploded by IRA sympathizers, murdering Lord Mountbatten and three others aboard.

The Hague

The next stop General Schilt made was in the Netherlands, where he visited Marine Corps General John C. McQueen, who General Schilt had known years before in Nicaragua, when they were both junior officers. After a distinguished combat career in the Pacific, and now a Major General, McQueen was ordered to The Hague in 1956, to serve as Chief of the Military Assistance Advisory Group. The International Court of Justice is the principal judicial body of the U.N., which is sometimes referred to as the "World Court." It is housed in the Peace Palace, in The Hague. The court was established in June, 1945, and began work in April, 1946. While at The Hague, Major Bailey and I were furnished a military sedan, and were driven throughout the countryside. We admired the Dutch cleanliness, and the beauty of hundreds of acres of colorful blooming tulips; many growing between operating Dutch windmills. The Netherlands was spotless, scenic, flat, and indeed beautiful.

Italy

In Rome, General Schilt met with the Chief of the Italian Navy (Marina Militare). The Italian Navy is the Maritime Defense Force of the Republic of Italy. Formed in 1946, the Italian Navy is one of the four military branches of the Italian Armed Forces. While in Rome, we also visited St. Peter's Basilica, an Italian Renaissance-style church built in Vatican City. The church is huge; and inside the Basilica is Michelangelo's Pieta statue of Mary holding the body her dead son, Jesus. The statue is spectacular; almost breathtaking. The Pieta statue measures about five by six feet.

Naples, Madrid, and Morocco

The next stops at Support Activity, Naples, Italy; and Madrid, Spain were made mainly to refuel the R5D. From Madrid, the next stop was in northwest Africa, at the Naval Air Station at Port Lyautey, French Morocco. Having long been governed by France and Spain, the government of Morocco was struggling to become an independent nation; free of being a Protectorate (colony) of France and Spain since 1912. General Schilt asked the Naval Air Base commander, a U.S. Navy Captain, whether Morocco would prevail. He said that he was betting on Morocco. In 1946 after forty-four years, Morocco gained its independence; and NAS, Port Lyautey was renamed after the nearby city of Kenitra. NAS, Port Lyautey was slowly turned over to the Royal Moroccan Air Force. The last U.S. Military personnel left Kenitra in 1977. This trip was my first, and only, visit to Africa.

The Azores

Departing Port Lyautey on 14 September 1946, General Schilt started his trip back to Washington, by first landing for fuel at Lajes Airfield on the Portuguese island of Terceira, one of several Azores islands. The Azores are in the North Atlantic Ocean, nine hundred miles west of Lisbon, Portugal, and two thousand three hundred miles east of Washington, D.C. Lajes Field, known as the "Crossroads of the Atlantic," provided a mid-Atlantic stopover point for the expeditionary movement of allied warplanes during and after WWII. General Schilt had deployed from Philadelphia to Punta Delgada in the Azores, in 1918, as an aircraft mechanic with the 1st Marine Aeronautical Company. General Schilt, now the Director of Marine Corps Aviation, returned to the Azores, thirty-eight years later. From Lajes Airfield, the General's flight stopped for fuel at NAS, Argentia, Newfoundland. Our flight then proceeded non-stop back to NAS, Anacostia, where the flight had originated fifteen days earlier, on 31 August 1956.

Chapter 19: General Schilt's Final Far East Trip

On 3 October 1956, General Schilt commenced his final trip to the Far East. From Anacostia, he flew to Tinker Air Force Base in Oklahoma, then to El Toro where he departed on 4 October for NAS, Barbers Point, Hawaii. The trip also included a visit to MCAS, Kaneohe Bay, located on the opposite side of Oahu Island from Honolulu. I knew that General Schilt had accepted an invitation to attend a dinner party at Kaneohe Bay, to be held at the Commanding Officer's on-base quarters. When I knew of such dinner party invitations, I would always get a message to the dinner host, advising them that eating shrimp cocktail made General Schilt very ill. I know that information was always appreciated; as shrimp cocktail never appeared on a dinner menu.

When the dinner party was over, I would go to the restroom, and write the names of the host, and other dinner party attendees, on my small pocket-size notebook. After departing Hawaii, on the next long leg of the flight to Wake Island, I would hand-write Generals Schilt's appropriate thank you letters on a yellow lined tablet. At Wake Island, I mailed the hand-written letters back to Lillian Mainhart, his secretary in Washington. She would type the thank you letters to the hosts, and have them ready for General Schilt's signature, as soon he returned to Washington from his long trip to the Far East.

From Wake Island our flight proceeded to Kwajalein, Marshall Islands, and then to NAS, Sangley Point, near the Philippine Islands city of Manila. From Sangley Point, we flew to the large U.S. Navy installations at NAS, Cubi Point, and the adjacent Subic Bay Naval Base. For the Navy to build a Naval Air Station at Cubi Point, an entire mountain had to be leveled. Leveling the mountain was the largest earth-moving effort since the building of the Panama

Canal. Both installations were located west of Manila, across Manila Bay in the Philippine Province of Bataan.

Corregidor Island, located near the entrance of Manila Bay, is where General Douglas MacArthur had departed on 11 March 1942, with his wife, his son, and their Amah (nurse) on U.S. Navy PT Boats for the Philippine Island of Mindanao. President Franklin D. Roosevelt, fearing that Corregidor would soon fall to the Japanese, and that MacArthur would be taken captive, had ordered him to escape to Australia. From Mindanao, after having spent two days at sea, MacArthur and his family were flown in a U.S. Army Air Corps B-17 bomber to Darwin, Australia, and they then traveled by train to Melbourne, the Capital City of Australia; arriving ten days after they had left the Philippines.

From the Philippines, General Schilt's flight proceeded to Kadena, Okinawa, and on to MCAS, Iwakuni, and to NAS, Atsugi, Japan. All of his previous flights to the United States from the Far East had returned through Alaska. However, this flight returned to Wake Island, Hickam Air Force Base in Hawaii, and MCAS, El Toro, California. His final flight to the Far East returned to Washington, D.C. on 28 October; twenty-five days after departing.

Helicopter and KC-130 Shopping

On 11 November 1946, General Schilt visited the Boeing Vertol Helicopter Plant near Wilkes-Barre, Pennsylvania, to learn more about a new jet-powered Boeing Vertol CH-46, which was designed by the Boeing-acquired Vertol Aircraft Corporation. (The Vertol name was an abbreviation for Vertical Take Off and Landing.) The CH-46 was then manufactured by Boeing. The twin-turbine tandem rotor designed helicopter has the same size lifting rotor above each end of its long fuselage. To alleviate torque, the rotors turned in opposite directions; meaning no available power was lost to driving a tail rotor. In addition, The CH-46 was a safer, and more efficient, helicopter. The allowable center of gravity travel was only two and one-half inches in the early Sikorsky HO3S; and in the HRS helicopters we flew in Korea, it was just eleven inches. When flying a helicopter loaded beyond its limited center of gravity travel, the pilot would be unable to have full control; which made careful weight distribution inside the helicopter critical. In the new Boeing Vertol CH-46, with its tandem rotor design, the allowable center of gravity was one hundred forty-four inches. Accordingly, the helicopter could carry loads placed in almost any section of its long cabin, with little concern that the pilots would have any weight and balance control difficulties. Additionally, by folding its rotor blades over the cabin, the CH-46 could also fit on aircraft carrier elevators.

The Marine Corps eventually took delivery of five hundred thirty-four CH-46 medium-lift helicopters, which had another important feature - an opening and closing rear loading ramp. The CH-46s were used extensively, to carry combat Marines in Vietnam.

In addition to selecting Marine Corps helicopters, General Schilt realized that a new and improved heavy-lift, fixed-wing transport aircraft was needed. The main large transport aircraft the Marine Corps was flying were old four-engine C-54s, which had been obtained from commercial airlines, and were converted DC-4s. The smaller, twin engine R4D-8 was an improved C-47 Gooney Bird, which was widely used in WWII.

General Schilt flew to Marietta, Georgia, and visited the Lockheed Aircraft plant that was producing C-130 Hercules transport aircraft for the U.S. Air Force. The Hercules was powered by four turboprop engines, driving the four propellers, which could be reversed, to accomplish short airfield landings. General Schilt wanted to know if the C-130 could be modified, to accomplish aerial refueling, and was assured that aerial refueling capability could be added to the C-130, without losing any cabin space. The refueling hoses, with attached large shuttlecock-like drogues, and hose reels, were carried in two large wing tanks; one on each side of the KC-130. The wing tanks allowed two receiving aircraft to refuel at the same time.

Lockheed arranged to provide a Hercules at MCAS, Cherry Point for a demonstration. General Schilt flew to Cherry Point, and flew the C-130 with the Lockheed demonstration pilot. I rode in the large troop-carrying cabin, that had a large rear-loading ramp for troops, cargo, and vehicles. I was very impressed with the large cabin size, and the tremendous Hercules turboprop power. The Hercules' short, reversible-pitch propellers permit it to land on very short runways.

General Nathan F. Twining, who was then the commander of Air Materiel Command, graciously agreed to an interruption of the on-going Air Force C-130 production at the Lockheed Marietta, Georgia plant, to produce three squadrons of KC-130s for the Marine Corps. It probably didn't hurt, that at the same time, General Twining's younger brother Merrill B. Twining was a Marine Corps Major General, stationed at Headquarters, U.S. Marine Corps. No doubt, the younger Twining continually reminded his older brother, that the Marine Corps sorely needed the KC-130. The "K" in the designation denotes tanker.

Because of General Schilt's diligence, Marine Corps Aviation was delighted to receive three squadrons of the new dual-capability (transport and tanker) Hercules KC-130s, which would replace all of its aging C-54 transport aircraft, in all of its four-engine transport (VMGR) squadrons based at Cherry Point, El Toro, and at NAS, Barbers Point in Hawaii.

One Marine Corps KC-130 is assigned permanently, to the Navy's Blue Angels Demonstration Team. The tanker is the only non-fighter aircraft in the team. The aircraft is beautifully painted; in the same blue and gold colors as the other smaller Blue Angel demonstration aircraft. The Marine Blue Angel Hercules normally opens each Blue Angels show with a short Jet-Assisted Takeoff (JATO), followed by a spectacular steep climb to several thousand feet, with several JATO bottles burning brightly on each side of the KC-130 fuselage.

When on long flights, the Hercules can aerial refuel all of the other Blue Angel demonstration aircraft. The Hercules also transports the Blue Angel support personnel , and all of the team flight line support equipment. The Marine Corps Blue Angel KC-130 is affectionately named "Fat Albert."

Occasionally the Secretary of the Navy (SECNAV) would request that prominent businessmen be taken on Marine Corps and Navy overseas flights. On one of his flights to the Far East, General Schilt was asked to take Mr. Fred Young as a SECNAV guest. Mr. Young owned the Young Radiator Company in Racine, Wisconsin. Of course, General Schilt complied, and Mr. Young joined General Schilt in California, and rode with him to Hawaii, Wake Island, Hong Kong, Korea, and Japan; returning to California through Alaska.

Mr. Young was a most personable individual, and I gladly extended some of my aide duties to him. His presence caused some concerns to the commanders of certain military installations. They did not know whether to extend honors to Mr. Young, including flying the blue SECNAV flag over their headquarters building, or to General Schilt, by flying his red, three-star Marine Corps flag.

At certain Marine Corps installations, General Schilt needed to have confidential Marine Corps conversations with other general officers. In those instances, I would usually take Mr. Young on a local interesting day-long shopping tour. The trip went well, as Mr. Young was a delightful man, who expressed his deep appreciation for General Schilt's hospitality throughout the flight, to the Far East and back. Mr. Young offered me a job at his Young Radiator Company if I did not choose to stay in the Marine Corps. I thanked him; pretended to thoughtfully consider his offer; and then politely declined his kind offer.

In other rare instances, Mrs. Schilt was authorized to accompany General Schilt on flights within the United States, where Mrs. Schilt's presence was expected. On one such flight, we were in a twin-engine Convair R4Y. The Convair was pressurized, so it could fly at high altitudes, generally in smooth air; thus making the flight much more comfortable. This flight to California from NAS, Anacostia, included refueling stops at Glenview, Illinois and Minneapolis, MN.

On the next leg of the flight to San Diego, I was flying the pressurized Convair, with Mrs. Schilt riding beside me in the co-pilot's seat. We enjoyed viewing the beautiful snow-covered Rocky Mountains from high above Colorado and Utah. Meanwhile, General Schilt and his staff pilot, Kel Bailey were enjoying a conversation in the Convair's comfortable cabin seats. The aircraft we were flying had engine cowl flaps that would not open. Normally, those flaps were opened during take offs, to keep cool air flowing past the hot engine cylinders. Malfunctioning flaps were not a problem when flying in the relatively cool air during the winter months. However, this aircraft was scheduled to fly to Panama, following our return to Washington. In Panama, the hotter temperatures would require the use of the cowl flaps. We landed at San Diego, and parked the airplane near the Convair plant, in the aircraft parking area. The next morning, there was a note in the cockpit, stating that the cowl flaps were now operating properly. It's amazing, how having a three-star rank, automatically accelerates aircraft repair, and other flight line services.

Our next stop was NAS, Point Mugu, where General and Mrs. Schilt were hosted by other civilian SECNAV military friends. General Schilt's flight then went to MCAS, El Toro; then to NAS, Dallas, Texas. From Dallas, General Schilt told Mrs. Schilt that we would be landing at NAS, Memphis, Tennessee for fuel. But he knew that the next stop was going to be at NAS, Pensacola, Florida where the Schilt's daughter, Alice, and her Navy Officer husband were stationed.

After landing in Pensacola, the portable visiting aircraft boarding ladder was moved to the open doorway of the Convair. Mrs. Schilt was descending the ladder when she spotted her daughter Alice, and her husband Ensign Greg Black, waiting below on the tarmac. Still thinking it was Memphis, Mrs. Schilt was surprised and said to them, "What are you doing here?" Alice replied, "Mom, where do you think you are?" Meanwhile General Schilt was chuckling above, from the open Convair door.

General Schilt's Retirement

My last helicopter flight with General Schilt was at Quantico, on 23 April 1957; a month before he retired from active Marine Corps duty, after having served since 1917. He retired with full honors; including a parade led by the President's Marine Corps Band at 8th & I Marine Barracks in Washington, D.C. He was promoted to a full General (four-Stars) at his retirement ceremony. When the parade was over, he turned to me and said, "Here Bob, take this thing" (his four-star flag) and handed it to me.

I attended his retirement ceremony with Millie, and our two children, Bill and Jeanne. The general's retirement was a bittersweet time for me, as he and Mrs. Schilt always treated us as family members. They were a very kind and gracious couple. Following his retirement, General and Mrs. Schilt returned to his Olney, Illinois home, where they lived for several years, before moving to Norfolk, Virginia. Millie and I visited General and Mrs. Schilt several times, at both their homes. General Schilt died in January 1987. Mrs. Schilt pre-deceased him in 1985. They are both buried in Arlington National Cemetery.

Major Kelvin Bailey

When General Schilt retired, his staff pilot Major Kelvin "Kel" Bailey was returned to inactive duty in the Marine Corps Reserve. Kel, and his wife Gwen, stayed in Washington, D.C., and Kel took a job flying for Butler Aviation, which was based at the Washington airport. Some of Kel's flights were to fly Presidential candidates; including Richard Nixon, Hubert Humphrey, and John Kennedy. He also flew candidate Barry Goldwater to the Republican National Convention in San Francisco. Flights carrying such important individuals were always controlled and monitored, by the Central Intelligence Agency.

Kel Bailey also flew on other missions in Europe; some highly classified. Meanwhile, his wife, Gwen, went to the offices of several conservative Senators and Congressmen almost every day, to work as a volunteer. The Baileys had no children; so they adopted our children Bill and Jeanne.

After I was ordered back to California with my family, Kel received a call from one of the principals in the Disney organization, wanting to know if he was interested in joining the Disney organization, to fly the new Walt Disney Productions' Grumman Gulfstream. Kel had only one job interview, and that was in New York City, with a single interviewer - Walt Disney. He told Kel that he wanted the best pilot, to be the chief pilot for Walt Disney Productions. Kelvin was hired, and flew the Disney Gulfstream for fourteen years. Most flights were to and from Florida where Walt Disney World was planned and built. On other flights, he took costumed Disneyland characters to cities where a new Disney movie was opening. After taking the job with Disney, Kel and Gwen moved to Burbank, California, near the Disney Studio and Burbank Airport. The Disney Gulfstream, along with several Sears & Roebuck and Union Oil jets, was based at Burbank.

Marine Lieutenant General Verne J. McCaul

Following General Schilt's retirement, I stayed on as aide to Lieutenant General Verne J. McCaul for several months. General McCaul had been ordered from Norfolk, Virginia to Washington, where he assumed his new duties, following General Schilt, as the Director of Marine Aviation. Those two considerate officers permitted General McCaul's aide - Major Bill Dwiggins - to remain in Norfolk, until his children had completed their school year. General Schilt arranged the same for me; by having me continue as General McCaul's aide, until our children, Bill and Jeanne, had finished their current grade school years in Springfield, Virginia.

One of my first duties as General McCaul's aide was to arrange a flight to the Far East, so General McCaul could become familiar with Marine Corps Aviation organizations and their deployments, which extended from Taiwan to Okinawa, the Philippine Islands, Korea, and Japan. On 20 May 1957, he departed Anacostia on the first leg of his flight to MCAS, El Toro, California. The next legs of his flight to the Far East were to Hawaii, Wake Island, and to the 3rd Marine Aircraft Wing headquarters, now at MCAS Iwakuni, Japan. From Iwakuni, his flight proceeded to Okinawa, Hong Kong, and NAS, Sangley Point, near Manila. From the Philippines, the flight returned to MCAS, El Toro with stops in Guam, Wake Island, and MCAS, Kaneohe Bay, Hawaii.

While General McCaul spent three days being briefed at El Toro, I went to nearby MCAF, Santa Ana, and completed my first one-hour flight in the new Sikorsky HUS-1. I was delighted with the aircraft, knowing that I would likely be transferred to that helicopter squadron, after my short temporary assignment as General McCaul's aide ended.

Chapter 20: Transfer to California

After completing duties as a general's aide, the aide can usually select his next assignment. I selected HMR(L)-363. General Schilt had arranged to have me transferred back to California. Therefore, I knew that my next PCS orders from Washington, D.C. would lead through the chain of command to helicopter squadron HMR(L)-363, based at MCAF, Santa Ana, California. That squadron was equipped with all new HUS-1 helicopters, and was slated to take part in a ship-to-shore landing exercise on the Philippine Island of Luzon. My assignment to HMR(L)-363 was even more pleasant, as I would again serve in the same squadron with my old friend and mentor, Major William P. "Mitch" Mitchell. We had served in the same night-fighter squadron at Okinawa. I also I served with him when he was the executive officer of Helicopter Squadron HMR-161, during combat operations in Korea. We also flew together on a downed-pilot rescue mission, forty miles behind enemy lines. I looked forward to serving, and flying again, with Mitch.

We listed our house for sale in Springfield, Virginia, and departed for California, before the house was sold. First, we traveled to Michigan, to see our families. Next, we went to Bloomington, Minnesota - a suburb of Minneapolis - to visit my Northwest Airlines Captain brother, Bill Dean, his wife Margaret, and their daughter Gretchen. We spent several enjoyable days aboard their yacht, and at the stables, where we all rode horses.

From Minnesota, we drove west across South Dakota; stopping to see Mount Rushmore, and to visit Rapid City. Then we were off to Cody, Wyoming, where during summer months, they stage a daily evening rodeo. We continued driving into and through Yellowstone Park, where we visited the beautiful Yellowstone Falls, and Old Faithful Geyser. Departing through the Yellowstone Park's West gate, we entered Montana.

We stopped at Dillon, Montana, to visit my former night-fighter squadron buddy Carl Davis, and his lovely wife Martha. Carl was practicing law in his Dillon hometown. Carl's sister, Annie had married Roy Forrester; our friend from Saipan. The Forresters owned a ranch about five miles from Dillon, which we often visited. We always had a wonderful time in Dillon; enjoying picnics at the Forrester ranch, and fly fishing.

From Dillon, the driving trip to California was across the desert, as described in previous chapters. The trip was long, hot, tiring, and uneventful. Upon arrival in California, we moved back into our home in Santa Ana, and were pleasantly reunited with neighbors and friends. The ever-faithful Hurds left our house clean, and ready for us to move in upon arrival. They moved to a nearby house in the same neighborhood. At the end of my allowed transfer, and my authorized leave days, during July 1957, I reported to HMR(L)-363 for duty. Our air group commanding officer was Colonel Ernest C. Fusan.

Helicopter Transport for President Eisenhower

In late September 1958, our squadron was alerted to provide helicopter lift for President Eisenhower, in the San Francisco Bay area. At that time, Presidential helicopter support, away from Washington, was provided from the closest military helicopter base. Our helicopter air group, based at MCAF Tustin, California was the only helicopter airfield in the western United States, with the Sikorsky HUS helicopters required for the Presidential mission in San Francisco.

Personnel from the Sikorsky plant in Connecticut arrived in Tustin, and installed flotation devices on the three wheels of the lead helicopter. The devices were a safety requirement, because most of the flight with the President aboard was planned to be flown over water, from the San Francisco International Airport to

Letterman Hospital airstrip, near the south end of the Golden Gate Bridge. A VIP kit was also installed in the cabin of the same helicopter, replacing several canvas-type bench troop seats, with more comfortable lightly upholstered seats.

Colonel Fusan gave me the responsibility to lead the HUS-1 Helicopters to San Francisco, and to carry out the mission. My lead helicopter—outfitted with flotation gear and the VIP kit—was especially configured for the president. The second, non-configured HUS-1, was a backup. The two helicopters selected were fairly new, and both had low time engines installed. Each helicopter had a crew chief who was directed to wear a clean standard flight uniform.

Since being alerted to perform the Presidential mission, we received more specific mission details and instructions. We were directed to proceed to NAS, Alameda, arriving no later than 8 October 1958. NAS Alameda, which is located in the city of Oakland, is directly across the bay from the San Francisco International Airport (SFO).

On 8 October 1958, five days prior to the mission date, I departed with two helicopters, from MCAF, Santa Ana, for NAS, Alameda. After one refueling stop, we proceeded to Alameda, where upon arrival, we were ordered to land directly in front of a specific hangar. The hangar doors were then opened, and our two helicopters were quickly towed inside. The hangar doors were then closed, immediately. The hangar was empty, except for the two tow tractors, each with its tow bar, a refueling truck, containers of sealed engine oil, new yellow Mae West life jackets, and two arrays of engine analyzing equipment.

We were billeted in a house on the base, and were provided two Navy sedans. We were instructed to fly the helicopters locally, every day, with the analyzing equipment installed. Following each flight, data from the engine analyzers was monitored by strangers, who were always accompanied in and out of the hangar by the NAS, Alameda Duty Officer.

On the day before the Presidential mission, we were directed to fly a complete rehearsal flight. We landed and parked at the U.S. Coast Guard Air Station, located in an isolated corner of SFO. We stopped the helicopter rotors, but not the engines, as this was the same procedure to be followed when the President, and members of his party, boarded my helicopter. I released the rotor brake, and engaged the rotors. I took off immediately; flying the same route we would follow the next day, when the president was aboard. We were told that taking photographs aboard the helicopters, by any member of our helicopter crew, was strictly forbidden.

On the day President Eisenhower arrived, we started the helicopter engines, and were monitoring the SFO Control Radio frequency, in order to know when the President's airplane landed. We watched the President's transport airplane - call-sign "Columbine Two" - land, and then taxi toward our position at the Coast Guard Air Station. Immediately after "Columbine Two" parked, and stopped its engines, a small Presidential party emerged, and quickly walked toward my helicopter.

One member in his party was Major Virgil D. "Virge" Olson, President Eisenhower's personal helicopter pilot. I had flown the helicopter from NAS, Alameda, with the enlisted crew chief in the cockpit with me. Major Olson was a good friend of mine, who was also the commanding officer of HMX-1 at Quantico; the helicopter squadron that provided Presidential helicopters in the Washington, D.C. area.

After landing, the crew chief quickly exited the cockpit, and waited below, to help the President and members of his party, minus Major Olson, put on their Mae West life jackets properly. As planned, Major Olson put on a Mae West life jacket; then quickly scrambled up the side of the helicopter through the open window, and into the open cockpit seat. After fastening his safety (lap) belt and shoulder straps, he put on the intercom/radio earphones. He leaned toward me, and we shook hands. On the Intercom he said, "Hi Bob, it's great to see you again. I told the President that he did not need to be concerned about having helicopter support at San Francisco, as everything needed for his arrival would have been arranged."

From the helicopter cockpit, I watched President Eisenhower walk toward the helicopter, and noticed him glance upward toward the cockpit and give a short wave; which to me represented his gesture of acknowledgment and appreciation. When the crew chief reported, via the intercom, that the passengers in the cabin were all seated and secured, I released the rotor brake and engaged the rotors, called the SFO control tower, and immediately was cleared for takeoff.

When we cleared the San Francisco Airport, Major Olson took control of the flight, and proceeded as planned, over water along the San Francisco City/Bay shoreline. No other aircraft was flying within fourteen miles of the helicopters carrying the President. Our flight route was north, away from SFO, so that it did not interfere with other arriving and departing SFO airline flights.

After passing Candlestick Park football stadium, and flying at five hundred feet, I switched radio frequency to the NAS, Alameda control tower, which monitored (and probably reported) our flight progress. I was amused when a Navy patrol bomber was denied takeoff clearance at NAS, Alameda. When the patrol bomber pilot, who did not know about the fourteen mile restriction, questioned the takeoff denial, the control tower stated flatly that there was high priority traffic, consisting of two Marine Corps helicopters, flying along the bay shoreline. Mentally, I could picture that patrol bomber pilot scratching his head and wondering why?

Major Olson just smiled as he was, no doubt, more used to this executive priority than I was. Approaching the San Francisco-Oakland Bay Bridge, we turned left to continue following the San Francisco Bay shoreline. Via the intercom, Major Olson and I briefly discussed how two pilots from Michigan were privileged to have the President of the United States as a passenger in our helicopter.

After passing Alcatraz Island on our right, we commenced our descent to the Letterman Hospital airstrip. The only picture of the helicopter with the President aboard, appeared in a San Francisco newspaper. The picture was taken during our landing approach. Although somewhat blurred, it clearly shows the flotation equipment on each of the three wheels. Alcratraz Island, and the Golden Gate Bridge, appear in the background of the picture.

President Dwight D. Eisenhower exiting HUS-1,
piloted by Bob Warren (13 Oct 1958)

Major Olson was giving instructions to our crew chief, who was riding in the cabin with the president. Basically, Major Olson instructed the crew chief not to let our passengers, including the President, emerge until the rotors were braked to a stop. When the president stepped out of the helicopter, he was immediately surrounded by uniformed motorcycle policemen, and a crowd of onlookers. Major Olson quickly shook my hand, and scrambled down outside of the helicopter.

With our mission completed, I watched the President and his motorcade -the president in a long Lincoln limousine with the top down - depart. I waited for the crowd to disperse. Then with the crew chief in the cockpit again, I engaged the rotors, took off, and reversed course back to NAS, Alameda. I reported the mission successfully completed, via radio to the NAS, Alameda control tower, and reported our inbound position. After landing at Alameda, we quickly removed the flotation boots; leaving them in the hangar as instructed. We then took off for the long and uneventful four- and one-half hour return flight to MCAF, Santa Ana. Our mission was successfully completed.

Rocket Engine Tests and Artificial Clouds

Another very interesting helicopter VIP flight that I was ordered to fly, was to the Los Angeles International Airport (LAX). I was to meet a passenger on the tarmac; not inside the airline terminal building. The VIP was Senator Lyndon B. Johnson; who had flown from Washington, to watch spaceship rocket engine tests. I flew Senator Johnson from LAX to the north side of the San Fernando Valley. As we approached the test area, I saw several rocket engines mounted vertically above their rock supports. I was fascinated to view the test rocket engine firing sequence of events, as follows:

- Just before the rocket engine fired, a geyser of water, resembling a huge waterfall, was released, and gushed below the rocket engine. The water prevented the extreme heat of the fired rocket engine from melting the rocks.
- As a result of the sudden heat and water mixture, white steam clouds, which rose above the rocky ridge lines, were created. In the arid desert air, the white clouds quickly dissipated.

Two weeks later, I was ordered to repeat my previous flight from LAX to the San Fernando Valley test site. On this second flight, the number of passengers viewing the rocket engine tests increased to six.

Visiting Parents

Millie and I invited her parents, Rudy and Mildred Weber, to visit us during the Thanksgiving Holiday season that year. They still lived in the little town of Covert, Michigan, where Millie and I had graduated from high school in 1941. We took them to nearby Disneyland, and to Knott's Berry Farm; which they thoroughly enjoyed. At Knott's Berry Farm, visitors were invited to visit the small jail, where a speaker was hidden. I had purposely lagged so that I could feed information to the man who talked to the jail visitors. When Millie's dad looked inside the jail door, the voice said in a surprised voice, "Why, here is Rudy Weber, visiting from Covert. When did you get here Rudy?"

Millie's dad was a home builder, who was wide-eyed when I took him to our helicopter base at Tustin, and he first saw the two identical immense blimp hangars. He was further fascinated when I pointed out that those hollow hangars - except for the massive telescoping doors - were constructed entirely of wood. Wooden stairs, catwalks, and crawl platforms were built along the two rows of windows, high on each hangar side, and they extended the full hangar length of one thousand feet. I explained that during certain weather conditions, fog would form inside those hangars. Rudy was further entertained, when he watched one of the dome shaped hangars being reroofed. The original tar paper roofing was being removed, and replaced with large sheets of aluminum.

Purple Thanksgiving Turkey

Our son, Bill was a student at the nearby Washington Elementary School, in Santa Ana. He said that he had a part in the upcoming Christmas story pageant at the school, and that he needed a purple robe, because he was going to be one of the "wise guys" in the Christmas story. Millie purchased a can of purple dye, and filled our garage laundry tub with warm water; added the dye, and immersed the entire robe in the dyed water.

We had purchased a large, frozen Thanksgiving dinner turkey that had to be thawed. The turkey was wrapped in tight plastic, except for its exposed turkey legs and the area around its neck. Millie carried the frozen turkey to the garage and set it on top of the laundry tub water faucets to thaw slowly.

A problem developed when part of the turkey carcass, which was resting on the hot faucet, thawed faster than the part resting on the cold faucet. The result was that the entire turkey toppled into the purple dye water. Millie came out to the garage, and saw the partially frozen turkey floating in the laundry tub. She lifted it out, and viewed the purple legs and neck area. It looked like someone had choked it to death.

Millie cried, as she thought the big turkey was ruined. Her mother laughed, as she knew the dye was a harmless product. We kidded Millie, by saying, "You should call the dye manufacturer, and explain the whole purple dye/turkey situation." Then, ask for their solution, because it says on the dye box to "Call Miss Writ" in Cincinnati, Ohio if you experience a problem with their product.

On Thanksgiving Day, the turkey was roasted, and it was delicious. Again, we had a lot for which to be thankful. Millie's dad summed up his feelings about his visit to our house when he said, "There are two United States - California, and then the rest of it."

Chapter 21: Philippines Operations

To the Philippines and Back

We knew that our squadron would be introducing the new Sikorsky HUS-1 helicopters to the Far East, by first participating in a landing exercise on the Philippine Island of Luzon. This exercise would be ship-to-shore from the Navy's first ship configured to operate only helicopters. The USS *Thetis Bay* was converted from an escort carrier (CVE) into a landing platform helicopter (LPH). The conversion removed all ship fixed-wing catapults and arresting landing systems, and added increased berthing and messing facilities for a full battalion of Marines. As the first to undergo such major transition, the USS *Thetis Bay* was designated LPH-I.

The Luzon exercise was planned to include our entire squadron of twenty-four HUS-1 Sikorsky helicopters, flying from the *Thetis Bay*. However, the *Thetis Bay* had to first sail from San Diego to NAS, Oppama, Japan with our squadron HMR(L)-363, with its full complement of helicopters. Then the ship had to sail to Naha, Okinawa. At Naha, the Marine battalion would embark, and participate as the ship-to-shore landing force in the Philippines.

Severe Storm at Sea

All went well on the voyage to Japan from San Diego, until the *Thetis Bay* approached Japan, and sailed through a very severe storm. Winds exceeded sixty-five miles per hour for thirty-six hours. Seven of the helicopters were protected in ship's hangar deck. The rest of the helicopters were carried on the flight deck. The on-deck helicopters were subjected to continuous saltwater spray, and at times to seawater that came over the ship's bow, onto the flight deck loaded with helicopters. Most of the helicopter cockpit glass protective covers were blown away. The helicopters were chained securely to the flight deck and rotors were folded and lashed securely over the helicopter tail cones to prevent rotor flopping and damage. Because of the storm, no personnel were permitted on the flight deck. The main damage to the helicopters was continuous exposure to salt water which, if not washed off, would quickly result in magnesium metal fatigue.

Upon arrival, the helicopters on the deck were unloaded at the nearby NAS, Oppama Seaplane Base where they were completely washed with fresh water. The seven helicopters carried in the protected hangar were inadvertently exposed to sea water, from the firefighting water nozzles that sprayed seawater all over the hangar deck during a ship fire drill. They, too, had to be unloaded and washed with fresh water.

Meanwhile, I was ordered to Okinawa ahead of the *Thetis Bay*'s scheduled Okinawa arrival. The reason for requesting a HUS pilot was to assist in writing the battalion landing plan. The capabilities of the new HUS, including fuel consumption per hour, airspeed and range, and troop-carrying capacity, were unknown to the Marine division. At Okinawa, I reported to the Marine Division Air Officer, Colonel Joseph "Joe" Renner, and was able to quickly provide the HUS-1 helicopter data required to complete the landing plan.

Performing All Manner of Things

I was waiting in front of a dockside warehouse at the Okinawa port of Naha, when the *Thetis Bay* arrived from Japan. I watched the ship enter the port. I was standing alongside the warehouse, waving at some of my pilot friends, who were standing on the flight deck, with our freshly washed helicopters. The port of Naha was operated by the U.S. Army. Suddenly, from the ship's bridge, a loud amplified voice commanded, "Major Warren, get a line handling crew, to tie up this ship." The irritated voice belonged to the captain of the *Thetis Bay,* and reflected his displeasure that someone in the Army had failed to send a line handling crew to tie up the *Thetis Bay*.

Regardless of who screwed up, I had my orders. So, I looked around and realized that I was alone; wondering where the hell I was going to find a line handling crew. Just then, here came "The Calvary." Trucks approaching the dock were filled with Marines, who would board the *Thetis Bay*.

I quickly found a Marine Second Lieutenant, who was a platoon leader, and ordered him to immediately send one of his three squads to the dock, to tie up the *Thetis Bay*. I assured him that I would tell his company commander later about what I had ordered one of his platoon leaders to do. He complied but in normal Marine infantry unit fashion, it was correct, measured, and slow. First, he had his platoon fall in, and then commanded open ranks. The squad selected was then ordered to stack arms and remove packs (backpacks). Next, a guard had to be posted to protect those stacked rifles and packs.

Meanwhile, the ship needed immediate help. But the Marines were a lot more concerned about protecting their rifles and packs, than about the dire needs of some "squid ship." Finally, after reaching the dock, the trained ship sea and anchor detail started tossing heavy lines from the ship to the dockside Marines. A lot of colorful language was expressed both ways, between the sailors aboard and my ad hoc Marine line-handling crew ashore. I didn't think this all boded well for a pleasant sea voyage to the Philippines. This event reminded me of the printed statement on rank promotion documents that charge the promoted Marine to: "Perform All Manner of Things." I guess that charge includes tying up a ship, before it cuts a slice out of some Okinawan pier.

A Large Navy Flotilla

With its Marine battalion aboard, the USS *Thetis Bay* departed Naha, Okinawa, and sailed toward the Philippine island of Luzon. Our ship joined a flotilla of eighty ships; the largest number of allied ships assembled since World War II. Sailing south, the flotilla passed the island of Formosa (named "Beautiful Isle" by passing mariners) and since 1945 officially known as Taiwan (meaning "Terraced Bay"). Taiwan is an island nation, two hundred forty-five miles long, and ninety miles wide. The water just offshore is very deep; allowing the ships in our flotilla to sail safely near the Formosa/Taiwan shoreline. The island was indeed a "Beautiful Isle."

Luzon Ship-To-Shore Landing Exercise

The roundtrip distance from the *Thetis Bay* to the helicopter landing zones on Luzon was a hundred miles. The distance was really an asset, because an orderly interval between the ship and helicopter landing zones (LZs) could easily be maintained. Most of our flights were over dense jungle, after passing the shoreline, and proceeding to the LZs. Following each round trip, the helicopter rotors were stopped for safety, while the next load of ten Marines boarded their helicopter. To save time, our helicopters refueled with the engine running, almost a prohibited procedure aboard aircraft carriers. However, all went well, and the use of helicopters, flying from dispersed ship platforms, was proven to be a new and a viable method of conducting amphibious operations.

After the battalion of Marines had been safely landed, the *Thetis Bay* sent all of our Marine helicopters ashore for several days, in order to perform some overdue repairs to the flight deck, and to other areas of the ship. We flew to the small village of Bitulok, which had a dirt-surfaced airstrip, and a generous local supply of San Miguel Philippine beer. The beer was sold by the single bottle, or in buckets containing five bottles. Our pilots had no alcoholic drinks after leaving Japan; so, they eagerly purchased the buckets. They were thirsty; and wholeheartedly engaged in beer drinking contests.

One thing led to another; and soon some of our pilots were bravely racing down the Bitulok dirt runway after dark. They were riding water buffaloes, in a hastily organized water buffalo derby. The next day, those pilots were a sad lot. Except for having splitting headaches lasting all the next day, there were no other discernible, serious casualties.

As other squadron pilots arrived at the Bitulok village, they were invited to view a Philippine folk dance called the "Tinikling," which originated during the Spanish colonial era. The dance involves two people beating, tapping, and sliding bamboo poles on the ground, and then against each other, in coordination with one or more dancers who step over, then in between, the heavy bamboo poles; always keeping perfect time to the music. After drinking a bottle or two of San Miguel beer, some of our pilots, much to the delight of the skilled dancers and the audience, learned to dance the Tinikling. Again, there were no serious injuries; only a few sore ankles, which were far less severe than the headaches suffered by those pilots who rode in the water buffalo derby.

Return to Japan

When the *Thetis Bay* repairs were completed, our helicopters were recalled to the ship, which had been detached from the flotilla; and we sailed directly back to Japan. Upon arrival, the helicopters flew ashore, where they all were transferred to a new squadron, in the Oppama based Marine Aircraft Group-16. I was on temporary orders. So, I had to return to the United States, and did not stay in Japan permanently.

Since Naval personnel were not permitted to have two permanent changes of station in a single year, I boarded ship at Yokosuka on 27 February 1958 and took command of HMR(L)-363. One hundred Marines, who had completed their Far East tours, were assigned to my squadron aboard ship, for transportation back to the United States. Having completed the change of command formality, we sailed for home aboard the *Thetis Bay;* arriving at the Southern California port at Long Beach three weeks later. A Marine squadron being transferred without airplanes, was referred to as a "flag and bible" transfer.

During the return voyage to Long Beach, I kept the Marines busy. Every morning, except Sunday, we had rifle inspections, physical exercise, and close order drill on the flight deck. The Marines were then assigned to afternoon working parties, to perform all manner of things aboard ship. Other than mess duty, I insisted that the working party Marines would be supervised by Marine NCOs, and not sailors. Navy personnel, usually ship division officers, would tell the Marine NCOs what needed to be done, furnish the supplies and equipment needed, and then let the Marine sergeants take charge. I could see no reason to waste manpower while sailing home. I knew the Marine help in sprucing up the ship was appreciated, and keeping Marines busy was, as always, the best way to keep them out of trouble.

Manning the Rails

When the ship was nearing Long Beach harbor, the ship's executive officer told me that sailors would man the rails when entering the harbor, by standing along the edge of the flight deck. He then said that my Marines could be in formation behind the deck edge sailors. He was a Navy commander; one rank above mine. I respectfully told him that I could not do that, but if the Marines could take their rightful place, as the senior Naval service on the sailor's right, we would be honored to participate in the traditional manning the rails. Otherwise, I would dismiss my Marines. I was correct and he knew it. He quickly relented; and we proudly manned the rails, positioned correctly on the right of the sailors. Before the *Thetis Bay* docked at Long Beach, I expected that some Lieutenant Colonel would meet the ship, to take command of my squadron. I was only a Major, and pilots of my rank were very seldom given a squadron command.

As soon as the ship docked, Colonel Robert Johnson, the helicopter Air Marine Group commander at MCAF, Tustin came aboard. I met him and he told me that he noted that my Marines were manning the rails in their correct position. I took Colonel Johnson to the ship's bridge, where I introduced him to the ship's captain. In addition, I took advantage of this opportunity to relate to Colonel Johnson, how professionally our helicopter squadron had been used during the exercise on Luzon Island. I did not mention the water buffalo derby. The Captain told Colonel Johnson about ordering me to get a line-handling crew to tie up his ship at Naha, Okinawa. I was surprised that he remembered that incident.

When those pleasantries were over, Colonel Johnson invited me to ride with him in his staff sedan back to Tustin. He told me that the other Marines in my squadron would be provided transportation back to MCAF, Tustin. His invitation to ride with him was somewhat puzzling, as I still expected that I would be relieved of my squadron command by some Lieutenant Colonel. Colonel Johnson then gave me the great news that I would remain in command of HMR(L)-363, albeit the squadron designation would be slightly changed to HMRI-363. The new composite designation reflected that the squadron would operate several types of helicopters; including the Sikorsky HRS, HUS, and the Kaman HOK. He said there were some Lieutenant Colonels inbound. Meanwhile, I was to remain in command. I told him that I was truly honored by his decision.

Chapter 22: Helicopter Squadron Command

Flag and Bible Marines

Most of the Marines aboard the USS *Thetis Bay* attached to my "flag and bible" squadron command from Japan to Long Beach had completed their Far East tours, and were due for transfer or discharge. I studied the Marine Corps' Table of Organization (TO) for a helicopter squadron. Then, I practically camped on the desk of the Air Group S-1 (Personnel Officer), requesting immediate assignment of more Marines to my squadron.

For a few weeks, we had no helicopters. So, I could devote most of my time to personnel organization, and non-flying training. I was assigned a very experienced Squadron Sergeant Major, who provided me with wisdom and insight regarding all enlisted men matters. For instance, he appropriately suggested that, because we had not yet received helicopters, we might concentrate on annually required rifle range qualifications for our troops, including officers. In addition, Major Lyle Tope who was a well-qualified S-3 (Operations Officer) was assigned to the squadron. In addition, my new squadron Executive Officer Major Duane "Red" Redallen joined. Redallen had just returned from a U.S. Embassy tour in Haiti.
ix

The first helicopters assigned to my squadron were Kaman HOKs. They were small, observation helicopters; with overhead interlocking rotor blades, that were mounted at the center, on lightly slanted masts. The blades were directly over the pilots' cockpit, and the passenger cabin. The two other helicopters were very familiar to me. I had flown the Sikorsky HRS in Korea and I transported President Eisenhower, at San Francisco, in the larger Sikorsky HUS. Some HOKs had been used to transport scientists, civilian engineers, and support personnel, during the placing, and test explosions of, the twenty-three atomic bombs at Bikini Atoll in the Pacific Ocean.

Squadron personnel buildup proceeded sharply, and soon we were included in exercises; flying from ships offshore to landing zones at Camp Pendleton. We transported medium artillery guns externally, and troops in the helicopter cabins.

During one ship-to-shore, I had our Marine Air Wing Commander as my co-pilot. Major General Thomas "Tom" Ennis was familiar with the drop-bow surface landing craft. However, the landing exercise with the troops transported by helicopter, was all new to him. I admired him for participating and learning as, after all, the helicopter air groups and squadrons were in his Air Wing command.

We flew out to the ship, and entered one of four holding pattern circles. We established fore and aft and port and starboard of the aircraft carrier. While in a holding pattern, as I was explaining the helicopter procedures to General Ennis, I received a call from the ship saying, "Your signal is Charlie." That's the age-old signal on all aircraft carriers meaning, you are cleared next to land.

Obviously, the ship's Captain realized that he had a two-star General in a holding pattern, waiting for a turn to land. Upon receiving that signal, we left the holding pattern, and landed immediately. I purposely let General Ennis fly to the flight deck, and land our helicopter on a forward designated landing spot. Our HRS helicopter had its blades folded, was towed onto a flight deck elevator, and quickly struck (lowered) below to the ship's hangar deck. The exercise then continued, with Major General Ennis thoroughly enjoying watching the flight operations, with the ship's Captain, from the bridge.

After several hours, the ship-to-shore operations were completed. I told Major General Ennis that I had filed a flight plan for our flight from the ship to MCAS, El Toro. He asked where our helicopter was located. I told him it would appear on the flight deck from the forward elevator in a few minutes. It did, and we climbed into the cockpit, started the engine, engaged the rotors, and took off; heading back to his headquarters at MCAS, El Toro.

Major General Ennis had obviously enjoyed participating as a pilot in a modern (helicopter) landing exercise. While flying back to El Toro, he reminisced about his early days, flying open cockpit airplanes. He recalled the days when it was normal to fly reasonably low, feel the air blowing through the open cockpit, and once again smell some engine exhaust fumes.

After landing, he thanked me, and told me that he would be calling again to set up additional flights. I knew then, that as with General Schilt years before, I was destined to once again be a helicopter flight instructor for a Flag Officer.[x]

Throughout the summer months my helicopter squadron was busy training new pilots to fly the helicopters assigned to our squadron; one model at a time. Starting with the small Kaman HOK, they gained experience, as they completed the training syllabus. They would graduate to the next larger and more load- carrying helicopters. For each of our squadron helicopters, the training syllabus included lifting heavy cargo net loads attached to the underside of the helicopters, thereby mimicking what we had done in combat during the Korean War. Supporting the ground troops at Camp Pendleton, only forty miles away, became an almost daily training ritual. Major Lyle Tope, the squadron S-3 (Operations Officer) did a masterful job of keeping the training records for each of three different helicopters, correctly including all pilot and aircrew training.

Late in July 1958, Lieutenant Colonel Elswin P. "Jack" Dunn reported to Marine Air Group-36 (MAG-36), to which my squadron was also assigned. Jack Dunn, and his lovely wife Ellie, were close friends of ours. But, when he started flying with my squadron almost daily, it was obvious that he was preparing to relieve me, and take over my squadron command. He did, and he requested that I remain as the squadron Executive Officer; second to him. He knew that I would provide helicopter squadron organization and flying experience that he had not yet gained. Accordingly, I was a valuable asset to him. I was happy to see Jack get a squadron command; meanwhile having some fixed feelings because I was losing my command. However, I also realized how fortunate I had been to command a squadron for about five months, while still a Major.

I was overdue for assignment to the Far East; and in August 1958, my former yearly PCS orders limiting transfer no longer applied. Lieutenant Colonel Jack Dunn intervened, to keep me around as long he could. Neither of us realized then, that very soon, our paths would cross many times in the Far East.

Fatal Crash

Not long after Lieutenant Colonel Dunn took command, HMRI-363 lost a HUS in a fatal helicopter crash. One of our lieutenant pilots flew into a fog bank, attempting to get to Camp Pendleton. The HUS helicopter could be flown safely when the visibility was a mile or more. However, almost daily, early morning sea fog formed along the southern California coast, and moved inland. The fog would burn off (dissipate) during the late morning hours. The pilots were briefed to return to base if foggy weather conditions were encountered, or even suspected. For whatever reason, the pilot of that helicopter did not heed those instructions, and flew into what we called "a cloud full of rocks." That error resulted in the crash, in which he, his co-pilot, and crew chief all died on impact.[xi]

When this terrible accident happened, I recommended to Lieutenant Colonel Dunn that he handle the funeral arrangements; including extending genuine sorrow to the families of the deceased. I knew that his wife, Ellie, would very capably assist Jack in expressing genuine heartfelt grief to the grieving families. I also recommended that I write the required formal Aircraft Accident Report; as I knew all the ramifications and details associated with the failed CG&A Boxes.

After writing and submitting the Formal Accident Report, I would then write the squadron Commanding Officer's forwarding endorsement. No accident cause or blame was due to anyone except the deceased pilot, who had clearly disregarded the many cautions presented at all our daily squadron pre-flight briefings. Losing a pilot, regardless of the circumstances, casts a squadron-wide pall over everything; and includes a mandatory flying stand down. Also affecting the overall squadron mood were the funeral services, held in the on-base chapel. Later, we received the replacement helicopter, with all the required Navy Bureau Number aircraft inventory logs and records. Next, the squadron identifying number was painted on the new bird.

During the time of the accident, the Air Wing Commanding General, Major General Tom Ennis was on leave. He normally called me at least two times each week, to fly the helicopter. He had returned from leave shortly after the helicopter accident. I stopped by his office at MCAS, El Toro and asked him when he wanted to fly again. He said that he would have to delay flying for a week or so, in order to catch up on some accumulated paper work. He then said, "Including forwarding endorsement of your squadron Accident Report."

I told him that I had written the accident report, while Lieutenant Colonel Dunn handled the many funeral details. I told him that I had been careful to omit some unimportant accident report detail. Omitting details would make it easy for the higher chain-of-command echelons to have a valid reason to include comments in their forwarding endorsements, before eventually forwarding the report to the Naval Aviation Safety Center in Norfolk, Virginia for final review and disposition. He looked at me knowingly and responded with "Get the hell out of here!" He knew that I had learned the Aircraft Accident Report forwarding drill very well. I also realized that it probably was not wise for me to pull the General's chain again.

We heard nothing more, regarding our squadron's aircraft accident. By the time Jack Dunn has assumed command, all of our Sikorsky HRS helicopters had been transferred to the Air Group-36 Headquarters and Maintenance Squadron. So, when General Ennis wanted to fly, I had to borrow an HRS helicopter, and its crew chief, from H&MS-36. For obvious reasons, I was never turned down.

Chapter 23: Oppama, Japan

Reassignment to the Far East

In March 1969, I was reassigned from MCAF, Santa Ana to the Far East; specifically to the 3rd Marine Aircraft Wing, headquartered in Iwakuni, Japan. From there I was assigned to MAG-16, which was based at NAS, Oppama; located adjacent to the large Naval Base at Yokosuka. Yokosuka is on the western shore of Tokyo Bay, about thirty miles south of Tokyo, and fifteen miles south of the city of Yokohama.

I left Millie and our two children, Bill and Jeanne, in our Santa Ana home, during March. My family was with our close friends, Rolene and Verdan (Buck) Bukove; who had lived next door for years.

I arrived in Japan, later in March; starting my fifteen-month tour away from home. This deployment was, at that time, the longest of my Marine Corps career. But, at least this time, was peacetime.

When I arrived at Oppama, Colonel George W. Herring was the Air Group Sixteen (MAG-16) commanding officer there. He formerly had commanded the helicopter squadron HMR-161 during its organization, its training in California, and its deployment to Korea. He commanded the squadron during several months of combat operations, as previously described.

Upon arrival at Oppama, I joined his MAG-16 staff as the S-1 (Personnel Officer). I remained in that assignment for several months. Then I was assigned MAG-16 Aviation Safety Officer. This job entailed flying with all the air group's numbered squadrons, and reviewing the squadron safety procedures with each squadron commanding officer. My job was to observe and make recommendations regarding any unsafe flying practices, and other unsafe helicopter maintenance or airfield conditions.

For instance, I recommended to Colonel Herring that all Air Group flying should be stopped immediately, because I noted that some refueling trucks were painted erroneously. The large, painted fuel identifying numbers did not match the fuel carried in the tanker trucks. Some fuel trucks were refueling helicopters with 115/145 octane fuel. While that was the correct helicopter fuel; the truck had MOGAS (motor vehicle gasoline) painted on the truck tank. MOGAS was a much lower-rated octane fuel. Had it been pumped into the helicopter fuel tanks, the results would, no doubt, have been tragic. On my recommendation, all MAG-16 flying was stopped, until the refueling trucks were repainted to properly identify the fuel in the trucks.

Meanwhile, my friend Lieutenant Colonel Jack Dunn arrived with HMR-363; the squadron I had commanded at MCAF, Santa Ana, until I was relieved by Jack. The Marine Major who relieved me as the MAG-16 S-1 had previously served on the staff of the Navy Air Force, Atlantic Fleet, where he was closely associated with Captain Paul D. Buie, USN who later commanded the Navy's largest ship, the aircraft carrier USS *Ranger* (CV-61).

Aircraft Carrier USS *Ranger* (CV-61)

When launched at the Newport News, Virginia shipyard in 1957, the USS *Ranger* was the largest ship in the Navy. After launching, it completed its required new-ship sea trials off the Virginia Capes. The ship's shakedown cruise included deployment to Guantanamo Bay, Cuba. The ship was then ordered to join the Pacific Fleet. As it was too large to transit the Panama Canal, the *Ranger* had to sail around Cape Horn, passing the southern tip of South America, in order to reach the Pacific Ocean. After sailing north, past the west coasts of South, Central, and North America, the *Ranger* docked at Alameda, California.

Alameda is located on the east side of San Francisco Bay. After briefly operating off the California coast, the *Ranger* sailed to Pearl Harbor, Hawaii. There, the ship officially joined the Pacific Fleet before sailing to Japan, where it further joined the U.S. 7th Fleet.

The *Ranger* arrived and docked at the Naval Base at Yokosuka, Japan. The Major's ship had just arrived from Pearl Harbor and docked at Yokosuka, and he had called Captain Buie, who immediately invited him to visit his ship. He accepted, and asked if he could bring another Marine Major with him. The Major invited me to accompany him to nearby Yokosuka, to meet his former staff associate, Captain Paul Buie, the USS *Ranger*'s Captain.

The *Ranger* was indeed massive; meaning we had no trouble locating her. The ship was hard to miss; tied up to the Piedmont Pier, Yokosuka's longest shipyard pier. The *Ranger*'s bow protruded one hundred thirty-five feet past the Piedmont Pier; requiring it to also drop its bow anchors. The largest pier cranes were even in height with the top the USS *Ranger* superstructure.

Promptly, at the scheduled visit time, we boarded the *Ranger,* by walking up its personnel boarding gangplank. From the top of the gangplank, we then stepped aboard the ship's quarterdeck. Following proper U.S. Navy boarding procedure, we stopped, stood at attention facing aft, and saluted the U.S. flag flying from the ship's stern. Then, following long held Navy tradition, we turned to the ship's Officer of the Deck (OOD); saluted, and requested permission to come aboard. Of course, it was granted; as the OOD already had been alerted that Captain Buie was expecting us.

Captain Paul D. Buie, USN

The Major and I were escorted though the ship to Captain Buie's sea cabin. We were asked to show our military ID cards to the ever-present Marine Corps enlisted sentry. After firmly rapping, the Marine sentry then opened the Captain's sea cabin hatch. He announced our presence by stating our ranks and last names. Captain Buie rose from his desk, walked to meet us, shook our hands, and welcomed us aboard.

We spent about thirty minutes chatting in his sea cabin, mostly recalling humorous experiences when the Major and the Captain previously had served together. He was a very amiable and gracious senior officer host. His unhurried manner seemed to veil the awesome responsibility that went with commanding the largest ship in the U.S. Navy. Yet, he still took time to welcome a couple of visiting Marine Corps majors. He also expressed his admiration for the permanent Marine Corps detachment aboard his ship.

Captain Buie was a WWII hero, who had organized Navy Attack Squadron Sixteen (VA-16). That squadron, flying from the USS *Lexington* (CV-16), shot down one hundred fifty Japanese airplanes, while under his command. For those and other actions, he was awarded the Navy Cross, the Silver Star, the Distinguished Flying Cross with two stars (two more DFCs), the Air Medal, and the Presidential Unit Citation.

Captain Buie arranged for us to tour the ship; including touring the ship's cavernous engine room, which housed four massive boilers, and four steam turbine engines. The engine room was the bailiwick of the Engineering Officer; a Navy Commander. He explained the functions of the major components in the engine room. The four turbines could deliver two hundred eighty thousand shaft horsepower. Each of the turbines turned long steel shafts, extending from turbine engines, through the ship's after hull. Each shaft drove an attached twenty-plus-foot diameter bronze propeller. Those propellers—called screws— could drive the *Ranger* to speeds of thirty-four knots.

From one of the *Ranger*'s upper decks, we looked down a long ship passageway, through dozens of oval shaped open hatches. They appeared to get smaller, when viewed from a distance. Like all shipboard hatches, each could be closed in an emergency, to prevent flooding.

After expressing our appreciation to Captain Buie for our welcome aboard, and for our tour of the ship, we requested permission to go ashore from the OOD, and receiving it, we again faced the stern, and saluted.[xii] We then walked down the gangplank, to the pier, and returned to NAS, Oppama.

Submarine USS *Ronquil* (SS-396)

During my career, I tried to add to the college credits I had attained at Michigan State College. When I was General Schilt's Aide, I enrolled in University of Maryland courses, taught in the evening at the Pentagon. Attending classes was difficult; as often I had to accompany the General on many of his long trips, including those long trips overseas. Therefore, it was futile to enroll in courses like College Math or Foreign languages. But at Oppama, it seemed that I might be able to complete more college courses offered by the University of Maryland College Overseas Extension Program. The courses were held in the evening, at the nearby Yokosuka Naval Base. I enrolled in a course offered there.

Another class attendee was a U.S. Navy Chief Petty Officer, who was a crew member on the USS *Ronquil* (SS-396), a U.S Navy submarine. I asked him how I could get a ride on his boat (submarines are the only U.S. Navy warships referred to as boats). He told me the *Ronquil* would often go to sea for a day, and return the same day. He suggested that I visit the *Ronquil,* and make a verbal request to the *Ronquil*'s Captain, a Navy Lieutenant Commander, (the same rank as mine).

I told Captain Herring that I'd like to have a one-day-only submarine experience. He gave me a quizzical look, shook his head, and verbally approved my request. The next morning at 0730 I boarded the USS *Ronquil*, ready for a new, day-long, undersea experience. The *Ronquil* was a diesel-powered boat, which had launched in 1944, at the Portsmouth Naval Shipyard, in Kittery, Maine. Compared to the USS *Ranger*, the *Ronquil* was tiny, and a far cry from the new, and much larger, nuclear-powered submarines.

The *Ronquil*'s mooring lines from the Yokosuka pier were cast off; thereby freeing the *Ronquil* to commence its journey on the surface, out of Tokyo Bay, before diving. At the same time, the cruiser USS *St. Paul* (CA-73) was sailing in the opposite direction, toward Yokosuka. The *St. Paul* flew a blue flag, with three white stars, indicating the Vice Admiral who commanded the U.S. 7th Fleet was aboard. When U.S. Navy ships pass each other at sea, they traditionally render honors back and forth, by momentarily dipping their national colors. In effect, the ships are saluting each other. The *St. Paul*'s rails were manned by sailors wearing white uniforms, and members of its Marine detachment. As we passed the *Saint Paul*, the *Ronquil* offered honors with only a couple sailors on deck, plus me, the one-man Marine Detachment.

To say that facilities and conditions in the *Ronquil* were small would be a real understatement. For instance, the only shipboard office was a cubicle just wide enough to accommodate a typewriter, with two file drawers underneath. Being aboard was like living in a tiny house. At any given time, at least one-half of the crew was on duty, and the sailors shared bunks. Crates of food were stowed in the forward torpedo room.

Dive, Dive, Dive

After sailing from the Yokosuka Naval Base, the *Ronquil* proceeded south on the surface, toward and past the entrance to Tokyo Bay. The submarine was now in the deep water of Sagami Wan, and the order was given to "Dive, Dive, Dive." The submarine then angled bow (nose) down, and slipped quietly under water. The dive continued until a depth of four hundred feet underwater was reached, and the submarine leveled.

The mission of the dive was then revealed to me. The main purpose of the dive was to check for any leaks, following its completed repairs at the Yokosuka Naval Base. There were a few leaks. At that pressure, the small leaks shot sea water horizontally across the submarine. In addition, torpedo loading drills were held; but the submarine torpedo doors were never opened. The submarine then rose to periscope depth, and more torpedo firing drills were held.

The submarine then surfaced, and sailed back up Tokyo Bay to Yokosuka. The OOD maneuvered the boat from his position behind a small windscreen located at deck level, just ahead of the submarine's vertical sail. I witnessed a firm verbal admonishment from the submarine's captain to the OOD, following his request to have the captain come topside, and direct how the submarine should pass through many Japanese fishing boats just ahead. The captain took one look and then said, "I've been called needlessly and further, you (the OOD) should figure that out because, after all, it is your responsibility to safely maneuver the boat." The captain immediately went below.

I assumed that he knew that the worst that could happen was the *Ronquil* would push some small fishing boats aside, out of the way. The *Ronquil* docking back at Yokosuka was uneventful. I thanked the captain for his hospitality, and I went ashore. I was satisfied with my first submarine experience. I do not intend to ever "dive" again.

Chapter 24: First Orders to Laos

The Commander in Chief, Pacific (CINCPAC) Admiral Harry D. Felt, USN was the senior U.S. Military Commander in the Pacific. From his Camp H. M. Smith headquarters in Hawaii, his command directed the major activities of the United States Army, Marine Corps, Navy, and Air Force aircraft, ships, and ground units operating in the Pacific Ocean area. At times, allied military units often participated in the combined exercises as well.

The two major subordinate Marine Corps organizations were, the 1st Marine Division based on Okinawa, and the 1st Marine Air Wing based in Japan. Each is commanded by a Marine Corps Major General. Depending upon which of the two was senior, his Marine Command was designated Task Force-116. The Aircraft Wing based at Iwakuni, Japan was commanded by Major General Carson A. Roberts. Roberts was senior, and designated Commander of Task Force (CTF)-116.

Major General Roberts was directed by CINCPAC to send an experienced helicopter pilot, to advise the local head of the U.S. Operations Mission in Laos (USOM-Laos), on the feasibility of using helicopters to support their planned support operations. Major General Roberts in turn, directed our Oppama-based helicopter air group (MAG-16) to send the selected pilot to Laos.

Colonel Herring submitted my name, and I received orders that read in part, "Proceed to Bangkok, Thailand, by commercial air, via Hong Kong; and to other places necessary in the execution of these orders." My orders also strangely specified that I take both a military uniform, and civilian clothing. First, I was directed to stop at the U.S. Embassy in Tokyo, where I would receive a passport. With those orders in hand, I rode the train thirty miles, from Oppama to Tokyo. At the U.S. Embassy, the receptionist handed an envelope to me that contained two U.S. passports. One had a photo of me in my

Marine Corps Major uniform. The other passport had a picture of me wearing a casual sport shirt, and identified me as a Department of the Navy employee. I was advised to use my military passport through Hong Kong, and to not attempt to fool the British government, which still administered the British Hong Kong Colony, under an extended ninety-nine year lease extension, from the government of China. The envelope also contained round-trip airline tickets to Hong Kong, Bangkok, and return to Tokyo, via Hong Kong.

From the American embassy in Tokyo, I proceeded to Tokyo's Haneda International Airport, where I boarded a Pan American Airways four engine Boeing Stratocruiser; leaving Japan for Hong Kong's Kai Tak International Airport. As the flight passed south over Okinawa, I thought about having flown from a small aircraft carrier, to Kadena Airfield, during the assault on Okinawa in April, 1945.

At Hong Kong, I had to wait several days for a commercial flight to Bangkok. So, I registered and stayed at the beautiful Peninsula Hotel in Kowloon, located in Hong Kong's New Territories. Every afternoon, tea time was announced, and hotel guests were invited to attend this traditional British event. Certainly not wanting to offend anyone, every afternoon I attended, and enjoyed the wonderful British Tea Time at the Peninsula Hotel. I was wearing my Marine uniform, and was quickly spotted by an elderly gentleman, who invited me to sit at his table. I learned that he had been a hotel fixture for several years. His table included a brass plaque with his name inscribed thereon; thus establishing his permanent, personal table reservation.

After waiting in Hong Kong for several days, I was notified that I had been booked on a non-stop flight to Bangkok. I felt like royalty, when I checked out of the Peninsula Hotel, and was driven to the airport in one of the hotel's fleet of beautiful Rolls-Royce automobiles. The route my flight took to Bangkok was well east of the Chinese owned Hainan Island, and then over the port city of Da Nang, Vietnam. I arrived in Bangkok at the Don Mueang International Airport; where my military passport was stamped, indicating my arrival date.

In the airport terminal, I was approached by an American of Chinese descent, who introduced himself as John Lee. He told me he was the pilot of the twin engine C-46 (Curtiss Commando) transport that would take me to Vientiane, Laos. The airplane was owned and operated by Air America, a Central Intelligence Agency (CIA) airline. He also told me to wear civilian clothes in Vientiane, the administrative capital of Laos.

Flying on an Air America Airlines C-46, and now wearing civilian clothes, were very positive indications that my mission was CIA directed. The pilot John Lee told me that because he had Oriental features, everyone expected him to communicate in a Far East language. He said that he could not; and added, "Hell, I was raised in Brooklyn."

I expressed concern that I had arrived in Thailand on a military passport, and now would be leaving on a civilian passport, with no Thailand arrival stamp; it could raise the question of how I could leave, when I had not officially arrived. John Lee took my civilian passport, and said he knew how to take care of the problem. When he returned my civilian passport to me, I noted that it now contained a Thailand arrival stamp.

Laos Overview

Though it can be found on a map, the country of Laos did not really exist. Many of its two million people would be astonished to be called Laotian. They know themselves to be Meo or Black Thai or Khalom tribesmen, living in small ethnic groups throughout the countryside. National identity was rare, because Laos had long been a territory of Thailand, a part of the vast French controlled Indochina. Laos is a land without a railroad, a single paved highway or a newspaper. The chief crop of Laos is opium. The French influence did not survive long after the French 1954 defeat at Dien Bien Phu.

When the French declared Laos independent, it had no cohesive government. Attempts to fill the vacuum were made by communist groups such as the Pathet Lao. Meanwhile, the CIA was trying to thwart those communist efforts, by setting up programs to deliver food to remote areas, and prevent starvation throughout Laos. Much of the food (mainly rice) delivery was accomplished by air drops, by Air America airliners.

Arrival in Vientiane

My Air America Airlines flight from Bangkok to Vientiane, Laos was uneventful. I was the only passenger. Many cargo items, foodstuffs, and mail were also placed aboard. After landing at Vientiane, John Lee escorted me to a small, modern house, where I was billeted. The house, owned by the U.S. Embassy, was fairly new, well lighted, and comfortable. The bedroom had a single bed, and a large ceiling fan. I was cautioned to sleep under the full, bed-length mosquito net. I slept very well.

The next morning, I was taken to breakfast, and then to the U.S. Embassy Programs Evaluation Office, where I was introduced to a Mr. Heintges and Mr. Sparrow. They were both very cordial and thanked me for coming to Laos. They were very aware that I was stationed in Japan, and that I was sent to Laos by CTF-116 to be their helicopter advisor.

I learned later that Mr. Heintges was U.S. Army Brigadier General John Heintges, and Mr. Sparrow, his chief of staff, was a

U.S. Army Colonel Herbert G. Sparrow. They headed what was called the United States Programs Evaluation Office. They told me to address them only as "Mister," and to make no references to any military rank, including mine. The caution was because, the official U.S. position was that, we had no military presence in Laos.

They asked a lot of questions regarding where available U.S. helicopters were located, and the load carrying capability of each type. They showed great interest in the Boeing-Vertol H-21, a tandem-rotor helicopter, operated in very limited numbers, by both the U.S. Air Force, and the U.S. Army. I cautioned them that although the H-21 had excellent load carrying capability, the helicopter had three transmissions, and that each had to be changed after every ninety flying hours. One transmission was located under each H-21 rotor. A third, much larger transmission was located over the helicopter engine, where it transmitted engine power through shafts, to each of the two smaller under-rotor transmissions.

They mentioned the need for helicopters to support Operation Hotfoot, a covert operation having no obvious U.S. connection. However, it was an operation intended to support Lao forces in their civil war against the Pathet Lao, a communist adversary. The plan included using the CIA proprietary airline Air America to deliver troops and air drop supplies. They suggested that I fly to one of the outposts in Laos, to learn more about the overall relief efforts to support the Lao Army.

I had the feeling that while I was away, the information I provided regarding helicopters in the Far East, and the load carrying capability of each type would be assessed. In particular, the CIA per hour estimated cost of operating the H-21 was being evaluated at some higher headquarters, for possible guidance and resolution.

I was shown some Embassy message traffic, reporting, "Maj Warren, CTF 116 helo advisor to PEO-Laos, stated H-21 helos require extensive ninety-hour maintenance...etc." Other embassy messages cited my evaluation of each helicopter load carrying capability. I rode a C-46 Air America airplane to Luang Prabang, where several Laotian soldiers and Americans—obviously CIA Operatives—were waiting to be paid. A small card table was placed inside the aircraft, and was used as a pay table, and to record the payments.

Luang Prabang, is the royal capital, whereas Vientiane is the administrative capital of Laos. I was driven the slight distance to the Royal Palace gate in a jeep. The Royal Palace was built beside the Mekong River, which flows past the palace at twelve miles per hour. The Mekong is two thousand one hundred miles in length, making it the twelfth longest river in the world. The river flows along the borders, or through six countries. I started to take a picture of the Royal Palace through the palace gate. But, when I started to aim my camera, a uniformed palace guard blocked my view, and menacingly raised his rifle. Not wanting to test his marksmanship, I returned to the jeep, and was driven back to the airport, where the Air America C-46 was waiting for my return flight to Vientiane.

Upon return, I was advised that unless I spoke French, I could return to Japan. However, if I did speak French, I would be retained in Laos. Thankfully, I did not speak French.

I learned that the CIA estimated the cost of operating the H-21 was $1,100 per hour, and that H-21 availability was very questionable. Accordingly, the entire effort to provide helicopter support had been placed on hold. With that, I expressed my appreciation, and said goodbye to Mr. Heintges and Mr. Sparrow. I sent a message to CTF-116 notifying that I had been released by PEO-Laos, and was returning to Japan.

I wrote to Millie, and told her that all my life, I had been searching for the end of the world, and in Laos, I had finally found it.

I then flew from Vientiane to Bangkok. From there, I continued my reverse course, and flew back to Japan through Hong Kong.

Return to Japan

After arriving at the Haneda Airport in Tokyo, I rode a commuter train the thirty-five miles back to my home base at Oppama. Colonel Herring assembled his MAG-16 staff, and the helicopter squadron commanders, for a briefing, in which I related my experiences in Laos.

I detailed most of my experiences, but said very little about my stay in the lush Peninsula Hotel, and nothing about my ride to the airport in the hotel Rolls Royce. I said that I felt that the United States was committed to supporting the Lao Army, at least partially by helicopter. However, the larger U.S. Operations Mission (USOM-Thailand) seemed to be waiting for instructions from CINCPAC, or possibly from some higher national authority.

Meanwhile, I wrote to Millie and suggested that she start making arrangements for her trip to Japan, for the permitted sixty-day visit. I also had a letter from Major Victor A. "Vic" Armstrong in Quantico who told me that my orders to Quantico were forthcoming. Further, I would relieve him as the HMX-1 commanding officer, and with that assignment, I would become the helicopter pilot for the President of The United States.

Chapter 25: Second Orders to Laos

Two weeks after I had returned from Laos to Oppama, Japan, I was summoned to Colonel Herring's Marine Aircraft Group 16 office at Oppama. He showed me a message just received from CTF-116.

Major General Roberts directed me to return to Laos. The main difference was that on this visit I would report directly to the U.S. Ambassador to Laos as his helicopter advisor. Further, the message also directed Colonel Herring to load eleven Sikorsky HUS helicopters aboard the USS *Thetis Bay,* at the nearby Yokosuka Naval Base. Colonel Herring had already notified Lieutenant Colonel Jack Dunn, the squadron commander of HMR-363, to ready eleven of his helicopters for deployment. We all wondered just why only eleven of the normal complement of twenty-four squadron helicopters was specified. I left Oppama for Laos; the second time still not knowing the reason.

My orders directed me again, as on my recent first trip, "To proceed to Bangkok, Thailand via commercial air, etc." But this mission did not require a stop at the U.S. Embassy in Tokyo, as I already had both my civilian and military passports. My round trip tickets were waiting for me at the Pan American Airways boarding desk, at the Tokyo Haneda Airport terminal. The flight to Hong Kong was uneventful. I did not remain in Hong Kong, because at the Kai Tak Airport terminal, I was able to board another airliner, departing for Bangkok almost immediately. Arriving at Bangkok's Don Mueang Airport, I passed through the arrival and departure gates effortlessly.

U.S. Embassy in Laos

I flew to Vientiane on a C-47 aircraft that belonged to the U.S. Embassy. I did not realize that it had been sent to Bangkok to transport me to Vientiane. Upon arrival, I reported to Ambassador J. Graham Parsons. It was a Sunday afternoon, and he was hosting a garden party on the Embassy lawn. He introduced me as a military aide who had just returned from a trip to Bangkok. While we were out of earshot from his other guests, we briefly discussed the situation. He revealed that any use of helicopters would be under U.N. auspices; painted white, and bearing U.N. markings. Now I knew why only eleven HUS helicopters had been specified. Eleven was the total number that could reasonably be transported out of sight in the *Thetis Bay* hangar deck, with none exposed on its flight deck.

The next day at the U.S. Embassy, Ambassador Parsons told me that even though my orders stated that I would be his helicopter advisor, he expected me to be in charge of all things having to do with the use of those U.N. helicopters, and to keep him informed. I told him that I would do my best to meet his expectations. He had just put me totally in charge. So, as any Marine would do, I took charge; albeit with many reservations and concerns.

My first concern was how to get those helicopters to Laos. Would refueling stops be necessary? If so, where? After arrival, who would direct their operations; and from where? Where would the helicopter crews be billeted, and what would they eat? How could I be sure that their drinking water was purified, to prevent them from getting the debilitating "Asian Belly?"

I considered the admonishment given to me years earlier by the Chief of Naval Operations Admiral Arleigh Burke, USN, when I was a student attending Amphibious Warfare School at Quantico. I recalled that he said, "Sometimes you may think that you don't know what to do." He then quickly added, "When that happens, just use your God-given American horse sense, and do what you think is right. You will be right; and we will send your orders later."

I was shown message traffic that revealed the *Thetis Bay* would be in position to launch helicopters--now being painted white—in five days. The launch position would be twenty-five miles east of Da Nang, Vietnam. The name of helicopter refueling locations was requested, as was their final destination. After measuring distances on maps, and knowing the range of the HUS, I concluded that the first refueling stop would be at the city of Savannakhet, Laos, and the second, at Vientiane, Laos, which as far as I knew, would be the helicopter flight's final destination.

I knew that the helicopter flight would require high octane fuel at both locations. Therefore, positioning high octane gasoline at the refueling stops would be my top priority. USOM-Laos could offer no help. So, I flew back to Bangkok, where I presented to USOM-Thailand my first request, namely getting helicopter engine high octane fuel positioned at Savannakhet, and at Vientiane.

I presented my verbal request to the head of USOM-Thailand, a uniformed U.S. Army Major General. After listening intently, he asked who was going to pay for the fuel. I told him that I did not know, however, I had seen a message from CINCPAC to the Captain of the *Thetis Bay*, forcefully stating, "If you don't get white paint yell; and yell like hell!"

Within hours thereafter, he told me that the fuel would be positioned, along with portable, manually operating aircraft refueling pumps at those locations, within two days. I thanked him, and could now shift to my other concerns associated with the arrival of those U.N. helicopters. So, I flew back to Vientiane from Bangkok.

Vientiane Airfield Helicopter Operations

My next concern was where on the Vientiane airfield would the helicopters land and park, when they arrived from Savannakhet. I noted three old, four-engine Laotian Airliners parked along one edge of the PSP (pierced steel planking) runway. The airliners had the Lao three headed elephant logo painted on each side.

I decided to have the helicopters land and park in the same area, as it was obvious from viewing those old civilian airliners that they had not been flown for a long time. No activity around them was evident; and I also noticed that most of the airliner tires were nearly flat. So, I knew that the arriving helicopters would not interfere with any on-going Lao Airline operations.

My next concern was billeting and health for the helicopter crews. I found, and rented, a three-story office building near the airport, that had adequate space to schedule operations, and provide adequate shelter for the crews. It also was close to the helicopter flight line, and alleviated the immediate need for vehicle transportation. Hen, the building owner, asked, "Who is going to pay the rent?" I crossed my fingers and responded, "Send the bill to the U.S. Embassy."

By now, I had enough experience to know that the State Department generally forwarded its bills for payment to USAID, the Agency for International Development. My priority now shifted to food and drink for the helicopter crews, as I knew they could not eat Lao Army rations, nor could they drink the local water. I surmised that I could depend on medical support from either the U.S. Embassy or from USOM-Laos, in the event of an accident or crew sickness. So, what else would I need?

After pondering further, I sent a message requesting help to CTF-116, the command that sent me to Laos twice. I stated a need for canvas Lyster bags[xiii], or other water purification equipment, including the water purification chemicals for Lyster bags, and for troop canteens. I included the immediate need for a thirty-day supply of U.S rations, cots, inflatable rubber mattresses (rubber ladies), and sleeping bags, as well as the all-important mosquito netting.

The building I rented had toilet, laundry and showering facilities; but both shower and laundry soaps would be required. I estimated that each of the eleven helicopters would have a crew of four. So, initial needs would be to provide for forty-four Marines.

I concluded that a guard detail would be necessary, after the helicopters landed at Vientiane. Accordingly, I requested weapons and ammunition. I was not concerned with training the helicopter crews as flight line sentries, because "every Marine is first, a rifleman." Every Marine has received weapons training and has achieved rifle qualification. I felt like I was running a MABS by myself.[xiv]

As my lists of support equipment grew, my messages to CTF-116 requesting support also grew. I was told later, that following receipt of my requests, loaded C-130 (Hercules) transport aircraft, loaded with my requested support items, waited on Okinawa, ready to deliver the equipment I had requested, directly to Vientiane.

I considered that it was time to pause, and report the actions I had taken, to Ambassador Parsons. He had directed me to keep him informed. When I arrived at the Embassy, I was told that Ambassador Parsons had gone to Bangkok for several days, to attend important high-level meetings.

While reviewing my sent and received messages at the U.S. Embassy in Vientiane, I noticed one that was rather unusual. It was sent from a language school headquarters in Okinawa. The message said that a U.S. Army officer was arriving on Laos, on a special assignment. When he arrived, he was to be billeted with me. This message was how I became acquainted with Captain Rene Defourneaux, U.S. Army.

When I met Captain Defourneaux, he revealed that he was fluent in French, having grown up in France, and that he still had relatives living there. During WWII, he joined the U.S. Army, and had received special training. Later, as a Special Assignment Operative, he had parachuted behind the German lines in France, to contact members of the French Resistance. He did not elaborate further, except that he worked from a language school in Okinawa, and that the people there would always know of his whereabouts, and would share his location with me, if I presented his code name properly.

He also told me that he knew the North Vietnamese leader, Ho Chi Minh, very well. Of course, that was surprising to me. Further, he said Chairman Ho had requested U.S. Assistance in the Vietnamese struggle against continued French colonization of Indo China, following WWII.

Rene Defourneaux never told me what he was doing in Laos. He would often disappear for a few days. During one of his mysterious disappearances, Ambassador Parsons returned to Laos. He then told me that the entire U.N. Helicopter effort had been placed on hold. With that information, I knew my mission was complete, and I could return to Japan. I sent messages to CTF-116, and to MAG-16, that I was returning.

Further message traffic I saw, revealed that the USS *Thetis Bay* had departed, and was sailing home to Japan, with a stop at Hong Kong. I never saw Captain Rene Defourneaux, in person, again.[xv]

After expressing my appreciation, I said goodbye to Ambassador Parsons. Before departing, he told me that the decision to cease the U.N. helicopter mission had come from Washington, D.C.; and the decision had been strongly endorsed by the CINCPAC Admiral Harry Felt, USN.

With that, I departed for Bangkok, and Hong Kong, where I wanted to review the whole situation with my friend, Jack Dunn. Jack was still aboard the *Thetis Bay* with his eleven HUS helicopters still painted white. I also needed to speak with the ship's captain. The *Thetis Bay* had just arrived in Hong Kong, and the white helicopters had all been screened from the sight of hundreds of Hong Kong hawkers by sewing together hundreds of *Thetis Bay* bed sheets, and draping the sheets over the helicopters.

I had arrived in Hong Kong ahead of the *Thetis Bay,* and was waiting on the pier when she docked. As soon as the ship's gangplank was lowered to the pier, I went aboard and was warmly greeted by my good friend, Jack Dunn. He told me that he had received permission from the *Thetis Bay*'s Captain to have me stay aboard the ship while I was in Hong Kong, and that the ship's captain had requested an informal briefing from me. Of course, I would gladly brief him.

Another reason I wanted to stop in Hong Kong was to send a wire message to Millie, telling her that I would be back in Japan within a week, and that she could now make her final arrangements to fly to Tokyo. She could start her permitted sixty-day Marine wife's visit to Japan. I left the ship after two days, and flew from Hong Kong back to Tokyo, then returned to Oppama on a train. I was happy that my second mission to Laos was over, and I could see Millie again very soon.

Chapter 26: Spouse Visit to Japan

Preparing for Millie's Visit

Anticipating Millie's visit, I purchased a reliable old Chevrolet sedan from an officer who was returning home from Oppama. I also contacted a Japanese lady, who agreed to rent her beach house to me for two months. Her name was Yaiko, and she lived a short distance from the beach house she rented to me. She was especially pleased, when she learned that my wife would be with me.

The house had a small refrigerator, stove, water heater, a western style bed with linens, and a dining table. I purchased a few basic china dishes, and some flatware not normally used by the Japanese. The basic Japanese dishes were bowls for rice and noodle soup, teapots, and teacups. The basic Japanese flatware was chopsticks.

When Millie arrived at the Haneda airport in Tokyo, she passed easily through Japanese customs. I led her to the old Chevrolet sedan, and told her that I had rented a furnished beach house, just down the beach from the summer home of the Emperor of Japan. That really was true.

She gave me letters and pictures that Bill and Jeanne had sent for their Dad. I was amazed to see how much they had grown since I left home, and started my fifteen month tour to the Far East, many months ago. Although tired from the long airplane ride across the Pacific Ocean, Millie looked just as pretty as when I left home.

The Japanese had copied the British in many ways, including driving on the left side of a road. Accordingly, their vehicles had the steering wheel and the other driving controls on the vehicle right side. I had driven jeeps and other military vehicles on Japanese roads and streets. So, I was quite familiar with their traffic patterns and rules. I noticed that Millie was very apprehensive at first, when I drove on the left side of the street.

Our rented house was less than ten miles from both Oppama and Yokosuka. We had the choice of eating at the Oppama Officer's Mess, dining at the Yokosuka Naval Base Officers Club, or going shopping for groceries at the Yokosuka Navy Base commissary, and the Japanese food markets.

Since I had to continue my duties at Oppama, I had to drive to and from our rented beach house. The route required driving through the small village of Zushi and the city of Kamakura. The main street through Kamakura passed by a large prominent, cast-in-bronze statue of the Great Buddha. This statue is one of Japan's fascinating historical landmarks. Built in 1243, the statue weighs one hundred twenty-five tons, and is over forty-three feet high.

While I was working at Oppama, Millie became quite friendly with Yaiko, our landlady. Yaiko invited Millie to her house, where she served cookies (more like crackers) and tea on a table raised slightly from the floor. They both sat on the floor, Japanese style.

Yaiko described her first encounter with American G.I.s, right after WWII ended. When the American troops first passed her house, riding in Jeeps and trucks, they whistled at her. Yaiko was an attractive Japanese lady, probably in her late twenties. She said that she never felt threatened by any occupying American servicemen.

One day, when I returned after my workday at Oppama, Millie told me Yaiko had sent a Japanese handyman to fix an electrical problem in our bathroom. The light did not turn on. The handyman was sitting, on the floor (Japanese style), beside a low table, eating some fresh fruit that Millie offered to him. When he finished eating, Millie tried to explain the light bulb in the bathroom had burned out. His face lit up when he finally understood, and he exclaimed, "Ah-so" (I understand). He then bounded outdoors, and jumped astride his small, noisy motorcycle, and put-putted away, to find a new light bulb for the bathroom.

When she told me about the language barrier she had with the handyman, I told her, using my limited pidgen Japanese that she needed only to say, "Binjo (bathroom), Dinki (electricity), Domi-domi (No good)."

About a week after Millie's arrival, the Marine Corps announced the results of the Lieutenant Colonel Selection Board. From one thousand six hundred forty eligible Majors, only two hundred forty-seven were selected for promotion. From our entire Marine Air Group-16 (MAG-16) at Oppama, only two of us were selected. The other was Major Frank J. Hubka who was stationed in our Observation Squadron, based in Okinawa. Of course, I was delighted to see my name on the list of those selected for promotion; but the mood at Oppama was understandably very grim. So, I decided to get away from Oppama, by taking leave, and traveling with Millie, away from the base, where we could celebrate together. We decided that our first trip would be to the city of Kyoto.

Visit to Kyoto

We drove to Tokyo, left the Chevrolet in a parking area, and rode a train through the beautiful Japanese countryside, to Kyoto. I had stayed in the city several times during the Korean War, at the designated R & R Miyako Hotel. The hotel had been upgraded, and was among several new hotels built since my last visit to Kyoto. We stayed in Kyoto several days, and enjoyed visiting the Japanese shrines, Torii Gates (Shinto Shrines), and the well preserved, centuries-old, thick roofed buildings.

Miyako Hotel Dining Room, Kyoto, Japan

    We were surprised, and fascinated, watching the Japanese fishermen in Biwa-ko (Lake Biwa). Each fisherman paddled his small boat into the lake. However, instead of using baited hooks, or other lures, fishermen used a tethered bird, called a cormorant. An aquatic bird, the cormorant dives, swims rapidly under water, and catches fish. But, before the bird dives, the fisherman places a metal ring around the bird's long neck so it cannot swallow the fish it catches. The tethered cormorant, with a fish in its beak, is then gently pulled out of the water, and into the boat, by the leash fastened around its leg. The fish is removed, and added to the fisherman's catch. The bird is then allowed to dive back into the water, to catch another fish. Occasionally, the bird is allowed to dive without the ring around its neck, so it can swallow the fish. Watching those small fishing boats at night is beautiful and peaceful. Each boat was lighted with a single, dim oil lantern.

    At Kyoto we could begin to sense the serene culture of Japan. Kyoto had been the capital city of Japan, before the capital was moved to Tokyo, in 1868.

Mt. Fujiama

Following our train trip to Kyoto, we rested and relaxed at our beach house for a few days. We then drove to nearby Odawara, a city near the base of Mt. Fujiyama (Fuji). We registered at a very nice hotel in the Mt. Fuji foothills. The bedrooms had both western-style beds and futons; soft cotton filled mattresses that can be unrolled, then spread on the bedroom floor for sleeping. Against the backdrop of the beautiful snow-covered Mt. Fuji, the hotel featured saunas, hot water tubs, and an exquisite dining room.

Soon after registering at the hotel, we met an American Army officer, and his wife, who were on their second visit to Japan, and staying at the same hotel. They were on leave from Seoul, Korea where he was stationed. We dined with them, and thoroughly enjoyed their company. They encouraged us to enjoy the talents of the hotel's well-trained Japanese masseuses. We did!

At the scheduled time, we met two Japanese ladies in a special massage room that had individual massage benches. I thoroughly enjoyed my massage, while lying on one bench. I don't think Millie enjoyed her massage as much, because she was curiously distracted and wide-eyed; trying to see what was going on at my bench.

Mt. Fuji, called Fuji-san by the Japanese, is the most famous symbol of Japan. At twelve thousand three hundred eighty-nine feet, it is the highest mountain in Japan, and dominates the surrounding landscape. It can be seen for hundreds of miles. The mountain is still considered to be an active volcano, though it has not erupted since 1707. Our hotel staff told us that it's not likely to erupt again without warning; as a team of geologists constantly monitors Fuji-san's volcanic activity. Rising high above a lower landscape, it is simply a beautiful Japanese icon. Fuji-san could easily be viewed from our beach house, from Yokosuka, Yokohama, Tokyo, and from miles beyond.

Sendai, Japan

Millie and I were so impressed with the excellent train service that we decided to visit another Japanese city. When discussing this with our landlady, she recommended a train trip from Tokyo to the city of Sendai; a distance of about one hundred eighty miles. We boarded an express train at the Tokyo station, and enjoyed the trip, traveling northeast along the east coast of Honshu Island, to the city of Sendai.

We were very impressed with the obvious efficiency of almost everything in Japan. Their trains were spotlessly clean, and they always departed and arrived exactly on time. Yaiko also recommended that we purchase packaged food called Ekiben - from the words 'eki' (railway **station**) and '**bento**' (boxed lunch) - meaning to train travelers, comfort food. Hawked by vendors shouting, "Bento-O-Bento" at train stations, these packaged lunchboxes are designed to be enjoyed on long train rides. The lunchboxes usually showcase the cuisine of the region. Each of our two Ekibens consisted of a lightweight container box, packed with pieces of meat, rice, pickled vegetables, and other foods, sized to portable portions. Using chopsticks over a freshly opened Bento while on an express train ride is almost an essential part of a train journey, for most Japanese travelers.

Sendai shares the same latitudes as Washington, D.C., and Athens, Greece. The city is modern, while being in harmony with nature, and surrounded by a splendid natural environment. A tree lined river, with very clear water, flows through the city. From the eastern edge of the Pacific Ocean, and west to the Ou Mountains, the people enjoy magnificent scenery; changing with each of the four seasons. Areas to the north and south are agricultural, and produce some of Japan's best rice.

Nearby Matsushima Bay is known as one of Japan's three most scenic locations. The bay is a haven from the harsh waves of the Pacific Ocean, and is famous for oyster farming. Our three day stay in Sendai added further insight into the serene and harmonious Japanese culture.

We rode the train back to Tokyo, each eating another delicious Bento with chopsticks, and surreptitiously, with our fingers.

Millie and I discussed our future plans, following my return from my current Far East tour. All that I could be sure of was that I would get a pay raise when, eventually, I would be promoted to Lieutenant Colonel. I did not tell her about the information I had from Major Vic Armstrong, (also selected for promotion), who was the Commanding Officer of HMX-1 at Quantico. I did tell her that I would probably be transferred to Quantico but, because I had not received orders, it was only speculation. I surmised that I might be assigned to the Educational Center at Quantico, to teach aviation subjects; specifically helicopter operations.

We did talk about our son, Bill, who would be starting high school, and that our daughter, Jeanne would also be attending a new middle school. We spent our last week together at our beach house.

In that Yaiko had been extremely helpful to us during our entire stay, we invited her to attend dinner with us at the Yokosuka Naval Base Officers Club. We were surprised and very pleased that she was dressed, Japanese style in a beautiful orange and black kimono, complete with the colorful waist belt called an obi. She also wore white stockings, and cloth-covered open-toed sandals, called getas. During dinner, she received many admiring looks, and many verbal compliments, regarding her beautiful Japanese attire. We were very proud to have her as our guest for dinner that evening.

A few days later, I drove Millie back to the Haneda Airport in Tokyo, where after a sad goodbye, she boarded a Pan American airliner for her flight back to California. Her wonderful visit had been for fifty-nine days, one day short of the Marine wife visiting limit. I know she was anxious to see Bill and Jeanne again, and to rescue them from our wonderful next door neighbors Rolene and Verdan (Buck) Bukove.

The next day I said goodbye to Yaiko, returned the key to our rented house, and thanked her for all her personal kindness. On the way back to Oppama, I stopped in the city of Zushi. I was about to cross the street when a Japanese policeman held up his hand, gesturing that I should not cross that street. In a minute I knew why. I looked down the street, and saw a motorcade approaching, with four motorcycle police outriders. As it passed me, I knew it was Hirohito, the Emperor of Japan; identified by prominent display of the Imperial Chrysanthemum Crest, the Imperial Seal of Japan. I was in uniform so, when the motorcade approached, I remembered the old military adage, "When in doubt, salute it."

Shortly after Millie left, I delivered a HUS helicopter to the 1st Marine Air Wing at MCAS, Iwakuni, Japan, where the helicopter would be used as a Search and Rescue helicopter, at that air station. After taking off from Oppama, I flew between the majestic snowcapped Mount Fujiyama on my right, and the Izu Peninsula on my left. The Izu Peninsula is warmed by water on three sides, and is semi-tropical. Citrus fruit is grown there. I made a refueling stop at the Itami Air Base, where we arrived and departed on R&R flights, during the Korean War. The entire flight to Iwakuni was over the Japanese Island of Honshu; the largest of Japan's four main islands. Flying at about five hundred feet, I could view the beauty of the Japanese countryside. Flying over several inland waterways, I saw barges loaded with many and varied newly manufactured items; including one loaded completely with new Japanese motorcycles.

After leaving the HUS at Iwakuni, I flew on a Marine transport aircraft back to Oppama, via nearby NAS, Atsugi, followed by a short helicopter flight to Oppama.

CINCPAC Helicopter Transport

One day I flew a HUS helicopter to Yokota Air Base, where I met, and transported Admiral Harry Felt, USN, CINCPAC, from Yokota to a helicopter landing facility called Washington Heights, near downtown Tokyo.

Maj. Bob Warren, pilot for Admiral Harry Felt, USN, CINCPAC (1957)

After takeoff, I wrote a penciled note, reached down into the helicopter cabin, and handed it to the crew chief. Using the intercom, I asked him to give it to our Admiral passenger. It read, "Admiral, I recently was your CTF-116 helicopter advisor in Laos. It's an honor to have you aboard." He wrote a note back to me on the other side of the paper, handed it to the crew chief, who handed up to me. It read, "Do you want to go back? I'm glad you are out of the U.N., and back in the Marine Corps." I noted that when the Admiral departed my helicopter, he was met at Washington Heights by the waiting U.S. Ambassador to Japan, and several other dignitaries; both American and Japanese. Obviously, as CINCPAC, Admiral Felt's status, and power, were widely recognized.

Air Group Commander Change

During the time I was on temporary orders away from Oppama, MAG-16 received a new commanding officer. Colonel George Herring, who sent me to Laos twice, had completed his tour, and was relieved by Colonel E. V. Finn, who told me that I was being transferred from Oppama, to our Observation Squadron (VMO-6) on Okinawa, which flew HOKs. He knew that I was a HOK qualified pilot, as I had HOKs assigned, when I commanded my squadron at MCAF, Santa Ana, California. Further, he told me that I would report to Lieutenant Colonel Fred Hughes, the VMO-6 commanding officer. At that time, I had three months remaining on my Far East tour.

Chapter 27: Transfer to Okinawa

Tachikawa Air Force Base - Japan

With my transfer orders in hand, I drove my old Chevrolet to the Tachikawa Air Force Base (AFB), located west of Tokyo. At the Air Freight and Passenger Office, I inquired about flights to Okinawa. The Air Force operated several Troop Carrier transport airplanes at Tachikawa, including very large C-124 Globemasters. When I asked about a change of station ride to Okinawa, they read my transfer orders, and agreed to take me on one of their aircraft training flights to Okinawa. They wanted to know if I would have any household items that I needed to take with me. Apparently, they were used to moving Air Force and Army families, and their belongings. I explained that all I wanted to take was my flight clothing and uniforms and, with tongue in cheek, my old Chevrolet. I was astonished and delighted when they agreed to take my automobile. Otherwise, I planned to abandon it, parked in the Air Freight and Passenger Office parking lot with its ignition keys intact.

The flight to Okinawa on 10 February 1960 was uneventful, except on that flight, I learned why the Air Force referred to the C-124 as "Old Shakey." My Chevrolet looked like a small toy in that Globemaster's cavernous cabin. After landing, I thanked to C-124 crew for my ride to Kadena; now an expansive air field with twin long runways. Kadena had become a major aerial port, serving all of our Armed Services. It was a far cry from the single, muddy Kadena runway, where I first landed my F6F Hellcat there on 9 April 1945.

Welcome to Okinawa

Lieutenant Colonel Fred Hughes, the Commanding Officer of Marine Observation Squadron Six (VMO-6), met me at the Kadena Air Force Base (AFB) terminal. First, he congratulated me on my selection for promotion. He then expressed surprised that I brought my Chevrolet with me. From Kadena, he rode with me to Camp Kawae, where VMO-6 was based. He told me that I would be his Squadron Executive Officer; replacing Major Frank Hubka who had just been transferred home. In addition to its OY-1 Sentinel spotter aircraft, VMO-6 operated HOK Helicopters. The Kaman HOK was designed and built as a synchropter. As mentioned in an early chapter, each of its two overhead rotor blades was mounted high, on separate overhead pylons, which tilted slightly outward. The two main rotor blades were synchronized so that one rotor blade would pass the other blade without intersecting (hitting) it.

Bob Warren flying Kaman HOK helicopter (1960)

I arrived at Okinawa on 15 February 1960 and departed for home on 15 May. During the three months I was stationed at Okinawa, I flew the HOK thirty- five hours on twenty-eight flights. I was never really comfortable, when flying the HOK. Its constant, severe vibration seemed to be a step backward, after flying the smoother, and more easily maintained Bell and Sikorsky helicopters. I felt it had a basic design flaw that made the helicopter dangerous, which had likely contributed to several fatal HOK crashes. A control rod failure could cause one of the blades to violently whip up and down, causing one blade to hit the other. After transfer from Okinawa, I flew the HOK as little as possible. I was relieved when all HOK helicopters had been stricken from the Navy and Marine Aviation aircraft inventories, and had been replaced by a more reliable helicopter.

WW II Okinawa Reminiscing

On weekends, I spent many hours driving my Chevrolet the full 60 mile length of Okinawa. One of the first places I visited was the old Yontan Airfield; now abandoned. That was where my close friend, Lieutenant Chuck Temple, had crashed, when taking off behind me, at night. His F6F Hellcat hit a bomb hole in the Yontan runway that somehow, I had missed. And, I recalled the heroism of our flight surgeon, Lieutenant Commander "Doc" Kelly, who lay down and shielded Chuck from the machine gun rounds 'cooking off' from his burning, crashed Hellcat. I also recalled the evening when four Japanese fighter planes flew low over Yontan Airfield, and one of our squadron pilots, Captain Jim Etheridge, shot one of those fighters down, right after take-off, and while his Hellcat's wheels were still retracting.

One weekend I drove to the northern end of Okinawa, to a very nice Armed Forces recreation area; complete with a mess hall, showers and sleeping tents. I thought about Lieutenant "Rocky"

Steele, another of our night fighter squadron pilots, who had been shot down in daylight by a flight of Marine Corsairs in that same area. And, I remembered Captain 'Gus' Arndt, who alone on a night heckler mission, flew north from Okinawa toward the Japanese Naval Base at Amami Oshima, and never returned.

At one point, I stopped to look at one of many Okinawan tombs that held the remains of Okinawan family members. I remembered our first night at Kadena, when our pilots tried to sleep on the tomb's front porch, four per porch, while tracer ammunition constantly streaked overhead. I recalled reading the name, Lieutenant Bruce Bonner, on his temporary grave site. Bruce was one of our squadron pilots, who was killed in a crash near Kadena Airfield. And, I wondered whatever happened to Lieutenant Chuck Engman, another of our pilots. He was evacuated to a hospital on Guam, soon after he had been shot down twice on the same day; once during daylight, and the second time, at night.

Return Home

A month prior to my scheduled return to the United States, I received an advance copy of my orders; specifically transferring me to Marine Corps Schools at Quantico, Virginia. The evening before I departed, I attended my going away party. I was presented with a small, carved wooden statue of a Honey Bucket Man, complete with a shoulder pole, and a Honey Bucket suspended from each end of the pole. The statue had a small plaque, on which was engraved my name, and the following statement: "Capable of Carrying Any Load, Anyplace, Anytime." The Honey Buckets are used throughout Asia to carry "night soil." The next day, I boarded a TWA Airliner, and departed Okinawa. I wondered if I would ever be there again. A few years later I was there; passing through Kadena Airfield, on my way to South Vietnam.

Millie, Bill, Jeanne and our friends, Art and Audrey Rawlings met me at the Los Angeles International Airport (LAX). We had a joyous reunion for a few days, before we packed our belongings, and rented our Santa Ana house, again to the reliable Hurds. After our household effects were packed, and driven away in a commercial moving van, we started our driving trip East; with stops to again enjoy visiting Carl and Martha Davis, and Roy and Annie Forrester in Dillon, Montana.

After leaving Dillon, we drove to Great Falls, Montana, where we stopped at a roadside restaurant for lunch, just before a violent thunderstorm hit the Great Falls vicinity. We chose seats well away from the large restaurant glass-front window. When the storm wind broke the front glass window pane, glass shards were scattered several feet into the restaurant. When that window pane broke, Bill was eating watermelon. He froze, with a piece of melon on his fork, halfway to his mouth. After finishing lunch, we continued driving east. We stopped to pick up several golf ball size hailstones, scattered along the highway, behind the storm.

We proceeded driving across South Dakota, to Bloomington, Minnesota, where my brother Bill still lived. He related a conservation he just had with his neighbor, who was a doctor. The doctor had commented that it seemed Bill was home an inordinate amount of time each month. Bill quickly responded, "Doctor, we are only allowed to fly 60 hours per month, in the airlines. That equates to about two flights per month to Hawaii, Japan, Hong Kong, and back. And, unlike your medical profession, in the airlines we don't get paid for "practicing."

Leaving Minnesota, we drove around the south end of Lake Michigan, to our family's homes in southern Michigan; where we spent a couple of weeks visiting our parents, and other relatives. We left our two children, Bill and Jeanne with Millie's parents, Rudy and Mildred Weber, and with their Uncle Walt and Aunt Marnie

Weber, on their nearby farm. Walt and Marnie had two girls, Patricia "Tish" and Cindy. Those four children always had great fun playing together. Bill also had a great time riding with his Uncle Walt, on the farm tractor, through the farm's apple and peach orchards. Millie and I drove, by ourselves, to our next duty station; the very familiar Marine Base at Quantico, Virginia.

Chapter 28: Quantico Education Center

Arrival Good News

Arriving at Quantico, I presented my orders for duty at the Marine Corps Schools Headquarters. I was told by the base adjutant that my promotion had been received, and as soon as I reported to the Educational Center for duty, I would officially be promoted to Lieutenant Colonel.

In preparation for my promotion, Millie and I went to the Marine Post Exchange, where I purchased my new Silver Oak Leaf rank insignia to be pinned on my uniform, as part of the promotion ceremony. Next, I checked in to the Education Center, and was welcomed by Major General Richard C. Mangrum, who, as a Lieutenant Colonel on October 30th, 1943, had pinned Navy Gold Wings on my new Marine Corps uniform, at NAS, Corpus Christi, Texas. General Mangrum warmly welcomed me, and told me that I would report to Colonel David C. Wolfe, as an instructor in the Education Center Aviation Branch.

General Mangrum then scheduled my promotion ceremony, to be held in his office, the following Monday. He said that Colonel Wolfe, and all of the Aviation Branch instructors, plus the heads of all the other Education Center Branches would attend. Further, Millie and our children were definitely invited. Bill and Jeanne had remained in Michigan, to spend the summer with their grandparents and at their Uncle Walt and Aunt Marnie's farm, nearby. At the office ceremony, my promotion document was read by General Mangrum's Aide. Then Millie pinned the new rank insignia on my uniform. It didn't seem possible, that five years earlier, a similar ceremony was held in the office of Major General Christian Schilt at MCAS, El Toro, California, when I was promoted to the rank of Major. How time had flown by!

Range of Aviation Branch Instruction

Colonel 'Dave' Wolfe introduced me to the other Aviation Branch instructors. He told me that before I could instruct in any class, it would be necessary to complete the two-week school for new instructors, and to have written lesson plans for the subject being taught, approved. He told me that instructors from the Aviation Branch would teach at several schools.

Those were, the Amphibious Warfare School (AWS) Senior Course, attended mostly by Lieutenant Colonels; The AWS Junior Course, attended by Captains; the Communication Officers School, where the students had ranks equivalent to the AWS, Junior Course, and where the instruction would be practically the same as instruction at the AWS Junior Course; and The Basic School (TBS), which was required for all new Marine Corps Second Lieutenants, who had completed the two six-week, summer Officer Candidate School (OCS) at Quantico, after earning their College degrees, and having been commissioned as Second Lieutenants.

Except for TBS, all other schools would start in September, and continue for nine months. TBS classes were of six-month duration; two per year. Other instruction during the summer months was devoted to Reserve Officers, who were on their two-week active-duty assignments, at Marine Corps Schools. I had no apprehension about 'being on the boards' in front of a class, as during the years I had spent as pilot in my VMP-354 at MCAS, Cherry Point, I had attended a six-week instructor's school, at the Naval Base in Norfolk, Virginia. I had also instructed in the Staff NCO Leadership School at MCAS, El Toro for ten months.

Colonel Wolfe told me to take a week to get settled in our newly assigned quarters at Quantico. I decided to visit Headquarters Marine Corps, to see Major General Keith McCutcheon, who was now the Director of Marine Aviation. General McCutcheon asked me what I was doing at Quantico. When I told him that I had been assigned to the Education Center, and was going to instruct in the Aviation Branch, he acted surprised, and said "I thought you were going to take command of HMX-1". He then called the Officers Assignment Branch and was told that Lieutenant Colonel Edwin Reed had taken command of HMX-1, because having been sent to Laos a second time, I could not have arrived at Quantico in time to relieve Lieutenant Colonel Vic Armstrong, who had received orders to the U.S. Embassy in the Far East, where he would be assigned as the Naval Attaché.

This would have meant the President of the United States would not have been assigned a new Marine helicopter pilot. Of course, the Marine Corps would never let that happen. That was all understandable to me, and I knew that Ed Reed would do an excellent job as the President's helicopter pilot. While Commanding HMX-1, he served very well, as the pilot for three U.S. Presidents. It was inconceivable to me, that the Director of Marine Aviation, would not know who had been assigned as the helicopter pilot for the President of the United States. Who did he think he was kidding?

Accordingly, I was very disappointed with General McCutcheon's obvious pretension. I respected him, and had served closely with him for years. I attended helicopter training with him at Lakehurst, and then served under his command at HMX-1 in Quantico, and a year later, I had served under him again in combat, after he had relieved Lieutenant Colonel George Herring as the Commanding Officer of HMR-161 in Korea. But, I think his reasoning was political. If anything bad, involving a Marine helicopter, happened to the President, he could then say that the Officers Assignment Branch had selected the President's new helicopter pilot. This was one of the few times during my entire career that I clearly recognized "politics." I guess it all paid off for General

McCutcheon, as he became the first Marine Aviator to wear the four stars as a Marine Corps General.[xvi]

Lustron Houses

When I arrived back to Quantico, Millie was unpacking our household effects in our newly assigned Lustron house, located in the very beautiful 800 Block of Base housing. Our house had woods on three sides, and had been built on a hilltop, just above one of the base eighteen-hole golf course fairways; indeed, a very lovely setting. The largest assembly of Lustron houses in one geographical location was at the Marine Corps Base in Quantico, Virginia, where sixty were assembled. I was assigned to one, as on-base living quarters.

Lustron houses were prefabricated, enameled steel houses, developed in the post-WWII era, in response to the shortage of homes for returning servicemen. They were invented by Carl Strandlund in 1947, and manufactured by the Lustron Corporation. With enameled panels inside and out, the Lustron houses were in sharp contrast to more traditional dwellings, made of wood and plaster. The outside panels came in four pastel colors. The inside wall panels were mostly gray. The house interiors were designed with an eye toward the modern, space age space-saving, and ease of cleaning. All models featured metal cabinetry, a service and storage area, and metal ceiling tiles. Ours had a living room, and three bedrooms. It was heated with an oil-burning furnace, which directed hot air into an enclosed space above the metal ceilings. The walls featured a one-inch blanket of fiberglass wool insulation.

We moved into our Lustron house in 1960, and we occupied it with our two children for the next four years.

The Basic School

The Education Center (ED Center) consisted of three separate campus buildings, conveniently located on the Quantico main base. The one exception was The Basic School, located in Quantico's live-firing Impact Area. Newly commissioned Marine Corps Second Lieutenants ordered to The Basic School were recent college graduates who had committed to The Platoon Leaders Program during their early college years. That program required attendance for two Officer Candidate summer sessions at Quantico. The first, between their Sophomore and Junior years, and the second, between their Junior and Senior years. Upon receiving their college diplomas, they also received their Marine Second Lieutenant Commissions. That was quickly followed by orders to attend TBS.

A few TBS students had graduated from one of the Service academies, such as the Naval Academy, or West Point. Others had graduated from Military colleges, like the Virginia Military Institute (VMI), or from The Citadel in South Carolina and, therefore were not in the Platoon Leaders Class (PLC). Regardless of where they received their college degrees, all newly commissioned Marine Second Lieutenants received orders to attend TBS at Quantico. TBS was held in a one-story building, with a one hundred fifty seat, theater-like classroom, and several smaller classrooms and offices. It was built near rifle ranges, and mortar and recoilless rifle firing impact areas, as these were important subjects taught at TBS. The familiarity and employment of these infantry weapons would prove vital to the soon-to-be Platoon Leaders.

The overall objective of TBS was to teach the new Second Lieutenants how to train their forty-seven Marine Platoon to fight smart, and to win! We informed each new TBS class that the Marine Aviation Close Air Support (CAS) foundation had started in the Banana Wars, fought in Central America, during the 1920s. CAS tactics, and new procedures, were developed much further during WWII, in the Pacific theater, as the Marines fought from island to island. Starting on the island of Guadalcanal, new procedures were continuously developed, to better control aviation fires, in close proximity to friendly troops. For instance, Air Liaison Parties, led by a Marine aviator, directed aircraft from radio equipped jeeps.

We explained the diverse aircraft capabilities designed to support them, and their Marines, including fighter, bomb carrying attack, transport/refueler, airborne electronic counter-measures aircraft, and now, helicopters. Our instruction included Marine Squadron, Air Group, and Air Wing organization. We instructed the TBS students on how to request air support and, if possible, to describe targets by radio, with reference to colored smoke. Students were shown pictures, and models of aircraft, and the main capabilities of each. Our instruction stressed that Marine Air Support "was always there for the asking." Further, that the only reason for having Marine Aviation at all, was to effectively support our ground Marines.

We cautioned them to accept any air support available, regardless of which of our armed services happened to be providing it. It sometimes worked the other way, too, as during the campaign in the Philippines, Marine aviation showcased its ability to integrate with the U.S. Sixth Army units, during fighting on Luzon; for which it received high praise from the Sixth Army Commander, Lieutenant General Walter Krueger, and for which the participating Marine Air Group was awarded the Presidential Unit Citation. Marine Air had provided security for the right flank of the U.S. Army 41st (Sunset) Division.

We always enjoyed teaching the Second Lieutenants at TBS, as they were all bright young officers; eager to learn how Marine Corps Aviation could support them. The TBS Commanding Officer was a full Colonel named Louis H. Wilson, Jr., who had been decorated with The Medal of Honor for heroism, when Marines recaptured the island of Guam, in WWII. The assignment to TBS as Commanding Officer was generally known as a "king maker," as almost always the TBS Commanding Officer would be selected for promotion to Brigadier General. Colonel Wilson was, and later he became a Four-Star General, and Commandant of the Marine Corps. While still commanding TBS, he told me that he was going to move my desk from the Ed Center Aviation Branch, to TBS. I guess that was his way of complimenting me; as he knew very well then, that he could not alter my instructor assignment to the Aviation Branch.

The AWS Junior Course

Lieutenant General Roy S. Geiger

The name "Geiger" was well known at Quantico. Years before, when a Major, Roy Geiger had organized and commanded the first Marine Corps aviation squadron at Quantico's dirt-runway, Brown Field. Over the years, he directed both air and ground Marine units and, was thus well known throughout all of the Armed Services, as an amphibious warfare expert. During the assault on Okinawa, Major General Geiger had been promoted to Lieutenant General, and assumed command of the U.S. 10th Army when its U.S. Army commander was killed. Named after this outstanding Marine Corps Officer, Geiger Hall was built to provide a permanent building for AWS Junior Course (JC) instruction. The distance from my Lustron quarters, to Geiger Hall, required a five minute drive, or a fifteen minute walk.

Attendance at JC was scheduled for nine months each year; from late September to June of the following year. Students ordered there were mostly Marine Captains, and a few First Lieutenants, who had been selected for promotion to Captain. Most had completed a combat tour in the Pacific, during WWII. It was a mid-level school, with courses designed to further the student's knowledge of how Infantry Companies and Aviation Squadrons were organized for combat operations, and how each was controlled by higher Marine Corps echelons (Battalions and Aircraft Groups); or at least how it was supposed to be done. Many lively discussions ensued, based on the student's actual combat experiences.

As instructors, we felt that the students who had served in combat had earned the right to be heard. We acknowledged that in combat, the best laid plans quite often deviate far from any "school solution" and, that the utilization of Marine Aviation, in unplanned and unconventional ways, was often necessary, in order to contribute to the overall objective, which was to win the Battle, and the War. For instance, during the Korean War, Marine Aviation received its daily missions, called "frag orders," from the Commanding General of the 5th Air Force. The main missions of Marine fixed-wing aviation squadrons in Korea, assigned by the 5th Air Force, were termed "rail cut" missions.

Accordingly, Marine F4U Corsairs and AD Skyraiders would attempt to cut the train tracks at both ends of North Korean train tunnels. If successful, they could trap a train, trying to hide inside of a tunnel. In Korea, a squadron of Corsairs was also flying from the USS *Badoeng Strait* (CVE-116), a small jeep aircraft carrier. Command relationships were complicated, in that some Marine Corps fixed-wing aircraft operating from Korean airfields, and some from U.S. Navy aircraft carriers, received their daily missions from the 5th Air Force. The main lesson is that Marine Aviation had to remain flexible, and prepared to do all manner of things; mainly to hit and destroy whatever targets they are assigned.

Further, in the 1st Marine Air Wing in Korea, the one Marine Observation Squadron (VMO-6), and later, the single Helicopter Transport Squadron (HMR-161), received their daily missions from the Commanding General of the 1st Marine Division, with little or no outside interference or competition. However, the 1st Marine Division, as one if it's several Divisions, was an integral unit of the U.S. Army 10th Corps (X-Corps). However, the responsibility of supporting its squadrons, by providing high octane aircraft fuel, aircraft engine and airframe spare parts, mandated engine and airframe maintenance checks, aircraft mechanics, maintenance officers, and trained helicopter pilot replacements, remained the responsibility of the 1st Marine Air Wing.

The main purpose of the AWS Junior Course was to present, at the company grade (Captain) level, better insight into the complications of Amphibious Warfare operations, and thus prepare those students for more responsibility. Hopefully, it would also assist in their promotions. The students also learned from their close associations with their classmates who had differing professional specialties. For instance, experienced artillery, tracked vehicles, infantrymen, communication, and aviation officers were immersed in the same classrooms for nine months. Accordingly, they learned a great deal from each other, and while there, gained respect for the accomplishments of each other. The students also developed personal and family friendships, which often lasted throughout their entire careers.

Teaching students from all of the Marine Corps schools was a real joy. The students arrived at class on time, and motivated by the possible life and death subjects being taught. The students attending any of the schools at Quantico appreciated the investment being made in their careers. In the four years that I instructed there, I never experienced a discipline issue.

The AWS Senior School

Thirty-five to forty students at a time, mostly Lieutenant Colonels, representing a cross section of the Marine Corps, both aviation and non-aviation officers, were ordered to Quantico for nine months, to attend the Senior School. At least one officer from each of the other U.S. Armed Services also attended. I recall one of my students was Lieutenant Colonel Sidney B. "Sid" Berry, U.S. Army; a West Point graduate. After graduating from Senior School, Sid attended the Army War College at Carlisle, Pennsylvania, and later, with the rank of Major General, he commanded a U.S. Army Infantry Division at Fort Benning, Georgia. Following very successful combat tours in Vietnam, he was promoted to the rank of Lieutenant General, and became the 50th Superintendent of West Point.

Another of my Senior School Officers was Lieutenant Colonel Robert H. Barrow. A superb Marine Officer, he rose in rank to become the 27th Commandant of the Marine Corps. Each year, the Marine Corps selected some of its brightest officers to attend the U.S. Navy War College, the Air Force Command and Staff College, and the U.S. Army Warfighting Center. Several officers from Allied Armed Forces also attended the Senior School, as students. Instructing in the Senior School required a different relationship between instructors and students; as Lieutenant Colonels were sometimes senior to the instructor.

This fact required a somewhat different teaching technique. Therefore, students were first called upon to take the instructors position on the stage, in front of their fellow students, and introduce themselves, and give a brief ten-minute account of some memorable military experience. They did not realize at that time, they were probably teaching each other; and probably some of their instructors, as well.

I always started my first Senior School class by stating that, except for the somewhat vague Marine Corps Assignment Officer policy in Washington, our assignment as instructors and students might well have been reversed. I expressed my belief that there were students in the class who knew more about some particular aviation subject than did I, except possibly for helicopter training, and use and control of helicopters during amphibious ship-to-shore operations. Planning for helicopter use, in amphibious landing instruction, often required coordination from an experienced infantry officer.

One was Lieutenant Colonel Samuel "Sam" Jaskilka who, as a Captain, had been decorated with the Silver Star medal for leading his Marine infantry company over the seawall during the Inchon landings in Korea. Sometimes he would complete his part of the planning, and I would write the helicopter portion at his desk, in another section of the Ed Center. It was always enjoyable (really, fun!) to work with Sam.[xvii]

Within a few weeks after a new Senior School started, the Allied students were sent on an escorted week-long field trip to Washington, D.C. and New York City, visiting the Pentagon, and Headquarters, U.S. Marine Corps, in Washington, and touring the United Nations building in NYC. While Allied students were away, students from the AWS Senior Course, AWS Junior Course, and the Communications Officers School, assembled daily in Ellis Hall, where they received classified briefings, presented by the Commandant of the Marine Corps, and his principal Deputies from Washington.

The main thrust of Senior School was to expose students to intricacies of Navy/Marine Corps relationships during amphibious landings on hostile shores; and included, for instance, an explanation of the responsibilities of the Amphibious Task Force Commander (Navy) and the Landing Force Commander (Marine Corps), and the conditions and achievements that must be met, prior to passing control of aviation assets from the Amphibious Task Force, to the Landing Force. The Navy/Marine Corps relationship would now include control of helicopters with Landing Force troops aboard, flying off aircraft carriers. Helicopter operations and control, was the main subject I taught at the Senior School.

In 1948, at the Marine Corps Schools, the first amphibious helicopter doctrine manual was published. It was titled Phib-31. This manual remained the standard Marine publication that described the tactical use of helicopters. Phib-31 described the "vertical envelopment," concept that was proven successful during the Korean War. The concept was expanded to include selection of helicopter approach and retirement routes (named after States), to and from the Landing Zones and ships at sea, and the selection, and naming of control points (named after Cities) along those routes (and alternate routes as well).

I challenged the students to devise a way that the ship, launching the low flying helicopters, could know the location of helicopters flying to the Landing Zones. Further, how the helicopters could be protected from hostile fire when approaching and retiring from the landing zones. These were tactics not yet fully developed.

Lessons taught at the various schools were repetitive. Except for updates, they changed little, from year to year. World events could cause some updating of lesson plans, but only if the U.S. Armed Forces were substantially affected.

Before graduation each year, the students had to plan for an amphibious attack on a hostile force. It was termed a Command Post Exercise, and involved all but TBS students. The fictitious "hostile force" selected, was based at Camp Lejeune, North Carolina. For the exercise, the students were loaded aboard Landing Ship Tanks (LSTs) at Quantico's Potomac River dock. After casting off, the LSTs sailed down the Potomac River, to where it emptied into the Chesapeake Bay. Approaching Norfolk, Virginia the ships turned, and sailed into the Atlantic Ocean, then proceeded along the Atlantic Coast, seaward from Cape Hatteras, to Camp Lejeune.

There, the students made a ship-to-shore landing, over the beaches, by both drop-bow landing craft and by helicopter.

To add more realism to the Command Post Exercise, all the radio communication nets (both aboard ship, and ashore) were manned by students attending the Communication Officers School. I did not ride the LSTs to Camp Lejeune, as each year I was sent to MCAS, Cherry Point to coordinate the planned air transport of students from the nearby MCAS, New River airfield, back to Quantico.

I would stop at the headquarters of the 2nd Marine Aircraft Wing, to pay my respects to the Commanding General; but mainly to let my presence be known, and to obtain permission to state the requirements for transporting the students back Quantico, to the Cherry Point based Marine Transport Squadron (VMGR). The aircraft used were Lockheed (Hercules) KC-130s from the VMGR Squadron at Cherry Point. It was a simple task for me to prepare manifests for each aircraft, which would determine how many aircraft were needed; and then to ensure the aircraft were loaded with the correctly manifested passengers. Many students transported back to Quantico by air, expressed their appreciation to me for arranging their short return ride.

Landing on the short runway at Quantico required the KC-130s to reverse propeller pitch upon touchdown; leading to some brief passenger anxiety, followed by relief after stopping, when the student passengers recognized that the aircraft was still under full control. Following the return to Quantico, the students' last lesson before graduation was a detailed critique of the Command Post Exercise; concentrating on the good and bad lessons learned. Graduation programs were held at each school. With that, students graduating from all three schools departed Quantico, for their next duty stations.

Chapter 29: Joy of Quantico Duty

Crossroads of the Marine Corps

The Marine Corps Base at Quantico is known as the "Crossroads of the Marine Corps". It is now best known as an Officer's training facility. Quantico was formerly a combat training facility. However, during WWII, ground combat training was moved to the Marine infantry divisions, located at Camp Lejeune and Camp Pendleton. Marine Aviation combat training moved to the Marine Corps Air Stations at Cherry Point, North Carolina and El Toro, California. Quantico was left with two main missions. The first was to train college students to become Marine Officers; and to continue to educate those Officers, throughout their careers, in war fighting, leadership, and other skills at advanced level schools. The second mission is to provide total helicopter support from the Quantico Air Station, for the President of the United States.

Quantico's seventy-five-thousand-acre Impact Area now houses a permanent school for newly commissioned Marine Corps officers. Rifle and pistol ranges are still located in the Impact Area. The FBI Academy, and its technical facilities, and live firing ranges, have also moved to the Impact Area.

A Unique Little Town

"Quantico" is said to mean "by the long stream," in a Native American language. In 1917, the government purchased land that, except for its riverfront, completely surrounded the town of Quantico. Its purpose was to provide a WWI training camp for the Marine Corps. Now known as a Marine Corps base, the land purchased, covered fifty-nine thousand acres. The town of Quantico, formerly called Evansport, covers slightly over forty acres of land area. The town is completely surrounded, by the Potomac

River to the east, and the Quantico Creek to the north, and the Marine Corps Base on the other sides.

The town of Quantico has only one main street. Potomac Avenue starts at the Marine Base main gate, immediately crosses the Richmond, Fredericksburg and Potomac Railroad (RF&P) track, and ends, straight ahead, at the Potomac River dock; a distance of only about seven to eight city blocks. All business establishments in Quantico are located on Potomac Avenue. Quantico has only about six hundred residents, most of whom are business owners and employees. The main businesses on Potomac Avenue when I was stationed there were a bank, a Masonic Temple, several thriving uniform sales stores, several restaurants, and dry cleaning establishments. Quantico residents leaving the town of Quantico, and returning home, had to pass through the Base main gate.

The main thoroughfare through the Marine base is Barnett Avenue. It parallels the RF&P railroad tracks, past the Marine Post Exchange, the Base Headquarters, a service station, the Base Commissary, and the Base power plant.[xviii] It then turns left, and crosses over the RF&P railroad track. It continues past the Quantico Air Station, while paralleling the railroad from the opposite side; crossing a low swampy area called Chompawansic Creek, then passing Larson Gymnasium, the Officer Candidate School, the old Brown Airfield, ending at the Base south border fence.

Dependent Schools

To provide education for the dependent children of Marines living on the base, and in the town at Quantico, two on-base schools were built, very close each other. Our son Bill started Quantico High School (QHS) as a freshman. His younger sister, Jeanne, started the 5th grade at the John H. Russell Elementary School. She later went to Quantico High School in the 8th grade; the same year Bill was a senior. Both became very active in school activities, and Bill graduated in 1964.

Both schools had recently been built, and were financed by the Federal Department of Education. The teachers at both schools were civilian Federal government employees. There was always close interaction between the Marines and the school teachers, because the Parent Teacher Association (PTA) and School Board members were Marines; appointed by the Commanding General, Marine Corps Schools.

Dependent School Activities

Daughter, Jeanne Warren

Starting In the 5th grade at Quantico, Jeanne also started swimming instruction. She excelled at swimming, and her team used one of the outdoor base pools to practice, and to hold competitive swim meets. She usually placed high, and sometimes, she even won. Jeanne was a fearless competitor; probably because she had to compete with her older brother, Bill. When she was a high school freshman, at Quantico High School, she also was invited to participate in varsity level relay races, because she could run so fast. She finally stopped swimming, because someone told her that her shoulder muscles were getting too big.

Cotillion dances were scheduled and held in Harry Lee Hall, one of the on-base all-purpose buildings. The cotillion dances for the grade school children were meant to teach them all how to dance. The young boys were also taught how to properly ask a girl to dance, and how to hold and lead her, as his dancing partner. It was amusing to watch as the little girls learned more quickly about dancing than did the boys. So the girls would maneuver their dancing partners (the boys) to positions where the girls could then have running conversations with each other. Most of the boys appeared to be very uncomfortable, and could not wait until the music stopped, and they could escort, as taught, their dance partner back to her seat and, as taught, thank her for the dance. Obviously, they couldn't wait to get rid of their dance partners. Between dances, most of the boys would disappear into the restroom, where they tried to hide, and not have to participate in the next dance. Their parents would have to flush the boys out of the restroom.

Millie would occasionally schedule a slumber party at our house for Jeanne and several of her little neighborhood girl friends. She usually did this when I was away from Quantico. The little girls would all bring blankets and pillows (and usually a small stuffed animal). They would sleep on Jeanne's bedroom floor in a circle, with their feet toward the middle. In reality, none of them slept much. Bill would always find a way to be gone during the nights of the slumber parties; usually staying at some friend's on-base house; often his football team buddy, Larry Walt.

Son, Bill Warren

Quantico High School Football Team

Mr. Gene Leonard was the High School football team coach all four years that our son Bill attended Quantico High School. Mr. Bill Marshall was the basketball team coach, and Mr. Barry Hall, the baseball team coach. The school principal was Mr. Burton.

QHS had a football field adjacent to the school building, which served very well as a practice field, but only had a few bleacher seats; so the High School football games were played at Butler Stadium. Several years before, a Marine Major General, named Smedley Butler, had supervised the building of a large on-base football stadium that the QHS Football team could also use for its home games. The Marines at Quantico also fielded a football team that played their home games in Butler Stadium; usually against other Armed Service football teams, and some college teams. When the games were scheduled on the same weekend day, the QHS football team kicked off at Noon; and the Marine team, later in the day.

Most of the Marine team players were Marine Second Lieutenants who were attending TBS as students. Some of those TBS students, who played football at the college from which they had graduated, would come to QHS and help Gene Leonard with coaching football. One was Francis E. "Ed" Huering,[xix] who had played for the University of Maryland in the Orange Bowl. He had a long scar on his arm, from an injury he had received on the Orange Bowl opening kickoff. He said after that, in the game, "things got worse". His admonishments to team player "goofs" were more severe, using more colorful language than Coach Leonard would use. After all, Coach Leonard was still a High School teacher.

Bill played on the High School football team his freshman year. At the end of that season, the team was entertained at a roller skating party which certainly was enjoyed and appreciated. But, I felt it did not give appropriate recognition or reward for all of the QHS football team seasonal efforts. So, working with the School Board and the football coaches, we planned a more appropriate Football Banquet, to be held at the end of each football season in Waller Hall, the base Officer's Club.

In addition to the team members, their parents and their coaches, each banquet was attended by several General Officers including Lieutenant General Edward W. Snedeker, Major General Lewis W. "Lew" Walt, and the Command Chief of Staff, Colonel Donn J. Robertson. The guest speaker was always a former college football star player who was selected from the students at TBS, and invited to speak. Three of the outstanding football team players were honored, and presented trophies. Bill was presented the Outstanding Lineman Award Trophy, three years in a row.

Bill also played some High School basketball. But, because opponent players were often viewed by him as football opponents, he usually "fouled out" early in each game. However, I think the varsity basketball coach, Bill Marshall, still viewed Bill as a nice kid. Bill also played varsity baseball at QHS. He was aggressive and strong; he hit for a decent average, and he could throw hard. But, when he threw hard, we never knew where the ball was going. Bill usually played 1st Base on the QHS baseball team, which held practice, and played games, at the on-base Freeney Baseball Field.

The football and baseball home games were usually played on Saturdays. If rainy weather caused either the Butler Stadium or Freeney Field playing surfaces to be wet, I would fly a helicopter, hover low over the playing surface and blow away the accumulated water puddles. I never received any objection for my playing field "drying" efforts.

Quantico High School Football Team, 1961 (Bill Warren #53)

The U.S. Air Force Aero Club

The original location of the U.S. Air Force Aero Club was at Bolling Field; located across the Potomac River from the Washington National Airport. Club membership included prominent U.S. Air Force and Army Air Corps officers such as Senator Barry Goldwater, and Chief of Staff of the U.S. Air Force, General Curtis E. LeMay. The club needed to find a new location, because of the imminent closing of Bolling Field, and the ever increasing Airline and General Aviation air traffic, in and around Washington National Airport. MCAS, Quantico, located thirty miles south of Washington, was chosen to be the new temporary location of the Air Force Aero Club. When the club moved to Quantico, I joined it immediately.

I already had my Commercial Pilot's License (No. 122042), which I had obtained at Grand Rapids, Michigan after WWII, when I was considering flying with Northwest Airlines. Ratings listed on my Commercial Pilot's License included; Single and Multi Engine Land – Instrument - Instructor, Fixed Wing and Helicopter. The Aero Club owned several small, civilian airplanes. The one I chose to fly was the Piper Tri-Pacer model, which had a tricycle landing gear. It had side-by-side dual-control pilot cockpits, and seating behind the cockpit for 2-3 passengers. Its engine could be started from inside the cockpit, by the pilot, using an electric starter. I usually flew at the Aero Club, before normal working hours on weekdays; leaving weekend flying for the Aero Club members who had to drive to Quantico from the Washington, D.C. area.

Several days each week, I would awaken Bill early, and give him basic flying lessons. This also provided more father/son time together. I felt that this was important, because of my long deployments, when Bill did not have his father around. When flying together, we usually crossed the Potomac River, and flew to a small airstrip near Potomac Heights, Maryland. There was no air traffic control tower there, and we always seemed to have the airstrip to ourselves. It was there I taught Bill takeoffs and landings. Following one of those Instructional flights, I told Bill to take us home, by flying along the Maryland river shore, and then crossing the river to Quantico. Apparently, he was concentrating more on properly flying the airplane, than on navigating. Bill finally realized that things were not right, when he saw the Potomac River make a sharp U-turn to the northeast, and the bridge crossing the river at Dahlgren, Virginia came into view. It reminded me of when my instructor, years before at Austin Lake, told me to fly us home, and I had no idea where we were, in relation to Austin Lake. I never pressured Bill to learn to fly, as I knew that his eyesight would not permit him to get a pilot's license.

One year, on Jeanne's Birthday, and with their parents' permission, I crowded five little girls into the Aero Club Piper Tri-Pacer, strapped them in, and took them on an airplane ride over Quantico. When Bill and Jeanne were in school, Millie and I would often fly to Fredericksburg, to have breakfast at the airport there; then fly back to Quantico. One morning I called our neighbor, Martha Shifflett to go with us to Fredericksburg, and have breakfast. Her husband, Ed Shifflett was away from Quantico, and their daughter, Missy (Evelyn), was in school. Martha accepted, and when I had driven downhill to the main on-base street, she wondered why I didn't turn right, drive off the base to Highway One, and then about twenty-five miles south to Fredericksburg. Instead, I turned left, and proceeded through the base to the airport, where we boarded a Aero Club Piper Tri-Pacer and flew to Fredericksburg for breakfast. A surprised Martha Schifflett could only mutter, referring to me in her Texas drawl, "that fool will do any-thing."

Lieutenant General Edward Snedeker was the Commanding General, Marine Corps Schools at Quantico. He commanded everything there. Like the majority of Marine Generals, he was a highly decorated infantry officer. His Aide was a Marine Corps pilot, and often they went flying together from MCAS, Quantico in a T-28 training airplane. The General/Aide relationship was almost like my association with Lieutenant General Schilt, when I was his Aide, and we often flew together.

However, there was a huge difference. General Schilt was a Naval Aviator, and General Snedeker was not. Therefore, General Snedeker was not allowed to fly solo in any military airplane. So, wanting to fly solo, he joined the Aero Club. So did his Marine Officer Naval Aviator Aide. But his Aide could not certify that General Snedeker was "safe for solo" in an Aero Club (civilian) aircraft, because the Aide didn't have a commercial pilot's license with an Instructor Rating. I did; and it was likely just a matter of time, until this would be known. Then I would be placed "on the spot," by being asked to certify General Snedeker "safe for solo," when I had never flown with him. To avoid all of this, I quietly dropped my membership in the Aero Club; meaning, of course, that I could no longer fly in any of the Club's airplanes. I was relieved that I had potentially "dodged a bullet."

QHS Senior Nick Fritz

Between his Sophomore and Junior years at QHS, Bill asked his mother if it would be alright if "Nick" moved in with us. Millie immediately responded with, "Nick who?" Nick Fritz was the son of a Marine Sergeant Major who had just received transfer orders from NAS Corpus Christi, Texas, to MCAS Cherry Point, North Carolina. His older son, Nick, needed a few more high school credits to graduate from high school. The QHS football coach, Gene Leonard, asked the members of the team if any of their families would consider having Nick live with them, so he could attend and graduate from QHS. That's why Bill asked his Mom if Nick could stay with us. Of course, Gene Leonard wanted to have Nick Fritz on his football team.

We talked to Nick, Bill, and Jeanne, about the possibility of Nick moving into our house. We explained to Nick that he would have to adhere to the same house rules that applied to Bill and Jeanne. Nick readily agreed with all that we proposed. We then discussed the situation with Nick's parents; to ascertain if they agreed with Nick moving in with our family, and to talk about how it might affect Nick's younger brother, Freddie, to be living away from his big brother, for the first time. They agreed to let Nick live with us; and we told them that if Nick moved in with us, it would be for his entire Senior high school year, and he would be treated as a member of our family, and therefore would pay nothing for his food, lodging or miscellaneous expenses.

When we were assured by the High School principal that Nick could continue as a QHS student, Nick moved into Bill's room in our Lustron house. Nick proved to be a wonderful asset to our family. He was always protective of Jeanne. He and Bill played on the QHS football team. They returned home after daily practice, in an old Chevrolet sedan that I had purchased as a "second" car. They were always hot when practice was over, so they drove home with the car windows down. Millie and I could never convince them to roll the car windows up, before leaving the car. So, the car seats were often wet, due to rain beating through the open car windows. After football practices, both Bill and Nick were always hungry, so they would quiz Jeanne, who was a finicky eater, who often tried to cover the food that she didn't eat with a paper napkin. Like two hungry wolves, they would ask, "Jeanne, are you finished yet?"

After High School graduation, Nick attended North Texas State University, in Denton, Texas. Based on the football films that had been taken at QHS, Nick was offered a football scholarship. He later joined the Marine Corps, and then transferred the U.S. Army, and successfully completed the Army helicopter training programs at Mineral Wells, Texas, and Fort Rucker, Alabama. Nick was later wounded in South Vietnam, while flying an Army Light Observation Helicopter.

Our Family Visits to Quantico

Several times during our four-year tour at Quantico, we enjoyed visits from our families; first from my parents, from their farm home in Coloma, Michigan. They were with us for Thanksgiving Day. Millie, for the first time, prepared dinner for my parents. All went well, until she tried to put whipped cream on the pumpkin pie dessert. She was using one of the new, aerosol whipped cream cans, and inadvertently, she "shot" my mother with whipped cream. Although Millie was mortified, all the rest of, including my mother, were very amused. The dinner was delicious; including the aerosol-charged whipped cream on the pumpkin pie.

Another visit was from Millie's family, when her older brother Walt, and his wife Marnie, arrived with Patricia "Tish" and Cindy, their two teenage daughters. Walt and Marnie were traveling with their close friends, Jim and Marian Case, and their teenage daughter Linda. The adult visitors all stayed on the base at Harry Lee Hall. Somehow, all the teenage girls managed to "fit" in Jeanne's bedroom. Bill arranged "dates" for all the visiting teenage girls. When Bill and the girls left the house, a thick layer of hairspray had settled on all of the bedroom surfaces. They all went to the bowling alley, in a side section of the base Post Exchange. Then, they migrated to the Teen Club, which was located behind the Post Exchange.

Other family members who visited us at Quantico included my sister, Helen McKean, and her husband, Eugene "Gene," and their daughter, Nancy. At times, I would fly from Quantico to Norfolk to take fuel samples from the President's helicopters, for testing. Once, while Nancy was engaged to Dean Reger, a crew member on the Navy Amphibious Forces Command Ship at Little Creek, Virginia, he was granted a short leave, and I brought him with me, on my helicopter return flight to Quantico.

The Teen Club

One of the most popular buildings at Quantico was the wonderful Teen Club. It was a special gathering place for teenagers. To be permitted admission, a teenager had to be a student, or a teen who was with a QHS student. It was open on weekends, and on Fridays, following varsity games or contests. The Teen Club operated under the watchful eye of 'Mom' Larson who was able to function as the chaperone for a very noisy bunch of kids. "Mom' Larson knew every one of the teens who attended. She offered advice for those who requested or needed it. Sometimes she became sort of a surrogate mother for troubled teens. She insisted on proper language, acceptable dress and decent decorum. She was the most important "teen" there, and was their special friend and confident. All the kids respected and valued her friendly guidance, and sometimes, mild discipline.

The Teen Club rules were rather informal, but were well known, and almost always closely followed. The kids all understood that the Teen Club could be closed at any time by the governing High School Board, and if that happened, they would lose their popular on-base gathering facility. Of course, our teens were permitted to bring teenage visitors to their parent's home. It was open on weekends, or "as needed" to thus accommodate any special event.

Major General Lewis Walt, USMC

I would be remiss if I did not include the positive influence General Walt had on the school sports at Quantico. He commanded the Marine Corps Development Center (MCDC) at Quantico; the organization that studied and developed new weapons, tactics for their use, and war fighting strategies. This did not include Marine Corps aircraft, or other aviation assets; as those, including Marine pilot flight and aircraft mechanic training, and the provision of aviation supplies, were the purview of the U.S. Navy's Bureau of Aeronautics (BUAER).

However, the aviation support of ground troops was always well known at BUAER, as several Marine Aviators served on General Walt's Development staff. They coordinated their work through the office of the Director of Marine Aviation, at Marine Corps Headquarters in Washington, D.C. General Walt had a brilliant war fighting record, and I will address some of that in a later chapter of this book when I write about serving on his staff in South Vietnam.

I became acquainted with General Walt at Quantico, when his son, Larry Walt, quarterbacked the QHS football team. General Walt recognized my efforts in organizing the annual post-season football banquets. When I wrote an article, titled *Maintain the Balance,* which was published in the Marine Corps Gazette, it received laudatory comments from General Walt. When I reported to him that the QHS coaches did not receive pay raises commensurate with pay raises for other teachers, he promptly stated that he would discuss the matter with the Commandant of Marine Corps Schools, Lieutenant General Snedeker. In the Naval Service, "request mast" is the principal means for a Marine to formally seek assistance from, or communicate a grievance to his or her commander. I don't know exactly what procedure on behalf of the coaches, General Walt used, but the coaches immediately received their pay raises.

I came to realize that my assignment as an instructor at Quantico, rather than an assignment as the President's helicopter pilot, was a blessing in disguise for me. I was able to spend most of my time with my family, in a fun, but disciplined, Marine Corps base environment. Additionally, I became associated with many Marines who I felt markedly enhanced my career. I was very proud to see one of my students (Robert H. Barrow), years later, appointed Commandant of the Marine Corps. And General Walt always befriended my family and me at Quantico. Later when I was assigned to his III MAF Staff in Vietnam, he was a definite career benefactor, both to me, and to our son Bill, who upon graduating from the Virginia Military Institute (VMI), was commissioned a Marine Second Lieutenant, completed TBS at Quantico, and served in Vietnam as a Marine Infantry Platoon leader.

I was concerned about being qualified for my next promotion to Colonel. I had been at Quantico, and had done nothing but teach school during the four years since being promoted to Lieutenant Colonel, upon my arrival at Quantico in 1960. I felt that career-wise, I really needed to be assigned to a Marine Air Group; so I requested, and received orders to the 2nd Marine Aircraft Wing at MCAS, Cherry Point, North Carolina.

End of Quantico Duty

The last months at Quantico were very busy; with Bill graduating from High School. He had applied for admission at VMI and was accepted. He was to report to VMI at Lexington, Virginia. Jeanne was anxious about where she would be attending school the next year. I really expected to be sent to MCAS, New River, North Carolina and hopefully, to take command of MAG-26, the helicopter air group based at New River, North Carolina. While I was at Cherry

Point, arranging air transportation for return of the graduating Ed Center students to Quantico, I called on the Air Wing Chief Of Staff, Colonel Andrew "Andy" Smith to discuss my assignment, when I would report for duty later that summer. Years before, Lieutenant Colonel Andy Smith had assigned me to VMP-354 at Cherry Point; a squadron that had F7F, twin-engine Tigercats. He was always a very amiable and intelligent.

But now, he very firmly told me that I would not be assigned to the MCAS, New River-based MAG-26, because another officer had been personally selected for that assignment, by the 2nd MAW Commanding General. That was somewhat puzzling, as the current MAG-26 Commander Officer, Colonel Frank C. Lang, later told me that everyone knew that I was the best qualified to relieve him, as the MAG-26 commanding officer. Everyone, I guess, except the 2nd MAW Commanding General, who was obviously trying to salvage the career of an officer who had just wrecked a fixed-wing airplane at Cherry Point.

So, the officer was sent to helicopter training, and then on to command an air group with several squadrons; no matter that he had very little helicopter experience. By transferring him to MAG-26, he would then be away from the Marine fixed-wing community, and therefore, would escape any close scrutiny. By contrast, I had flown helicopters for over ten years, as described in earlier chapters of this book. I also learned that this officer's wife, and the 2nd MAW Commanding General's wife were very close friends, and were devout members of the same church.

Colonel Smith told me that I could select assignment to any air group in the 2nd MAW except the helicopter group, MAG-26. I returned to Quantico exasperated and angry. But, realizing that I would enter the Colonel's promotion zone in about a year, I thought I'd best get over it. I decided to request duty at MCAS, Beaufort, South Carolina, where two jet-equipped air groups were based.

They were MAG-31 and MAG-32. Each of those air groups had F8U (Crusader) fighter jet squadrons, and A4 (Skyhawk) jet attack squadrons. That meant that I would have to transition back to flying fixed-wing airplanes; this time to jets.

I selected MAG-31, as its Commanding Officer, Colonel Edmund P. "Ed" Hartsock was well known as an outstanding Marine pilot, and an excellent and fair leader. Also, Lieutenant Colonel Donald "Don" Fisher was being transferred from the Quantico Ed Center, Logistics Branch, to MAG-31. Don was a skilled fighter pilot, who had been a member of the famous "Black Sheep" Squadron, in the South Pacific. I knew that I could learn a lot by serving next to Don Fisher. Don and I would both be in the zone to be considered for promotion to Colonel, during the next year. He was senior to me, so I assumed he would become Colonel Ed Hartsock's MAG-31 Executive Officer. I pondered where that would leave me. I knew that I would have to go through some kind of a jet transition course, before I could effectively take over the number three job on the MAG-31 staff, which was the Operations Officer (S-3).

Before the end of our time at Quantico, we took leave, and drove to Michigan to visit our families. We knew that this might be the last time, for a long time, that we would all get together as an immediate family. That proved to be sadly true. After returning to Quantico, we had our household items packed for shipment to Beaufort. On the way to Beaufort, we dropped Bill off at VMI, where he was to begin classes shortly. It was a gray, rainy, and sad day, when we left our son at VMI. But we knew that within a few days, thing would sharply change at VMI, when the parade ground, now empty, except for the imposing statue of the former VMI Professor and Civil War General Stonewall Jackson, would be filled with cadet close order drill activity. The Civil War vintage buildings would soon be filled with "Rats," and upper classmen, who harassed the new uniformed VMI Rats unmercifully.

After leaving Bill at VMI, Jeanne was very quiet. She was, no doubt, realized that she had just lost her close association with her older brother. As a teenager, she was somewhat apprehensive about what was ahead for her at Beaufort High School.

Chapter 30: MCAS, Beaufort to Spain

Brief History of MCAS, Beaufort

The Beaufort Air Station nicknamed, "Fighter Town," holds a significant place in the history of South Carolina. The Air Station site was formerly the location of several plantations. In the summer of 1941, the Civil Aeronautics Authority proposed to establish an airport at the present Air Station site. In August 1942, five thousand eight hundred acres of land was purchased for the construction of a Naval Auxiliary Air Station. Construction began in December 1942, and was completed in August 1943. The airfield was commissioned NAS, Beaufort on 15 June 1943. During WWII, the Naval Air Station supported advanced training, and operations of anti-submarine patrol squadrons, over the southeastern seaboard of the United States. Deactivated in 1946, it was closed, until reactivated ten years later as a Marine Corps Auxiliary Airfield.

While assigned as Lieutenant General Schilt's Aide, I attended that reactivation ceremony, and I recall the admonishment given to the citizens of Beaufort, by their Congressman, L. Mendel Rivers, when he said "I know y'all are happy that this Air Station is opening again. But, when the Marines bring in their noisy jets, and you want to complain about the noise, call your Senator; don't call me".

The Marine Air Station was designated a Marine Corps Air Station in March of 1960. The Air Station operates as one of the satellite bases under the Marine Corps Air Bases Command at Cherry Point, North Carolina. Likewise, the Air Groups and squadrons at Cherry Point, New River and Beaufort are under the 2nd Marine Air Wing command, also headquartered at Cherry Point.

Operation Steel Pike In Spain

When we arrived at MCAS, Beaufort, we stayed in the on-base Hostess House, until our household effects arrived from Quantico. We then moved into our newly assigned quarters in the very nice Laurel Bay housing area, located four miles from the Air Station.

When I reported for duty at Marine Aircraft Group-31 (MAG-31), I was welcomed by the Air Group Executive Officer, Lieutenant Colonel Don Fisher. He told me that the MAG-31 Commanding Officer, Colonel Ed Hartsock was in the Caribbean Sea area, umpiring the aviation participation in a Marine Corps Landing Exercise. Further, I would be assigned as the Air Group S-3 (Operations Officer). Also, my transition to flying jets would be delayed, because MAG-31 had been tasked to deploy to Almeria, Spain where a Navy Construction Battalion (CB) would prepare a smooth surface for a Short Airfield for Tactical Support (SATS).

The main components of a SATS were four thousand feet of runway, constructed using interlocking aluminum panels, and MOREST arresting equipment, with cross-runway cables to stop a landing airplane short, as on an aircraft carrier. The expeditionary SATS airfield at the Bogue Auxiliary Airfield near Cherry Point, had been disassembled, loaded aboard ships at Morehead City, North Carolina, and shipped to Spain, where it would again be assembled, and used in Operation Steel Pike; a Navy/Marine Corps exercise that would take place on the Mediterranean coast of southern Spain, about 150 miles east of the Straits Of Gibraltar.

The plan was to transport the SATS on U.S. Navy ships. However, when a hurricane kept those Navy ships from reaching Morehead City, very quickly, contracts were negotiated for the use of two civilian United States Line cargo ships. The ships loaded the palleted aluminum planking, catapult and arresting components, along with a portable aircraft control tower. With only a few Marines aboard to supervise the SATS equipment loading and unloading, they crossed the Atlantic Ocean, sailed through the Straits of Gibraltar, and on to Almeria where offshore, they dropped their anchors, and unloading of the transported SATS equipment began immediately.

Meanwhile, the MAG-31 staff, with tents, cots, portable field furniture, field rations, potable (drinking) water, radio-equipped jeeps, and other related equipment and necessities were transported four miles to the Port Royal dock. Our MAG-31 staff and equipment were loaded aboard the USNS *Geiger*, a Military Sea Transportation Service ship, which incidentally had been named for General Roy S. Geiger, whom I've mentioned earlier in this book.

Lt. Col. Bob Warren aboard USS Geiger enroute to Spain (1965)

The *Geiger* was primarily used to transport U.S. Servicemen, and their families, to and from overseas assignments. We were surprised to see printed meal menus that included a variety of food being served; with each printed menu also mentioning the name of the ship's Master, and the Chief Steward.

En route to Spain, we had all of our MAG-31 personnel, including the officers, practice climbing down cargo nets, which we hung along the *Geiger* bulkheads. This was how we would be required to disembark over the side of the *Geiger*, into landing craft, when we reached our Almeria destination.

SATS Construction

The USNS *Geiger* anchored offshore from the Almeria SATS site, with MAG-31 ready to participate in Operation Steel Pike. The CB battalion was already at the site; busy grading, rolling and smoothing the surface, in preparation for laying the interlocking aluminum panels, and aluminum aircraft parking surfaces. The surface in the Almeria area was like some desert areas in the Western United States. It was flat, very dusty, and completely devoid of water and trees.

We went ashore, where there was an active lighthouse. The large lighthouse building housed the entire family of the lighthouse keeper. A large stone and concrete oil tank surrounded the lighthouse building. The lighthouse had no electricity. The light atop the lighthouse tower, and the building lights, were all oil fueled. When the palleted aluminum planks were moved to the shoreline, rough terrain forklifts lifted the palleted aluminum planks, and other SATS components, from the surf and carried them to waiting CB trucks. In turn, the SATS equipment was unloaded, right where it was needed, to continue runway construction. The CB installed SATS was completed by the end of the third day.

Marine fighter squadron 451 (VMF-451), led by our MAG-31 Commanding Officer, Colonel Ed Hartsock, had flown from Beaufort to NAS, Lajes, near Lisbon, Portugal, where they landed at the end of their trans-Atlantic (TRANSLANT) flight, and waited for completion of the SATS installation, at Almeria.[xx] The VMF-451 commanding officer was Lieutenant Colonel Dellwyn L. "Del" Davis, who led his squadron, arriving from Lajes, at the SATS, ready to land, late in the afternoon of the third day, following SATS installation. However, they were waved off and returned to NAS Lajes, because a white stripe, marking the center of the SATS four-thousand-foot runway, was still being painted.

The Crusader Squadron returned to the Almeria airfield the next morning, and each made an arrested landing on the SATS runway. After parking, the pilots assembled in a tent, where I briefed them on the SATS operational procedures; which would include their participation the next day, in a show for many North Atlantic Treaty Organization (NATO) visitors. At the SATS installation, MAG-31 installed bleachers beside the SATS runway for several NATO country onlookers. On the second day of operations, several KC-130 Hercules transport aircraft, carrying our NATO visitors, landed on the SATS runway. As soon as each KC-130 landed, and their NATO passengers were unloaded, each KC-130 took off and circled offshore at different, pre-planned, altitudes. Then VMF-451 put on a SATS utilization show for all of the NATO visitors. Each Crusader, with extended tail hooks, made an arrested SATS landing, followed by a short takeoff, using the Crusader afterburners.

After the show was completed, a joint U.S Marine/Guardia Civil Honor Guard was featured. I thought it interesting that we were putting on a NATO air show in Spain, which was still a non-NATO country. Following a week of busy SATS use, VMF-451 returned to NAS, Lajes, and then made their TRANSLANT flight back to MCAS, Beaufort. The SATS components were all disassembled, and loaded aboard the same civilian cargo ships for return.

My duties as the Air Group Operations Officer (S-3) were over. So, I went aboard one of the cargo ships, which was now busy re-loading SATS equipment. I met the ship's Master (Captain), who told me that he had been a PBM (Mariner) pilot in the Navy. I related to him that I had almost shot down a PBM, north of Okinawa in 1945.

A HUS helicopter from one of the Operation Steel Pike landing force aircraft carriers had been furnished to MAG-31 at the SATS site for Air/Sea Rescue purposes. After VMF-451 and departed, I flew the HUS to Malaga, Spain and back twice, to return Spanish Air Force personnel to their home airfield at Malaga. At Malaga, I was able to view some Spanish Air Force fighter planes. They were old WWII German ME-109 Messerschmitt fighters, repainted with Spanish Air Force insignia. Those trips to Malaga and back were one hundred mile long flights, along the southern Spain coastline. Those helicopter flights also met my pilot, four hours per month, flying requirement. Before we could reload our equipment on the USNS *Geiger*, we had to solve the only real problem we encountered; which involved custody of a small, freshwater pump. It became the only bane in the entire MAG-31 SATS effort.

The Fresh Water Pump Woes

The first I heard of the Marine well-digging crew, was when one of the CB petty officers reported to me that a well digging crew was in the path of the SATS runway construction. I immediately went to the site, where the crew had started drilling a well. I explained to them that they had to move, and suggested they move their well-drilling operation to a rise above the SATS activity, where some goats were munching some dry brush. They explained that they had been sent to Spain by a Marine Corps engineer unit.

They promptly moved their operation uphill, and started to drill again. At about 50 feet their drill encountered solid rock. They reported that this would slow their operation somewhat, but that the drill could penetrate the solid rock. It did; and after drilling through the rock, a huge cavern of fresh water was found. Their next well-digging requirement was to sink a casing through the well hole, to prevent cave-in when the drilling bit was removed. A new unexpected problem now arose. The drill bit was the same diameter as the ID (inside diameter) of the casing. To go through the rock, an OD (outside diameter) hole was required. The only option left was to sink the smaller pipe through the well hole, directly into the water source.

That pipe was then attached to the small pump, to bring the fresh water to the surface. The well, supplying fresh water to a near useless dry desert, could potentially change the economy in that area of Southern Spain. If the water pipe became detached from the water pump, it would fall into the water cavern below, and would be of no use. We recommended that we leave the pump, with pipe attached; but we received no authority to do so.

The next communication regarding the pump, involved the Ambassador to Spain, who demanded that the pump be left. The next I heard of the pump was several months later, when I was deployed to NAS, Roosevelt Roads, in Puerto Rico. Lieutenant Colonel Don Fisher had taken command of MAG-31, after Colonel Hartsock had been transferred to Washington. Don Fisher flew down to Roosevelt Roads from Beaufort to visit my jet squadron. While there, he remarked, "Bob, I think we finally got rid of that goddamn pump."

Return to Beaufort

While at sea on the USNS *Geiger* carrying MAG-31 home, we were out of the military communications message loop. Those passenger ships received only routine weather reports, and of course, emergency communications, when necessary. We loaded a MAG-31 radio jeep on a *Geiger* top deck. But, that radio had a limited range. So, we were virtually out of communication for almost the entire trip back to Port Royal, and then home to Beaufort.

When we were about 100 miles from Beaufort, I received the news, via the radio jeep, that Millie's mother had died. Millie had flown back to Michigan, and was with her mother in the hospital at the time of her death. Bill was in his first year at VMI, and Jeanne was a sophomore at Beaufort High School. After the funeral, Millie flew back to Beaufort. Colonel Ed Hartsock had returned to Beaufort with VMF-451, ahead of the *Geiger*. The Hartsocks took Jeanne with them to meet Millie. But, when Colonel Ed Hartsock turned toward Charleston, Jeanne told them that they should go the other way, because her Mom would be arriving in Savannah. So, the Hartsocks changed their destination from Charleston to Savannah, where they met Millie. I really felt bad to have been at sea, and out of communication, during this entire sad episode in our family's life.

Chapter 31: Transition to Jets

During the first week of December 1964, I reported to VMT-1 at MCAS, Cherry Point, for transition to flying jets, after fourteen years of flying helicopters. I was a Lieutenant Colonel, and most of my instructors were Majors and Captains, with a lot of jet flying experience. In such situations, the transitioning pilot leaves his rank on the ground. The 12-week Transition Course included flying Grumman TF9F-J Swept-wing Cougars, and attending related ground school, five days a week.

I drove our little Volkswagen, to and from Cherry Point each week, leaving Cherry Point for Beaufort after my morning flight each Friday, and returning to Cherry Point on Sundays. It was a trip of 300 miles each way, on Highway 17. I would leave Beaufort, and drive back to Cherry Point on Sunday mornings. I timed driving through Charleston during Sunday morning church services, when the traffic would be light. At Cherry Point, I stayed in the Bachelor Officer Quarters (BOQ).

The Jet-Powered F9F Cougar

The Cougar is powered by a single Pratt & Whitney J-48 turbojet engine that developed seven thousand, two hundred pounds of thrust. It featured folding wings, and was the U.S. Navy's first successful swept-wing fighter aircraft to operate from aircraft carriers. The Cougar's top speed was six hundred fifty mph, with cruise speed of five hundred sixteen mph, and a range of one thousand miles. It was armed with four 20mm cannon mounted in its nose, and could carry two one thousand pound bombs, or two one hundred fifty gallon fuel tanks, attached to its wings externally.

The F9F Cougar was built at the Grumman Aircraft plant at Bethpage, New York. Its first flight was in September 1951. Its empty weight was eleven thousand, four hundred, eighty-three pounds. It had a one thousand, sixty-three gallon internal fuel tank. An aerial refueling probe projected from the Cougar's nose, and extended the overall length of the Cougar from forty-two to forty-eight feet. Its unfolded wingspan was thirty-four feet, and its height (at the top of the tail) was twelve feet. A perforated speed brake was mounted at the bottom of the Cougar fuselage.

Three hundred, seventy-seven of the two-seat TF9Fs were produced for the Navy. They served, for two decades, as advanced weapons systems trainers, for aircraft carrier landing training, and for transitioning Naval Aviators from flying other types of Navy aircraft to flying swept-wing jet fighters.

VMT-1 was the Marine Corps training squadron charged with transitioning and training jet pilots. The squadron had a dozen TF9F-J Cougars; painted orange and white, the standard high-visibility colors for all Navy training aircraft. The VMT-1 Cougars had two cockpits. A single pilot, or the student pilot, always occupied the front cockpit. Before flying, a comprehensive ground school, lasting several days, was held to explain the Cougar safety and emergency procedures, jet engine starting and shut down, and general aircraft airborne handling, and aircraft limitations.

For instance the Cougar was limited to 7.2 Gs, measured on a cockpit G-Meter that could not be reset from the cockpit. At sea level, a standing person weighs about 1.0 G. If, in a jet, the pilot pulls 7.2 Gs, he will weigh about 7.2 times his normal weight. To prevent blackouts when pulling high Gs, a jet pilot wears a fitted G-Suit, That G-suit pushes blood from the pilot's legs and abdomen toward his brain, and thus prevents blackouts during high G maneuvers. I had never worn a G-suit before flying the Cougar, and I quickly found it very comforting. I could feel the G-suit inflating, even in a tight turn.

On 8 December 1964, I flew my first instructional Cougar jet flight. I expected to be taken for a simple backseat jet ride. That expectation was way off! When approaching our assigned Cougar, my instructor led me on a walk-around outside inspection of our Cougar; then he told me to get into the front cockpit. The enlisted "plane captain" assisted with properly strapping me into the front cockpit, attaching the G-suit to the pre-packed parachute harness, connecting the oxygen hose to my face mask, pointing to the ejection seat handle, and connecting my face mask radio cord to the Cougar radio/intercom system.

By then, my instructor had climbed into the rear cockpit, and commenced giving further instructions to me, using the jet's intercom system. He told me how to adjust the cockpit seat height, adjust the two rudder pedals for proper lengths, and how to close the cockpit canopy. He then told me to insure that the enlisted plane captain was clear of the jet, and that the parking brake was "on." He then "walked me through" the Cougar jet engine start procedures; telling me after the engine started, to adjust the engine throttle to IDLE, and to check all the engine and oxygen flow gauges, and complete the printed cockpit Take Off Check List.

Next, using the radio, I called the Cherry Point airfield control tower, requesting clearance to taxi for takeoff. The control tower then directed me to taxi to the center of the airfield, and to line up outward toward the active runway. MCAS, Cherry Point is a beautifully designed airfield. All aircraft takeoffs start at the center of the airfield with eight-thousand-foot runways extending from the center. Approaching aircraft land on the runway toward the airfield center. The airfield center is a circular hard surface mat, about two thousand feet in diameter. I was surprised that, in the jet, I sat so low over the parking mat surface. That was because the Cougar jet engine was behind the pilot's cockpit, at about the same level. I was used to climbing high up the side of a troop-carrying helicopter to reach the cockpit, which was usually mounted higher than the helicopter engine.

Flying the TF9F-J

The details of my initial Cougar taxi and takeoff were transmitted over our connected intercom, by my instructor in the rear cockpit. He told me that I would make the takeoff, but that he would follow my actions by also monitoring, and lightly holding the rear seat dual controls ready, if necessary, to take control. First, while holding the jet's brakes, I advanced the throttle to 100% power, and released the brakes. I was surprised at how fast the jet accelerated. When it reached the runway airspeed of one hundred, fifty knots, he told me to raise the nose slightly, and we immediately left the runway, and became airborne. Next, I raised the jet's wheels.

When the wheels were retracted, I noted a perceptible lightness, in elevator control pressure. The jet nose began to porpoise up and down slightly. That was a normal experience for transitioning pilots, as the standard elevator control gave way to a "full flying tail," when the wheels were retracted. Thus, the pressure required to control the aircraft at all speeds became considerably less, after the wheels were retracted. On landing, when the wheels were lowered, the elevator control reverted back, and again seemed slightly "heavy."

On my first flight, my instructor had me climb to twenty thousand feet, and then stall the airplane. This was done by reducing the engine throttle to IDLE, then while holding the nose of the jet level, the airspeed quickly "bled off,"' until the aircraft lost wing lift and "stalled." There was no tendency for the Cougar to enter a "spin," as long as the rudder was held in a neutral position. Like any fixed-wing airplane when stalled, the rudder is the only effective control. Therefore, a pilot can induce a spin, or stop the spinning turn, with the aircraft rudder. When entering and recovering from a simple stall, the jet lost several thousand feet of altitude, whereas a propeller-driven combat airplane could recover in about a thousand feet.

The remainder of my first flight was spent navigating along the North Carolina coastline, noting the location of the mouth of the Cape Fear River at Wilmington; the mouth of the Neuse River, that flows past MCAS, Cherry Point, and Cape Lookout; to where the Carolina Coast turns sharply to the north, and extends over Pamlico Sound, to Cape Hatteras; and on to the North Carolina Outer Banks. We then turned, and started our descent back to Cherry Point, where there was an established approach and landing pattern.

Jets entered the landing pattern, always over Runway 5 at fifteen hundred feet, with airspeed of two hundred, fifty knots. After passing the airfield center, the jet would break sharply to the left, and the pilot would sharply reduce throttle, and open the jet speed brake, until the aircraft slowed to one hundred, fifty knots, paralleling the landing runway downwind. At one hundred fifty knots, the speed brake would be retracted, and the wheels and landing flaps lowered.

The pilot would call the control tower and report, "three (wheels) down and locked." In turn, the tower would say, "Marine jet (call sign), cleared to land." While turning to the landing pattern base and final legs, the throttle would be adjusted as necessary, to reduce altitude, to reach the final landing approach just over the Runway end number(s). After landing touchdown at one hundred, thirty-two knots, the throttle would be reduced to twelve percent (IDLE), until the landing roll-out was completed. With its tricycle landing gear, and the absence of propeller torque combined, the Cougar had no tendency to swerve as in some single engine propeller-driven aircraft. The landing flaps were then raised, and the jet would be directed back to the squadron flight line or, upon request, back to the takeoff runway. Visiting aircraft would be directed to park near the control tower, on the designated Visiting Aircraft parking area to be refueled.

Jet Transition Flights

As mentioned above, My first jet flight was on 8 December 1964; two days before my 41st Birthday. I made three takeoffs and landings. My next daily instructional flights were largely to teach me routine, home airfield, safe jet flying, airfield patterns and procedures. For instance, during my first five days, my instructional flights totaled 28 takeoffs and, fortunately, the same number of safe landings. On 15 December, I flew the Cougar alone; my first solo flight in a jet. But, the instructor flew a second Cougar alongside me, to closely monitor my jet flying procedures; still concentrating on ensuring that I followed proper airfield patterns, including safe takeoffs and landings. I had my last jet flight of 1964 on December 17th. I then drove back to MCAS, Beaufort to spend the Christmas and New Year holidays with my family.

While in Beaufort, I flew the twin-engine R4D to Roanoke, Virginia to bring our son, Bill home from VMI for the Holidays. He was a member of the ROTC at VMI, so I assumed that authorized him to ride in a military airplane. I hope that assumption was correct; but I never really checked to see if it was. Bill wore his VMI cadet uniform on the flights to Beaufort and back.

During the Christmas holidays, I had my first real chance to discuss my future assignments with my Air Group Commanding Officer, Colonel Ed Hartsock. I had only first met him in Spain during Operation Steel Pike, so I did not know him well. I learned that he was very aware of the situation that prevented me from being assigned to MCAS, New River to take command of the helicopter air group there. He said that he told the 2nd Marine Air Wing Commanding General that he was going to make sure that I went through jet transition, either at NAS, Pensacola, or at VMT-1 at Cherry Point. He also related to the Air Wing commander that I was too well-qualified to be assigned lesser duties than that of a flying squadron commander. I told Colonel Hartsock that I felt he had really stuck his neck out on my behalf, and that I really appreciated it. He then told me that Marine Attack Squadron 331 (VMA-331), also known as "The Bumblebees," would depart the aircraft carrier, USS *Forestall*, after returning soon from its nine month deployment to the Mediterranean Sea area.

Further, Colonel Hartsock told me that VMA-331 was due to return from the USS *Forestall* to Beaufort at about the same time I would complete jet transition. And, if I completed the jet transition course successfully, I would take Command of VMA-331. Wow! I thanked him sincerely for all of his consideration and efforts on my behalf. I now thought that I might still have a chance to be selected for promotion to Colonel the next year.

After spending the Christmas season in Beaufort, I reported back to VMT-1 at Cherry Point on 3 January, 1965. My next instructional flight was on January 4$^{th.}$ I was told to stay in the airfield flight pattern, and shoot landings. I stayed in the pattern, and made 7 takeoffs and landings on that flight. I had learned long before that, when considering flight safety, the number of landings should always equal the number of takeoffs. During January 1965, I logged 30 more hours flying the Cougar. For the most part those flights, extending through February, were routine.

There were, however, a few significant exceptions. One was a cross-country flight that required two scheduled stops at airfields away from Cherry Point; one of which had to be at a civilian airport. The second exception was a "tail-chase;" and the third, an instrument flight, to and from, a distant airfield. I'll briefly describe each.

Cross-Country Flight

On 5 February 1965, I filed a cross-country flight plan, directly to Battle Creek, Michigan; a civilian airport. Before departing, two auxiliary one hundred fifty gallon wing fuel tanks were fitted, and filled. That additional fuel increased the overall available fuel from one thousand sixty five, to one thousand, three hundred fifty gallons. With my instructor in the Cougar rear seat, I took off on a two hour, non-stop flight to Battle Creek; cruising at just over five hundred miles per hour.

I had called my sister, Helen the day before, and told her that I would arrive in a jet, at the Battle Creek airport, about noon the next day. She and her family lived a few miles away from Battle Creek, near Kalamazoo, Michigan. It was an easy drive for her to meet me at Battle Creek. When I landed the Cougar, she was waiting at the airport terminal. We had a nice forty-five minute visit, while my instructor supervised refueling our jet, leaving a standard government form used to pay for the fuel. He then filed an instrument flight plan to NAS, New York (Floyd Bennett Airfield), located in Brooklyn. Approaching New York, we were being controlled by New York Center, the FAA aircraft controlling agency. We arrived over New York at Flight Level 390 (39,000 feet).[xxi]

Arriving over New York, we were advised that, starting at ten thousand feet, solid clouds rose to our Flight Level. New York Center then directed us all the way down to ten thousand feet, by radar; constantly changing our headings, airspeed, and altitude, to avoid other air traffic in the New York area. At times, when directed to descend rapidly, it was necessary to deploy our speed brake to reduce airspeed. We broke out under the clouds over Long Island and were then vectored (turned) toward Floyd Bennett Airfield. When on an instrument flight plan, the air controlling agency must direct the airplane all the way to runway touchdown. In our case, we would have been directed to change radio frequencies from New York Center to Approach Control, then to the Airfield Control Tower radio frequency, for final landing instructions

Canceling an instrument flight can only be done by the aircraft pilot; never by any controlling agency. After we broke underneath the cloud deck at ten thousand feet, the visibility was excellent; so I asked New York Center (my current control agency) if they would like me to cancel my instrument flight plan. Our very busy controller answered, "I sure would appreciate it." I did; but by doing so, I then took the responsibility of flying visually; sometimes threading my jet through other low flying aircraft, from several busy New York City and New Jersey airfields. We landed at Floyd Bennett Airfield and, after taxiing to the Visiting Aircraft parking area, we Remained Overnight (RON).

It had been a long day for me, and I had no problem sleeping in the Floyd Bennett BOQ that night. The next day, February 6th, 1965, we flew non-stop back to Cherry Point. The flight home took just under two hours. As always, after landing at Cherry Point, we had an extensive post-flight briefing.

The Tail-Chase

Most of our flights during February 1965 ended with a confidence-building, two-plane tail-chase. It was scary at first, to fly just a few feet from another jet, but it soon became a real confidence builder. To fly in the correct position behind the flight leader, the chasing pilot used the oval shaped section in the center of the Cougar windscreen, for correct position. The Cougar had a centered, oblong-shaped, thick, bullet proof glass windscreen, centered at the front of its larger glass canopy. By using the oblong, glass portion for reference, the chase pilot flies to the correct tail-chase position; which places the tail of the lead airplane at the top of the oblong glass, with its wing tips on the outer edges of the glass. That put the chase Cougar five feet below, and three feet behind, the lead aircraft.

In that position, the pilot of the chasing aircraft can look into the tailpipe of the lead aircraft, and see the fire ring around the lead Cougar engine turbines. No matter what the lead aircraft does, the chasing Cougar pilot keeps the same oblong, glass sight pattern. The lead airplane does smooth acrobatics, including loops, and high wingovers, with the chase Cougar tucked in closely behind. It was terrifying at first, but it soon became routine, and a lot of fun.

Of course, it was necessary for the lead pilot to avoid any abrupt maneuvers, and to never sharply slow down, which could cause a mid-air collision. One tail-chase flight became very memorable to me. My instructor, a Major flying in the lead Cougar, led me into a cloud bank, and then sharply turned right, and lost me. While maintaining his proper chase position, the chase pilot cannot read his aircraft instruments, as he is busy maintaining the required sight pattern. So, there I was - somewhere over North Carolina - not knowing whether I was flying up or down, because I was flying in a cloud. The last glance I had at the altimeter, I was flying at eighteen thousand feet. I quickly realized that my recovery would depend on an old flying recovery procedure that I had learned years before.

It's called Needle, Ball & Airspeed. There is a single cockpit instrument that houses a turn indicator needle, and a floating ball, inside a glass. When disoriented, a pilot first centers the turn Needle, then centers the Ball, and next, controls the airplane airspeed by use of the engine throttle and, if necessary and practical, the aircraft speed brake. It became a truly wild ride. I first saw the ground, when I broke through the bottom of the cloud deck; going like hell, and headed straight down into the North Carolina farmland. I needed to pull out and get level, so I opted to not use the speed brake, as it was located under the Cougar fuselage. I thought this might further add to my Cougar's already steep, nose-down attitude, and I desperately needed to bring the Cougar nose up to level flight.

I quickly reduced the throttle to IDLE, and pulled the control stick back, which induced a High G load on the Cougar, and on me, as well. I finally got the Cougar level at an altitude of three thousand feet. The High G-Load had fully inflated my G-Suit, and partially pulled my sweaty oxygen mask off my face. When flying level again, I noted that the Accelerometer (G-Meter) showed a maximum of 7.5 Gs. That exceeded the 7.2 maximum allowed for the Cougar; meaning that I had over-stressed the airplane beyond its allowable G-limits.

I joined my instructor over Edenton, North Carolina. He knew I was angry with him, when I told him to join on my wing, and directed him to move around my Cougar, to look my airplane over to see if any excess G-damage was evident. There was none, so I assumed the lead, flew back to Cherry Point and landed. Close inspection of my Cougar revealed there wasn't even a popped rivet. I guess that is how Grumman Aircraft gained the reputation of being built by the Grumman Iron Works. I conducted the post flight briefing and told the instructor that he almost got me killed; and to never sharply change directions in a cloud again, when leading a student in a tail-chase, or for any other reason. He knew that he had really screwed up. Now on the ground, and Lieutenant Colonel to Major, I told him that I never wanted him to be scheduled as my instructor again.

Instrument Flight

My final required jet transition flight was a non-stop flight, on instruments, to Houston, Texas. For instrument training, the Cougar front cockpit is fitted with a retractable cloth hood, which requires the student to rely completely on the airplane instruments, while also managing, and changing to the radio frequencies of the various FAA controlling agencies along his flight route. We could have easily reached Cherry Point non-stop on our return flight but, mysteriously for me, we landed at Jacksonville, Florida before returning to Cherry Point.

The standard instrument (bad weather) approach to Cherry Point starts at a known position off-shore, called the Cape Lookout Thirty Nautical Mile Fix; flying at twenty thousand feet. From that point, we turned to the heading of the Cherry Point bad weather Runway 32, and commenced our descent. The weather was bad; with heavy rain all the way down, with very low clouds, and some fog forming at Cherry Point. Visibility was about one-half mile. I was no longer flying under the hood, because the weather was so bad. We broke out underneath the low clouds with wheels and flaps down, ready to land on the now visible, wet, lighted runway, dead ahead. However, just before touchdown my backseat instructor advanced the throttle, raised the wheels and flaps, and directed me to climb back to the Cape Lookout Thirty Nautical Mile Fix, and start another instrument approach. We repeated the instrument approach five more times before making our final landing.

Then, I realized that our stop at Jacksonville was to get more fuel; allowing us to make six instrument approaches, rather than being satisfied with just one. Having made those several, real instrument approaches, I was convinced that I could fly the jet successfully in any kind of bad (Bird Walking) weather. On 23 January 1965, I flew my last flight at VMT-1, making 11 takeoffs and landings. I had successfully completed the Jet Transition Course in two and one-half months. During forty-one day and night flights, I had logged seventy Cougar jet flying hours. I thanked the VMT-1 commanding officer, Lieutenant Colonel Clark E. Merchant, and all of my flight instructors. I drove out the gate at Cherry Point, and returned to Beaufort on 21 February 1965, wondering if I would ever return.

Chapter 32: Change of Squadron Command

When I arrived back at MCAS, Beaufort, VMA-331 was still at sea, aboard the aircraft carrier USS *Forestall*. When that ship neared Norfolk, Virginia, it launched the VMA-331 Skyhawks, for return flight to their home base at MCAS, Beaufort. When the squadron returned, many of the squadron wives, children and other members of the family, along with close friends, were waiting near the flight line, to welcome the squadron pilots home. One of the A4-E Skyhawk jets had a crossed ski pole and a crutch, painted on the jet nose. That represented the only accident the squadron had during its nine month deployment; and it had nothing to do with flying. It represented an accident in which one of the pilots broke his leg, while skiing in the Alps.

The next day, the non-flying members of the squadron arrived aboard a Marine KC-130. They had debarked from the USS *Forestall* when it docked at Norfolk, and were transported by bus to NAS, Norfolk, where they boarded the Marine KC-130 transports for the flight back to Beaufort. I noted that the VMA-331 Squadron Commander and his wife mingled with the waiting dependents, to meet the KC-130 at the MCAS, Beaufort terminal. The VMA-331 Commanding Officer, Lieutenant Colonel Stanley H. "Stan" Carpenter, and his wife, were there to welcome the all-important jet mechanics, and other enlisted members of the squadron, home to Beaufort. VMA-331 had done a superior job aboard the aircraft carrier USS *Forestall*. The squadron operated without a single accident, or a lesser incident, during its entire nine month deployment; operating in the Mediterranean Sea, as members of the U.S. Sixth Fleet.

Change of Command Party

The night before I took command of VMA-331, relieving Lieutenant Colonel Stan Carpenter, a party was held at the Beaufort Officer's Club. Stan thanked the assembled pilots, and their wives, for all the support they gave to him during their outstanding performance aboard the USS *Forrestal*. He welcomed Millie and me as the party's honored guests, and Bill and Jeanne as well. It was really a bittersweet party, as VMA-331 would quickly break up. Many of the pilots had already received orders to other stations and duties. Stan had been ordered to Washington for further duty. A dozen new pilots, mostly Second Lieutenants were joining the squadron, and had to train, and become proficient in flying the A4E Skyhawk.

Change of Command Honored Guests

It was a pleasure for me to invite my old boss, General Christian Schilt, USMC (Ret), then living in Norfolk, Virginia, to the Change of Command ceremony. He accepted; and when I asked him if there was anyone special he would like to see, he named a lady now living in Beaufort named "Bunty" (Mary Elizabeth Bunting) Pate, spouse of the late General Randolph M. Pate, who had been the 21st Commandant of the Marine Corps. General and Mrs. Schilt were next door neighbors of the Pates, at the historic old Marine Barracks at 8th & I Streets, SE, in Washington, D.C.

I called Mrs. Pate in Beaufort, and extended an invitation to her; stating that General Schilt would attend, and that he asked me to extend his invitation to include her. I told her that if she could attend, I would be pleased to send my son Bill, who was a VMI cadet, to escort her in a staff car to the Change of Command ceremony. General Pate had graduated from VMI in the Class of

1921. Mrs. Pate graciously accepted; and was very appreciative, and pleased.

Traditional Changing of Command

After the guests were seated, Lieutenant Colonel Stan Carpenter and I took our places; both facing the formation of squadron Marines. I stood on his left; denoting that he, on the right, was still the VMA-331 Squadron Commander. He first put the participating troops at ease. He then called the formation to attention, and the adjutant marched forward, carrying the squadron flag attached to a flag pole. He halted in front of Colonel Carpenter, while the orders directing the change of command were read. Colonel Carpenter then took the flag from the adjutant, turned and faced me, and presented the flag and pole to me; symbolizing the change of command. Meanwhile, the adjutant did a right face, took a step in front of me, did a left face, and stood in position, ready to receive the flag from me. I handed the flag back to the adjutant who, holding the flag, did an about face, and marched alone back to his previous position, with the squadron staff.

Using the public address system, I invited Stan, as the outgoing Squadron Commander, to make any remarks that he desired. He first properly addressed the honored guests, and thanked the Second Marine Air Wing representative, Colonel Stoddard Courtelyou, for attending. He then thanked the assembled troops for all of their loyal support and hard work. He wished me well as the new VMA-331 Squadron Commanding Officer. I then commenced my remarks, by first telling both General Schilt and Mrs. Pate that it was a personal honor for me to have them attend. From those remarks, I generally parroted Stan's remarks, and thanked him for turning over such a fine squadron to me. I again turned and saluted him, as my gesture of admiration for him.

I then announced that upon dismissal from this Change of Command Ceremony, liberty would be granted to the squadron, ending at 0800 two days later. I then gave my first Squadron Command, "Officers and men of Marine Attack Squadron Three, Three One, DISMISSED". I received a message from Colonel Ed Hartsock that read, "Congratulations Bob, you now have the greatest job in the world; don't screw it up"

Chapter 33: Jet Squadron Training

Getting VMA-331 Organized

The day after taking command of VMA-331, I asked Major Edgar K. "Ken" Jacks to call the squadron's Majors into my office for a meeting at 2:00 pm. I opened the meeting by thanking all of them for coming. I then told them that the squadron needed re-organization, and I thought we should start now. So, I assigned each of them their duties. First, the squadron Executive Officer, Major Ken Jacks, would receive the reports from the Squadron Duty Officer and the squadron Sergeant Major Evans as the first order of business, in Ken's office every morning at 8:00. Also, in my absence, Ken would always have my authority, if needed; as I intended to check out in our A4-E Skyhawk, and fly as much as possible.

Second, the Squadron Operations Officer, Major Bob Sheehan, who would publish the flight schedule for the following work day, and direct and oversee all squadron flight operations, including required training (syllabus) flights at Beaufort, and during all squadron deployments. Third, was the squadron Engineering Officer, Major Mack Lewis, who would schedule and monitor all squadron aircraft maintenance, including mandated aircraft maintenance checks accomplished both at VMA-331 and, at the next higher Headquarters and Maintenance Squadron of MAG-31. Further, Major Lewis would advise Major Sheehan of the number of squadron aircraft ready to fly the next day.

Fourth, the Squadron Material (Supply) Officer would procure all aircraft maintenance parts, pilot fight suits, G-Suits, ejection seats, oxygen bottles, and all other flight and ground support equipment, and enlisted uniforms. I charged all of these Majors to recommend his assistant(s) to the Executive Officer for consideration, and/or approval, within a week. I told Major Ken

Jacks that I wanted to meet the rest of our squadron pilots in the squadron pilot's ready room at 0900 the next day, and that the meeting uniform would be clean flight suits.

First All Pilot's Meeting

My first meeting with the squadron pilots was held in the Squadron Pilot's ready room, the next morning at 0900. First, I announced a ten-minute coffee break, to be followed by the pilots comfortably being seated with their coffee. I then introduced myself, and all of the Majors I had met with on the previous day. I then asked each of those Majors, starting with Ken Jacks, to introduce themselves, and to state what their general duty assignments were, starting the day before.

I briefly gave the assembled group my aviation background, which included combat at Okinawa and Saipan in WW II, followed by my experiences as a helicopter pilot in Korea. I briefly described my duties as General Schilt's Aide at El Toro and later, for two more years in Washington. At both locations, I had taught General Schilt to fly the helicopter.

I also told them I had been fortunate to have commanded a helicopter squadron for nearly a year in California. More recently, I had instructed all levels of students at Marine Corps Schools in Quantico for four years. Now, I was looking forward to being a student pilot again; learning to fly the A4-E, just as I had recently completed the jet swept-wing transition course, flying the F9F-J Cougar. Further, I told them I intended to start my A4E Skyhawk training by flying "Tail End Charlie," until Major Sheehan said that I was now qualified to move up to leading a two-plane section, in our four-plane Skyhawk formations. Further, that through ready room pre-flight briefings, while flying, and in post-flight briefings in the pilot's ready room, I told them that, for now, I was just another student pilot, learning how to most effectively fly the A4-E Skyhawk.

So, if anyone in the flight noted any error I made, or was about to make, to let me know immediately.

I cited the loss of our squadron commander at Cherry Point, when all of us, as Second Lieutenants, knew that he was incorrectly "metering" his oxygen bottle dial to save oxygen. But, because of his rank, we were hesitant to tell him that his diluter/demand oxygen mask already "metered" his oxygen. He got anoxia and dove his Hellcat, straight down into North Carolina. We took a ten-minute pilot's meeting break.

Next I told them that our squadron would most likely be deployed away from Beaufort, because the entire airfield was due to be closed for extensive maintenance, but as of yet, no specific dates were known. I told all of the pilots who had not yet flown the Skyhawk, that I would meet them on the flight line at 1400, to view a proper pre-flight walk-around aircraft inspection, conducted by the Squadron Engineering Officer, Major Mack Lewis; who at the completion of his walk-around inspection, would answer any of their questions. I concluded the meeting, by also stating the probability that within a year, most of us would be transferred to South Vietnam (SVN). So, the Marine Corps expects us to prepare here, for combat there.

A4-E Skyhawk History

The Skyhawk was a delta-wing aircraft, designed by a Douglas Aircraft engineer named Ed Heinemann. It was sometimes referred to as Heinemann's "Hot Rod," or "The Scooter." Regardless of its nickname, the Skyhawk was built for the Navy and the Marine Corps, as a light, jet-powered attack bomber. It was aircraft carrier compatible. Two thousand, nine hundred and sixty A-4s were built by Douglas Aircraft, and deliveries of the A-4s began in 1962. Its top speed was six hundred, seventy mph; and loaded, it flew at a top speed of five hundred, eighty-six mph. Before the sound barrier had been broken, the A-4 held the official closed-course speed record of six hundred, ninety-five mph. The A-4 engine had been changed from the Curtis-Wright J-65, to the Pratt & Whitney J-52; thereby providing more jet engine thrust, and greater reliability. The empty (dry) weight of the A-4 was nine thousand, eight hundred, fifty-three pounds. Its normal take-off weight was eighteen thousand, three hundred, eighteen pounds. Its maximum takeoff weight was twenty four thousand, five hundred pounds. It had an internal fuel tank capacity of twelve hundred U.S. gallons; and could increase that fuel amount to eighteen hundred U.S. gallons, by externally attaching two, three hundred gallon tanks at wing hard (attachment) points.

The A-4 could accomplish aerial refueling through its built-in extended aerial refueling probe. The A-4 did not have an on-board starter. Instead, when starting its jet engine, a small, hand-towed, battery powered blower was wheeled under the A-4 fuselage, and connected to the airplane by a flexible duct, which blew air up into the jet engine, through the engine rotor blades and vanes. The moving air caused the engine to start turning, and when the engine reached a cockpit reading of twelve percent, the pilot moved the engine throttle to the left, against some electrical contacts, that "lit the fire" in the A-4 engine. The portable blower was then quickly shut down, detached, and hand-towed from underneath the now running A-4 engine.

Skyhawk Familiarization and Training Flights

My first familiarization fight in the A-4E was, as scheduled, a local flight of one and one-half hours, at MCAS, Beaufort on 5 March 1965. At first, the little Skyhawk seemed rather fragile and flimsy, compared to the F9F Cougars that I had recently flown at Cherry Point. That comparison started when I entered the Skyhawk cockpit. I had to climb up an access boarding ladder to reach the cockpit level. By comparison, I could easily reach the Cougar cockpit level, by merely stepping from the parking surface into a single fuselage foot door while simultaneously grasping a higher hand access panel. Then, merely by hanging on and stepping up once, I could swing my leg into the much lower, and seemingly more secure, Cougar cockpit.

As I gained experience flying the Skyhawk, I learned to appreciate its' exceptional characteristics. The Skyhawk wingspan was just slightly over twenty-six feet. But, by using multi-carriage bomb racks attached to hard points underneath the Skyhawk wings, eighteen pre-loaded, two hundred fifty pound bombs could quickly be attached. Or, by attaching two, three hundred gallon external fuel tanks, at the same wing hard points, the Skyhawk would prove very valuable, when extended flights were required. The Skyhawk armament also included two 20 mm machine guns, and a variety of air-to-air missiles, including the "Sidewinder."

My first Skyhawk flights at Beaufort were mainly familiarization flights, which required the pilot to remain in the MCAS, Beaufort traffic pattern. But, those flights required more than "touch-and-go" landings. An experienced squadron Skyhawk pilot stood at the edge of the runway, and monitored each Skyhawk flight, for traffic pattern correctness, proper radio discipline, and landing approach airspeed, with wheels and flaps down.

Soon after we arrived in Beaufort, my sister, Helen, her husband, Eugene "Gene" McKean and their teenage son, visited us at Beaufort. I asked the pilot monitoring one of my flights to take my brother-in-law Eugene, and my nephew Dick, with him out to the runway in his radio jeep, to watch my several landing and takeoff performances. Their position was right beside my jet landing touchdown spot; where immediately after touchdown, there would be a burst of noise, as I added full throttle, to take off, and go around the traffic pattern again. I think my relatives enjoyed watching my screaming jet flash past them, and slam down on the runway at 4-Gs. My nephew Dick still remembers being there, fifty years later.

Bob Warren, Commanding Officer VMA-331, Beaufort, SC (1965)

As I gained experience flying the Skyhawk, I realized why so many other Allied Nations had purchased the Skyhawk; including Argentina, Australia, Brazil, Germany, Indonesia, Israel, Kuwait, and Malaysia. Those nations obviously learned that the Skyhawk was easy to maintain, and it had a variety of excellent ordnance delivery capabilities. Its short wing span did not require wing folding for aircraft carrier operations. But, it also had a large wing area. That feature alone, gave the Skyhawk the ability to turn sharply, and to quickly recover from very steep bombing and rocket runs. For instance, when diving the Skyhawk toward a surface target, I could release the bombs or rockets in a forty-five degree dive at twenty-five hundred feet, then sharply pull 4 G-s, and the Skyhawk would be flying level, or climbing again, at no less than two thousand feet.

The Skyhawk was a very nimble little attack aircraft that could out-turn every other jet warbird, at low altitudes. For that reason, both the United States Navy Top Gun School at NAS, Fallon, in Nevada, and the Israeli Air Force, used Skyhawks as adversary aircraft. Not all of the Skyhawk ordnance deliveries were from steep dives. They could also perform what was called the "loft maneuver." To execute that maneuver, the Skyhawk would approach the target, flying at maximum speed, at tree top level. When attack Initial Point (selected by intelligence sources) was reached, the attacking Skyhawk would pull up into a 4-Gs vertical climb. When the sharp climb passed eighty-five degrees, the bomb automatically released, and continued its upward flight, until gravity caused it to drop down vertically on the target.

After the bomb release at eighty-five degrees, the Skyhawk continued pulling 4-Gs until it was completely inverted. It would then roll upright, and dive steeply, and at full throttle, toward the ground; away from the target being attacked. This flying maneuver was also called the 'Half Cuban Eight. It, hopefully, would allow the Skyhawk to be underneath the line-of-sight blast from the exploding bomb.

To allow adequate clearance for loading the bomb, the Skyhawk had unusually long landing gear struts. For years, the U.S. Navy Sixth Fleet in the Mediterranean Sea the aircraft carriers were prepared to launch their Skyhawks on missions that required the loft maneuver.

In December 1974, the U.S. Navy's flight demonstration team replaced their F9F Cougars with A-4 Skyhawks. The National Museum of Naval Aviation, located at NAS, Pensacola, Florida, features four Blue Angel Skyhawks hanging overhead, in their tight air show formation positions, from the reinforced glass roof, over the Museum's beautiful Blue Angel Atrium.

Chapter 34: Puerto Rico Deployment

Naval Station Roosevelt Roads, Ponce, Puerto Rico

On 13 June 1965, I deployed with my VMA-331 Skyhawk squadron to the Naval Station, Roosevelt Roads. It was a return to familiar territory for me. I had deployed there several times with my former squadrons at MCAS, Cherry Point. The last time was while I was a member of Marine Photo Reconnaissance Squadron (VMP-354); flying Grumman twin-engine F7F (Tigercats). Most Marine Corps pilots, at one time or another, have deployed to Puerto Rico. Another time, I had deployed to Puerto Rico, with VMP-354, to an airfield near the Puerto Rico south coast city of Ponce. Ponce is well known by generations of Marine Corps pilots, as the site where Don-Q-Rum distilling and bottling takes place.

In the 1930s, before the existence of Roosevelt Roads, many Marine Aviators flew from Ponce, and from the neighboring St. Thomas Island airfield, as well. The Naval Station at Roosevelt Roads is commanded by a non-aviator U.S. Navy Captain. So, there is not a designated NAS, Roosevelt Roads, even though a modern Naval Air Station actually exists <u>within</u> the confines of the Naval Station. Instead of having a Naval Air Station command there, the responsibilities for all of the Navy and Marine Corps squadrons using Rosy Roads, even for short periods of time, lies with the designated Commander, Fleet Air Detachment (CFAD).

The CFAD is the senior Squadron Commanding Officer of the permanent, or temporarily-based, Navy or Marine Corps squadron, using the facilities at Roosevelt Roads. When I arrived there, commanding VMA-331, I became the CFAD. Two U.S. Navy squadrons were based at Roosevelt "Rosy" Roads. One was a Navy Patrol Squadron, and the other a squadron that operated unmanned aircraft, flying over the vast 600 x 600 mile Navy weapons ranges located east of Puerto Rico. Those two Navy squadrons were based permanently, and occupied large hangars there. Our relationship was casual, and largely consisted of exchanging flight schedules.

Lt. Col Bob Warren addresses VMA-331 personnel
at NAS Roosevelt Roads, Puerto Rico (1965)

The Naval Station, Roosevelt Roads was built in 1943, at the extreme east end of Puerto Rico. It housed a two-runway Naval Air Station. Its main runway was eleven thousand feet, and the other was fifty-eight hundred feet. Squadron Aircraft parking, and maintenance shelters, were in permanent tents erected at the end of the unused fifty-eight hundred foot Rosy Roads runway. Our enlisted Marines lived in two-story barracks, and the Officers in the BOQ.

Some Marine Corps expeditionary items were also being field tested there. Examples were forty thousand gallon rubberized bags laid flat on the ground, then filled, through floating sea transmission lines, from off-shore tanker ships. At Rosy Roads, all of our jet refueling, was from experimental rubber bags. While there, four-star Admiral Thomas H. Moorer, the Commander in Chief of the U.S. Atlantic Fleet, visited my jet squadron.[xxii] To observe refueling, he ducked under the wing of one of our Skyhawks with me, and watched it being refueled from a forty thousand gallon rubber bag. Before leaving, he thanked, and shook hands with the very busy Marine Corporal who was in charge of refueling our A-4E jets from the rubber bags. Ordinarily, the Marine Corporal did not have a four-star Admiral looking over his shoulder.

Personnel and aircraft of VMA-331
at NAS Roosevelt Roads, Puerto Rico (1965)

    Another distinguished visitor at Rosy Roads was Marine Brigadier General Ormand R. Simpson, who at that time, commanded the 2nd Marine Division at Camp Lejeune, North Carolina. I had known General Simpson at Headquarters, Marine Corps, when he was a Colonel, assigned as Military Secretary to the Commandant of the Marine Corps, and I, a Major, was assigned as Lieutenant General Schilt's Aide. Our offices were near each other.

    During General Simpson's visit, I had my squadron put on a timed, bomb-loading demonstration. We started a stopwatch when two, multi-carriage bomb racks, pre-loaded with bombs, were wheeled, and attached underneath each of our demonstration

Skyhawk's wings. Next, the bomb dropping circuitry was checked, while the pilot entered the Skyhawk cockpit, strapped in, and started the jet's engine. To reach the takeoff runway, the pilot had to taxi over a mile. Following takeoff, he flew past General Simpson in less than 5 minutes since the bomb loading began. Later, in a thank you letter to me, dated 25 July 1965, he wrote that he saw what he expected - that I was running a first class outfit; and, that the ordnance-loading demonstration was one of the most impressive things he had ever seen.

About midway through our VMA-331 deployment, the Squadron Executive Officer, Major Ken Jacks, suggested that I should change my Military Occupational Specialty (MOS), from Helicopter Pilot to Jet Attack Pilot. I thanked Ken for his suggestion, but I thought it would be more attention-grabbing for my promotion board members to note that I was a designated helicopter pilot, but now was commanding a deployed jet attack squadron. I never knew whether or not the two MOS's were noted. However, something had obviously worked for me; and my selection for promotion to Colonel was announced a few weeks later.

Flying the little Skyhawk at Rosy Roads was fun. We could take off, and in just a few minutes we were cleared (by radio) to commence bombing or rocket attacks on targets located on Vieques Island; only five miles southeast of Rosy Roads, in steep 45 degree dives on targets named "Twin Rocks" and "Fungi Bowl." Reaching twenty-five hundred feet, the Skyhawk pilot could fire his rockets, or release his bombs, pull 4-Gs, and his Skyhawk would stop its dive, and be climbing again at fifteen hundred to two thousand feet. Flying at these low-altitude attack levels, the Delta A-4 wing performed exceptionally well.

Lt. Col. Bob Warren jet-assisted take off in an A-4
NAS Roosevelt Roads, Puerto Rico

On the 29th of July 1965, I flew three flights in support of a Marine Battalion landing exercise on the island of Vieques. The commanding officer of the Battalion was Lieutenant Colonel Robert D. "Dewey" Bohn. We had met previously, when we were both Captains, and General's Aides, in California. He was Aide to Major General John T. Selden at Camp Pendleton, and I was Aide to Major General Christian Schilt at El Toro. I contacted Colonel Bohn aboard the command ship of the Amphibious Task Force, where he was with Commander Julian T. Burke, Jr. USN, who held the Title of Commodore.

I related to them that I would like to support the Marines who would be helicoptered to the landing zones on Vieques Island, by serving as a TACA Tactical Air Coordinator (airborne), while flying a jet from nearby Rosy Roads. Controlling a helicopter landing operation from a jet was something I had always wanted to try, since I had taught protection of vulnerable troop carrying helicopters at Marine Corps Schools in Quantico. I guaranteed that if allowed to participate, I could easily and correctly report the position of every helicopter wave from "feet dry," where it crossed from the sea to land, and at every control point along the approach and retirement routes, to and from the ship. I also commented that if approved, we all would be contributing further to the successful history of vertical envelopment, albeit on a larger scale than when we proved years earlier in Korea that we could supply a Marine battalion, IN COMBAT, by helicopter.

They both approved it and I flew back to Rosy Roads (in a helicopter). I had already planned to have other of my squadron Skyhawks "attack" simulated enemy targets at various control points along the approach routes, from "feet dry," to the landing zones. The squadron S-3 (Operations Officer), Major Bob Sheehan, planned other squadron flights to attack "enemy" gun positions. The squadron, deployed away from Beaufort, felt a very real sense of accomplishment. When flying my three TACA (A) flights on 29 July, I logged 6.4 flying hours in three separate squadron Skyhawks.

Surprise Arrival of VMF-451

By the end of July 1965, when we were preparing to leave Rosy Roads and return to our home base at Beaufort, I received a message from our 2nd MAW Headquarters at Cherry Point, notifying me that VMF-451 would arrive, and would co-locate with my Skyhawk squadron at Rosy Roads. I called a quick meeting of my principal squadron staff officers, read the "co-locate" (shared space) message to them. I told them that the VMF-451 Commander, Lieutenant Colonel George A. Gibson, was a very capable officer who would, no doubt, accept most, if not all of our co-locating suggestions, as long as those suggestions were fair, and beneficial to both squadrons.

I told the assembled group that I intended to move Lieutenant Colonel Gibson into my Commanding Officer's tent, and that I expected the same cooperative courtesy be extended by all of our VMA-331 to their VMF-451 counterparts. The VMF-451 fighter aircraft were the Chance-Vought F-8 (Crusaders), which were equipped with afterburners that would enable the Crusaders to reach speeds of MACH-1 and more.

We had completed our training cycle, so we could turn over bombing target priority at Vieques to VMF-451. We received the schedule for our squadron return to Beaufort in two weeks; so we had plenty of time to prepare for our return. At Commodore Julian Burke's suggestion, we selected one hundred of our squadron's enlisted Marines to embark on his ship, for a "liberty run" to the Dutch Island of Aruba in the Southern Caribbean Sea. They would then return them to Rosy Roads a week later. We had another liberty contingent fly to Jamaica on our Air Group twin-engine transport for a few days; another well- deserved "liberty run" for our squadron Marines.

For the members of our squadron who could not go on one of those "liberty runs," we organized a big squadron beach picnic party, complete with wonderful burgers and hot dogs. After some effective "beer courage," the Marines played their favorite game, called "throwing their Commanding Officer into a tub of iced beer, so he wouldn't have to go far, just to get a beer."

Each day I arrived at our shared tent about an hour after Colonel Gibson's arrival. I felt he should have some time alone to organize his day, before I arrived. One morning when I arrived, George greeted me warmly, saying, "Congratulations, Bob, you have just been selected for promotion to the rank of full Colonel". He then stated that his squadron, VMF-451, was organizing a promotion party for me at the Rosy Roads Officers' Club. I thanked him profusely, and suggested that the party be on the normal Wednesday "Free Rum Night" at the Rosy Roads Officer's club.

I did not receive a message of congratulations from Colonel Don Fisher, my Air Group Commanding Officer. Don's name was not on the promotion list, so my promotion created a very a awkward situation for both Don and me. Basically, I was selected for promotion, but my boss was not. So, what would be our future relationship? I didn't really know. I had a deep respect for Don Fisher.

He was an ace (five Japanese airplanes shot down), in Major Gregory "Pappy" Boyington's "Black Sheep" Squadron, in WW II. He recently led the ground contingent of our Air Group from Beaufort to Spain, and directed the building of a functioning expeditionary SATS airfield in three days. He was an excellent instructor at Marine Corps Schools in Quantico. Of course, I didn't know why he had been passed over for promotion. I honestly thought he should have been selected. Don had assumed command of MAG-31 when Colonel Ed Hartsock had been transferred to Washington. I sent a message to Don Fisher in which I pledged my complete support, stating that as long as he was Commanding Officer of MAG-31, he would continue to have my complete loyalty.

We also had a short-notice visit at Rosy Roads from Lieutenant General Alpha L. Bowser who, at Norfolk, Virginia, commanded Fleet Marine Force, Atlantic. His command included the 2nd Marine Air Wing at Cherry Point, and the 2nd Marine Division at Camp Lejeune, North Carolina. He visited both VMF-451, and my squadron. I had one of my squadron Warrant Officers, Chris Eck, organize a fun-filled "dining in" party at the Navy Officers Club. I also invited Don Fisher, my Air Group Commander to attend. Don flew down to Rosy Roads from Beaufort, and arrived before General Bowser; so he was on hand to greet General Bowser when he arrived.

As CFAD, I served as the dinner master of ceremonies, First, I welcomed the Navy Captain who was the commanding officer of the Naval Station, Roosevelt Roads; then my MAG-31 Commander, Don Fisher; followed by the commanding officers of our two neighboring Navy Squadrons; and, of course, I honored General Bowser by asking him to be the "dining in" guest speaker. He gave a very inspiring talk, regarding the importance of Marine Aviation. He mentioned the ordnance-loading demonstration that my attack squadron had put on for General Ormand R. Simpson a few weeks earlier at Rosy Roads, as an example of Marine Corps air/ground cooperation.

Return to Beaufort

On 24 August 1965, VMA-331 departed Rosy Roads for our non-stop flight to Beaufort. Our route home was west over Puerto Rico and the Dominican Republic. To avoid flying through Cuban airspace, we turned northwest, passing Great Inauga Island, over Nassau, then Grand Bahama Island; where we turned west and made landfall near Cape Canaveral, Florida. From there, we simply flew along the Florida coastline; over Jacksonville, then Savannah, where we started reducing altitude for our landing at Beaufort.

Upon landing, I was met on the flight line by Millie, Bill, and Jeanne. Bill was now a second year cadet at VMI. Jeanne was a Beaufort High School Junior. After my selection for promotion to Colonel, and before I returned from Puerto Rico, Millie had been moved into one of the beautiful larger quarters overlooking the Broad River, in the Laurel Bay housing area. Therefore, it appeared that I would be relieving Don Fisher, as the Commanding Officer of MAG-31, and thus would occupy one of the three Colonel's houses overlooking the Broad River. The other Colonel's quarters were reserved for the Beaufort Air Station Commanding Officer, the soon to arrive, Colonel Joseph R. "Joe" Warren.

Jeanne, Millie, Bob and Bill Warren (with Bob's A-4)
NAS Beaufort, SC (1965)

I thought it unusual; and I was surprised, and disappointed, that Colonel Don Fisher did not meet and greet VMA-331, one of his MAG-31 squadrons, as was traditional, on their fight line after returning home from their extended deployment in Puerto Rico.

The next day I reported to Don Fisher in his office that my squadron had returned to Beaufort in good order, after completing its training syllabus at Roosevelt Roads. I expressed my disappointment to him that he did not meet our returning squadron. He completely dismissed that comment. I also expressed my surprise that Millie had unexpectedly been moved into Colonel's quarters in Laurel Bay, without my knowledge. When I asked if any orders had been received regarding my future, he served me a large plateful.

He informed me that I would temporarily retain command of VMA-331, and would participate in a planned U.S. Sixth Fleet exercise in Greece; scheduled to start in about two weeks! In that only a few of our pilots were experienced in aerial refueling, he had arranged to have a KC-130 tanker in Beaufort, to practice aerial refueling on 2 September. He then told me that I would fly with him, in the Air Group twin-engine R4D-8 transport to Cherry Point on 2 September, where I would attend a briefing on the upcoming exercise in Greece.

By 2 September, the day my squadron was supposed to practice the aerial refueling that Don had scheduled, there was little doubt that he wanted to make everything as difficult as possible for my squadron; without appearing to do so. I didn't have an appreciation for the deep feeling of bitterness that Don Fisher held, because he had failed selection for promotion. I was truly sorry that our association, and respect for each other had deteriorated so far, so quickly. I realized that he wanted to remain at Beaufort, and wondered what else he would maneuver next, to assure that he would stay there. It didn't take long for me to find out.

On 2 September, I rode as a passenger in the Air Group twin-engine R4D-8, flown by Don Fisher, to Cherry Point where, at the 2nd MAW Headquarters, I would be briefed on the forthcoming 6th Fleet Exercise in Greece. I met with the 2nd MAW Staff, and noted that the Commanding General was absent. The senior officer who chaired the meeting was Colonel Stoddard Courtelyou, who I first thanked for representing the 2nd MAW, when I took command of VMA-331 at Beaufort six months before. He then requested that I give a brief report concerning our squadron activities at Roosevelt Roads.

I started by relating the visit of the Commander in Chief of the U.S. Atlantic Fleet, four-star Admiral Thomas Moorer, USN, who witnessed refueling our Skyhawks from a forty thousand gallon rubber bag. Next, was the visit of Major General (Selectee), Ormand R. Simpson, Commanding General of the 2nd Marine Division, who was accompanied by the Rear Admiral who commanded the Naval installation at Guantanamo Bay. I described the Skyhawk ordnance-loading demonstration we had provided for General Simpson. I then described the visit from Lieutenant General Alpha Bowser, the Commanding General, Fleet Marine Force, Atlantic. I noted some squirming on the part of the 2nd MAW staff, when they realized that those high ranking staff officers had visited my squadron at Roosevelt Roads, but none of them had.

The briefing on the upcoming maneuver in Greece then commenced. The two MAW G-3's (Operations Officers) said that twelve of my VMA-331 Skyhawks would participate, by first flying across the Atlantic Ocean. The first leg would be a non-stop flight of about two hours, from Beaufort to Kindley Air Force Base (AFB), Bermuda on 15 September. The second leg, on 16 September 1965, would be from Bermuda, to Torrejon AFB at Madrid, Spain; approaching landfall in Europe over Lisbon, Portugal. The non-stop flight to Torrejon would take 7.2 flight hours, and would require 3 aerial refuelings. The refueler aircraft would be Marine Corps KC-130s, operating from MCAS, Cherry Point. After its last aerial refueling, one of the KC-130 would remain with the Skyhawk squadron, throughout the exercise, to provide any service needed.

On 23 September, VMA-331 would fly to Larissa, Greece, its final destination; and from where it would participate in support of Greek and other Allied Force landings, near the Strymonas River, in northern Greece. Greek Air Forces, equipped with Republic-built F-94s, would also be operating from Larissa, in support of the exercise. The total exercise would take three days; after which VMA-331 would return home via Rota, Spain and Lajes AFB in the Azores, located twelve hundred miles west of Lisbon. From Lajes, 5 flying hours, and two aerial refuelings, would be required to reach Kindley AFB in Bermuda, on 3 October 1965. The G-3 wanted to know if I had any questions regarding the briefing.

I told him that I had several questions. In that the KC-130s were at Beaufort that day, for aerial refueling practice with my squadron pilots, could another KC-130 be spared for me to practice? I had never had a live aerial refueling opportunity, so I asked when I would get my turn. The G-3 said that he would check on that, and let me know. The 2nd MAW Chief Of Staff suggested a fifteen-minute break, and asked Don Fisher to accompany him from the conference room where the briefing was being held. I will never know for sure, but I sensed the Chief Of Staff took Don Fisher to the "woodshed."

When the briefing continued, I noted that Don Fisher did not return. The Chief Of Staff announced that Colonel Fisher was arranging for me to practice aerial refueling, and further, that Don Fisher would be contacting the MAG-31 Headquarters & Maintenance Squadron, to make sure that twelve of the VMA-331 Skyhawks had low-time jet engines, and to ensure that all twelve had perfectly functioning systems; including the all important aerial refueling probe valves.

I had more concerns, which I directed to the G-4 (Supply and Logistics), who was not a Naval Aviator. First, I wanted to know the source of available JP fuel at Larissa, for my twelve VMA-331 Skyhawks. I also wanted to know what type of ground equipment was available at Larissa to tow the Skyhawks in and out of existing airfield revetments; the availability of battery-operated blowers, used to start the Skyhawk jet engines; and the unique Skyhawk pilot boarding ladders. I also wanted to know the source of Skyhawk spare parts in the U.S. Sixth Fleet operating area, and who would be responsible for delivery of the needed spare parts to our squadron.

The 2nd MAW G-4 partially answered my briefing questions as follows: At Larissa, Greece, the U.S. Air Force had stored what was referred to as their War Reserves. That included one tanker (refueler) truck, filled with JP fuel, plus many items of wheeled airfield equipment. When I asked how long (days, weeks, months or years) those Air Force "War Reserves" had been stored at Larissa, he stated that he "would attempt to find out." I was obviously very apprehensive; especially about the spare parts availability, as I had already noted slowdown in Skyhawk spare parts availability to or squadron, due to the increased tempo of Marine Corps Skyhawk land-based operations in Vietnam. Priority was rightfully given to the Skyhawk combat squadrons fighting there.

After the briefing at the 2nd MAW conference room, I rode back to Beaufort in the same R4D-8, piloted by Don Fisher. We had no conversation during the flight, except that he told me that a "buddy store" flight had being arranged for me to practice aerial refueling.[xxiii] On 10 September, 1965 I flew a Skyhawk, and "plugged and unplugged" the "buddy store" ten times, at an altitude of twenty thousand feet; the same altitude that aerial refueling would be done during our forthcoming TransLant flight to Spain the following week.

During the week prior to departing Beaufort for Bermuda, the squadron made many decisions regarding the TransLant flight to Torrejon AFB near Madrid, Spain, and the non-stop twelve hundred mile flight to Greece, passing through Spanish, French, Italian and Greek airspaces. The route to be followed had already been determined by higher headquarters. Entering another country's airspace requires permission - usually per-arranged - and expected in the form of a Standard Position Report by radio, that includes flight composition, time, position, altitude, and the next anticipated reporting position.

For ease of aerial refueling, the twelve Skyhawks would proceed in flights of four; refueling from the KC-130, two at a time and, weather permitting, at twenty thousand feet. To extend the Skyhawk range, a fuel flow of thirteen hundred, twenty-five pounds per hour - rather than airspeed - would be monitored, and followed. Our Skyhawks would commence tanking with about thirteen hundred, twenty-five pounds of fuel aboard, and break away, fully loaded, a few minutes later, with nine thousand pounds of fuel aboard. After all four in each flight had been fueled, the flight would depart the KC-130, climb to a cruising altitude above thirty thousand feet, and proceed on course to the next aerial tanker position.

Meanwhile the KC-130 tanker would reel in its array of refueling hose and attached shuttlecock-shaped cones, into its large "wing tanks," and would reverse course, and await the next flight of four, due to arrive and commence refueling. The KC-130 that would accompany our squadron would carry our highly skilled enlisted mechanics to Bermuda, and wait at Kindley AFB for our arrival. It would carry twelve battery-operated blowers, used to start our Skyhawk jet engines, and twelve pilot boarding ladders; and wait there before further following our flight to Spain, and on to Greece.

Chapter 35: Jet Squadron TransLants

East-Toward the Rising Sun

On 15 September 1965, our squadron departed MCAS, Beaufort on a two hour, non-stop flight to Kindley AFB, Bermuda. We departed in flights of four, at thirty-minute intervals. Those intervals provided adequate time for landing and parking the first four Skyhawks, before the second four arrived. All twelve Skyhawks arrived on time, and in good order. Kindley AFB was a fully operating Air Station, so all parking and aircraft services were available; but under the watchful eye of our squadron Marines who had landed earlier on the KC-130. That completed the first leg of our TransLant flight "toward the rising sun."

The squadron enlisted men were billeted in Air Force barracks and the pilots in the Transit Officer's Quarters. I rested well; pleased to have completed the first leg successfully. The following morning, 16 September 1965, I led the first flight of four Skyhawks departing Bermuda, on the second leg of our flight to Torrejon, AFB near Madrid, Spain. That leg would require aerial refueling three times. My flight logbook shows that I flew 7.2 non-stop hours between Bermuda and Spain. My first aerial refueling (when I actually received fuel from a Marine Corps KC-130 tanker, the first time), was at our initial ARCP (Aerial Refueling Control Point), four hundred sixty-five miles east of Bermuda.

We met our KC-130 tanker at the pre-planned altitude of twenty thousand feet; flying on our course that moved our flight along more than one hundred miles, while my flight of four jets refueled. My aerial refueling was easy. One of the pilots in my flight, observing my refueling, by radio said, "It looked just like a aerial refueling training film, Colonel." The fuel flowed through my refueling probe, past the cockpit. I could hear the noise of the fuel gushing past the cockpit. It took only a few minutes to reach a full fuel load of nine thousand pounds, including the two wing tanks, which were automatically filled. As soon as the first two Skyhawks were "tanked," they moved off to the side, while the next two refueled. When all four of our jets had completed aerial refueling, we climbed in formation, back to our cruising altitude; then later descended back down to twenty thousand feet to meet our second tanker. After the second refueling, we continued our flight toward the third KC-130, where we completed our last refueling between the Portuguese Azores Islands, and the city of Lisbon, Portugal.

Lt. Col. Bob Warren aerial refueling in his A-4, on the way to Greece

As we approached the Portugal/Spain border, we transmitted our required position report, and commenced a slow altitude reduction, letting our jets slow to five hundred miles per hour, as we crossed Spain, flying toward Torrejon, AFB near Madrid. We had plenty of fuel to complete the flight, so we increased our airspeed considerably; not concerned anymore with fuel flow rate. Our first flight of four Skyhawks landed at Torrejon, AFB about an hour before the second flight, led by Major Ken Jacks, arrived on schedule. The third flight of four, led by Major Bob Sheehan arrived next. Upon arrival, all of the pilots were taken to the Officer's Mess for a meal; then to the Visiting Pilots Quarters to shower and sleep, sleep, and sleep-- for hours!

Our squadron remained at Torrejon, AFB for a week, before we departed for the last twelve hundred mile non-stop leg to Larissa, Greece. Over Spain, we were under Barcelona Air Control. Then, we gave our next Position Report to French control. We did not fly over France, but their sovereignty reached south, into the Mediterranean Sea; so a Position Report was required. One of the pilots in my flight was Captain Bill DePietro who was of Italian descent. Bill spoke fluent Italian; so he asked if he could give the next Position Report, when we reached Italian Airspace. I gave him permission to do so. I thought it would be an unusual radio communication, as air control language, worldwide, is English. Crossing into Italian Airspace, Bill called (In Italian) "Roma Control, Roma Control, entering Roma Airspace at Time, Position and Altitude, next reporting to Hellenic Control, over." Roma Control quickly answered Bill's Italian message (in perfect English), "We don't need to talk to you," I thought it was amusing; but I think Bill was somewhat disappointed, if not crushed. When we crossed into Greek Airspace, I gave the position report to Hellenic Control, and our flight landed at the Greek Air Base at Larissa. The second and third flights landed later; thirty minutes apart.

Larissa Air Base

The Greek city of Larissa is located about one hundred fifty miles north of Athens, on the main highway between Athens and Thessaloniki. That coastal road passes a myriad of bays, and inlets, that mark the western border of the Aegean Sea. We landed at Larissa Air Base on a runway about eleven thousand feet long. It had been construction by the Germans during WW II, to provide a bomber base in that area. The runway was lined with large aircraft revetments, in which the German Heinkel bombers, and other German aircraft, could be parked and protected. The revetments were so large that our twelve Skyhawks required only three revetments; with parking space left over in each.

The Greek Air Force was also operating from Larissa. They were flying former U.S. Air Force fighter aircraft of the F-84 vintage. They landed so fast that most of the eleven thousand foot runway was used. By contrast, when landing our A-4 Skyhawks, less than half of that long runway was used.

After our arrival, and parking in one the revetments, we occupied tents that had been erected for us. One sign over a tent opening had Greek lettering. Underneath on the same sign was printed, in English, VMA-331. I didn't really know what the Greek lettering meant at that time. But after bringing the sign back to Beaufort, I took it to a Greek restaurant, and asked for a translation of the Greek lettering. Translated, it meant "the Officer in Charge." We had arrived several days before our part in the Exercise began; so, I had our accompanying KC-130 take me to Athens, to learn as much as possible about details concerning the Exercise, but even more importantly, to learn when we could expect the arrival of the spare parts we had requested. I was told that our spare parts requests were, or would be, sent to the Sixth Fleet Aviation Depot in Rota, Spain.

While in Athens, I had time to visit the Parthenon, overlooking the city; built in honor of Athena, the Greek Goddess of Wisdom. I marveled at the eight massive, tapered columns along the Parthenon front, and seventeen on each side. I also shopped at one of the thirty or so furrier stores in Athens. I purchased a beautiful Stone Marten stole, and a Persian lamb coat for Millie. I also bought an Athens Palace Guard Greek hat, which I brought it back to Beaufort in my jet. I wore it when I met Millie on the flight line, in Beaufort. The Greek Guard hat was red, with a long gold tassel; and was usually worn atop a white palace guard uniform.

I sent my other fur purchases back to Beaufort on the KC-130, along with items purchased by our squadron personnel, who visited Athens after the Exercise was completed. I had sent the KC-130 to Athens again, and to Remain Overnight (RON), so more of our personnel would have a chance to relax, sightsee, and shop. Most of the Athens furriers received raw furs in bales from Canada.

I was given the choice of returning to Larissa by flying, or by riding in an American Military Staff Car. I opted for the staff car, and thoroughly enjoyed the day-long ride. In many ways it reminded me of driving across the United States. We passed seaside resorts, areas resembling the Piedmont, tobacco farms, and beautiful rolling hills, all in one day.

U.S. Air Force War Reserve Equipment

We were horrified, when we first saw the Air Force War Reserve equipment that we were supposed to use during this Exercise. The wheeled towing equipment had not been used for years; evidenced by the fact that the wheels could not be turned. Our squadron mechanics quickly removed the wheels, cleaned the wheel bearings, added new grease, and made them operative and useful again. Next, we inspected the one U.S. Air Force War Reserve refueling truck. The fuel it contained was contaminated, as large globs of bacteria were present. That could be expected, when fuel is unused, and stored for long periods. We could do nothing by ourselves to remedy that contaminated fuel situation. We needed an immediate new source of JP fuel for our Skyhawks.

I reported this to our 2nd MAW Headquarters and further, that we were contacting the Greek Air Force to see if their JP fuel would be compatible. It was; and we arranged for one of their refueling trucks to be available to refuel our Skyhawks, during the Exercise. When I reported this back to the 2nd MAW at Cherry Point, the G-4 bean counters wanted to know the unit of Greek JP fuel, and the cost per unit. Further, they wanted to know who was going to pay for the Greek fuel we used. Running out of patience, and tired from the long flights from Beaufort to Greece, I curtly answered back, "Probably the American Taxpayer, as usual."

Having solved most of our squadron's local problems, which had been created by the long-time neglect of The Air Force War Reserves, we flew all of our flights in the Scheduled 6th Fleet Exercise, with no further problems. Another concern for me was that the Skyhawk parts we had requested, immediately following our arrival in Europe, were never received. The A-4 Skyhawk is a wonderful airplane, with excellent capabilities. However, it is very small; so there is little space for redundant (back up) systems.

For instance, all the electronic components are housed in a single, round "biscuit," which has to be pressurized. It is placed just ahead of the pilot's feet, literally inside the Skyhawk cockpit. Without pressurization, the whole electronic biscuit shorts out, and immediately becomes useless. So, if a cockpit seal develops a leak, the pilot has no communication, and is very uncomfortable. Without cockpit pressurization, the pilot remains conscious because he is still getting oxygen through his face mask, but none of his attitude instruments function properly.

I had earlier contacted an aircraft carrier that was also participating in the 6th Fleet Exercise, citing the list of parts we needed. The carrier responded that they had no spare A-4 parts, as they were no longer operating the Skyhawk. Without spare parts, the maintenance problems would multiply quickly, and very soon. There were already several Skyhawks parked on the flight line, in non-flyable condition. I was pondering how I could get twelve Skyhawks to fly safely non-stop to Rota, Spain, where I had been told the Aviation Supply Depot for the U.S. Sixth Fleet was located.

I was considering meeting with my squadron staff officers as soon as they returned from Athens. Together, we could possibly figure out a safe solution. I was considering that situation when a KC-130 landed at Larissa. I thought it was the "liberty" flight returning early from Athens. It was not. But aboard was Lieutenant General Alpha Bowser, the Commanding General, Fleet Marine Force, Atlantic, from Norfolk, Virginia, along with my 2nd MAW Commander, Major General George Bowman, from Cherry Point. They arrived at Larissa from Thessaloníki, where they had observed the amphibious landings, in which we had provided "Exercise" air support. I quickly briefed them on the landings, from our viewpoint. They seemed satisfied that all had gone quite well. General Bowser told me that he was somewhat surprised to see me again, as he had just seen me only a few weeks ago at Roosevelt Roads in Puerto Rico.

I described the deplorable condition of the Air Force War Reserves, and how our aviation mechanics had managed to clean and grease the wheel bearings, so that those equipment items could be used. I told the Generals that I just couldn't believe seeing the globs of contaminated fuel stored in the War Reserve fuel truck. I considered refueling from a Marine KC-130, but twelve Skyhawks would need more than the available amount of fuel in a KC-130. So, I had gone "hat in hand" to the Greek Air Force at Larissa to see if the jet fuel they were using, was compatible with the fuel used by our Skyhawks. Fortunately it was, and the Greeks had loaned a refueling truck to us, with an invitation to refill the truck from their sources when needed.

I told General Bowman about his staff wanting to know what the Greek unit of fuel measure was, plus the cost per unit, and other petty details, including them wanting to know who was going to pay for it. General Bowser then asked me, "What did you tell them?" When I told him that, as usual, "probably the American taxpayer" would pay for it, he smiled and said, "Good Answer." With that, I felt that General Bowman was undergoing a "slow burn," regarding the pettiness of his 2nd MAW staff.

I then expressed my concern over not receiving the badly needed spare parts, and not being confident about safely flying from Greece, non-stop, twelve hundred miles to Rota, Spain, where I was told aviation spare parts for the Sixth Fleet were stored. Knowing that we could not stay in Greece much longer, I told the two Generals that we would have to fly to Rota under visual flight conditions, and that some of our Skyhawks would be not fully equipped. I told them that I would ensure that at least the leader in each flight of four would have all of his Skyhawk systems fully functional; and that each of the flights would be led by one of my squadron's experienced Majors.

Knowing that I was putting him on the spot in front of his boss, I then asked General Bowman if he concurred with my plan. He obviously had no choice but to say that he appreciated my predicament, and that he did concur. He told me that all of our Skyhawks would be fully equipped before our TransLant west, no matter where the spare parts came from. I tucked that statement into my memory bank, for possible future use. I knew that my popularity with the 2nd MAW Staff, and their commanding general, was probably slipping fast. I did not realize that it would get even worse after we arrived in Rota, Spain, and after General Bowman had returned to Cherry Point.

After the two Marine Generals departed, the KC-130 "liberty" flight landed at Larissa, and the squadron pilots emerged presenting a sorry sight. Each carried a named furrier box, containing a fur to be brought to Beaufort for their wife. Each pilot also appeared to have a severe hangover, caused by drinking an excessive amount of Ouzo, the anise-flavored. lip-smacking delicious, Greek National Drink. After discussing the makeup of each Skyhawk flight, we departed Larissa several days later; although several Skyhawks lacked the repairs critical for flight safety. However, all reached Rota safely, with a lot of good weather, and no doubt, the Lord's Blessing as well. Once again, I felt that He was never far away, when I needed Him most.

Naval Station, Rota, Spain

The U.S. Naval Station (NAVSTAROTA) is stationed on a beautiful, sixty-one hundred acre Spanish Naval Base. Sitting on the Atlantic Coast in Southern Spain, it is located only a few hours from the Straits of Gibraltar. It is sometimes called "The Gateway to the Mediterranean." Driving north, it is only a few hours to Portugal. Rota supports U.S. and NATO units, transiting the region with fuel, cargo and logistics, and serves as an Aviation Supply Depot for The U.S. Sixth Fleet. I was anxious to reach the source of Aviation supply at Rota; hopeful that that my growing list of needed Skyhawk spare parts would be filled. But, I was told the Skyhawk squadrons fighting in South Vietnam had taken all of the parts previously stored in Rota. Learning this, I transmitted the list of the spare parts that I needed, by message, to the 2d MAW Headquarters at Cherry Point. I added that I would not attempt a TransLant without fully functioning airplanes in my squadron.

I also requested approval of my plan to move my squadron, piecemeal, to Lajes, AFB, located in the Azore Islands, by sending at least two aircraft at a time, after the anticipated parts had been received and were installed. Moving my squadron to Lajes, twelve hundred miles west of Rota, would have the advantage of reducing the number of aerial refuelings from three to two, while en route to Kindley AFB in Bermuda. I received approval for my plan; but the source of spare parts was not yet revealed to me.

Translant West-Toward the Setting Sun

I was stunned, when I learned that an A-4 Skyhawk squadron, located at Cherry Point, had been grounded, so the parts I needed could be removed from its Skyhawks, and delivered to my squadron at Rota. The procedure of taking parts from another airplane is called "cannibalization," and except for in dire emergencies, is forbidden; because it short circuits, and seriously disrupts, the entire Naval Aviation support and supply chain. I received a message from the 2nd MAW at Cherry Point, advising me of the "cannibalization" source of supply. I was advised that the list of spare parts my squadron needed would arrive in Rota within 2-3 days. The parts did arrive, on a Marine KC-130, on the third day. Its pilot gave me an unsigned message, demanding that the spare parts be returned to Cherry Point within 48 hours after my squadron landed back at Beaufort.

It seemed to me that someone considered a few Skyhawks sitting on the flight line for a few days without parts, was much more serious than my squadron's need to safely transit the Atlantic Ocean on a trip long enough to require multiple aerial refuelings. I immediately tore up the message, and threw it away, with the KC-130 pilot watching. I was hoping he would report my action to the same person who gave him the message, and who didn't have the guts to sign it.

I remained in Rota, and flew one of the last two A-4 Skyhawks to reach Lajes. I reported to the 2nd MAW Headquarters in Cherry Point, that VMA-331 was ready for TransLant to Bermuda. I also requested from MAG-31, that its Headquarters and Maintenance Squadron remove all of our "borrowed" spare parts, as soon as possible, after we landed at Beaufort; and return them to Cherry Point, "within the 48 hours" specified in the unsigned note delivered to me at Rota, by the pilot of the KC-130.

The next day, 3 October 1965, my squadron departed Lajes for Bermuda and, after aerial refueling twice, arrived after non-stop flights of 5.2 hours. Our accompanying KC-130 was a designated aerial refueler for our flight. Some of our "passenger" mechanics took pictures out of the KC-130 windows, of our jets "plugged in" to the tanker refueling hoses. After Remaining Overnight at Kindley AFB, we departed as a single, twelve-plane flight, to MCAS, Beaufort. Millie met me on the VMA-331 flight line. I removed my jet helmet, and donned the gold tasseled, red Greek hat, before I climbed out of the cockpit, and descended the boarding ladder to the tarmac, where she welcomed me home with her special kiss.

I was relieved that VMA-331 was safely home. Again, I thanked the Lord for His divine guidance to VMA-331 (Bumblebees), all the way to Greece and back.

When removing my G-Suit and Flight suit in the pilot's ready room, Lieutenant Colonel Gordon V. Hodde met me, and told me he was transferred to Beaufort, and had orders to relieve me as Commanding Officer of VMA-331. I expected to be relieved by somebody, as I had been selected for promotion to the rank of Colonel. I congratulated Gordon, and told him that he was getting a well- trained A-4 Squadron, and that I was surprised that I had not been relieved when I brought the squadron back to Beaufort from Puerto Rico, as I had been selected for promotion to Colonel. Too, my wife Millie had been moved into the large house in Laurel Bay, before I had returned with my squadron from Puerto Rico. I had a suspicious idea about who was behind all of that chicanery. Our new house was next door to Colonel Joe Warren's house, who was the new Commanding Officer of MCAS, Beaufort.

After resting for a few days, I had an 'all pilots meeting" in the squadron Ready Room. It was intended to be my farewell speech to my squadron's pilots. I told them how proud I was of all of them, and thanked them for helping me become a better jet pilot. I revealed to them that our squadron had to overcome some major obstacles during our deployment to Greece, and return. Some of the problems were withheld from them, and that probably, at times, was at least puzzling to them. I told them that the command problems were mine. Further, the problems always belong to the unit's Commanding Officer and, if he passes them along, he is only destroying the morale in his unit. I emphasized this by admonishing them to remember the long standing military adage, "The Commander, and the Commander alone, is responsible for everything his unit does, or fails to do. He may delegate his authority, but never his responsibility." I told them that their new VMA-331 Commanding Officer would be Lieutenant Colonel Gordon Hodde, who they would meet at the end of this meeting. Further, that several of them would, no doubt, receive orders to South Vietnam very soon. I reminded them that was the real purpose for all their Skyhawk training. I then asked them to please stand, and greet their soon-to-be, new VMA-331 Commanding Officer, Lieutenant Colonel Gordon Hodde.

I left the meeting, and went outdoors to say goodbye to the squadron enlisted men, who were assembled in formation. I expressed my thanks to them, and to their NCO leaders, for the success of their squadron through many trying times, and told them that I knew I could always depend on them. I told them that I knew they would give their same support and loyalty to their new VMA-

331 Commanding Officer, Lieutenant Colonel Hodde, who they would meet in a few minutes. I also told them that their outstanding performance of duty during our deployments to Puerto Rico and to Greece, were no doubt major factors in VMA-331 just receiving the Attack Squadron Naval Aviation Safety Award for Year 1965. Thank you, fellow Marines, and Semper Fidelis!

Millie and Bob; VMA-331 returns from Greece
NAS Beaufort, SC (1965)

Chapter 36: Beaufort to Cherry Point

Change of Station Orders

The day before my meetings with our squadron pilots and enlisted men, I had received my copy of message orders from the 2nd MAW, which are cited briefly as follows:

(1) Directed Colonel Mahafee to proceed to MCAS, Beaufort, and relieve Lieutenant Colonel Fisher as the Commanding Officer of MAG-31.

(2) Directed MAG-31 to assign Lieutenant Colonel Hodde as the Commanding Officer of VMA-331, relieving Colonel (selectee) Robert Warren.

(3) Directed Colonel (selectee) Robert Warren transfer to the 2nd MAW at Cherry Point, for further assignment, with 30 day annual leave authorized.

The orders further specified that the changes cited in this order would be effected without ceremony. Sadly, this meant that there would be no traditional troop formations, to include passing of the unit's flag from the old to the new Commanding Officer. Millie also wondered why they had moved her into a new on-base house for only three months. The Base public works department again made arrangements with a local Moving Company, to pack our household effects, and load and transfer them to MCAS, Cherry Point.

We decided not to take annual leave at that time; so Jeanne could quickly transfer from Beaufort to Havelock High School. The town of Havelock was located just outside the MCAS, Cherry Point main gate. Jeanne coped very well with the news of my transfer; knowing she would miss her Beaufort High School classmates. But, she also knew that service kids are used to unexpected transfers, and she was able to quickly adapt to making new friends. I was anxious to leave Beaufort, because in the 14 months that I was stationed there, I had been deployed for 10½ months. Before departing Beaufort, I had called the Cherry Point Hostess House, and made reservations for our temporary stay, while officially checking in at Cherry Point.

Millie was at Beaufort High School to get Jeanne's school records, for her transfer to Havelock High School. Meanwhile, I was saying goodbye to neighbors and friends at Laurel Bay. Our son Bill was on leave from VMI, and was available to help drive our VW "Bug," and our Oldsmobile convertible, the three hundred miles to Cherry Point. Bill and Jeanne rode together most of the trip in the VW, and thus had some good brother/sister time together. While I was transitioning to swept-wing jet flying at Cherry Point, I had driven that same route twice a week; so I was very familiar with U.S. 17, the coastal highway which passed from Savannah, near Beaufort, through Charleston, Myrtle Beach, past the Camp Lejeune Marine Base at Jacksonville, North Carolina, and then on to New Bern, only seventeen miles from Cherry Point.

While staying in the Hostess House before officially reporting to the 2nd MAW Headquarters for my duty assignment, we were notified that our on-base quarters were not ready for occupancy, and we were assigned to temporary on-base quarters. We enrolled Jeanne in Havelock High School, and made a driving trip to Morehead City. We passed the house we had rented years before, on Evans Street. We reminisced about Bill taking his first steps in the house next door, which was owned by Percy and Roxie Holland. The Masonic Hall, located behind our house, was still standing, and appeared well kept.

After several weeks, I was assigned a very nice two story brick house, in a U-shaped wooded neighborhood. It was commonly known as the senior officers housing area. Two houses at the end of our street had a commanding view, overlooking the very wide Neuse River. They were assigned to the two General Officers stationed at Cherry Point. The Quonset Hut housing area, where we had previously lived for 3½ years, when I was a Lieutenant and Bill was a busy toddler, no longer existed.

Our house had been built before central air conditioning had been developed. So, window air conditioners had been installed on each floor. I also recall that a truck dispensing a DDT fog would drive through our neighborhood each week during the bug season. The neighborhood kids had great fun running behind the dispensing truck through the DDD fog. Ginger, our dachshund, would often show up at our door with a badly swollen face. We surmised that she had gone hunting in the wooded area near our house, and had burrowed into a bee or hornet nest in the woods, or possibly into one of many ant hills. We would give her some anti-inflammatory medicine to reduce her temporary, pitiful appearance, and her obvious pain.

As expected, Jeanne adapted to Havelock High School conditions quickly, and soon developed new, close friends. After six weeks, we offered to send her back to Beaufort for a short visit with her old friends. She said that she would rather stay at Cherry Point, with her new friends. In her Junior year, she became a cheerleader at Havelock High School.

Promotion and Staff Assignment

On 4 December 1965, in the office of the Commanding General, 2nd MAW, I was promoted to the rank of Colonel. His Aide read the 15" x 10" promotion document. Over the Presidential Seal is printed, "The **PRESIDENT** of **THE UNITED STATES OF AMERICA**". The promotion document was signed by General Wallace M. Green, Jr., Commandant of the Marine Corps, and by Paul H. Nitze, Secretary of the Navy. It established 1 December 1965, as my new

Colonel's date of rank. I was then told that my 2nd MAW Staff Assignment would be the G-2 (Intelligence Officer), as soon as my Top Secret security clearance was verified.

I don't know why I was assigned that staff job, except that 1951, just before our helicopter squadron sailed for Korea, Lieutenant Colonel Herring sent me to NAS, Alameda, California to attend a six week long Air Intelligence School. That probably was still in my personnel record. However, I was more inclined to think that maybe the 2nd MAW had a G-2 staff opening for a full Colonel, and I just happened to be available.

My assistants in the G-2 section included a skilled Major named Howard Albright, and a Second Lieutenant named Doug Hurd, who had been promoted from his former enlisted rank. Both had been trained, and had flown as Radar Intercept Officers, in several Marine Photo Reconnaissance Squadrons. Howard had also completed a year-long exchange tour, with the Royal Air Force in England. While flying there, he had to ejected from his jet, which was equipped with a Martin-Baker Ejection Seat. The parachute functioned properly, and thus, Major Howard Albright automatically became a member of the Martin-Baker Ejection Seat Society.

The G-2 Staff also included several top enlisted men, all of whom possessed Top Secret security clearances. Intelligence gathering activities came under G-2 staff cognizance at the 2nd MAW. Most intelligence gathering flights from Cherry Point were flown by Marine Photo Reconnaissance Squadron-1 (VMCJ-1). Flying new, supersonic, twin-jet McDonnell F4 (Phantoms), each carried no guns, but instead, had a whole array of intelligence gathering equipment, including aerial cameras, and sophisticated radars.

After daily missions, the data gathered was removed quickly from the VMCJ-1 Phantoms, and delivered immediately to a higher military headquarters. That is about the limit of information I feel comfortable to reveal. I was surprised to learn the extent of the local intelligence gathering efforts accomplished daily, by VMCJ-1. In addition to the daily intelligence gathering we provided, we also received worldwide classified information, most of which would be included in our once-a-week, early morning staff briefings. I can clearly recall my briefings, including events leading up to the overthrow of the Shah of Iran, and him being replaced with the Ayatollah Khomeini; who later established the Islamic Republic of Iran.

Iran is the second largest country (by area) in the Middle East. Saudi Arabia is first. I also gained a wealth of knowledge about coast and landing beaches throughout the world, where Marine Corps Amphibious Operations could feasibly be conducted. My head was spinning, trying to absorb all of the new information I received. At the time, I did not realize how much that knowledge would later affect my duty assignments in South Vietnam.

Temporary Orders to Europe

The 2nd MAW was directed to send two representatives, holding Top Secret clearances, to attend an Electronics Intelligence Conference in Oberammergau, Germany - a small village near Germany's southern border. I was allowed to take Millie, but I had to pay for her travel expenses. I also selected Major Albright to attend the Conference. He certainly had the background to absorb the classified material presented, and to contribute the results of his experiences as well. He chose to have his wife, Charlotte, accompany him.

We flew via commercial airliner to London. Major Albright and I were briefed at the U.S. Naval Headquarters, regarding our participation at the Oberammergau Conference. As I had never been stationed in Europe, Millie and I felt fortunate to have the Albrights with us. They had served in England for over a year. When Howard was "posted" with the British Royal Air Force, they traveled extensively throughout Europe. Following our briefings at the Naval Headquarters in London, the four us flew to Frankfurt, Germany. We arrived several days ahead of the Oberammergau Conference, so we would have time to enjoy driving our rented car between Frankfurt and Munich; which added greatly to our enjoyment, especially having the Albrights as our driving "tour guides." We were impressed with the neatness, cleanliness and organization that was very evident, even in the smaller German towns, as we drove through the German countryside.

Munich, Germany

With a population of around 1.5 million people, Munich is the second most populous city in the German Federal state. Only the German Capital city of Berlin has a larger population. Munich is known as the "Beer Capital of the World." Each year, in September and October, during the annual sixteen-day Oktoberfest held in Munich, over a million and a half gallons of beer is consumed. There are multiple beer taverns in Munich; the most famous of which is the Hofbrauhaus which opened in 1589. Munich is home to numerous museums and centuries-old buildings. And new ones, like the modern BMW Auto Museum can be visited, as well. The Munich Central Plaza contains the popular Glockenspiel Show, in which daily, high above street level, promptly at 11:00 am, the glockenspiel chimes, and through moving parts, tells stories from the 16thcentury. From Munich, we drove about fifty miles south, to Garmisch-Partenkirchen, located near the German/Austrian border.

General George S. Patton Hotel

While attending the Conference in Oberammergau, we stayed at the General George S. Patton Hotel, in the city of Garmisch-Partenkirchen. A huge, framed, and lighted mural of General Patton hangs prominently on a hotel lobby wall. Several feet high, the painting depicts Lieutenant General George S. Patton, standing in front of several tanks, with dismounted crews. Riding crop in hand, he is resplendent in his uniform; with highly polished boots, and leather leggings that reach his Army Uniform britches, just below his knees. His gleaming helmet is Army green, and displays the three silver stars of his Lieutenant General rank, also displayed on his uniform shoulder epaulets. At his waist, his two pearled-handled revolvers can be seen.

During WW II, under General Omar Bradley, Lieutenant General Patton had brilliantly commanded the U.S. 3rd Army. He did not come home after the German forces surrendered, as he died of wounds received while riding in his Staff Car, which was mysteriously hit by a large U.S. Army truck. He died a four-star General, on 21 December 1945, and is buried in the American Cemetery and Memorial, in Hamm, Luxembourg.

Oberammergau

Located in the beautiful Bavarian Alps, Oberammergau is known primarily as a wood-carving town. Also, in 1634, the townspeople started what became known as "The Passion Play." It began at the town cemetery, where hundreds who had died from a pestilence (plague) sweeping Europe, were buried. The "Passion Play," now performed every decade, depicts the suffering and death of Jesus Christ on the Cross. Seating capacity at the "Passion Play" is limited to fifty-two hundred people, and requires reservations to attend. Up to three hundred actors are on the stage at one time. Only Oberammergau's permanent citizens may participate. A "Passion Play" lunch intermission is declared half way through the three hour performance. Attendee reservations include the name and location of the restaurant where the attendee must have lunch. The "Passion Play" is performed in German. However, attendees are given easy-to-follow translation booklets.

The Conference

The Electronic Intelligence Conference site, at Oberammergau, was only a twenty mile drive from the Patton Hotel. Major Albright and I drove to the Conference site each day, leaving Millie and Charlotte at the Patton Hotel, to shop and to sightsee in the quaint city. As Conference attendees, we were required to present our Military ID Cards, and verification of our security clearance, every time we entered the Conference site. We were warned to never discuss our Conference experiences in our automobiles, or outside the Conference site, for any reason.

For the most part, the information presented was for only attendee consumption and use. By contrast, Major Albright and I had the opportunity to describe how we gained intelligence locally, then how the distribution process worked. Having done that, I felt that we had contributed materially to the Conference agenda. Once again, this is all of the Conference information I can comfortably discuss.

Garmisch-Partenkirchen

This picturesque city is nestled in a valley near the Germany/Austria border. It was the site of the 1936 Winter Olympic Games. The mountain scenery is magnificent, and may be enjoyed from all directions. Just to the south of the city, the Zugspitze, Germany's highest mountain, rises to nine thousand, seven hundred, eighteen feet. The Germany/Austria border runs over its summit. Cable cars connect to the top of Zugspitze where, on a clear day, the mountain peaks of Austria, Italy and Switzerland can all be seen. Accessing the cable cars was easy, and they operated daily from 8:30 am to 4:45 pm. It was a fifteen-minute ride up to the mountain top, with the cable cars rising vertically six thousand, five hundred, sixty-two feet. The view from the top is spectacular in all directions, including a view of Lake Eibsee, far below. The moving cable cars stop climbing momentarily, as they pass over the flat, tower-supporting array of "bogey" (alignment) wheels. From inside the cable car, passengers first feel a slight rocking motion, followed by the sensation of falling; thus adding further to the cable car-riding thrills.

Conference End - Return to the USA

With the Electronic Intelligence Conference over, we commenced our return trip to the United States. We first drove our rented car to the Munich airport, where the Albrights left us to fly directly to London, where they would spend time with their Royal Air Force friends. Millie and I continued driving our rented car back to Frankfurt. As we neared each German town, we would see posted signs that read "WILLKOMEN" above the city name, also printed in German. We had fun trying to pronounce each German city name. When departing a city another sign read "AUF WIEDERSEHEN" above the city name. Those signs made it easy to follow our German road map, back to Frankfurt.

Arriving in Frankfurt, we turned in our rented car at the airport and then flew to London where we anticipated rendezvousing with the Albrights, and flying back to the United States together. However, the Albrights were not there. In London, we learned that they had returned home early. Howard had been notified that his brother, Second Lieutenant, Walter L. "Walt" Albright had been killed in South Vietnam, while flying as the radar intercept officer in a Douglas F3D night fighter squadron. It was a sad end to what otherwise, had been a wonderful trip to Europe. Upon arrival back at Cherry Point, I briefed the 2nd MAW Commanding General on the agenda of the Conference in Oberammergau.

The rest of my duties, as the 2nd MAW G-2, were busy and enjoyable. To meet my flight proficiency requirements, I would often fly to distant cities to pick up components needed for a Marine squadron deploying to South Vietnam. I recall one such flight to Manchester, New Hampshire, and returning to Cherry Point on 19 October, 1966. That two-way flight required a total of 8.4 hours of flight time. On the flights when the cargo did not require a larger, four-engine KC-130 Hercules, we used a smaller, twin-engine Douglas R4D-8, now re-designated the C-117. I alternated my flying to remain current in both fixed-wing and rotary-wing aircraft.

Just before Christmas in 1966, on a pre-arranged flight to Roanoke, Virginia, our son Bill, who was on Christmas leave from VMI, was waiting in his cadet uniform. He climbed aboard, for the flight back to Cherry Point. During the Christmas and New Years Day holidays, I joined three other officers who had recently been promoted to Colonel, in planning, and sharing the cost of a promotion party at the Cherry Point Officers Club.

It was a grand buffet, with mountains of food. The buffet table centerpiece was a 2-3 foot high mountain-like fountain, with iced punch flowing down over three Colonel's rank shoulder insignia, simulating the "waters" of the Atlantic, Pacific and Indian Oceans. It was a joyous time for our family, our guests, and the other two newly-promoted Colonels as well. Bill wore his VMI Cadet Dress Uniform to my promotion party.

Year 1967

Before Bill returned to VMI, following his Christmas leave, he told us that he was applying to be commissioned in the Marine Corps, upon his college graduation. He had enrolled in Army ROTC at VMI, so he would not be required to attend the two six-week summer Officer Candidate Classes at Quantico. If accepted for a Marine Corps commission upon graduation, he would be ordered directly to The Basic School (TBS) at Marine Corps Schools in Quantico. He told me that he had contacted General Walt concerning his application for a Marine Corps commission. General Walt's response was, "Bill, <u>we</u> think the process has been delayed because it has been working its way through Army ROTC channels. However, the Marine Corps' Regular Commission Selection Board has assured me that your application will receive immediate attention, upon receipt." It did; and Bill was notified that he had been selected for a regular Marine Corps Commission upon his graduation from VMI. I don't think that Bill had to be concerned. Sometimes, it is reassuring to have friends in high places.

In January 1967, I was notified by the 2nd MAW G-1 (Personnel) that I could expect orders transferring me to SW Asia (Vietnam) the following May; more specifically, for assignment for duty with the III Marine Amphibious Force (III MAF). My transfer was a cause for some serious decisions for Millie and me. Jeanne would be a High School Senior during the next year, while I was deployed. Rather than having Jeanne move to another High School, we decided to rent a house off-base in the town of Havelock. Jeanne could keep her classmates and other friends, and in June of 1968, graduate from Havelock High School. Bill would also graduate from VMI in June, 1968. We rented a nice three-bedroom house in Havelock, and moved off-base in late April, 1967.

Also in late April, 1967, I said goodbye to my family, and departed for South Vietnam (SVN). I had no idea what my assignment would be, upon arrival. General Walt now commanded III MAF in Vietnam.

Chapter 37: Transfer to Vietnam

On 13 April, 1967 we celebrated Millie's 43d birthday, and our 44th Wedding Anniversary (the next day), at a party at the MCAS, Cherry Point Officers Club. During the following week, I said goodbye to my family, who had moved off base into a rented house in Havelock, North Carolina. I departed, to start my thirteen-month tour of duty in South Vietnam (SVN). I flew on a commercial airliner, to Honolulu, Hawaii. After reporting to our Fleet Marine Force, Pacific Headquarters in Hawaii, I was booked on a military flight to Kadena, AFB on Okinawa. At Kadena, the U.S. Air Force operates an aerial port, the agency that schedules all U.S. Military Passenger Flights to and from SVN from Okinawa. When I presented my orders, directing me to III MAF in Da Nang, the aerial port personnel wanted to know when I wanted to depart. I chose 29 April, so my thirteen-month tour in country (Vietnam) would commence no later than 1 May 1967, and would end 13 months later, on 1 June 1968.

      I was met at the DaNang airport by Colonel John Mahon. I had known him at Quantico, where our son, Bill had dated his daughter in High School. We rode together in a military jeep across a long, modern bridge that had been built recently by a Philippine company, over the Han River. I saw only two docks along the river that had boats in them, among hundreds of empty docks. John took me to a barracks-type building inside the III MAF military compound, where I was billeted in my own room. He pointed to a "hot box" in the closet, in which I was to store my dress shoes, to prevent them from growing mold in the prevailing humid conditions. He took my orders, so they would be endorsed correctly, reflecting my arrival date, and he said the orders would be returned to me. He also told me that General Walt wanted to see me, as soon as I was settled in. The III MAF compound had formerly been a French military facility, built around a very large parade ground. It had been constructed under French colonial rule. It fronted the Han River, which flows through the Port of Da Nang, and empties into the South China Sea.

Recent Vietnam Political Background

In May 1964, the French garrison at Dien Bien Phu had fallen to communist Viet Minh forces, which were commanded by General Vo Nguyen Giap. That French defeat effectively ended the French colonial rule in Vietnam. Meeting in Geneva, Switzerland in 1954, several countries participated in framing and signing the 1954 Geneva Accords, which divided Vietnam into North and South sectors. The Accords established a cease-fire line between the two sectors, along the 17th parallel. The United States was not a signatory of the Geneva Accords, mainly because the Accords provided for eventual unification by election, and the United States did not know which side would win. The North Sector was ruled by communist Ho Chi Minh. The South Sector leadership was somewhat murky, following the assassination of President Ngo Dinh Diem. Nguyen Cao Ky, a South Vietnamese Air Force Officer, served as Premier from 1965-67, and as Vice President, until he retired in 1972. His manner was flamboyant, and his risky, brash behavior gained him the title of "an unguided missile." He wore a black flight suit, white scarf and sunglasses. Accordingly, he was often referred to as "Captain Midnight."

United States-South Vietnamese Military Relationships

The senior U.S. Military officer in South Vietnam was U.S. Army General William C. Westmoreland. For the purpose of this writing, I will limit descriptions of my events, largely in South Vietnam, and more specifically, within the III MAF, which was commanded by General Walt, and later during my thirteen-month tour, by Lieutenant General Robert E. Cushman, Jr. Both of those Marine Generals commanded III MAF at Da Nang, in the (I) Corps Tactical Zone. III MAF served under the operational command of General Westmoreland, whose headquarters was in the Capital Special Zone, near Saigon. His official title was: Commander, U.S. Military Assistance Command, Vietnam (COMUSMACV). General Westmoreland's Air Force Deputy was headquartered in Thailand. All other MACV Deputies were headquartered in one of the four South Vietnam Corps Tactical Zones.

The (I) Corps Tactical Zone was located in nearest North Vietnam, and was adjacent to the Demilitarized Zone (DMZ), which extended about one mile on either side of the Ben Hai River, and west-to-east, from the border with Laos to the East China Sea. In the (I) Corps Tactical Zone, the northernmost province was Quang Tri. It bordered the entire length of the DMZ. Moving south, the next province was Thua Thien, followed by Quang Nam, Quang Tin, and at the southern end of the (I) Corps Tactical Zone, Quang Ngai province. The provinces could be somewhat likened to States, only instead of State Governors, the Provinces each had a Vietnamese Province Chief.

The French colonial government trained no Vietnamese civil servants. Accordingly, the majority of leadership positions, which would normally have been filled by qualified civil servants, were filled by Vietnamese military officers, who had little or no experience in directing civilian governmental affairs. For instance, the Mayor of Da Nang was Army of the Republic of Vietnam (ARVN) Lieutenant Colonel Le Chi Cuong. To coordinate Vietnamese programs instituted by the Province Chiefs, with on-going U.S. operations, a U.S. Province Senior Advisor was assigned to work with each Vietnamese Province Chief. Those advisors came from a variety of U.S. Sources. In I Corps, one was from the CIA; another was from "The Voice of America" (the radio broadcasting network of the U.S. government); another was a Marine Corps Lieutenant Colonel, and two others were from other U.S. Agencies.

The (I) Corps Tactical Zone was commanded by a Vietnamese Major General named Hoang Xuan Lam. His headquarters was in the city of Da Nang. His U.S. military counterpart in (I) Corps was General Walt, the Commanding General of III MAF. General Walt's headquarters was across the Han River, about a mile from General Lam's. To ensure Marine-ARVN artillery fire, Naval gunfire, and air support coordination, a U.S. Army advisor was assigned to each staff section in General Lam's headquarters. Major General Lam was only 38 years old.

Though General Walt was technically the MACV Adviser to General Lam, there was no doubt as to who was really in charge of combat operations in (I) Corps. And, just prior to my arrival in South Vietnam, President Lyndon Johnson had placed all of the U.S. nation-building efforts in South Vietnam under the charge of the U.S. Military. Now, in (I) Corps, the protection and security of each Province Headquarters, as well as the security of many provinces, became an added responsibility of the III MAF. Against the brief history of SVN cited above, it was difficult to recognize and grasp the many complications of the U.S. efforts in SVN.

In northern (I) Corps, the U.S. Marines and ARVN were fighting a near conventional war against North Vietnam. Regular Army forces wore distinctive uniforms, including steel helmets with a single red star painted on the front of each. In the three southern provinces of (I) Corps, more of a guerrilla war against local Viet Cong (VC) forces was being fought. The VC would meld into the normal population by day, and then at night, organize and infiltrate into SVN villages to terrorize village families, and dig new camouflaged tunnels and pop-up spider holes. The VC wore black pajama-like clothing with conical shaped straw hats, which made it almost impossible to distinguish who was, and who was not, a VC. During my tour, uniformed North Vietnamese Regular Army penetrated farther south from the DMZ, in ever increasing numbers, to augment local VC units.

      Remembering that General Walt wanted to see me as soon as I was settled in; I walked to General Walt's office, where I was told that he was away; but that he would return by helicopter later that evening. While waiting, I renewed my acquaintance with another Marine Corps pilot, Major General Robert G. Owens, Jr., who now was General Walt's Deputy for Military Operations. When I asked him about my assignment, he said that General Walt would tell me personally, and that probably I would be surprised. He said that General Walt would return in about an hour, and would land on the III MAF helipad at the edge of the Han River; where I waited.

Chapter 38: III MAF Assignment

Reporting to Lieutenant General Walt

At dusk, I waited for General Walt to arrive. I watched his Marine turbine-powered, UH-1E (Huey) helicopter circle in the dark, with its navigation lights blinking, then land on the helipad, which was now brightly lighted by the helicopter's landing light. General Walt debarked from the helicopter, and after turning and gesturing his thanks to the helicopter pilot, and to the door gunner, he saw me approach. I saluted him, and he said, "Hi, Bob. Welcome to Vietnam." His next question was, "How is Bill?" I told him that Bill graduated from VMI, and was now attending The Basic School at Quantico. I told him that Bill's Military Occupational Specialty (MOS) was to be Infantry. He seemed pleased with that MOS assignment for Bill. I told him that Millie sent her best wishes, and we exchanged other small talk about our families, while we walked to his office. He then said that he needed to talk to General Owens, who was waiting there. He asked me to return to his office the next morning after the 0700 daily staff briefing to discuss my new assignment. He smiled and said, "Again, Bob, welcome to Vietnam".

My III MAF Assignment

The next morning, after the 0700 briefing, I entered General Walt's office. He then introduced a civilian, Ambassador Barney Koren who was the III MAF Deputy for Civilian Operations. He told me that Ambassador Koren was a State Department Foreign Service Officer, with the equivalent rank of a Major General. He then told me that I will be working with, and for, Ambassador Koren. Since President Johnson gave the responsibility for nation-building in SVN to the military, we agreed that Ambassador Koren should now have a senior Marine Officer on his staff, performing the duties as his

Chief of Staff. General Walt smiled and told Ambassador Koren that the right Officer had now arrived. Ambassador Koren shook my hand, and greeted me warmly. General Walt added that the civilian nation-building requirements would have Combat Essential priority - the highest Military priority - right up there with beans and bullets.

General Walt then asked me if I had heard of the incident during the Korean War, when the Marine Air Wing Chief of Staff had been shot down, captured, and forced to confess to using germ warfare. I told him that I had, and that Major General Schilt, for whom I served as his Aide, was a member of a special board, convened at Headquarters, Marine Corps to investigate and determine whether or not the captured Colonel had resisted interrogation properly. After returning to his El Toro headquarters, General Schilt told me that he was convinced the North Koreans could make a captive say anything, without ever touching him. General Walt then told me that, due to my recent duty as the 2nd MAW G-2 at Cherry Point, the III MAF had been directed to not assign Colonel Warren to duty that had a potential for him being captured.

Ambassador Koren asked General Walt if I could attend the daily 0700 staff briefings. General Walt said that was a good idea. He then asked Ambassador Koren to show me the III MAF Combat Center, before we left. With that, Ambassador Koren and I briefly visited the Combat Center. It was a beehive of activity. Day and night, the war in (I) Corps was being monitored or directed from that Combat Center. Continual radio communication chatter with combat units in the field, and with higher headquarters, could be overheard.

Ambassador Koren and I then caught a shuttle boat for a five minute ride across the Han River to the City of Da Nang. His black, unmarked sedan was waiting, and we rode less than a city block to his office. I was surprised that his office was in a new riverfront four-story office building. He was interested in my Marine Corps background, and where I had known General Walt. I told him that General Walt's son, Larry and my son, Bill had attended Quantico High School, and had played football on the same Quantico High School team.

He then took me inside the office building, and introduced me to several office occupants, where USAID civilians shared office space with Vietnamese, who also worked there. He repeatedly said that I was going to be his Chief of Staff. I was pleased to see that Ambassador Koren maintained a friendly, harmonious relationship with his civilian USAID staff, and their Vietnamese counterparts. I was really surprised to see so many Vietnamese employees working in the new office building.

With no elevator, we slowly made our way up the stairwell to the building's top (fourth) floor. We entered an office that he told me would be mine. Inside, I met four U.S. Military personnel; one U.S. Army Lieutenant Colonel named George Myers, a Marine Staff Sergeant and two Marine corporals. They would all be working for me, and accordingly, would be near my office, where our close association would be required. I was impressed by the fact all were quite fluent in the spoken Vietnamese language.

For transportation, I was given keys to a British Land Rover, a truly versatile vehicle. A ½ ton truck, a pickup truck, and a jeep were also assigned for use by my staff. I turned down the offer for a Vietnamese driver for the Land Rover; preferring to drive it myself or, if necessary, have one of my staff drive it, until I became familiar with my new surroundings. All of those military vehicles would be maintained and operated from the III MAF motor pool. My staff members were all billeted in the III MAF compound, and all ate in the III MAF mess facilities. The Officers mess was located on the edge of the Han River. General Walt lived, and often dined with principals of his staff, and sometimes with visiting dignitaries, in his well guarded bunker. Dining with General Walt was by invitation only.

Ambassador Koren lived across the Han River, in a house in Da Nang that was provided by the U.S. State Department. It was guarded around the clock by City of Da Nang Police, who wore white uniforms. Vietnamese cooks, housekeepers, maintenance staff, and an array of servants, were assigned to work at Ambassador Koren's house. He would often host dinners for various distinguished visitors, which often included high ranking U.S. and Vietnamese military officers, and civilian officials.

A few days after my arrival, I received a written invitation to an informal, working dinner at Ambassador Koren's home, in Da Nang. The dinner invitation was also received by my Army assistant, Lieutenant Colonel Myers, who said he had never been invited to the Ambassador's home for dinner before. Another working level guest who arrived for dinner was Mr. Bill Johnson, the USAID agriculture advisor, who had previously served in Korea. He remarked that the Vietnamese farmers were more flexible, and very easy to work with, as compared to the Koreans, who he described as "real stone heads." We really enjoyed the dinner, and we all complimented the smiling cooks, and serving staff.

The Ambassador told us that he traveled to the Philippines about every six weeks, to visit his wife and family, who lived there. I decided that the U.S. State Department whirled in a different orbit than did the U.S. Military. He told me that I would know when he was away, and at the 0700 briefings at III MAF, I would represent him. His black sedan would also be available for my use, when he was away. He said that on his trips to the Philippines, he always departed and arrived at the military airfield in Da Nang; also the headquarters of the Marine Air Wing (1st MAW).

Before departing that evening, I told the Ambassador that I planned to visit some of the nearby Marine Corps aviation commands, including the Marine Aircraft units at the Da Nang Airport, and the Helicopter Air Group at nearby Marble Mountain, and when possible, the First Marine Division, commanded by Major General Herman Nickerson. I also told him that it would be necessary to meet my minimum four flight hours per month as a pilot, and further, that I did not want to lose my fixed-wing and helicopter pilot ratings. So, by renewing pilot friendships, it would be much easier to maintain my flight proficiency.

The Ambassador agreed, and told me that the CIA also operated aircraft, in and out of (I) Corps. Further, he told me that I should contact Mr. Jack Horgan, the CIA Officer in Charge of the (I) Corps regional area, to schedule their use. I would soon be flying with, or scheduling, Air America Airline supply flights in (I) Corps. At the 1st MAW I learned that daily KC-130 flights were scheduled between Da Nang, Quang Tri and Khe Sanh, often with additional stops at Phu Bai and Hue, in Thua Thien Province. The KC-130 Hercules was ideal for these missions; often landing on dirt runways, and by reversing its propellers after initial touchdown, its roll-out distance was very short. Its rear ramp made loading and unloading aircraft relatively easy, when transporting troops, cargo and military vehicles.

Daily 0700 III MAF Staff Briefings

The staff briefing room was dominated by a large V-shaped table. At the rear, at the point of the V, the briefing table split into two thirty-degree angled sections, opened at a small, slightly raised lighted stage, large enough for the staff briefer and a flip map case stand, which permitted the briefer to display maps or charts, one at a time. General Walt sat at the point of the briefing table. He usually opened each briefing with pertinent comments regarding III MAF or (I) Corps combat actions; sometimes referring to the message traffic file he carried. On his immediate left was Major General Owens, his

Deputy for Military Operations, and on his right Ambassador Koren, his Deputy for Civil Operations. His staff G-1, G-2, G-3 and G-4, and other principal staff members present, sat on the outside of the V-shaped table; thus giving General Walt an unobstructed view of the stage briefings. Behind General Walt there were several comfortable chairs, for occasional visitors.

One visitor, who always sat behind General Walt, was Jack Horgan, the CIA (I) Corps Regional Area Officer in Charge. I often wondered for whom did Jack work? Was it General Walt, Ambassador Koren, or the Station Chief at the American Embassy in Saigon? Or, was it General Lam, the Vietnamese (I) Corps commander? Jack Horgan worked from a special CIA compound on the outskirts of Da Nang, and from all appearances, he had a lot of authority. I never visited the CIA compound, as I really had no reason to go there. Security at the camouflaged CIA Compound was tight; guarded by very tall Hmong Guards from North China.

If Jack Horgan attended the 0700 briefings, he varied his method of transportation, thereby avoiding any set daily transportation pattern. In addition to probable clandestine operations, the CIA played a very active role in (I) Corps pacification efforts. It was no surprise to me, that they used several types of aircraft; from large twin engine C-46 Curtiss Commandos, to C-47s, and even smaller C-45, twin-engine Beechcrafts. I had ridden in most of these Air America aircraft years before, during my two trips into Laos. The CIA also operated a few Bell Huey helicopters on very special and limited missions; usually for visiting VIP transport. One of the twin engine Beechcraft pilots was my former Marine Major friend, Vernon E. "Jack" Ball, who had resigned his Marine commission, and now flew for the CIA.

Jack Ball offered to fly any items for me, from Saigon to Da Nang. I took advantage of his offer, and he flew two small, ceramic, highly painted elephants which I purchased in Saigon. I still have them.

CIA Pilatus PC-6 Turbo Porter Airplane

In Vietnam, the CIA operated a strange single-engine Swiss built, high-wing Pilatus PC-6 Turbo Porter, with a very durable, fixed landing gear, and a sturdy steerable tail wheel. I had never seen one. It was powered by a single, very noisy, turbo-shaft engine, which developed six hundred eighty horsepower. It had a large, single, high wing. It could be flown by one pilot, and could carry up to ten passengers; one sitting beside the pilot. It had Short Takeoff and Landing, (STOL) capabilities; nearly the same as a large, loaded transport helicopter. With a payload of twenty-five hundred pounds, a Turbo Porter could take off in six hundred forty feet, and land in four hundred thirty feet.

With those STOL capabilities, these aircraft could deliver bags of rice, caged pigs and chickens, plus a myriad of cargo, including Nuoc Mam, a favorite condiment dipping sauce, for fish and chicken wings. Deliveries were to remote, sometimes isolated Vietnamese villages. Province and Village Chiefs submitted requests to the Province Senior Advisor, for screening and priority assignment. The Military airfield at Da Nang was used for loading Pilatus Porters with mixed cargo, arriving from larger CIA transport aircraft. The sliding cargo doors on each side of its cargo space, made loading and unloading the Pilatus Porter very easy. It was originally designed to provide rescue operations at high altitudes. Its record was a successful rescue at over eighteen thousand feet, in the mountains in Nepal.

DMZ Refugee Crisis

One morning, at a 0700 briefing, General Walt, expressed concern that a problem was developing in Thua Thien Province. Marine commanders there reported that hundreds of Vietnamese people were moving south from the DMZ, into the village of Dong Ha, in ever increasing numbers. General Walt asked Ambassador Koren to check into the situation, and further suggested that he send me on my first trip up there, to determine the reason for the increased arrivals of several hundred people. That is how I had my first ride in the Pilatus PC-6 Turbo Porter airplane. I sat in the right cockpit seat, adjacent to the pilot. My first view of the situation was from the air. I saw hundreds of Vietnamese gathered around a single fresh water trailer, which normally was used to fill individual Marine canteens.

After landing, at Dong Ha, we learned that the Vietnamese families we saw were only a small part of the ten thousand Vietnamese who had been ordered to move out of the DMZ, by Prime Minister Nguyen Cao Ky. Typically, he didn't bother to warn the Province Chief, the Province Advisor, or the Marine Division nearby. I reported the situation to Ambassador Koren by radio; recommending an emergency delivery of fresh water and food from any source, by fixed-wing aircraft, helicopter or both; that to be followed by an emergency evacuation of as many as possible of these new refugees from the DMZ area, into another refugee camp, away from the DMZ. To add to the refugees' misery, the weather was hot and humid. I carried two canteens of fresh water with me.

While at Dong Ha, I contacted Bob Brewer, the American Province Advisor in Quang Tin Province, and told him my recommendations to Ambassador Koren. He was somewhat skeptical, and wanted to know how much authority I had to do that. I told him, "Quite a bit, including the highest (Combat Essential) priority for whatever I needed to help the Vietnamese people." Further, that priority was granted to me personally, by the III MAF Commanding General when he assigned me to be Ambassador Koren's Chief of Staff. I told Bob Brewer that he need not notify any Marine Units from the Third Marine Division, who were deployed in the area. Those units had probably already been told what actions they should take, to provide emergency deliveries of water and food for the DMZ refugees, and for refugee evacuation airlift.

While there, I did note what appeared to be a massive engineer effort along Route 9, which generally paralleled the DMZ, west toward Khe Sanh. I wondered if it would be possible to hire some of those refugees to work with the engineers on Route 9. I made a mental note to check with Ambassador Koren, regarding that hiring possibility. On the flight back to Da Nang, the Turbo Porter pilot diverted to Hue, and landed to deliver some cargo. The Tay Loc Airfield at Hue, was located inside the high-walled city known as the Citadel. After departing Hue for Da Nang, I noted a convoy of large trucks, driving north over the Hai Van Pass toward Hue, and the DMZ. When I returned to Da Nang, Ambassador Koren said my report had been correct, and that my recommendations were underway, jointly by III MAF and (I) Corps. He said that hiring refugees to work on the Route 9 upgrade could not be approved, if it was only to improve military fortifications. However, if the requests specified work to improve Route 9 for future commercial use, refugee labor was always encouraged. He said, however, it would be up to the unit performing the work, to specify the intended civilian hiring purpose.

Each evening I went to the III MAF Combat Center, to learn the progress of on-going military operations, or the plans for future operations. I would then select days when the equipment I needed could be spared. My needs usually included use of watercraft, transport aircraft, trucks, water trailers, well-digging equipment, and portable water pumps to operate rice paddy drainage during the harvesting season, or flooding during the planting season. I often forwarded requests for arms, ammunition, barbed wire and other security equipment requested by the American Province Senior Advisors, to the appropriate III MAF staff members; especially to Colonel Fred Haynes, the G-3 (operations) who stated he appreciated my non-interference requests, during times of very busy III MAF military operations. I really learned a lot more about day-to-day ground operations, when visiting Colonel Haynes in the busy Combat Center. I also made new friends and acquaintances, every night I was there.

There were many memorable days during my thirteen-month tour with III MAF. One was in June 1967, when General Walt was relieved by General Cushman. The relief ceremony was held in the III MAF compound parade ground. Four-star General Westmoreland was the senior Officer present, and he, along with Vietnamese General Lam, decorated General Walt with several medals and ribbons, reflecting his bravery and service, in Vietnam. Then General Westmoreland said that General Walt is not only a "Marine's Marine," but, was also a "Soldier's Soldier."

He said that General Walt had completed two complete tours as the III MAF Commander in Vietnam, and that he wanted General Walt to stay for a third tour. But, he was told that the Secretary of The Navy had to have General Walt back in Washington. There, he would be promoted to a four-star General and assigned as Assistant Commandant of The Marine Corps. The III MAF Adjutant read the orders, relieving General Walt of his duties in Vietnam, and assigning General Cushman as the new Commander of III MAF.

Additionally, the document promoting Major General Cushman to his new rank of Lieutenant General, signed by the Commandant of the Marine Corps, was read. General

Westmoreland then asked General Walt to assist him in pinning on Lieutenant General Cushman's new three-star rank insignia. Of course, General Walt complied, and then moved to his former staff. He firmly shook hands with each of us; thanking each staff member for their hard work, and dedicated service. He then boarded his helicopter, for the short flight to the Da Nang airfield where he departed for home. The next time I saw General Walt, now a four-star General, was when he visited me, over a year later, at MCAS, Tustin where I commanded Marine Air Group-56 (MAG-56).

Chapter 39: Distinguished Visitors

General and Mrs. Omar Bradley

One evening, General Cushman summoned me to his bunker. I entered it for the first time, and he cordially invited me to have a seat. He told me that the next day, III MAF would host some distinguished visitors, and that he wanted me to accompany him to the Da Nang airfield to meet them. He then told me that their visit would last about a week, and that I was to accompany them, show them everything; but keep them safe. Also, they would return to III MAF every evening, in time to have dinner with him, unless they were scheduled to eat elsewhere. He said that his G-3, Colonel Haynes, had prepared a daily schedule, and they would be furnished helicopter transportation. He said that he had informed Ambassador Koren that he was borrowing me, for a week. Filled with curiosity, I finally asked who these "distinguished visitors" were. His answer was, "General and Mrs. Omar Bradley." Wow! Now I was going to be an escort; probably more like be a body guard, for a five-Star General of the Army and his accompanying wife, "Kitty" Buhler Bradley.

The next day, I rode with General Cushman to meet the Bradleys. Remembering my days as General Schilt's Aide, I arranged to have a covered pickup, to transport the Bradley's luggage from the airplane to General Cushman's bunker. The Bradleys arrived at Da Nang, in a U.S. Navy twin-engine anti-submarine airplane, which had been converted to a Carrier Onboard Delivery (COD) aircraft. A COD was widely used to fly mail, aircraft parts, and personnel between ships at sea, or to shore air stations. The Bradleys arrived at Da Nang, from the aircraft carrier, USS *Constellation*.

General Bradley was bareheaded, and he wore a loose-fitting, khaki-color jacket, with no rank insignia. I noted that his bare head was badly sunburned. As seasonal rain showers were passing, I held an umbrella over him as we walked away from the COD plane, and toward General Cushman's staff car. Mrs. Bradley, an attractive younger woman, wore a pant suit, and walked with General Cushman, behind General Bradley and me. While leading them to the staff car, I asked General Bradley how many suitcases and clothing bags they had. General Bradley and General Cushman rode in the rear seat, and Mrs. Bradley rode in the front seat, with the staff car driver. To avoid staff car crowding, I asked General Cushman if I could load the Bradley's luggage into the pickup, and follow them over the Han River Bridge to General Cushman's bunker.

Col. Bob Warren escorts General of the Army Omar Bradley, Danang, Vietnam (Sep 1967)

Upon arrival, General Cushman's two enlisted Marine stewards served the Bradleys cool drinks and lunch. I assumed they wanted to rest, so I excused myself, and told them I would meet them the next morning, after breakfast. I also asked General Bradley if he would like to have a cap, to protect his head from further sunburn. He said that it would be appreciated. General Cushman also left his bunker after lunch, and returned to his office, while the Bradleys rested. He told them dinner would be served at about 1800, when he returned to his bunker, and if they needed anything, to just let the stewards know. I went to the Combat Center where Colonel Fred Haynes gave me the Bradley's printed schedule for the next several days. I noted that the schedule did not show any trips north to the dangerous Third Marine Division (3DMARDIV) areas near the DMZ.

      The schedule commenced the next morning, with a visit to the Navy Hospital Ship, USS *Repose*; then a briefing by a Scout Sniper unit; followed by a stop at a refugee camp; then dinner at the First Marine Division (1MARDIV) Command Post. I called the III MAF supply office and asked them to send a size XL Marine utility cap to me, at the Combat Center, for General Bradley. It was delivered to me at the Combat Center, by the Supply Officer, in less than twenty minutes. I contacted the Helicopter Air Group at Marble Mountain, to verify the time the helicopter was scheduled for the Bradley's transportation from the III MAF helipad to the hospital ship, *Repose*, and the estimated arrival time at the Hospital ship anchored off-shore. I asked that clean life jackets be provided, and that the helicopter crew chief assist the Bradleys with wearing and inflating the Mae West life jackets. I also asked that the Sikorsky HUS-1 Helicopter be fitted with two temporary seats; more comfortable than the standard combat troop benches, with netted nylon backrests. Mrs. Bradley carried a large handbag, from which she withdrew a pad, and constantly wrote letters and notes.

      The next morning after breakfast, I met the Bradleys, and handed General Bradley a utility cap, with a black Marine emblem stenciled on the cap front. I told him that there were no other cap choices. He just smiled, and put the cap on his head. At 1000 (10 am), we walked across the parade ground, to the III MAF briefing room, where General Cushman and his staff were all waiting. Showing respect, they all stood when General Bradley entered. General Bradley sat in the seat normally occupied by the Military Deputy. I sat with Mrs. Bradley in the back of the briefing room. General Cushman asked his staff to be seated, and he then took the stage.

  He welcomed General and Mrs. Bradley and told them that III MAF was honored that their first stop in Vietnam was to visit Marines. He referred to the schedule prepared for their visit, and asked General Bradley if he desired any schedule changes to please tell him. General Bradley said that he was satisfied with the printed schedule; and that he appreciated all the kindness and effort extended to Mrs. Bradley and to him, including receiving a free Marine Corps cap.

  General Bradley then added that many probably wondered about the purpose of their visit to Vietnam. So, he told the staff that President Johnson sent him to Vietnam, to view and assess the military and pacification progress. Further, that the President was within his Commander In Chief authority to do so, as officers with Five-Star rank never retire, and thus, remain on active duty for life. He referred to the schedule, and noted that until noon, he would be pleased to listen to the III MAF staff briefing. The G-2 then briefed on the military situation in the two northern provinces, and the North Vietnamese Army (NVA) buildup along the entire length of the DMZ. Next, was the briefing by the G-3, who related recent and on-going battles Dong Ha, Con Tien, and Khe Sanh, which tested the resolve of the Third Marine Division forces in that area. He explained that the main pacification effort in the two northern provinces, was the Combined Action Program (CAP), which was made up of a squad of Marines, that with a hospital corpsman, were assigned to each of several villages. Also, the CAP was augmented with a platoon of Vietnamese Popular Force troops. The CAP was designed to deny sanctuary for the NVA troops in that village; repulsing attacks on the village as well. After each staff presentation, the briefer asked if General Bradley had any questions. General Bradley asked who was in charge of each CAP. The answer was that it was the Marine Corporal Squad leader.

General Cushman then introduced Ambassador Koren, the III MAF Deputy for Civil Operations and Revolutionary Development Support (CORDS). Further, in that Ambassador Koren had no secure briefing area, his briefing would be here in the secure III MAF briefing facility. But first, he said there would be a fifteen-minute facilities break, allowing Mrs. Bradley time to go to General Cushman's bunker, and return to the briefing. Also, a short break would give the staff members time to personally meet and shake hands with this famous Five-Star General who, during the D-Day landings 1944, had commanded the U.S. 1st Army, which included the American troops who landed on the Omaha and Utah beaches.

Following the break, Ambassador Koren took the stage; adding his welcome, and personal appreciation for the Bradley's visit. He referred to the written schedule; noting that, following the briefing, the Bradleys would have lunch in the Officer's mess, next door. That would be followed by a visit to the Ambassador's office, across the river in Da Nang, with a brief stop at Vietnamese General Lam's (I) Corps headquarters. Then they would proceed to the Da Nang City Hall; calling on Vietnamese Colonel Le Chi Cuong, the city's Mayor. From City Hall, they would go to Ambassador Koren's house in Da Nang, where after a rest and freshening up period, he would host an informal dinner. Additional dinner guests would include General Cushman, General Lam, Da Nang city mayor, Colonel Le Chi Cuang, and Mr. Jack Horgan, the Regional CIA Officer whose headquarters was also near Da Nang. Following dinner, the

Bradleys would ride back across the river with General Cushman, to his bunker quarters, where the Bradleys were staying. General Bradley expressed appreciation for all the planning done to accommodate their visit.

Ambassador Koren used large flip charts on the stage, to help explain the increased pacification efforts in (I) Corps. He described that a renewed effort was started when President Johnson placed all nation-building responsibility under the charge of the military. General Cushman's predecessor, General Walt had responded, by beefing up the Ambassador's staff with the assignment of a Marine Colonel, to be his Chief of Staff. He explained that I was the newly arrived Colonel, in Vietnam. The Ambassador went on to say that General Walt had also increased the priority for pacification needs to "Combat Essential."

General Cushman had maintained all of those support actions, including continuing the CAP efforts in each of the III MAF regions. In some cases he had increased them, especially adding weapons, barbed wire, mines and personnel to protect each of the Provincial Headquarters. He reviewed the pacification effort in the northern two provinces, which were largely limited to the CAP program. He explained that the CAP program was very meaningful, as by assigning a Marine rifle squad to remain in those villages permanently, it represented our firm commitment to protect them.

Ambassador Koren then flipped to the next chart, which was a map showing the three southern provinces of (I) Corps. He pointed out that the First Marine Division area that includes Quang Nam, Quang Tin and Quang Ngai provinces, where pacification efforts were largely limited to Civic Action projects, of a temporary nature. However, NVA troops, supplies, arms, and ammunition - including rockets - were continuing to flow into South Vietnam, down the Ho Chi Minh Trail. When passing (I) Corps, the trail swings west into Laos, where we were not allowed to conduct air strikes, or other interdicting operations. The NVA selected certain mountain passes, leading from the Ho Chi Minh Trail in Laos, into SVN, where they planned and conducted small- and large-scale insurgency operations. He explained that, in some cases, NVA battalion-size forces had been defeated by Marine and ARVN forces.

He went on to report that when and where possible, Marine troop units at platoon and lower levels were assigned specific Civic Action projects, to help farmers with their pig farms, and with their duck and chicken flocks. Others troops dug wells, then assisted farmers with flooding fields to plant rice; then during harvest season, the rice fields were drained. The water pumps were provided by the U.S. Agency for International Development (USAID). Our troops usually did not assist with large animals, such as water buffaloes. The Vietnamese farmers were already water buffalo use experts. In the relatively pacified southern provinces, the U.S. Army 29th Civil Affairs Company was helping local governments with voting to choose their village chiefs, utility use, sanitation and organizing fair bartering and tax systems.

Ambassador Koren then explained why many ARVN officers were appointed to governmental positions, such as the Mayor of Da Nang; positions that would normally be filled by an elected civilian. In trying to regain sovereignty over all of Indo China following WW II, the French effort, backed by the United States, trained only a few civil servants. Following the defeat of French forces at Dien Bien Phu, administration of Vietnam was simply, and quickly, turned over to the Vietnamese, who were totally unprepared for accepting that civil government responsibility. That gave rise to the likes of Nguyen Cao Ky, a politically ambitious Vietnamese Air Force Officer, who became President of South Vietnam. His actions were unpredictable, and erratic.

For instance, just a few months prior, he had ordered ten thousand people to move out of the DMZ, without notification to the Third Marine Division, or any authority in (I) Corps. Suddenly, thousands of these refugees were fighting for water from a single Marine water trailer, near the city of Dong Ha. It was necessary to react immediately, by ordering emergency deliveries of food and water. After that emergency, their relocation to refugee camps began. Ambassador Koren noted that stopping at a refugee camp located nearby, was a stop on the Bradley's scheduled visit. He also mentioned that the next day, the Bradleys were scheduled to visit the Hospital ship *Repose*. He told them that I had made arrangements for a helicopter to take them to the ship, and that I would accompany them on the Hospital ship. He mentioned that the Bradleys would be guests of the Captain of the *Repose* for lunch; and that then they were scheduled to fly back to III MAF, to have dinner with General Cushman. The following morning, the Bradleys would be free to do as they pleased, as nothing was planned for them.

At the scheduled time the next morning, I accompanied the Bradleys to the III MAF Helipad where the Sikorsky HUS-1 was waiting, with engine running, and rotors stopped. Before entering the helicopter, the Bradleys put on new "Mae West" life jackets. After the Bradleys were seated inside the helicopter cabin, with seat belts fastened, the pilot engaged the rotors, took off, and we flew east for about twenty minutes, until the *Repose* was spotted. It was painted glistening white, with prominent red crosses. Before landing aboard, the pilot circled the ship with the helicopter cabin door open, so the Bradleys would have an unobstructed view of the Hospital ship. The pilot had contacted the ship by radio, and had been given clearance to land on the ship's helicopter platform, which had been constructed above the ship's stern. As the helicopter pilot approached for a landing aboard, he followed the hand signals of a ship's crewman, to fly slowly toward the ship's stern, hover, then touchdown.

The helicopter wheels were chocked, and its rotor was braked to a stop, before the Bradleys were allowed to un-strap from their seats, and step out onto the ship's deck. The ship's Captain walked across the platform, to meet and welcome the Bradleys. I stayed aboard the ship with the Bradleys, while their helicopter returned to Da Nang, with a specified time to return. In less than fifteen minutes, the *Repose* would again have room on its helicopter platform for additional medevac helicopters, arriving with wounded.

After clearing the noisy helicopter platform, the Bradleys were escorted to the comfortable ship's wardroom, where they were introduced to the Commanding Officer of the Hospital, the senior hospital Nurse, and the ship's senior Chaplain. General Bradley introduced his wife, and then me; as his Marine escort, charged with keeping us safe. Smiling, he added "so far, he has done a good job." With that, General Bradley said he needed to visit a head (latrine), and that Mrs. Bradley would also appreciate a few minutes to freshen up before lunch. The head nurse took Mrs. Bradley in tow, and together, they left the wardroom; returning about fifteen minutes later. Lunch was served at a table set up at one end of the wardroom. During lunch, many medical personnel, wearing their scrubs, entered the wardroom; quietly ate lunch, then returned to their medical duties. Other Navy Officers, wearing khaki summer uniforms, did the same.

The ship's Captain asked General Bradley if he would present Purple Heart medals to some of the wounded patients. General Bradley said he would be honored to perform that solemn duty. And, instead of viewing an array of hospital equipment, he said that he and Mrs. Bradley would also be pleased to meet as many of the medical staff as possible, during the patient visits.

During lunch in the ship's wardroom, the Captain briefly cited the proud record of the Hospital ship *Repose*. She was nicknamed, "The Angel of the Orient," for good reason. She served as a base hospital ship at Shanghai, and later at Tsingtao, for the U.S. occupation forces in north China, following WW II. She remained in Asian waters with an occasional return trip to the United States. She was decommissioned in San Francisco in January, 1950. That out-of-commission period lasted only about 9 months; as she was reactivated for service at the outbreak of the Korean War, and sailed for Pusan, Korea on 26 August 1950. After picking up a hospital staff at Yokosuka, Japan, she sailed in Korean waters, and evacuated patients to Japanese ports. She returned to San Francisco, from February to March 1953, for a brief repair and modification period, which included the installation of the helicopter landing pad on which we landed that day.

The *Repose* was again decommissioned; this time at the Hunters Point Naval Shipyard, in December 1954. After eleven years, the *Repose* was, once again, re-commissioned in October 1965, for service in Vietnam. Operating mainly in the (I) Corps area, she had treated over nine thousand battle casualties, and twenty-four thousand inpatients while deployed in this area. Among many other awards, the *Repose* received nine Korean, and nine Vietnam Service Medals. The Hospital Commanding Officer added that the ship had an eight hundred patient bed capacity, with a complement of ninety-five officers, and six hundred enlisted men including his medical staff.

General Bradley expressed admiration for the ship's superb record. He then asked to meet and thank the ship's Petty Officer, for the delicious lunch. He said that it just proved that Navy chow was always superior to Army rations. Following lunch, the group departed for a Hospital ward, where General Bradley presented each wounded patient with his Purple Heart Medal. He expressed personal thanks to each wounded recipient, and posed for picture with each, displaying the patient's Purple Heart Medal. Mrs Bradley requested a list of the patient names, and the home addresses of the Purple Heart recipients. The list had already been prepared. Mrs Bradley expressed her appreciation, and said she would use it to send personal letters to patients' parents and wives.

General Bradley's expression of thanks to the entire ship's complement was then transmitted throughout the ship, over the speaker system. The Bradleys then thanked their hosts, and boarded their helicopter for their return flight to Da Nang, and later, dinner with General Cushman. Nothing was scheduled for them the following morning, so Mrs. Bradley had time to write notes to the parents and wives of patients she had met the previous day, aboard the Hospital ship.

Scout-Sniper Platoon Visit

The following afternoon, we boarded a helicopter, and flew south to a 1st Marine Division Regimental Command Post, for a Scout-Sniper briefing, by a Marine sniper Sergeant named Shell. The 1st Marine Division was now commanded by Major General Donn Robertson; and the 1st Marine Regiment by Colonel Herbert Ing. Sergeant Shell's Scout-Sniper platoon was administratively attached to Colonel Ing's regiment, so the briefing was conducted in a squad tent at Colonel Ing's Regimental Command Post. The tent had three sides rolled-up, to permit hot air to escape, and permit some air circulation. General Bradley sat at a table placed next to the closed side of the tent. Sergeant Shell removed a sniper rifle from its box placed on the table. Then he paused, and gave General Bradley a quick briefing regarding the war, from his viewpoint. In Vietnam, the surgical marksmanship of the snipers, and the inability to locate them, had a significant impact on the morale of an enemy unit. It also added a psychological aspect, and contributed to the stress of battle for the enemy. Sniper missions have been described as "kill one; terrify one thousand." Further, when properly positioned, a sniper can be one of the most dangerous weapons on the battlefield; just by causing the enemy to never feel safe.[xxiv]

Sergeant Shell then showed General Bradley the special Winchester Model 70 Sniper Rifle; pointing out its long distance accuracy. He followed by describing a typical mission of a Scout-Sniper team; explaining that each sniper team consisted of two Marines; a Spotter and a Shooter. Their roles were interchangeable. Their missions were usually in response to a request by a Marine Infantry platoon leader.

The two-man teams operated independently; flown by helicopter as close as possible to the requesting Marine Infantry unit. Upon arrival, they would remove the sniper rifle and field glasses, and a few rounds of sniper rifle ammunition from a felt-lined box, which was left with the Infantry platoon, until their return. While the location and situation that required their spotting and sniping specialty were described, the teams wore special camouflage suits. Then, they disappeared, sometimes for days. They often studied their target for hours before shooting, and afterward, they crawled (called "Worming"), along escape routes, leading back to the platoon.

Other Briefing Tent Occupants

On the opposite side of the squad tent, facing inward toward the briefing table, folding Directors chairs with canvas backs and seats had been placed. Mrs. Bradley's chair was centered. The next two chairs, flanking Mrs. Bradley - two feet apart on either side - were the 1st Marine Division Commanding General Donn Robertson, and the 1st Regiment Commander, Colonel Herb Ing. Mrs. Bradley was so impressed with Sergeant Shell's presentation, she turned to General Robertson and loudly said, "Promote him General; you have a lot of authority around here."

Then that embarrassing situation for all present instantly changed, with Mrs. Bradley's frightful scream; issued when she turned, and was looking eye to eye with a huge, pregnant, Vietnamese sow pig, at a distance of about ten inches. The pig had wandered into the tent, under the rolled-up tent flap behind Mrs. Bradley.

Vietnamese pigs appear ugly as their foreheads extend above, and half way to the end of, their snouts. Mrs. Bradley was terrified when she saw that ugly beast only ten inches away, at her eye level, exchanging glances. Sergeant Shell remained in charge of the situation. He turned to Mrs. Bradley and told her that helping a local farmer raise his pigs was the Civic Action Project assigned to his Scout-Sniper Platoon. Also, he noted that the wandering sow pig was very gentle, and the troops had named her "Lady Bird."

Colonel Ing responded to her request for Shell's promotion by saying, "Mrs. Bradley, you obviously recognized the excellence in Sergeant Shell's briefing. He is an outstanding Sergeant, and I am blessed by having an entire regiment with very capable Sergeants just like him, assigned to important duties throughout my regiment." With the briefing finished, General Bradley shook hands with Sergeant Shell, and thanked him for the excellent briefing. Meanwhile "Lady Bird" had wandered out of the tent under the watchful eye, and much to the relief of Mrs. Bradley. General Robertson departed, and told the Bradleys that he and his staff were looking forward to having a pleasant dinner with them at the 1st Marine Division Command Post that evening.

Refugee Camp Visit

On the twenty-minute return flight back to Da Nang, we stopped at a refugee camp located south of the city of Da Nang. It was always disheartening to see the refugees, crowded together in makeshift shelters with their families. They sadly looked at us with anticipation, hoping for a better life we might bring to them. Actually, they had been herded together and moved into camps for their own safety and protection. At best, their situation could only be described as pitiful. Wherever possible, ARVN guards were assigned to guard the refugee camps. Food and water were available, to adequately maintain life.

When the French gave up, and turned governmental administration over to the Vietnamese, only two hundred doctors were left to practice medicine in all of South Vietnam. Most of the Vietnamese doctors had stayed in France, after completing medical school. Various relief agencies, the Red Cross, and some dedicated missionaries, attempted to help the refugees. Care Packages were often delivered to the refugees. The major problem that existed at all of the refugee camps was not the lack of food and water. It was the feeling of helplessness in the refugee men, due to their inability to any longer look after their wives and children. That quickly became the dominant refugee camp tragedy.

Most of the refugees were dressed in black pajama-like clothes, and most wore woven, conical-shaped, straw hats. It was the traditional Vietnamese dress. After viewing the refugees, Mrs. Bradley asked me what item the refugees really needed. I told her that they all needed a magic drug called "SOAP." With that, she turned to General Bradley, and asked who he might know at Proctor and Gamble. She later told me in a letter, that she had mentioned my refugee soap need to General Westmoreland in Saigon. He responded that the refugee need for soap was real, and if they had a source to provide soap, they could have it sent to his Headquarters, so he could then make equal distribution. In her letter she cited General Westmoreland's response, and added that I had been outranked. She really didn't need to tell me that four-star generals outranked colonels. I had known that for a long, long time.

"Kitty" Buhler Bradley was the second Mrs. Bradley. General Bradley's first wife had died of leukemia. "Kitty" Bradley's graciousness always included kindness, consideration, and genuine appreciation for all of the courtesies extended to her. I was honored to accompany both of them during their visit to III MAF. After her visit, she wrote my wife in North Carolina, telling Millie that I was well; and anxious to return home. When I told her that our son Bill was a student at VMI, she said that General Bradley was scheduled to be at VMI in about three weeks, to dedicate the new George Marshall Library.

Two statues now permanently overlook the parade ground at VMI. One is General Thomas J. "Stonewall" Jackson, and the other is General George C Marshall, Jr.; both graduates of VMI, also known as the "West Point of the South."

During my week with the Bradleys, I asked him what the length of his front line was in Europe, when WW II ended. He said that it was over six hundred miles, from one end to the other, and that it would take over two hours to fly from one end to the other in a C-47. The 12th Army Group he commanded had several numbered field armies; at its peak, totaling nine hundred thousand troops, serving in twenty-seven Divisions.

General George Patton's Third Army was under General Bradley's command. Although he lavished high praise on General Patton's professional ability, for turning his entire Third Army ninety degrees; changing directions from attacking east, to attacking north, where his soldiers broke through and rescued a surrounded U.S. Division during the Battle Of The Bulge; I suspected he did not admire General Patton's flamboyancy. Initially, I thought it best to tip-toe around the General Patton subject. However, one day he mentioned that he had recently talked to "Ike" about General Patton. They agreed that within ten years, if anyone mentioned the Second World War in Europe, the only General remembered would be Patton. He then said, "Give him a headline, and he would go thirty miles."

I asked General Bradley if he recalled having visited my helicopter squadron in Korea, when he was the first Chairman of the Joint Chiefs of Staff. He was surprised that I remembered that he was there, with Anna Rosenberg, the Assistant Secretary of Defense, to see first-hand, what new things the Marines were accomplishing in Korea, using helicopters.[xxv]

After a short helicopter flight to III MAF from the refugee camp, the Bradleys rested for an hour. It was then time to depart for the dinner, hosted by General Robertson, at his 1st Marine Division Command Post. General Robertson was very gracious, and expressed his honor that they could have dinner with him and members of his 1st Marine Division staff. Further, he expressed that they had, no doubt, already been subjected to many briefings, thus far during their III MAF visit, and he thought they would probably enjoy some lighter dinner conversation.

He said that he realized that the Bradleys had probably already recognized that Marines are pretty modest. He then surprised me, by stating that he had known me since the early 1960s, when he was Chief of Staff of the Marine Corps Educational Command in Quantico. He recalled that I had organized several Quantico High School Football banquets, which he attended when both General Walt's son and my son were members of the Quantico High School football team. For the benefit of members of my staff who had not previously known, General Robertson went on to tell them that, as a Captain, I was an HMR-161 pilot when General Bradley was the Joint Chiefs Of Staff Chairman, and visited my squadron in Korea. He also told them, that in my career, I had commanded both a Marine Helicopter Squadron and a Marine jet attack squadron. He then paused, smiled, and told the Bradleys that they probably recognized the china dinner dishes, as they had been borrowed from Ambassador Koren's house in Da Nang, where they had dined a few nights earlier.

He then described the humorous pig incident that occurred earlier that day during the briefing at the Scout-Sniper Platoon. He told Mrs. Bradley that he hoped she had recovered from her meeting with "Lady Bird." Mrs. Bradley said she could not wait to tell Mamie Eisenhower about her eye-to-eye meeting with "Lady Bird." More enjoyable pleasantries were exchanged, including General Bradley's thanks to General Robertson for their very informative and enjoyable visit to the 1st Marine Division area, and for the delicious dinner.

We then boarded the waiting helicopter, and flew back to the III MAF helipad at Da Nang. I knew the Bradleys were leaving for Saigon the next day, so I told them how much I had enjoyed their visit, and that it was a real honor for me to be assigned as their escort. Further, I would be sure that their luggage was put safely aboard the small Air Force business jet that General Westmoreland would send for them. The next morning, they both rode with General Cushman in his staff car to the airport. I followed them to the airport, with their luggage in the covered pickup truck. The business jet was waiting, and I watched the jet crew chief load the Bradley's luggage on board.

I saluted General Bradley and he told me that I had been a great escort. He asked General Cushman at plane side, if he could keep the Marine utility cap he was still wearing. General Cushman's answer was "yes;" but only if he wore it "when meeting General Westmoreland in Saigon." Mrs. Bradley gave me a hug, and said she would write to my wife. She also said she would try to contact our son during their forthcoming visit to VMI for the General George Marshall Library dedication.

I walked away from the jet, leaving General Cushman alone at plane side, to bid the Bradleys goodbye. When the Bradleys got aboard, and the passenger door closed, General Cushman walked to his waiting staff car. He waited outside of his staff car, while the small jet's engines started, and he watched it taxi to the takeoff end of the runway, where it commenced its takeoff roll. When it was airborne, the staff car driver opened the right rear door. General Cushman got into the backseat. I rode with him back to III MAF. He asked me how long their flight would take, to reach Saigon. I told him that the Learjet cruised at slightly over five hundred miles per hour, so it should land at Tan Son Nhat Airport in Saigon, in a little over one hour.

      He asked how the Bradley's visit to the *Repose* had gone. I told him it all went very well; and that General Bradley had presented Purple Heart medals to several Marine patients, and had posed with all of them for presentation pictures. Also, during lunch, the *Repose* Captain cited the wonderful history of the *Repose* and all of its accomplishments, including nine battle stars for service in Korea, and so far, nine more for Vietnam service.

      He had also heard something about the pig incident that occurred during the Scout-Sniper Platoon briefing. When I described it, he laughed out loud. When we arrived back at III MAF, General Cushman asked me to stay for lunch, because there were a few things he wanted to ask me. First, he wanted to know if I had heard anything about Ambassador Koren leaving. I had not heard anything; except that some of my friends on General Westmoreland's staff in Saigon had told me that a new Foreign Service Officer was joining Ambassador Komer's staff in Saigon. He then told me that the CIA Regional Area Officer, Jack Horgan was definitely leaving; but that he did not know who his relief would be.

      He told me that Ambassador Koren was very pleased with my work. He added that he had seen my Fitness (efficiency) Report, which required his endorsement. In the required handwritten section of the report, Ambassador Koren had stated that "most of the pacification efforts in (I) Corps could not have been accomplished without Colonel Warren." I told General Cushman that I spent each evening in the Combat Center, so that I could make requests for pacification support, when and where there was a minimum of intense military activity. I said that I usually coordinated my requests with the G-3, Colonel Haynes, before making specific requests for trucks, engineer support equipment, aircraft, boats, and other commonly used equipment, of other III MAF staff members. I told General Cushman that one thing that Ambassador Koren did not seem to understand was that I had to fly at least four hours per month, to maintain my Naval Aviator currency. Otherwise, it was a pleasure to work with him; though he often expressed concern that working with him might be detrimental to my career. I told him that I did not think it would.

General Cushman relayed the Bradley's appreciation for my escort efforts on their behalf. He asked me to report anything that I felt was significant. He then told me that I could return to my regular CORDS duties, but asked me to report directly to him, in the future, anything that I felt was significant. I thanked him for the lunch, and for his interest; and told him that while I was grateful for his appreciation for what I was accomplishing, the successes were largely due to coordination with Colonel Haynes, and other key members of his III MAF staff.

Chapter 40: Australia R & R Leave

After six months of deployment to Vietnam, U.S. troops of all ranks could request a one week Rest and Recuperation (R&R) Leave, to visit one of the following cities: Honolulu, Tokyo, Hong Kong, Singapore, Bangkok, Taipei, Taiwan, Kuala Lumpur, Malaysia, Manila, or Sydney, Australia. By letter, Millie and I discussed the possibility of meeting in Honolulu, for my R&R leave. We decided against that, because Jeanne was a high school Senior, and Bill was approaching his graduation at VMI. Those considerations, plus the distance and the expense of Millie flying from North Carolina to Hawaii and back, made us rule out Honolulu.

I had always wanted to find out if even some of the storied tales told by Marine pilots who had flown in the South Pacific, and had gone on R&R in Australia, were true. I was always fascinated by their stories about the automobiles in Sydney and Melbourne; that had an array of tanks that held the gas generated by the vehicle's onboard coal or wood-burning. The wonderful examples of Australian hospitality that had been related to me were fascinating, and almost unbelievable. So, partly to satisfy my curiosity, I requested Sydney for my R&R leave destination.

Various commercial airlines obviously learned that being assigned R&R flights was profitable. My flight to Sidney was on a Pan America Boeing 707. Our flight left from Da Nang with a majority of Marine passengers, as Da Nang was surrounded by two Marine Divisions, and a Marine Air Wing. After leaving Vietnam, the first leg was a five hour, non-stop flight to the city of Darwin, located on the north coast of Australia. Our non-stop flight to Darwin passed over Malaysia, Borneo, Celebes and Timor. In that Darwin was a refueling and service stop for our Pan American 707, we only had time to have a quick meal at the airport, and in the restaurant, change our Military Payment Certificates (MPC) to

Australian dollars, before departing for our Sydney R&R destination. Darwin was the capital city of the Northern Territories. It had been bombed by Japanese airplanes in WW II. I was surprised that the flight across a corner of Australia from Darwin to Sydney took almost the same length of time as the flight from Da Nang, Vietnam to Darwin. Upon arrival in Sidney, our aircraft landed at the Sydney International Airport, which was named after a Pioneer Australian pilot, Charles Kingsford Smith.

Charles Kingsford Smith

In 1928, Smith made the first trans-Pacific flight, from Oakland, California to Brisbane, Australia, in a slow, tri-motor Fokker, high wing airplane named "The Southern Cross." The total distance from Oakland, California to Brisbane, Australia was seven thousand, two hundred, thirty-eight miles. It was a fight with three planned stages: Stage 1. Oakland, California to Hawaii; a distance of twenty-four hundred miles, that took 27.5 flying hours. Stage 2. Hawaii to Fiji; a distance of three thousand, one hundred, fifty-five miles, that took 34.5 flying hours. Stage 3. Fiji to Brisbane, Australia; a distance of one thousand, six hundred, eighty-three miles, that took twenty hours. The total flight time was eighty-two hours; with the speed averaging about eighty-nine miles per hour.

The Southern Cross had a crew of four. Australian Pilot, Charles Kingsford Smith; Australian Relief Pilot, Charles Ulm; American Radio Operator, James Warner; and American Navigator and Flight Engineer, Harry Lyon. The trans-Pacific flight departed Oakland on 31 May and landed in Brisbane on 9 June 1928. The crew was met by an estimated twenty-six thousand people. In August, 1928 pilots Smith and Ulm made the first non-stop flight across the continent of Australia; from Melbourne on the southeast coast, to Perth on the west coast. On the evening of 12 September 1928, Smith and Ulm departed on a fourteen-hour flight across the

Tasmanian Sea, to New Zealand. Landing mid-morning at Christchurch, they were greeted by a crowd of thirty thousand people. On 8 November 1935, Charles Kingsford Smith was lost on a flight between Allahabad, India and Singapore. His airplane crashed in the Andaman Sea, near Burma. His body was never recovered. At the time of his death he was 38 years old.

Sydney Welcome Center

From the Sydney International Airport, we were all bussed to the R&R Welcome Center, located in the Chevron Hotel, in downtown Sydney. In the Hotel Lobby, a Money Exchange Booth had been erected, as a permanent Australian Bank, to serve all international travelers. Other temporary booths had been erected, and were manned by the very hospitable Australians. Each booth had a sign, displaying possible interests for the arriving troops from Vietnam. One sign read "INFORMATION." Another sign read "STATIONS," (the Aussie word meaning "RANCH"). If interested, arrangements could quickly be made to pick up the troops, and take them to a Ranch, or other choices. Additional signs read "Golf," "Swimming," "Zoo With Kangaroo Watching," "Theater and Opera House Tickets," and others advertised inexpensive car rentals. A list of nearby restaurants, motels and Australian Pubs, offering affordable menus prices, was provided. The Chevron Hotel Welcome Center was very well organized. However, I think that most of all, the troops enjoyed being among very friendly people, who spoke English, albeit laced with enjoyable Australian phrases; and most had round eyes.

When it was my turn to select a choice of activities, I chose to register as a guest, right there in the upscale Chevron Hotel. It had a very nice lounge and dining room, with a typical Aussie earthy name: "THE SILVER SPADE." When I entered the dining room and was seated for dinner, I still was wearing my summer Marine uniform. Almost immediately a gentleman approached and introduced himself as Mr. Hamilton. He invited me to join him and his wife to have dinner, as their guests. He said they were on Holiday (vacation) from their home in the city of Newcastle. They suggested a steak dinner; as Australian beef was excellent. While enjoying a glass of Australian wine, I ordered my steak to be cooked medium.

During dinner, the Hamiltons wanted to know the size of my family, and how long I had been married. I told them that Millie and I were married at Vero Beach, Florida in 1944; that our son, Bill would soon graduate from the Virginia Military Institute, and upon graduation, would be commissioned a Second Lieutenant in the Marine Corps. Our daughter Jeanne would graduate from high school in North Carolina. They also wanted to know how long I had been in Vietnam, and when I expected to be transferred back to the United States. They seemed reluctant to discuss much about themselves; but chose instead, to learn more about me.

I asked them about some Australian terms I had overheard. While enjoying the delicious Australian steak, and another glass of Australian wine, I told them that I understood "Gd-Day Mate," but not "Walkabout." They laughed, and explained that the term "Walkabout" referred to the Australian Aborigine population. The Walkabout meant that, no matter how successful an Aborigine became, they felt great loyalty, almost an obligation, to revisit their tribe whenever possible. That helped me understand their common term, "The bloody Aboriginals are on the Walkabout, you know."

While finishing dinner, they asked me if I would like to ride with them to Wollongong and back, the next day. Wollongong is a coastal city, with an Aborigine name, located about one hundred miles south of Sydney. I accepted, and agreed to meet them for breakfast. The weather was warm and pleasant so I wore casual civilian clothes. I quickly became aware that Australia is south of the equator, so summer and winter seasons are reversed from those in the northern hemisphere. After breakfast I got into their automobile, a mid-sized British Holden; a General Motors automobile, licensed for manufacture in Australia. We left Sydney, and drove past the Sir Charles Kingsford Smith airport. They wanted to know if I had heard of him. I told them that I was a Marine Corps pilot, and had heard about his historic flight from the United States to Australia in 1928. After passing the airport we drove along the coast, in and out, through rain forests.

They referred again to the Aborigines who, at six hundred thousand people, were about three percent of the total population of Australia. They said that the Aborigines were starting to assimilate into various governmental positions. But, for the most part, they still served as "stockmen" on various sheep and cattle stations (ranches). I enjoyed a very nice driving trip to Wollongong and back to Sidney, with the Hamiltons. They extended their hospitality to me, by offering another ride in a few days, back to their home in Newcastle; a coastal city located about one hundred miles north of Sydney. Meanwhile, they suggested that I enjoy the sights of Sydney.

Sidney, Australia

In many ways, Sydney reminded me of certain cites in the United States; especially San Francisco, as both featured beautiful bridges, and shipping docks adjacent to oceans. Sydney's harbor was small and compact, but very clean and beautiful. It appeared to have been planned carefully, with large marinas filled with boats, all along the Sydney Harbor shoreline. The Sydney Opera House, located on the edge of Sydney Harbor, is one of the world's most famous buildings. I did not have time to visit the magnificent Sydney Opera House, with its multiple white sail architecture, but sailed closely in front of it, on a water taxi to Bondi Beach, and return.

Bondi Beach was guarded by a permanent off-shore metal shark fence, which was constructed with sturdy round vertical rods, approximately four inches apart. The shark fence rose several feet above the ocean surface.

Another evening, when I entered the "SILVER SPADE" for dinner, I noticed a table with a party of five couples, who were seated and ordering dinner. As soon as I sat down, a member of that party, this time a woman, approached and asked me to join them for dinner. This was so typical of the hospitality I enjoyed during my entire stay in Sydney. I gratefully accepted, and joined them for dinner. As the evening progressed, I learned that each couple were owners of television stations in Adelaide, Melbourne, Canberra, Sydney and Brisbane. They said that had all assembled in Sydney to discuss television business.

They seemed genuinely interested in how I felt, concerning the news coverage of the war in Vietnam. I told them that largely, it was inaccurate, and at times disloyal, and often, downright deceitful. They asked me if I would agree to be interviewed, to express my views. I politely refused, stating that my trip to Australia had been for R&R, and not to give my analysis of the combat situation in Vietnam. I told them that the U.S. Military in Vietnam had recently been given the responsibility for pacification, due to the need for more security, for all nation-building efforts. One man asked me if I knew the name of the U.S. General who had just been killed in Vietnam. I had not heard anything about that bad news. However, due to the large U.S. Army presence, I felt that it was not likely to have been one of our relatively few Marine Corps General Officers. It turned out that I was wrong.

With one day left in Sydney, the Hamiltons contacted me, and invited me to ride with them to their home in Newcastle. I told them that I would have to catch a train back to Sydney that evening, as I had to start my return flight to Vietnam the next day. The drive to Newcastle was another enjoyable trip. We stopped for lunch at a restaurant where the Hamiltons knew the owners. After lunch, I learned another common Aussie phrase, when Mrs. Hamilton asked her husband if he had heard the lady owner say that her husband had left her after being "shot straight through" by the waitress. In non-Aussie English that meant that her husband had run off with a restaurant waitress.

When we arrived at their home I was amazed at the opulence of their house. There was a grand piano in the large living room, a large outside patio between their house and a swimming pool. It was indeed a beautiful home, with a magnificent view of the South Pacific Ocean shoreline. While there, I learned that Mr. Hamilton was a prominent steel manufacturing corporation executive. That evening they drove me to the train station. After thanking them profusely for all of their hospitality and kindness, I said Goodbye, and boarded the train for my two hour ride back to Sydney.

The next morning, the troops arrived back at the Chevron Hotel in good order, and on time to catch the buses back to the Sydney airport. After boarding our Pan American airliner for the flight back to Vietnam, I took muster, and every one of the Marines was aboard. I then asked them to raise their hands if they had gotten married while in Australia. They all laughed, when I said I was surprised that I saw no raised hands. I told them that if they had any money left, they would have time to change it back to MPC in the Darwin airport terminal. Further, they would not have to buy lunch in Darwin, as the Australians had prepared a sandwich meal that would be handed to each of them, as they boarded their Pan American airliner for the flight to Da Nang. Soft drinks would be distributed by the airline hostesses. Upon arrival in Da Nang, they would be met, and directed back to their Marine units.

I did not know until I returned to Da Nang from my R&R leave in Australia, that Major General Bruno A. Hochmuth, the Commanding General of the Third Marine Division was the General Officer killed in Vietnam. The UH-1E (Huey) helicopter in which he was a passenger, exploded in mid-air, about six miles north of Hue. It crashed, inverted, in a flooded rice paddy; killing General Hochmuth, the helicopter pilot, and four other passengers. The remains of General Hochmuth were recovered, and returned for burial in the Fort Rosecrans National Cemetery, near San Diego. To date, he was the most senior U.S. Officer killed in Vietnam, and he was the first and only Marine Corps Division Commander to be killed in any war.

In the III MAF Combat Center, I learned of increased traffic on the Ho Chi Minh Trail; most of which continued south, skirting (I) Corps to the west through Laos. But, there was also a definite buildup of NVA forces across the DMZ from Khe Sanh Combat Base.

Chapter 41: 1968 Tet Offensive

The Tet Offensive in 1968, was a turning point in Vietnam. It was masterminded by North Vietnamese General Vo Nguyen Giap. Reference is made to The Viet Cong (VC) in the west, The People's Army of Vietnam (PAVN or NVA) in the north, and the U.S. led South Vietnamese Army (ARVN) opponents. Terms like VC, NVA, PAVN and PAVN/VC are used interchangeably to identify all Vietnamese enemy forces. The U.S. troops simply referred to the enemy as "Charlie," their short, common term for Viet Cong.

General Giap's objective was to start a general uprising in South Vietnam. The North Vietnamese chose the Lunar New Year (Tet Holiday) to strike because Tet is a traditional "time of truce." Many Vietnamese travel, to spend the week-long Tet Festival with their relatives. That provided the perfect cover for the infiltration of communist forces. The North Vietnamese violated the long-standing Tet "time of truce," by launching coordinated attacks on major South Vietnamese cities, with eighty-four thousand troops, in three phases.

The first phase of the assault began on 30 and 31 January 1968, when PAVN/VC forces struck populated areas, with heavy U.S. troop presence, in and around the cities of Saigon and Hue. The second phase, launched simultaneous attacks on smaller cities and towns; commencing on 4 May, and extended into June. The third phase commenced in August, and lasted six more weeks. The Battle of Hue raged, over three weeks. The communist forces initially occupied a walled section of the ancient city known as the Citadel. They struggled fiercely against Marines and ARVN troops.

The Marines had not taken part in urban warfare, since they had captured Seoul during the Korean War. Opposed by superior artillery, tank and air, the PAVN/VC were finally dislodged and beaten. In Hue, the PAVN/VC forces lost an estimated five thousand troops. The Marines lost one hundred fifty, and the ARVN, four hundred. Such PAVN/VC losses were not sustainable, and in the months that followed, the U.S. and South Vietnamese forces retook the towns that PAVN/VC forces had previously secured during the 1968 Tet Offensive; but not without heavy military and civilian casualties, on both sides. In the end, U.S. and ARVN forces were able to crush the attacking enemy forces. But the scale of the unexpected attacks unnerved the U.S. political and military leadership in Washington. Thus, they were never able to convince the U.S. public that we finally had won. Although we did win the military war, we lost the war of public opinion. Once again, the media thrived on negative news because, as always, bad news sells.

My observations of the Tet Offensive were largely viewed from the III MAF Combat Center. All pacification efforts, except for the III MAF CAPs, had ceased. Therefore, I will limit my commentary on the 1968 Tet Offensive, to effective actions, as I viewed them in and around the five (I) Corps Tactical Zone provinces that received less publicity. Volumes have been written regarding heroic troop, and military actions, during the 1968 Tet Offensive. So, I'll not waste the reader's time by attempting to duplicate, or embellish, the writing of so many skilled book authors. But, I will attempt to provide some background information, to briefly describe the initial introduction of U.S. combat forces in South Vietnam in 1965, the birth of III MAF, and growth and changes in military command.

Background-Introduction of U.S. Forces Vietnam

On 8 March 1965, the Ninth Marine Expeditionary Force made an amphibious landing at China Beach, near Da Nang. The thirty-five hundred Marines were the first U.S. combat troops to arrive in South Vietnam. They joined the twenty-one thousand Advisors who were already there. The mission of the Marine

Expeditionary Force was limited to defending the American Air Base in Da Nang. Then on 5 May, the Joint Chiefs of Staff relayed President Johnson's approval to establish a force headquarters in Da Nang, to include the Third Marine Division and the First Marine Air Wing. By the end of 1965 the troop buildup reached thirty-eight thousand Marines in the Third Marine Amphibious Force (III MAF) under the command of Major General Lewis Walt who, on 4 June had succeeded Major General William R. Collins, who had reached the end of his overseas tour. Major General Walt had been selected as the new III MAF Commander by General Wallace M. Green, Jr., Commandant of the Marine Corps.

With his new assignment, came his promotion to Lieutenant General. The Change of Command ceremony was held indoors, because the American flag was not permitted to be displayed outdoors in SVN. The U.S. relationship with the Vietnamese military was very sensitive. Because the Americans were guests, they could only give advice; but could not compel action. A way had to be devised so the two military forces could cooperate, but also remain independent. General Westmoreland coined the intriguing phrase "tactical direction," a phrase identical in meaning to "operational control." But, the phrase "tactical direction" seemed more acceptable to the Vietnamese.

"Arc Light" Missions

Starting about three months prior to the 1968 Tet Offensive, The U.S. Air Force commenced flying their B-52 bombers against known communist troop buildups, and other targets. They were called "Arc Light" missions. The targets ranged from bombing targets in and around Hanoi (the North Vietnam capital city), and the nearby Haiphong Harbor, to troop air support missions in South Vietnam. The B-52 missions were initially flown from Guam to Vietnam; a round trip distance of forty-nine hundred miles.

Eventually, the B-52 flights were initiated much closer; from Air Force Bases at Kadena, Okinawa and U-Tapao, in Thailand. The shorter distances made more Arc Light missions possible.

I recall the III MAF concerns for troop safety when the Arc Light B-52s approached. Over one hundred bombs were dropped from each B-52 in the bomber stream. To assure troop safety, every ground unit in the B-52 target area had to be certain that all of their ground patrols had been safely recalled. The Arc Light missions also had to be carefully coordinated with other air support missions by Air Force, Navy and Marine Corps aircraft, including helicopters.

In the III MAF Combat Center, the coordination became a virtual nightmare. It seemed that the whole war had to stop in order to accommodate the B-52 bomber streams, approaching unseen from thirty thousand feet. On the other hand, B-52 bombs dropped all along the north side of the DMZ were very effective. The devastating effect of hundreds of high-explosive bombs, dropped in rows toward the western end of the DMZ, was often referred to as: "Spring Plowing At Khe Sanh."

The 26th Marine Regiment of the 3d Marine Division at Khe Sanh was commanded by Colonel David E. Lownds. His Khe Sanh location came under increasing artillery fire from communist forces, firing from the north across the DMZ, and from the west from positions in Laos. The Khe Sanh airstrip was under constant artillery and mortar fire. Air Force C-123 twin-engine transport aircraft, trying to deliver supplies were shot at, and even shot down, at Khe Sanh. A Marine four engine KC-130 transport, trying to deliver tank, flame-throwing fuel, was hit, and blew up, when attempting to land on the Khe Sanh airstrip. The Khe Sanh ammunition dump was also blown up. In effect, Khe Sanh was under seige. It became necessary to ease the dire situation at Khe Sanh by moving some 3d Marine Division troops west, along Highway 9, toward Khe Sanh, from the Quang Tri City and Dong Ha.

Drawing those Marine and ARVN forces away from the coastal cities of Quang Tri and Dong Ha was exactly what the PAVN/VC wanted, to support their Tet Offensive plans. The buildup and shelling of the Khe Sanh Marine combat base by the PAVN/VC was to give the impression that a major Tet Offensive attack would be against Khe Sanh. It was not; but was a PAVN ruse, intended to lure Marine troops away from the Quang Tri City area. Quang Tri City was a small city, with only sixteen thousand residents; but it was the capital of Quang Tri Province, the northernmost Province in South Vietnam. The 26th Marine Regiment became "cornered" on the west (at Khe Sanh) by Laos, and on the north (also at Khe Sanh) by the DMZ, and North Vietnam. Khe Sanh was constantly under attack, receiving enemy mortar and artillery fire from two directions.

Like the City of Hue, Quang Tri City is only six miles inland from the South China Sea; and within the range of Naval gunfire from supporting U.S. Navy ships firing inland, from the East China Sea. Quang Tri City is along Highway 1, a two-lane paved highway that parallels the South China Seacoast, south of the DMZ to Hue. As an important symbol of South Vietnamese authority, Quang Tri City became a prime target of the PAVN/VC during the 1968 Tet Offensive. Capture of Quang Tri City would ensure that Highway 1 to Hue, thirty-one miles to the south, could provide a direct open route to Hue, for the easy movement of troops and weapons from the north.

On 26 January, the 812th PAVN regiment moved across the DMZ, and entered Quang Tri City, which now was only lightly defended by the troops of the 1st ARVN Division. On 31 January, Robert Brewer, the CORDS Senior Advisor to the Quang Tri Province Chief, met with Colonel Donald V. Rattan, who was the American advisor to the ARVN 1st Regiment. An assault on Quang Tri, from the north, prevented the PAVN/VC from bringing additional forces into the city; and would also trap them, when trying to escape back to the DMZ.

The American military attributed the decisive PAVN/VC defeat to a strong ARVN offense, the effective intelligence on enemy movements provided by the CORDS advisor Robert Brewer, and the airmobile tactics of the 1st U.S. Army Calvary Division, commanded by Army Major General John J. Tolson. Between 31 January and 6 February, an estimated 914 PAVN/VC were killed, and another 86 were captured. The swift defeat of the PAVN/VC preserved an important symbol of South Vietnamese national pride, and allowed our allied forces to devote more resources to other battles in northern (I) Corps, particularly in Hue. General Tolson always gave great credit to the Marines, for their innovative use of helicopters in Korea.

One of the great ironies of the 1968 Tet Offensive was that the North Vietnamese may have been their own worst enemy. In late 1967, PAVN/VC troops laid siege to the Khe Sanh combat base in a deliberate effort to draw allied forces into the Quang Tri Province back country. The growing danger to the Marine base so alarmed General Westmoreland, that he directed III MAF to rush the 1st Cavalry Division into northern (I) Corps, a full month ahead of the planned schedule. And, instead of moving it out to Khe Sanh, he put the Division in the coastal low lands, where it could respond quickly to PAVN/VC attacks on Quang Tri City and Hue.

The Division had four hundred fifty helicopters, which were used to secure Bases, and to accommodate a huge supply flow, not possible in the Khe Sanh region, because of its remoteness, and the high level of enemy activity. The 1st Cavalry Division arrived just in time to save Quang Tri City, and to help the Marines and ARVN drive the enemy from Hue. Because of the soundness of the enemy defeats at Quang Tri and Hue during the 1968 Tet Offensive, another four years would pass; and the Marines had departed

Vietnam, before the North Vietnamese would try to take Quang Tri and Hue once again.

Throughout July 1966, accumulated evidence showed a VC buildup in the Southern provinces of Quang Tin and Quang Ngai. To counter and match the VC buildup, the 1st Marine Division (MARDIV) landed in Quang Tin province, and set up its headquarters at Chu Lai, during March 1966. The 1st Marine Division landing sharply increased the Marine combat presence in South Vietnam, by another twenty thousand troops. The (MARDIV) was commanded by Major General Herman Nickerson until 1 June when, at the end of his tour, he was replaced by Major General Donn Robertson. The newly arrived 1st Marine Division, and the U.S. Army Americal Division, commanded by Major General Samuel W. "Sam" Koster, were given the responsibility for all combat operations, including the addition of Quang Nam Province, in Southern (I) Corps Tactical Zone.

Both Division Commanders were in the III MAF Command, and their combat responsibilities included the protection of both the (I) Corps (General Lam) and the III MAF (General Walt) headquarters; as both are located in the important seaport city of Da Nang - second in size only to Saigon, in South Vietnam. Also, they were responsible for the protection of the 1st Marine Air Wing airfields at Da Nang and Chu Lai, the Monkey Mountain-based Marine Helicopter Air Group, the Navy Construction Battalion, the Korean Marine Brigade,[xxvi] located on Cape Batangan, plus all of the various hospitals and refugee camps located in and around Da Nang.

Both the airfields at Da Nang and Chu Lai received multiple rocket attacks. The existing aircraft parking revetments at Da Nang protected most of the parked aircraft. However, the newer airfield at Chu Lai had only minimum protection, and the headquarters of two Marine Aircraft Groups were attacked by multiple rocket attacks. Rocket attacks against the city of Da Nang were sporadic. However, one rocket hit a barracks in the III MAF Compound, and killed or wounded several Marine NCO's. Another rocket exploded at the (I) Corps Headquarters; where the only discernible damage was to an American Advisor's coffee pot. Several rockets exploded harmlessly, in the river between the City of Da Nang and the III MAF Compound. One harmless non-rocket explosion was on the sidewalk in front of the CORDS office building in Da Nang.

My opinion is that Army/Marine Corps Command Relations were being severely tested, when General Westmoreland intervened, and ordered the early movement of the 1st ARCAV into northern (I) Corps. The 1st ARCAV Division was already under the command of III MAF. As the COMUSMACV, General Westmoreland could, of course, assert his authority at any time. However, the Marines sometimes viewed General Westmoreland's orders as reflecting nervous interference from his MACV staff in Saigon; which somehow translated into a personal mistrust of some Marine military activity in the two Northern provinces of (I) Corps.

In retrospect, I feel that the early movement of the 1st ARCAV Division into the Quang Tri area, as previously described, was timely and correct. Further, the Army Americal Division's coordination and with the 1st Marine Division served the protection of Da Nang, and other joint division combat operations in Southern (I) Corps, very well.

My view was that the MACV/III MAF command relations were further strained when General Westmoreland announced that he was creating a MACV (forward) Command, to be headed by his MACV Deputy, General Creighton W. Abrams, Jr. The new command would be responsible for all military operations north of the Hai Van Pass; essentially all military activity in the two northern (I) Corps provinces of Quang Tri and Thua Thien.

The general feeling of Marines was a loss of confidence on the part of General Westmoreland in the III MAF Commanding General that, if so, was grossly unwarranted. General Westmoreland tried to soften the effect, by stating that the creation of MACV (forward) was just a "temporary" move. Apparently the announcement was made at a meeting with General Cushman, General Abrams and General Westmoreland at the Phu Bai Combat Base, near Hue, in Thua Thien Province. Once General Westmoreland returned to Saigon, Generals Abrams and Cushman worked well together.

Beginning in 1968, General Cushman's III MAF command numbered more than one hundred thousand soldiers, sailors and Marines. Since the previous June, he had under his command, two reinforced Marine Divisions, the U.S. Army Americal Division, the 1st Marine Air Wing, the Force Logistics Command, and the U.S. Pacific Command Reserve, with its three thousand Marines, in two battalions along with a helicopter squadron. In addition, he had "coordinating authority" over the four battalions of the Republic Of Korea Marines in the (ROK) Marine Brigade.

Including the ROK Marines, Lieutenant General Cushman had forty infantry battalions, and twenty-three aircraft squadrons in the III MAF area of operations; which extended from the DMZ south, for two hundred twenty miles, through five Vietnamese provinces, to the northern border of the (I) Corps Tactical Zone. He also had the new mission of protecting the headquarters of all five (I) Corps Tactical Zone province headquarters.

In effect, General Cushman commanded a field army, in size. He had many responsibilities, which had kept pace with the expansion, following the Ninth Marine Expeditionary Force landing in 1965. He wore many other "hats" including being the (I) Corps Senior Advisor to (ARVN) General Lam, and the CORDS Senior Advisor to Ambassador Koren in (I) Corps. General Cushman was well respected in the Marine Corps; with a reputation for political shrewdness. He viewed the new MACV command arrangement as a lawful order, and would therefore do his part to make it all work in harmony with the new MACV (forward) Commander General Abrams.

Of course, General Cushman and his subordinate were understandably unhappy with the new command arrangement, as it implied that General Westmoreland lacked confidence in III MAF; a motive that General Westmoreland steadfastly denied. General Cushman was also very cognizant that President Johnson's determination to halt escalation, after the Tet Offensive, was a crucial turning point of U.S. participation in the Vietnam War.

The U.S. Generals were convinced that, with additional troops, a new an accelerated pacification program would end the war. President Johnson did not agree. Instead, he tried to set parameters for peace talks; which consumed several more years, and caused thousands more military and civilian casualties. Then, in March, President Johnson announced that he would not seek reelection and, in effect, handed the whole Vietnamese situation off to the newly elected President, Richard Nixon. From my viewpoint that essentially ended the Vietnam War; although intense fighting continued for several more years, including the year that our son, Bill, a Marine Infantry Platoon Leader in Fox Company, 2d Battalion, 7th Marine Regiment, 1st Marine Division (Fox 2/7, 1stMarDiv). With only two months left in my 13 month tour, I went back to work in the CORDS headquarters in Da Nang.

Chapter 42: End of Vietnam Tour Events

Event One: Ambassador Koren's Retirement

After the 1968 Tet Offensive ended, I returned to my office in the CORDS building in Da Nang. My CORDS boss, Ambassador Koren, told me he was returning to the United States in a few weeks, and would retire from active duty with the U.S. Department of State. We had a long conversation about the future of Vietnam and CORDS. President Johnson's announcement that (1) he would halt further combat escalation, and (2) he would not seek re-election, and (3) he had halted all B-52 bombing missions below the 20th parallel, made the future of any meaningful pacification appear grim to both of us.

Too, that General Westmoreland's MACV Deputy for CORDS (DEPCORDS), Robert W. "Blowtorch Bob" Komer, had quickly skedaddled from Vietnam, following the start of the 1968 Tet Offensive. He later was assigned U.S. Ambassador to Turkey. I thought to myself that it was a good riddance. I told Ambassador Koren that working with him had been a real pleasure, and that I was sorry to learn that he was leaving before my tour in Vietnam would end, in two months. Further, I told him that, before he left, I would like to have an afternoon "Going Away Party" for him on the roof of our CORDS office building in Da Nang. All of the personnel in the CORDS office building could attend, and have the opportunity to thank him, and to bid him Goodbye. He approved the Rooftop Party Plan.

The Vietnamese CORDS employees were obviously amazed to receive an invitation to a party, to which invitations had also been extended to General Cushman, the III MAF Commander, the ARVN (I) Corps Tactical Commanding General Lam, and Da Nang Mayor, ARVN Colonel Le Chi Cuong. I also invited Mr. Bill Johnson, the CORDS Agriculture Advisor, as he and General Cushman had both graduated from the University Of Minnesota. Ambassador Koren said the party would be nice, and then told me to relay all party supplies needed to his residence staff; including the food and drinks. It all worked well, and the party was enjoyed by all who attended. A week later, I accompanied Ambassador Koren to the Da Nang Airport, where he would make his final departure from Vietnam. I asked him who his relief would be. He told me that he was not certain but, meanwhile I should represent him at the morning III MAF briefings, until his relief arrived. I had already done that several times, when he was temporarily away, visiting his family in the Philippines.

A week after I said goodbye to Ambassador Koren, I received a call from General Cushman, who asked me to come to his office. He smiled at me and said, "You have business in Saigon tomorrow, don't you?" Then he told me what this was all about. He said that he had just received a call from General Westmoreland stating that ARVN Commanding General Lam had been summoned to Saigon for an important meeting. The crux of the meeting was to vote on whether Nguyen Cao Ky would continue as the President of South Vietnam, or would he be replaced by Vice President General Nguyen Van Thieu.

General Westmoreland said that he did not want to start sending small jet airplanes to provide transport for Vietnamese Generals. He then said that if III MAF had an Officer who needed to visit Saigon, he would send the jet for him; and General Lam could ride along. Actually, I did have business, but it was in Da Nang. My long time friend, Colonel Stanley V. "Stan" Titterud, was arriving in Da Nang, that evening. Stan Titterud and I had flown together in Korea. I apologized to Stan, by telling him that my boss, General Cushman, was sending me to Saigon the next day in response to a request from his boss, General Westmoreland.

I surmised that General Lam voted correctly, as he flew to Saigon wearing two stars, the rank insignia of a Major General, and he returned to Da Nang wearing three stars, the rank insignia of a Lieutenant General. General Thieu won the "election," and became the new President of South Vietnam.

A few days later, I received a call from the Da Nang airfield stating that a Mr. Charles Cross had arrived, and requested a ride to the State Department House, in Da Nang. I was not surprised, as MACV in Saigon was continually sending "official visitors" to III MAF, when they didn't know what else to do with them. However, I was surprised when I arrived at the airport, and found that Mr. Cross (not Ambassador Cross) was Ambassador Koren's relief. I drove him to the State Department House in Da Nang that had been occupied by Ambassador Koren. He met the household staff there, and wanted to know if Ambassador Koren had a staff car and a driver. He also so wanted to know the source of food and drinks at his new residence.

He said that he would make his own arrangements to make his presence known to General Cushman at III MAF. I advised him that he could avoid early morning traffic on the bridge over the Han River, by leaving his staff car at the CORDS office building, and riding the military boat that shuttled back and forth across the river to the III MAF headquarters. He gave no indication that he appreciated my meeting him at the airport; nor my sharing with him how he could easily cross the Han River. He didn't ask about security arrangements for his house. I felt obligated to tell General Cushman that Mr. Cross had arrived, so I called his office and left the information regarding the arrival of Mr. Cross with General Cushman's military Aide.

A few weeks later, when I was at the III MAF Combat Center, General Cushman asked me how I was getting along with my new boss, Mr. Cross. I told him that Mr. Cross was a Foreign

Service Officer, who was recently transferred to South Vietnam from the U.S. Embassy in London, formally titled "The Court Of Saint James," and that Mr. Cross appeared to put his personal creature comforts above all else. I told him that as a Marine we expected combat assignments ahead of creature comforts. General Cushman just smiled and reminded me that as a Marine, I was trained to act; but that U.S. State Department Foreign Officers were trained to negotiate.

I reminded General Cushman that my tour in Vietnam was nearly over, and I told him that I would appreciate it if he would submit my final Marine Corps fitness (efficiency) report, rather than having Mr. Cross do so. He said that he would. I also recommended that my relief be assigned from CORDS in Saigon, rather than being selected by the III MAF. He agreed, and told me that he would have the assignment of my relief changed from III MAF, to MACV in Saigon.

Event Two: Arrival of the *Helgoland*

In September 1968, the German Hospital Ship *Helgoland* arrived in Saigon, after sailing seventy-five hundred miles from Germany. The vessel was built in 1963, to transport tourists from the German Port of Cuxhaven, to the North Sea island of Helgoland; a distance of forty miles. It was a party boat, that entertained children traveling with their parents, friends and relatives. When America entered the war in Vietnam, pressure was applied to NATO ally West Germany to assist. But, instead of sending troops, Germany chose to participate with a humanitarian effort; by converting the *Helgoland* to a German Red Cross Hospital ship. At Hamburg, the *Helgoland* underwent outfitting, and other conversion, necessary to make it a modern Hospital ship. The conversion included adding a helicopter landing platform on the ship's stern, as well as outfitting the ship with exemplary medical equipment.

Instead of tourists, there were ten doctors and thirty nurses on board, from the German Red Cross. Since the ship was under the protection of the Geneva Convention, it was considered to be strictly neutral. The ship had one hundred fifty patient beds. By comparison, the hospital ship USS *Repose* (AH-16) has 800 patient beds. Other U.S. Hospital ships, including the USS *Sanctuary* and USS *Consolation* were similar to the USS *Repose* in size, and in number of patient beds. Upon arrival in Saigon, the German doctors and nurses were not prepared for the horrors that were awaiting them, when the first wounded civilians were brought aboard. Their floating hospital became the most modern clinic in South Vietnam. Otherwise, medical care for civilians was a disaster; with only one doctor per seventeen thousand Vietnamese people. The Vietnamese called the *Helgoland* the "White Ship of Hope." The final Helgoland harbor was the city of Da Nang. For the doctors and nurses, working with so many civilian patients was physically and mentally challenging. They amputated limbs from children, women and men who had been shredded by gunshot wounds, and mines. Many others patients had Napalm burns on their bodies.

At Da Nang, the *Helgoland* tied up only a few blocks from the CORDS office building where I worked. I knew that the ship treated only Vietnamese civilians. However, I also knew the ship would need some emergency medical supplies, such as whole blood, which was not readily available from the local Red Cross, or any other source. So I asked the III MAF Communications Officer to have a military telephone installed on the ship, with a direct line to the military Da Nang Surgical Hospital where, if necessary, emergency medical supplies could be "borrowed." When the Marines arrived to provide and install a telephone, they wore standard issue utility uniforms. When the *Helgoland*'s chief surgeon spotted the Marines he became angry and let them know, in no uncertain terms, that only civilians were treated on board, not soldiers! The Marines retrieved their telephone equipment, and quietly left the ship. They really didn't care, as they only wanted to see as many female German nurses as possible, anyway.

Two days later, my assistant came into my office and said that there was a German officer requesting to see "the officer in charge." I invited him into my office, where he introduced himself as the Captain of the *Helgoland*. I asked him to be seated, and offered him a cup of coffee. He accepted, and then, comfortably seated, he apologized for having our Marines removed from his ship. He bluntly stated, "Sometimes, I have trouble with my chief doctor." He asked if it were still possible to have a military telephone on board, with a quick disconnect of the line, thus leaving the military telephone aboard, when he took his ship to sea. I assured him that I could easily make those telephone arrangements.

I then asked him why he would want to take his ship to sea. He responded that it was the rockets that were occasionally being fired into the area; some exploding in the Han River where his ship was moored. I became curious and asked him how he knew when to have his ship cast off, and go to sea. I thought he might have some kind of "back channel" information. But, he said that he could only guess; and wondered if I could provide any information regarding the predicted rocket-firing schedule. I told him that, officially, I could not, but at the briefings I attended every morning, the enemy rocket attack threat was discussed. The enemy still had some capability to occasionally fire eleven-inch rockets but, without aiming and launch equipment, the rockets had to be elevated manually to firing positions; usually tilted upward on logs, and generally pointed toward Da Nang. If fired, it would be soon after sunset, thereby giving the firing crews all night to escape.

I shared this information with him, and told him if he could visit my office each morning, I could share the likelihood of rockets being fired that evening, by simply stating, "I think if I were Captain of the *Helgoland*, I would take my ship out to sea this evening." Nothing more needed to be said. Sometimes when the rocket threat was high, the *Helgoland* would be seen in the early evening, sailing past the III MAF mess hall on the other side of the Han River, where I was eating my evening meal. Noting that the *Helgoland* was headed toward the harbor entrance to the East China Sea, someone with whom I was having dinner would wonder aloud, where the *Helgoland* was going.

I would mutter some non-nonsensical thing like, "Perhaps back to Germany," knowing all the while I was calling the shots daily, for or against, the evening sailing of the *Helgoland*. Hearkening back to the advice given to Marine officers in Quantico, Virginia years before, by the Chief of Naval Operations, Admiral Arleigh Burke, I recalled he said, "Sometimes you will not know what to do. When that happens, just use your God-given American horse sense, and do what you think is right. You will be right; and we will send your orders later."

Event Three: The Elephants of Tra bong

Indian elephants are indigenous to Vietnam. Their natural habitat is in the mountainous food-rich rain forests, away from the rice growing coastal plains. The much preferred beasts of burden are smaller water buffalo, because they are more docile, and easier to train than are elephants, and they eat considerably less. The water buffalo is a near perfect animal for rice farmers throughout all of Southeast Asia.

The village of Tra Bong is located in Quang Ngai, the southernmost province of (I) Corps. The Tra Bong villagers operated a self-contained sawmill that could cut through logs two feet in diameter. It was manufactured by the Mighty Mite Sawmill Company in Portland, Oregon. The sawmill had been purchased by the United States Agency for International Development (USAID) and sent to Vietnam. It was powered by an air-cooled Volkswagen engine that, through anchored pulleys and cables, moved a log on a moving carriage to, and through, the spinning saw; cutting the logs into boards of pre-set widths. The boards (largely Teak and Mahogany) were then loaded on powered barges, and taken down the Tra Khue River, to a waiting lumber market in Quang Ngai, the province capital city.

    I received a call from the American Province Advisor, who reported that the USAID Sawmill in Tra Bong was no longer working. The Quang Ngai Province Chief told him that the sawmill engine was still running, but when a log contacted the saw, the blade simply stopped spinning. I called the Marine Helicopter group (MAG-36) at Marble Mountain, and requested a small, dual-controlled Bell helicopter to take me to the Tra Bong sawmill site the next day. Besides inspecting the non-working sawmill, I needed to log some pilot flight time. The next day, a small, Bell (bubble canopy) HTL helicopter met me at the III MAF helicopter pad, and we flew to Tra Bong, where the Vietnamese Province Chief was waiting with the sawmill crew.

    While viewing the saw mill, I quickly discovered the problem. The three V-Belts driving the saw from the engine were slipping, because they had slowly loosened, through extended wear, and they had never been tightened. Although somewhat burned on their driving surfaces, the belts still appeared operable when tightened. The Gates Brand, with its belt number, could still be read. I showed the Province Chief and the sawmill crew how to make the belts tighter. Afterward, the sawmill engine was started, and the saw was properly spinning. The saw was shut down, and I found and copied the information shown on the V-Belts, and the sawmill

Model and Serial Number, from the small nomenclature plate that was affixed permanently to the sawmill log carriage. When I returned to Da Nang, I wrote and mailed a letter addressed to the President of the Mighty Mite Sawmill Company in Portland, Oregon. In the letter I listed the Gates V-Belts needed, and briefly described the sawmill location, and its important use. I told them that I would pay for the belts personally, as knowing the Federal Stock System payment delays, probably this, and the next war would be over, with his company still unpaid.

I was surprised by the Mighty Mite Company reaction to my letter, when two weeks later I received a call from MACV in Saigon, stating that a representative of the Mighty Mite Sawmill Company had arrived at Tan Son Nhat Airport in Saigon, on a scheduled Pan American Airways flight, with some equipment that I ordered. The caller wanted to know where he should send him. I asked the caller to have him register in the American-run REX HOTEL in Saigon, where he would be contacted. The caller did not know the representative's name. But, I knew his name would be revealed when he presented his required passport for hotel registration. Now What?

At the following daily 0700 III MAF staff briefing, I related the story concerning the Mighty Mite Sawmill Company Representative arrival in Saigon, and that I had asked the caller to have the Representative register in the REX HOTEL. But, because he was a civilian, he would not be permitted to ride in a military airplane or helicopter. General Cushman turned, and asked Jack Horgan, who headed the CIA Regional office in Da Nang, if he could handle this situation. Without hesitation, Jack Horgan said that would handle the whole thing; including getting the V-Belts to the Tra Bong sawmill. Once again, high priority was given to Vietnamese civil operations when needed.

Before leaving Tra Bong the previous day, I noted another potential problem which would likely arise with the heavy rains expected with the approaching Monsoon season. I asked the Province Chief how the logs would be skidded to the saw mill, when the heavy rains came, and trucks, and even water buffalo, would become mired in the soft surface between the forest and the sawmill. He knew the saw mill could not be moved into the forest, as the Viet Cong would likely destroy it during the night. He just shrugged his shoulders, indicating that he did not know. Neither did I.

I do not know where the idea of using elephants to skid logs originated. But on one of my visits to the Marine Helicopter Air Group (MAG-36) at Marble Mountain, I learned that a new Marine squadron had just arrived, equipped with the first large Sikorsky HR2S turbine-powered helicopters. These new Marine helicopters had the power needed to lift an elephant. But the elephants would have to be carried externally, because an elephant was too large to fit inside the HR2S helicopter cabin. If we could somehow procure two elephants, and have them moved to Tra Bong, they could be used to pull logs from the forest, across the open soggy field, to the saw mill.

I requested a meeting with General Cushman, so I could present the problem, and a partial solution. I told him that lifting an elephant, slung underneath a helicopter, seemed to dictate that the animal would first have to be sedated, and carried on a very strong pallet. He listened intently, then said he would contact MACV in Saigon, to request help from General Westmoreland's staff. He did, and the response was almost unbelievable. First, a request for serum, in quantities to knock out two medium-sized Indian elephants was ordered from a London zoo. Two trained elephants were rented, along with two large harnesses, and two experienced

Mahouts (Elephant handlers) were hired to accompany and guide the elephants, from the forest to the Tra Bong sawmill.

After being anesthetized, and while resting on pallets at Saigon's Tan Son Nhat Airport, the elephants would be loaded on a fixed-wing military transport aircraft, and flown several hundred miles north to the Marine airfield at Chu Lai. From Chu Lai, two large Marine Sikorsky HR2S helicopters would fly to Tra Bong, carrying the elephants, slung underneath, on a pallet. Amazingly, it worked. The elephants were put to sleep at Tan Son Nhat airport, in Saigon. They woke up in Tra Bong; not knowing that they had ridden several hundred miles in a fixed-wing transport aircraft, and had been carried on pallets, slung under helicopters, into the forest of Tra Bong.

While watching the helicopters approach, each carrying a pallet, with a still anesthetized elephant, one sawmill worker said to another that he wondered why the Americans brought them dead elephants. This successful endeavor to help the Vietnamese people, represented only one coordinated effort between several branches of the U.S. Military, the ARVN, the CIA, USAID, the U.S. State Department, and just a few U.S Allies (Korea, Germany and Australia), in a combined effort to protect, and bring a better life to the Vietnamese people. Canada contributed nothing. As I prepared to leave Vietnam, I was proud of my efforts to help win the hearts and minds of the Vietnamese people, over North Vietnamese communist tyranny.

Event IV: Junketing Politicians

During my entire assignment to III MAF in Vietnam, we were constantly called upon to host visits from politicians, mostly U.S. Senators. We had to stop our work and brief (entertain) them. To save time, we actually staged a show in the III MAF briefing room that practically repeated the same information to each visiting

Senator. Most went away, satisfied. However one Senator actually demanded that he be taken to the DMZ, so he could be photographed pulling the lanyard (firing) a howitzer at the DMZ. Fortunately, it did not trigger enemy counter-battery fire, as it could easily have done. I'm sure the picture of the senator "bravely" firing a cannon at the enemy in Vietnam, was used repeatedly in his next political campaign. A favorite expression of those politicians was, "When I was in Vietnam" or, "I just returned from Vietnam." I noticed that all of those political visits stopped abruptly with the onset of the 1968 Tet Offensive.

Although the political visits were annoying; for the most part they were harmless. For that reason, I have not named any of them, with one exception. I studied Senator Edward Kennedy of Massachusetts for a about week, when he visited South Vietnam. He was a member of the United Nations Refugee Commission. Kennedy sent two attorneys from his Washington, D.C. office to Vietnam, to schedule an itinerary for Senator Edward Kennedy, who would arrived in Da Nang a week later.

In setting a schedule with the two Attorney General lawyers we learned quickly that Senator Edward Kennedy had no interest in a III MAF military briefing. Instead, visits to two Refugee Camps in (I) Corps were planned. We felt refugee camp visits would be more in keeping with Senator Kennedy's UN Refugee Commission interests. The two attorneys made quick visits to the refugee camps, came back to Da Nang, and canceled the Senator's trips to the camps, stating, "There was nothing to see." What they really meant was that there was nothing bad to see. I then wondered why the hell he would come all this way to visit nothing. But, I guess he could return home and exclaim, "When I was in Vietnam..." While in Da Nang, the two attorneys stayed in Ambassador Koren's State Department house in Da Nang. When Senator Kennedy arrived, he also stayed there.

Occasionally, Marines got to enjoy a one-day, in-country R&R at China Beach, where the troops passing through the Da Nang area could drink ice cold beer, relax, swim, and usually drink more beer. Some of our Marines had an unexpected visit from a U.S. Senator, when, somehow, Senator Edward Kennedy found China Beach, and entered the tent where the Marines were drinking beer. They quickly glanced at him, uttering muffled expressions of disgust, and turned back to their more important beer drinking. My quick appraisal of the Senator caused me to surmise that with his huge head, covered with his long white mane, he just plain looked "goofy."

Ambassador Koren insisted that Senator Kennedy call on the Vietnamese (I) Corps Commander, General Lam who, very graciously invited Senator Kennedy into his (I) Corps headquarters office. General Lam presented Senator Kennedy with a round twelve-inch plague painted red, with a raised yellow Roman Numeral (I) centered on the Plaque. Corps Insignia are always depicted in Roman Numerals. General Lam handed the plaque to Senator Kennedy, stating that it was a gift, to remind him of his visit to Vietnam. The Senator refused to accept the gift, rose, handed the plaque back to General Lam, and departed from General Lam's office with no expression of appreciation of any kind. By refusing to accept the gift, he could not have insulted General Lam any more deeply. Senator Kennedy's actions during his entire trip to Vietnam bordered on idiocy. When he left Vietnam, we were told that his next stop would be Bangladesh. Another good riddance! He was an elitist snob; overblown with his family and self-importance. Truly, he was just plain rude and ignorant.

Event V: Departure from Vietnam

On 31 May 1969, I packed my suitcase, put on my summer uniform, and said Goodbye to General Cushman and his III MAF staff. I stopped by my old office in the Da Nang CORDS building, and said Goodbye to my military staff members. I thanked them for all they had done. Mr. Cross was out of the office, so I never did bid him Goodbye. On my way to the Da Nang airport, I also stopped at the Da Nang City hall to say Goodbye to Colonel Le Chi Cuong, the City Mayor.

At the Da Nang Airport, I gave my detachment orders to the Air Force Aerial Port personnel. I asked about the Air Force C-141 jet transport that was leaving for Okinawa after midnight on 1 June. They said I could not ride that airplane, as it was carrying a dozen caskets. I located the Air Force Major who was the C-141 pilot. I asked him about his Block (Departure) time. He told me that he was flying to Kadena, AFB on Okinawa, and that I could ride on his airplane. So, I retrieved my orders from the Aerial Port personnel, and with my orders and suitcase in hand, I climbed into the massive, C-141 cabin. I think I fell asleep before the C-141 wheels were up.

I woke up when the airplane started its descent to Kadena AFB, on Okinawa. I couldn't really believe that my thirteen-month tour in Vietnam was over. The time in Vietnam passed so quickly for me, that my tour of duty seemed more like five months. When I arrived in Okinawa, I called my close friend, Colonel Bob Simmons, who was the Commanding Officer of MCAS, Futenma, Okinawa. Bob Simmons and I had been Lieutenants in the "photo" squadron at Cherry Point, years before. Bob had been assigned to MCAS, Futenma, following his tour in South Vietnam. Bob, and his wife "Shortie," and Millie and I had been life-long friends, who had enjoyed many squadron parties at Cherry Point. One memory was when our toddler son, Bill fell into a tub of icy water at a picnic building called the Hancock Lodge. Bill contributed to his mischievous reputation early.

When I arrived at Kadena, I was advised that I could leave for home on another C-141, non-stop via the great circle route, to the Dover, Delaware Air Force Base. However, all Marine Colonels leaving Vietnam were required to report to the Fleet Marine Force Pacific (FMFPAC) Headquarters at Camp H.M. Smith in Hawaii, for the purpose of debriefing, and to make an oral history contribution, regarding their experiences. My debriefing was by another long time friend (and Marine Corps Aviator) Colonel Charles H. "Chuck" Ludden. The debriefing was recorded, and lasted most of one day. Chuck was fascinated by my assignment as a Marine pilot. While I was at FMFPAC, I was housed in the Transient Officer's Quarters, at Camp Smith. I stretched out on the lawn for a few hours, listening to the Hawaiian birds sing. One was the Nene, a Hawaiian goose. I couldn't recall ever hearing a bird sing in Vietnam.

I departed Hawaii on a commercial airliner to Los Angeles. After takeoff, the airliner had an electrical problem, and had to divert and land at Hilo, Hawaii, where it remained overnight for repairs. That delay caused me to miss our daughter Jeanne's Havelock High School Graduation. But my return also had its rewards. Many servicemen returning from Vietnam were jeered at by unthinking, cowardly idiots, who gathered in groups at the airline terminal; often calling the returning troops "baby killers," and shouting other epithets as the troops passed through airline terminals. Instead of being welcomed home, as the brave, surviving war heroes they really were, some were subjected to shameful ridicule. This was one of the worst episodes in our Nation's history. How utterly stupid it was, to blame the surviving troops, for the war they fought in Vietnam.

I returned to the Los Angeles International Airport (LAX), where I was greeted, and welcomed home by our friends Art and Audrey Rawlings. I had flown helicopters with Art Rawlings during the previous war in Korea. We gathered my luggage, and after passing the U.S. Customs inspection, we drove north a few miles to the Burbank home of Kelvin and Gwen Bailey. Kelvin had been the staff pilot for General Schilt all five years that I was General Schilt's Aide, and now Kel was the chief pilot for Walt Disney Productions. I thanked the Rawlings for the ride from LAX, and told them that Millie and I would see them, as soon as my orders specified permanent transfer to MCAS, El Toro, California, for duty with the 3d Marine Air Wing, following a 30 day leave. Meanwhile, I had to return to Havelock, North Carolina, and move my family to California.

The Disney Gulfstream Kel Bailey piloted was based at the Burbank Airport; close the Burbank Headquarters of Walt Disney Productions. The same hangar housed business jets owned by Union Oil, and a Sears & Roebuck corporate jet. The Gulfstream was often used to carry famous Disneyland characters, in costume, to cities where new Disney Movies were opening. It was used extensively to shuttle Walt Disney, and other Disney notables, to Kissimmee, Florida, and return, during the construction of Walt Disney World (WDW). Kelvin Bailey flew the Gulfstream to Kissimmee, on multiple trips, with Walt Disney as the only passenger.

During the ongoing negotiations to purchase the land for Walt Disney World, the purpose of the Gulfstream flights to Florida remained a secret. Often, before landing at Kissimmee, Kelvin would circle an area far from the WDW site, at low altitude, in case anyone became suspicious about the presence of this strange business airplane. When Kelvin landed the Gulfstream, he would taxi and park it with the passenger door away from the Kissimmee terminal, so it was not possible to identify anyone getting on or off the Gulfstream. Then, Kelvin would rent a car, and drive it to the Gulfstream door; ostensibly to load personal baggage, but a disguised Walt Disney would quickly get into the rental car back seat; where he would hunker down, to escape possible recognition. Kelvin would whisk the rental car away from the airport; first driving a few miles in a direction leading away, then turning back to the

WDW site, while Walt Disney explaining where the iconic Disney castle, other attractions, and themed hotels would be built. Walt was very proud of his plans for the Experimental Prototype Community of Tomorrow (EPCOT) creation.

At that time, the Disney Gulfstream bore only standard, FAA assigned identification; but its call sign was changed to "234 Mickey Mouse" after the land for WDW was purchased, and construction was well underway. The day I arrived back in California, a Disney Executive needed to fly from Burbank to Atlanta on the Disney corporate jet. Kelvin purposely delayed the flight, until I arrived home from Vietnam. After my arrival, Kelvin drove me to the Burbank airport, where I met the Disney Executive, and we flew non-stop to Atlanta. From Atlanta, I flew on a commercial airliner to New Bern, North Carolina, where Millie and Jeanne met me. My free ride to Atlanta aboard Walt Disney's personal Gulfstream; flown by his personal pilot, Kelvin Bailey, was an unusual and special "Welcome Home" for me.

Chapter 43: Final Career Transfer

When I arrived at the New Bern, North Carolina airport, I was greeted warmly by my wife Millie, and our daughter Jeanne Kay. Jeanne had just graduated from Havelock High School, and had pre-enrolled at East Carolina University, in Greenville. She would start her college courses there, at the end of summer. Meanwhile, she would drive with us to my next duty station, in California. Millie had our household effects already packed, and sent to California. She had moved from our rented house in Havelock, to a Motel in New Bern, where we really celebrated my homecoming. It was just great to be home with my wife.

Jeanne drove our Volkswagen back to Havelock, where she stayed overnight with friends. Millie had arranged to have a U-Haul automobile towing hitch attached to our Oldsmobile. With the small Volkswagen hitched behind our Oldsmobile, we started our driving trek to California. Due to Jeanne's High School Graduation, followed by Bill's VMI Graduation a few days later, we were on a tight driving schedule. We were headed to California, albeit in a round-about way, through Lexington, Virginia; Michigan; and Bloomington, Minnesota. Lexington is a small town in Virginia's Shenandoah Valley; home to both VMI, and Washington and Lee University; the latter founded during the colonial era, in 1749. It is the ninth oldest institution of higher learning in the United States. Its campus abuts VMI in Lexington.

We stopped in Lexington to, attended Bill's Graduation from the Virginia Military Institute (VMI), followed by his Commissioning Ceremony, as a Marine Second Lieutenant. Our driving speed through the hilly countryside was steady, but slow. The Interstate Freeways were not yet completed, so I was very conscious about the overall length of our two cars hitched together. After graduation, newly commissioned Second Lieutenant Bill Warren was ordered to Quantico; to attend the next Basic School class. He had purchased a new Volkswagen Karman Ghia, which he drove to Quantico, and we officially said Goodbye to him there, the next day. Then Millie, Jeanne and I departed for southwestern Michigan, where we visited our parents' homes in the small towns of Coloma and Covert.

I decided that I had enough of driving one car, and towing the second. So, before we headed on to Bloomington, Minnesota to visit my older brother, Bill Dean, his wife Margaret, and their teenage daughter, Gretchen, we traded in our two cars, and purchased a new Chrysler sedan. Because I was leaving Michigan, and would soon register the Chrysler in California, I did not have to pay Michigan Sales Tax. For a nominal fee, I was issued a special, low cost, temporary license plate for our new car. When I reached California, and while going through the motor vehicle licensing process, I had to surrender my temporary Michigan license plate. It was assumed that I had paid Michigan sales tax, when we purchased the new Chrysler. Of course I said little, but I was very grateful for the unintended sales tax omission.

My older brother, Bill, was very well paid, as a senior Northwest Airlines Captain. Further, due to his airline seniority, he could select his flights, which were usually to Tokyo, through Los Angeles and Hawaii; with an occasional flight to Hong Kong, and return to Tokyo. He then flew a reverse course, back to Minneapolis. Due to airline Captain flight hour limitations each month, Bill enjoyed considerable free time. He had purchased a houseboat, which he kept at a marina on the St. Croix River. Millie, Jeanne and I moved aboard Bill's houseboat, with his wife Margaret, and daughter Gretchen, the day after we arrived. The houseboat had several cabins, and we sailed for several days on the St. Croix River, Mississippi River tributary.

It truly was a luxurious experience, and a rare opportunity for us to have time together, and to reflect on our very different flying careers. Bill was a very successful airline Captain, and I, a Marine Colonel. We both gave much credit for our success to Mr. Forrest E. Totten, our one-room, Ingraham School teacher, in Coloma, Michigan; also to our wonderful adopted parents, the Warrens, and the Deans; but most of all, to the full measure of Divine Guidance we both enjoyed. I felt that for a couple of orphaned kids to have reached a decent level of success, it could have happened ONLY IN MY AMERICA.

From my brother's home, in the Minneapolis suburb of Bloomington, we drove west, through South Dakota, Wyoming, and Yellowstone Park. After a fly-fishing stop at Dillon, Montana, we drove through Twin Falls, Idaho, and Salt Lake City, Utah, and entered California, after crossing the hot desert during the daytime, in perfect comfort, due to the Chrysler's very efficient air conditioner.

When I reported to MCAS, El Toro, I was assigned a 4-bedroom house on the Base. Our next door neighbor was a U.S. Navy Captain, who was a physician, and the Commanding Officer of the MCAS, El Toro hospital. The El Toro Air Station was commanded by Major General William Gay Thrash who, when a Lieutenant Colonel, had been shot down and captured during the Korean War. He was tortured in a prison camp, and held for two years, by his North Korean captors. Among other things, they made him strip naked in bitter cold, Korean winter weather, while they clipped electrical wires to his body and, after pouring water on him, turned the electricity, on and off.

A couple of my friends who had also been shot down, and captured, were in the same prison camp with Lieutenant Colonel Thrash. They described his brave defiance, saying that when the electricity was turned on, then off, his entire body would shake. His

North Korean captors were attempting to make him confess that the Americans were using germ warfare tactics. I mention this very upsetting torture, to describe the brutal nature of communist dictatorships, and to express my admiration for Major General Thrash, for never confessing to the ridiculous North Korean, communist allegations. He will always be remembered as a very accomplished Marine pilot, and a truly brave Marine.

Marine Helicopter Air Group Fifty Six (MAG-56)

When I reported to the 3d Marine Air Wing (3rd MAW), I was ordered to take command of MAG-56, based at MCAF, Tustin, located only three miles from El Toro. My orders specified that I would relieve the Commanding Officer of MAG-56, who would then be transferred to the 3rd MAW Headquarters at MCAS, El Toro, where he would join the 3rd MAW Staff as the Comptroller (Finance Officer). In reality, I was relieving my old friend and companion, Colonel Keith W. "Cos" Costello, with whom I had flown as helicopter pilots in the same squadron (HMR-161) during the Korean War. In the Vietnam War, "Cos" had been wounded. When flying on a combat mission, a round, fired from the ground, penetrated the helicopter deck, and hit his heel. He recalled that when hit, the first thing he remembered was that his knee had violently jerked up, and hit his face.

Our Change of Command Ceremony took place on the large mat between the two massive LTA Hangars that I described earlier, in Chapter 12. Personnel from the entire Air Group, consisting of six flying squadrons, and two support squadrons, stood in formation during the ceremony. Then after Colonel Costello received the MAG-56 flag from the Air Group Adjutant, we faced each other, and he presented the flag affixed to a short pole, to me, symbolizing change of command. I received the flag, turned, and passed the flag back to the Adjutant who did an about face, and carried it back to the troop formation. After passing the MAG-56 colors (flag) to me, we exchanged positions and made our brief remarks.

The order was loudly barked out to "Pass in Review." The 3rd MAW band took position, and commenced playing martial music. As the band approached the reviewing stand, the Drum Major, leading the band, rendered a salute with his baton. He held the baton salute, until the entire band marched past the reviewing stand. Next, the four-Marine Color Guard, carrying the United States and MAG-56 flags, marched past. The Commander of Troops (the Air Group Executive Officer), and members of the Air Group staff marched past, in front of the reviewing stand.

As each squadron approached the reviewing stand, its Commanding Officer gave the order "Eyes right." He and his officers saluted simultaneously, by quickly raising their swords high from their right shoulder, marching, then in a single motion, lowering their swords, with the tip in front and above their right foot. As the reviewing officers, Colonel Costello and I, returned salute. The band

Drum Major then saluted the passing colors. We returned the salutes of the Commander of Troops, and each Squadron Commanding Officer, leading his squadron on review.

Marine Corps Change of Command ceremonies are symbolic of Marine Corps professionalism, discipline, and esprit de corps. In the interest of brevity, many smaller details of a Change of Command ceremony and the "Pass in Review" parade have been omitted. I was extremely proud and appreciative, to take command of so many disciplined and well-trained officer and enlisted Marines.

The Air Group that I now commanded had one Observation Squadron at Camp Pendleton, equipped with both small Bell Attack Helicopters and OV-10 fixed-wing North American Broncos. The remainder of MAG-56 was based at MCAS, Tustin. It included a squadron of Sikorsky H-19 helicopters, two squadrons of Boeing-Vertol CH-46 tandem-rotor, medium-lift helicopters, and two squadrons of the new Sikorsky HR2S heavy-lift helicopters. Each HR2S was capable of transporting up to thirty-five troops, or equivalent loads of several thousand pounds, internally if possible, or externally if necessary. (The twin-turbine powered HR2S was the helicopter used to carry the sedated elephants as described in Event Three of the preceding Chapter.)

The other two support squadrons were the Headquarters and Maintenance Squadron (H&MS-56) and Marine Air Base Squadron 56 (MABS-56). H&MS personnel included my MAG-56 headquarters staff, along with skilled maintenance personnel, who provided mandated engine, transmission and rotor systems changes and repairs, beyond what the flying squadrons were equipped to do. H&MS always had helicopters that required post-maintenance test flights, which also provided helicopters for pilots from the MAG-56 staff. Every helicopter had its individual maintenance log, detailing what and when, all maintenance was accomplished.

By flying H&MS helicopters, the staff pilots did not have to bother the flying squadrons, by trying to get on their flight training schedules. The Marine Air Base squadron provided all of the "logistics stuff," like food, purified drinking water, high octane aviation gasoline (AVGAS), tank trucks, ambulances, portable control towers, radios, medical equipment, and much more, to support the entire air group in combat for at least 30 days. Sometimes I still marvel that, during operations in Korea, HMR-161 could provide all of the H&MS and MABS capabilities, using only the resources of one squadron. However, when necessary, Marines can become innovative experts at "midnight requisition."

MAG-56 Mission

The main mission of my Air Group was to train and equip helicopter squadrons, for combat in Vietnam. Secondary missions included training OV-10 pilots to perform as Forward Air Controllers (FACS) Airborne. That secondary mission was flipped to a primary mission, when the Director of Marine Aviation, Lieutenant General McCutcheon, called me personally, to ensure an all-out effort to get the Marine OV-10s in Vietnam, ahead of the U.S. Air Force. I called the very capable Lieutenant Colonel Phillip P. "Phil" Upschulte, who commanded the Observation Squadron at Camp Pendleton. He reported that his OV-10 pilots, and their crews, were fully trained, and ready for combat. He alerted his OV-10 crews, pilots, and mechanics to expect transfer orders very soon.

I then went to see the 3rd MAW Commander, Major General Arthur H. Adams, at his MCAS, El Toro Headquarters, and apprised him of General McCutcheon's call to me, and the result of Colonel Upschulte's report, relative to OV-10 aircraft and crew readiness. When I asked if he wanted me to report the OV-10 readiness directly to General McCutcheon, or did he, as the 3d MAW commander, desire to do it, he immediately said he would pass my report to General McCutcheon. I told him that Colonel Upschulte had a complete list of the names and ranks of all the OV-10 pilots, observers and mechanics who would require overseas orders; and that they had all been alerted to expect their orders. General Adams asked for the list; so that it could be forwarded to General McCutcheon at Headquarters, U.S. Marine Corps, where the transfer orders would be issued.

It was obvious that I knew General McCutcheon, so General Adams asked me, where I had known him. I related that I had gone through helicopter transition training with him at Lakehurst; then at Quantico, I was one of his instructor/demonstration pilots at HMX-1. Then later, in Korea, I had flown with him almost daily, after he relieved Colonel Herring as Commanding Officer of HMR-161. General Adams told me that he appreciated my relating my telephone call with General McCutcheon to him; along with Colonel Upschulte's OV-10 readiness status. He then placed a call to General McCutcheon in Washington. I called Colonel Upschulte, and asked him to transmit the names, ranks and serial numbers to the 3rd MAW headquarters at El Toro.

Within a week, the ten OV-10 were flown to NAS, North Island, where they were hoisted aboard a small aircraft carrier, for transport to Vietnam. The OV-10 crews boarded, and sailed for Vietnam on the same ship. Their squadron commander, Phil Upshulte and I said Goodbye to them at dockside, and wished them well. We then rode together in my staff car back to Camp Pendleton. We discussed how long it would take to train more OV-10 pilots and crews, which certainly would be needed to reconstitute his gutted squadron OV-10 program. I revealed to him why I contacted my boss, General Adams, rather than dealing directly with General McCutcheon. I returned to my quarters at El Toro; hoping to get back to performing the primary mission of MAG-56.

In preparing squadrons for overseas deployment, a formalized training program was followed. It included several weeks of individual pilot checkout (instruction) fights, if they had not flown that type of helicopter before. Then each squadron used the nearby Sana Ana Mountains to learn how to fly in and out of rough terrain, while sometimes flying in strong Santa Ana winds. All of the transport helicopters we flew had dual controls, so a new helicopter pilot flew with a more experienced pilot who, in effect, became an instructor.

Transporting and supporting troops during training, was always given high priority. The squadron pilots learned to use cargo nets to deliver supplies, where no suitable landing spots existed. We practiced attaching cargo nets to the helicopter-suspended cargo hooks, hanging beneath a hovering helicopter. Especially valuable were opportunities to operate from aircraft carriers, operating off the Southern California coastline, between San Diego and Los Angeles. When possible, troops from Camp Pendleton would be bused to NAS, North Island, where they boarded an aircraft carrier. A few hours after sailing, our helicopters would arrive overhead during the daytime, and sometimes at night. The ship reported its readiness to have helicopters start landing aboard, by broadcasting, "Your Signal Is Charlie." The helicopters would then leave their holding patterns, land aboard, and commence transporting the Marines ashore.

The 3rd MAW coordinated such operations between the Navy ships, the participating Marines from Camp Pendleton, and MAG-56. The MAG-56 S-3 (Operations Officer) would respond to a daily Fragmentation (FRAG) Order from the 3rd MAW, which provided specific commitments. It was a daily "who, what, when and where" directive. If no exercises were planned, it would simply read, "Continue Daily Flight Training."

Army-Trained Marine Helicopter Pilots

The rapidly expanding Marine Corps Helicopter Program created need for more helicopter pilots than could be trained at NAS, Pensacola. All Marine helicopter pilots were initially trained in fixed-wing aircraft. Initial helicopter training had been transferred from Lakehurst, New Jersey to Pensacola, Florida, where considerably more Navy and Marine helicopter pilots could be trained. The Navy also had an increasing need for helicopters pilots; mainly to support their worldwide anti-submarine warfare efforts. That high priority need superseded the competing Marine Corps need for helicopter pilots to transport combat Marines. So the Marine Corps asked the U.S. Army if it could help by providing some initial helicopter training for Marine Corps pilots, transitioning from fixed-wing to helicopters.

In MAG-56 we joined twenty Marine Lieutenants who had completed the U.S. Army helicopter training at Fort Rucker, Alabama, where they flew Bell HUEYS. A majority of the graduating classes at Fort Rucker were Army Warrant Officers. At their class graduating ceremony, the graduating Warrant Officers had Army Wings pinned on their uniforms. But, the graduating Marines were handed the Army Wings, as they were already wearing their Navy Gold Wings. It was obvious that those young pilots had received excellent, initial helicopter training; so they had no trouble adapting to flying our Marine Corps HRS, CH-46 and HR2S helicopters. Those who were assigned to our Observation Squadron, at Camp Pendleton, were also trained to fly OV-10 Broncos. There was no stigma detected, due to those Marine pilots having learned to fly helicopters in an Army Helicopter Training Program. It was a temporary stop-gap helicopter training program, that served the Marine Corps very well; by preventing a serious helicopter pilot shortage, in our expanding Fleet Marine Forces.

Annual Rifle Range Qualification

All Marines are required to qualify, annually, on a rifle range. During my career, the first rifle I used was the bolt-action Springfield 03. That was followed by the Garand M-1 and M-14, and the Colt M-16. Each major Marine Corps base has one or more rifle ranges that are standard in design, and vary only by the number of targets. Annual rifle range weapons training lasts a week; with marksmanship scoring and recording, on the last of five days. Weather was of little consequence, because of the long held belief that "it never rains on the rifle range." Rifle range instructors were serious Marine veterans, who stressed range safety, and individual marksmanship, above all else. Training included practice sighting, and firing your rifle while prone, and from varying distances measured in up to five hundred yards. Rifle slings were used, to provide for more stable rifle aiming and firing.

Rifle range targets, numbered to match individual firing positions, were raised simultaneously, from below ground safety pits, prior to the following loudspeaker command: "Ready on the right. Ready on the left. Ready on the firing line. Watch your targets. Commence Firing!" The targets were numbered circular bulls-eye rings. After each shot, the target hit could be seen from the pit. The pit target-operator would then raise a round disc, fastened to a long wooden stick, and hold the disc over the bullet penetration hole in the target for about twenty seconds. Then both target and disc were lowered, and the target bullet hole was pasted over before raising it again. If the target had been completely missed, the disc was replaced by a waving red flag called "Maggie's Drawers." It was raised, and vigorously waved for all to see.

Between shots, the firing Marines had time to adjust their rifle sights for elevation and windage, before the entire firing sequence of events was repeated. Along with pilot training, weekly rifle range schedules were published, the week before assignment to the rifle range for annual qualification. Our MAG-56 squadrons at Tustin used the MCAS, El Toro rifle range, and our observation squadron at Camp Pendleton, used the rifle ranges there. I wrote about the annual rifle range requirement, to provide the background for what happened next.

Thousands of Field Jackets

When I commanded MAG-56, I lived at the El Toro Marine Corps Air Station. Every morning I would drive the three miles to my headquarters at MCAF, Tustin. Early on Monday mornings, I would often see a truck, loaded with Marines in my command, headed in the opposite direction, toward the El Toro rifle range. Early mornings in Southern California can be very cold, until the sunshine penetrates the early morning sea fog. Then, during late mornings, the temperature rises quickly. Some of the Marines riding on the truck wore issued, warm field jackets, and others did not.

When I noticed this, I turned around, and followed the truck to the rifle range, located on the rear perimeter of the El Toro Air Station. When their truck arrived, and the Marines got off the truck, I asked several, why they had not worn their field jackets. Their answers were quick and simple; there were no field jackets to be issued. I returned to my headquarters, and asked my staff why field jackets were not available. It was because the number of field jackets available, could not exceed the number shown in the units Table of Organization. I ordered the staff to contact each of our squadrons, to determine the number of field jackets needed. The total requirement was five hundred and fifty four.

I determined that no more Marines would be sent to the Rifle Range without a field jacket. If necessary, starting with me, then my staff, would surrender their field jackets, until the situation was corrected. An urgent request for five hundred, fifty-four mixed sized field jackets, was transmitted by the 3rd MAW to the Commandant of the Marine Corps, with an information copy sent to the Marine Corps Supply Depot in Philadelphia.

I heard nothing further, until I received a call from my friend, Colonel 'Cos' Costello, about three weeks later. He was now the 3rd MAW Comptroller at El Toro. When he called, he asked me if there was still a railroad train gate over there at MCAF, Tustin. I affirmed the gate presence, he said, "Well, You better open it, because <u>five hundred and fifty-four thousand </u>field jackets will be shipped by railroad to MAG-56 at Tustin." I said back to 'Cos', "I'm betting they will all be size Large". I thought that I would "pull his chain" a little more, by asking him if paying for that train load of field jackets would have an appreciable effect on the budget of the 3rd Marine Air Wing. He answered that many Air Wing Marines would probably starve, but they would die warm. His telephone call, and my response, were typical of the friendly back and forth between 'Cos' and me. I did not know who modified our field jacket order back to our original request for five hundred, fifty-four. I suspected that it was "Cos." Anyhow, the "train gate" at Tustin remained closed. Shortly thereafter, the field jackets arrived, and were issued.

During my tenure as the Commanding Officer of MAG-56, two squadrons achieved full combat readiness, and were sent to Vietnam. One was a Boeing-Vertol CH-46 medium-lift squadron, and the second, a Sikorsky HR2S heavy-lift squadron, with the ten OV-10 Broncos, and crews, from our observation squadron, (VMO-6) at Camp Pendleton. With the phase out of H-19s, that squadron no longer had a mission, and it was disbanded. The squadron H-19's were flown to Arizona, and placed in permanent outdoor storage at Yuma, and Litchfield Park.

General Lewis Walt Visit

It was a special, and most pleasant for me, when General Lewis Walt visited MAG-56. I had not seen him since he departed Vietnam in late 1967. He was now the first four-star Assistant Commandant of The Marine Corps (ACMC). He came to my office, and spoke informally to our assembled squadron commanding officers, and members of my staff. We then proceeded to one of the large blimp hangars. From atop a raised, flat bed semi-trailer, I introduced him, and he addressed the squadron pilots, and enlisted Marines, who were crowded around the trailer. He addressed them for about thirty minutes. We then visited the free- standing air control tower, where a Marine photographer snapped our picture, shaking hands.

I told him that I was honored, personally, by his visit to the Air Group I commanded. He wanted to know where my son, Bill, was serving in Vietnam. I told him that Bill was a Platoon Leader in Fox Company of the Second Battalion, Seventh Marine Regiment

(Fox 2/7), deployed in the Da Nang area. General Walt said that he would try to visit Bill. He did.[xxvii]

General Walt then said that he thoroughly enjoyed his visit to MAG-56. He thanked me for assembling my MAG-56 Marines, so he could talk to them. After returning my salute, he entered the rear seat of a waiting Marine Corps staff car and was driven three miles back to MCAS, El Toro. His four engine Marine KC-130 transport airplane was waiting for him to take off for Vietnam. He had previously completed two tours in Vietnam, as Commanding General of the Third Amphibious Force (III MAF), headquartered in the city of Da Nang.

I always wondered just why General Walt visited MAG-56, which I commanded, and no other unit at El Toro, or at nearby Camp Pendleton. As time passed, I suspected that he wanted to see me in a command environment before the Brigadier General Selection Board met, later that year. He headed that selection board, which was officially convened by the Secretary of the Navy (SECNAV). The board makeup included members who were all Marine General Officers; and included Major General Arthur Adams, who was the 3rd MAW Commanding General, and my boss, at El Toro.

Retirement Decision

Assuming that if I was selected for promotion to Brigadier General, it would have become the pinnacle of my Marine Corps career, Millie and I discussed the situation at length, and I finally concluded that I should submit my written retirement request to the SECNAV. It was a tough decision, but for some of the following reasons, I decided to retire from active duty. I had been decorated for combat service in three wars. But, whether in combat, or many other exercises and long deployments, Millie was always left home to raise our children, while I was away. Now, our children had flown from the nest.

When I had returned from Korea in 1952, Jeanne was about two years old. She clung to my leg and wouldn't let go. On the other hand, Bill's typical boyhood pranks made him live under a "wait until your Dad gets home" cloud. He said that he wasn't really worried, because he knew his Dad was in Korea. But, when Millie admonished them, using their first and middle names, "Jeanne Kay" or "Billy Dean," they knew they had better shape up, immediately. Once, when Millie started to spank Bill with a yard stick, it broke in half, causing them both to laugh.

Bill was a Marine Second Lieutenant, leading an infantry platoon in Vietnam. Jeanne was attending college; studying to become a Registered Nurse. I was only forty-six years old, leaving plenty of time for traveling together, or employment that would be free from, at times, requiring life and death decisions. I would never again have to leave Millie home by herself to make all of the many decisions of household financing and raising our children. She had always been the perfect Marine wife; and I wanted to be with her. She had an engaging personality, and a cute, innocent, non-threatening way about her, that made friends and strangers alike, almost always smile at her. Our children grew up, always knowing that their Mom loved them; and they looked forward to the joy of my returning home.

We were always very proud of all that Jeanne (a Nurse) and Bill (a Marine) had accomplished. Both earned college degrees. Jeanne later graduated from Southeastern University in Hammond, Louisiana with her Registered Nursing (RN) degree, and Bill had graduated from VMI with a Degree in History, and upon graduation, had been sworn in as a Marine Officer.

Chapter 44: Retirement

My Certificate of Retirement from the United States Marine Corps was dated the First of September, One Thousand Nine Hundred and Sixty Nine. It was signed by General Leonard Chapman, Jr., Commandant of the Marine Corps. In addition, he sent a separate letter to me, in which he cited my service in WW II, Korea, and Vietnam. He also listed my personal combat decorations, and expressed his appreciation for my long and honorable service. (See Appendix I)

A retirement parade was held for me, on the mat at the end of Blimp Hangar #1. I learned that my career-long friend, Colonel Keith "Cos" Costello would retire on the same date, so I invited him to join me in reviewing the retirement parade, which was almost identical to the parade described earlier, when I took command of MAG-56 from him, during the previous year. We invited our families, friends, and many Marine associates. One was Major General Robert Owens, the 3rd MAW Commanding General. Also there, retired Army Colonel Sidney Mashbir, and his wife Alice. Colonel Mashbir authored the book, *I Was An American Spy*, which he had autographed for Millie and me years before, when I was a Marine Captain.

Ron Dominguez, the manager of Disneyland, attended as my guest, as did Walt Disney's pilot, my long-time friend, Kelvin Bailey and his wife Gwen. Our daughter, Jeanne was there, dressed in a pretty, polka-dot dress, and wearing white shoes, on which she had painted polka-dots to match her dress. Our son, Bill was deployed; so he was not able to attend. The parade review was followed by a low-altitude flyover of twenty helicopters, four from each of the five flying squadrons, flying in tight formation. Following the retirement ceremony, a lavish retirement party was held at the MCAF, Tustin Officers Club.

After the party, we invited Cos and his wife, Marty to join Millie and me, at our new house in Tustin, to relax in our pool. While Cos and I were floating on rafts, I asked him how he liked being in the Army. Puzzled, he asked what I meant. I told him that we had just joined the Army of the Unemployed. However, my respite was short-lived, as a week later I started my new job at Disneyland in nearby Anaheim, California. I happily taught in the on-site University of Disneyland for the next two years.

Neil W. Moore, Millie Warren and Alice Moore Mashbir
Air Force One; MCAS El Toro, CA (1969)

Chapter 45: My Son's Career Synopsis

Introduction

In writing my book ONLY IN MY AMERICA, I decided my son's exciting career description should be included, especially his combat experiences in Vietnam. In so doing, I saved the best for last. Thank you, Bill, for a well-written synopsis of your fascinating Marine Corps career. As always, you made your Dad very proud. Thank you for your dedicated service.

Bill Warren's USMC Career – In His Own Words

I graduated from the Virginia Military Institute (VMI) on 9 June 1968, was commissioned as a Marine Corps Second Lieutenant on the same day, and reported to Marine Corp Base, (MCB) Quantico, Virginia for Basic School, on 10 June 1968.

Bill Warren in VMI Uniform   Sgt. Maj. W. Warren, VMI

The Marine Corps did not really know what to do with me for the three weeks or so before my Basic School class started, but it was decided that my VMI experience qualified me to do one useful thing...run parades!

Since there was only one parade scheduled during that three week period, I had a lot of free time to get fitted for my uniforms (at AM Bolognese, in downtown Quantico). I was dismayed to learn that my uniforms would cost more than my car; and was thankful that there was a bank a block away from the Bolognese store! As a regular commissioned officer, I did not rate a uniform allowance; but Mr. Bolognese took care of me, as well as he took care of my father before me! And while uniforms could be found that cost less, I never purchased a uniform from anyone other than Mr. Bolognese, because of the high quality, and his consistent kindness.

The Basic School started on 9 July 1968, and graduation was 4 December 1968. I received my Military Occupational Specialty (MOS) as an infantry officer and also received orders to the 1st Marine Division in Vietnam. After taking some leave, to drive from the east coast to the west coast, spending three weeks as a Company Commander of a three hundred Marine draft unit undergoing Pre-Vietnam deployment orientation training at Camp Pendleton, CA, and a week on the island of Okinawa, I finally arrived in Vietnam.

I was assigned as the Platoon Commander of the 1st Platoon, F Company, 2nd Battalion, 7th Marine Regiment. At that time, a Marine Corps platoon consisted of forty-seven Marines. The majority of my Battalion was deployed in the "rocket belt," west of Da Nang. My Company, however, was located south of the Da Nang airfield, and provided a rapid reaction force, designed to defend against, or counterattack enemy forces anywhere in the Da Nang area. Significant contact occurred in early February 1969, during the Vietnamese New Year holiday known as Tet.

My platoon was attacked by an NVA force, trying to attack the southern Da Nang airfield area. My platoon was the first unit they encountered. The platoon sustained no casualties, while killing two hundred sixty of the attacking NVA unit. During the ensuing week, our Company mission was to clear the urban areas of south Da Nang, where enemy fighters penetrated populated areas. During that week, we had no casualties, but killed another one hundred thirty-six NVA soldiers. During this time, we were required to dig up numerous NVA graves, in order to search dead enemy bodies for intelligence information. That was a most grisly and horrific experience in so many ways. It was also apparent that the NVA killed, and buried, their most seriously wounded because they slowed down the movement of their units. For me, this became the stuff of recurring nightmares, even to this day. Finishing this grisly task, we thought the battle was over, but it was only a prelude of what was to come.

Within a few days, my Company was relocated, by truck convoy, north and west of Da Nang, to an area known as the Di Loc Pass, which was the location of our Battalion headquarters. After a hot meal, a shower, and a few drinks of scotch, we began to believe the worst was over. Instead, we were told to finish our drinks, get our gear, go to the supply point to receive more ammunition, and get ready to move within an hour, to reinforce one of our Companies that was under fire, at a small defensive perimeter around an artillery unit, which was about ten kilometers west. We were also told that three other perimeters, which were manned by Marines from the remainder of our other Companies, were all under fire.

We moved out in a Company-sized combat patrol, and made it to our new area without incident. The Company we were to reinforce was actually being moved to reinforce another Company, so this area became our property to defend. Our area was nothing more than a mound of dirt, and a perimeter of about one thousand yards in diameter. Each of our platoons was assigned approximately one quarter of the perimeter to defend. An artillery battery of six howitzers was arrayed in the center of the hill, in sand bagged revetments. Within the perimeter were also the artillery, and our Company command posts. A few other large tents served as quarters for the artillery unit, but most of their Marines "camped out" with their howitzers, since they were constantly responding to fire missions.

A small helicopter landing zone (LZ) served as a supply and evacuation point. Our perimeter fighting positions were fox holes, with sand bagged culvert halves covering them. Around the entire perimeter, were massive amounts of barbed wire, broken glass, trip flares, claymore mines, and barrels filled with old motor oil, diesel and gasoline (known as "foo-gas") which could be ignited if necessary, as part of the defense. We also patrolled outside of the perimeter, to try to detect any enemy staging for an attack.

On the second evening, one of the patrols exchanged fire with an unknown- sized enemy unit. Two of our Marines were gunshot casualties, and we called for a medical evacuation helicopter. A big Marine Corps helicopter showed up quickly. The casualties were loaded, and as it flew off, it took fire, was hit, and tried to make it back to our position. The pilots were able to make it back within about eight hundred yards, before the helicopter crash-landed, and rolled over on its side. I immediately sent out a patrol, and when they got to the crash site, the pilot had gotten everyone out, including our two casualties. We were going to remove machine guns mounted inside the helicopter, but it caught fire, and exploded. No one was hurt.

It was pretty quiet for a while, but around midnight, we came under an intense mortar attack, followed by a ground assault by enemy infantry. As the sky was being lit by flares, it was apparent that the enemy had breached our defenses, and were inside the perimeter, attacking our fighting positions from the rear, and trying to blow up buildings and bunkers with satchel charges. Everywhere you looked, people were running, and shooting; some NVA and some Marines. I saw the pilot and co-pilot shooting their .38 caliber pistols, and someone managed to get them a couple of assault rifles. It looked like the NVA were trying to leave, when a huge explosion rocked the hill. One of the artillery ammunition bunkers exploded; destroying one of the howitzers, killing the entire crew, while raining shrapnel and debris all over the hill. Someone ignited the foo-gas, and then it seemed everything got quiet, except for an occasional gunshot.

    I returned to my platoon command post, to find it blown up. My corpsman was wounded; shot through the upper leg. It was weird; what seemed like just a few minutes of madness, was really nearly six hours of hard fighting, starting at midnight and lasting until dawn. When it got light enough to see, it looked like the entire war had been fought there. There was evidence of hand-to-hand combat, and bodies everywhere. My platoon was very fortunate, we had only seven minor wounded, and none killed. The enemy lost about one hundred fifty killed; and that is how Tet 1969 ended for us. Our remaining weeks at that position were filled with endless patrolling, and reconstructing fortifications. We never did get back to the scotch; at least, not for a while.

    Late in March, and in early April, the Company participated with the remainder of the Battalion, and five other infantry battalions, in an Operation named "Oklahoma Hills," by attacking east to west, in a mountain area known as "Charlie Ridge" which was west of Da Nang. Near the beginning of the operation, half of my platoon was detached, to provide security for a radio relay station, so I had only twenty-six Marines, including two machine gun sections, attached from the Company weapons platoon. Our

Company was the southernmost friendly unit during the operation, and my Platoon was the southernmost element of the Company.

One evening, being such a small unit, we set up an ambush at the intersection of six different trails, in the triple-canopy jungle. At about 2100 hours, we were engaged by an enemy force of unknown size; but judging from the noise of people moving through the jungle, I knew the enemy unit was much larger than mine. Fire discipline saved us from disclosing our exact location and size. We engaged, using no rifle fire; only hand grenades and our claymore mines. We threw a good number of hand grenades at the enemy, and they answered with a large volume of AK-47 fire, and hand grenades, aimed toward our general location.

I was convinced that the enemy unit did not know exactly where we were located; but seemed to be skirting our ambush to the south, while moving west. Calling for reinforcements, I was told that the remainder of the Company was not going to be able to help, because of the risk of engaging an unknown-sized enemy unit, while maneuvering in the dark. I was advised that I was on my own. However, I think that my half-platoon was the only unit in contact with the enemy that evening, because I had what seemed to be EVERY supporting arms asset in our area of operations at my disposal, including on station AC-47 (Spooky) gunships, which we used all night to fire in support of us.

We were able to use the gunships constantly; and in a constant "danger-close" environment (firing as close as seventy-five yards…at night…from our position, using their on board mini-guns (super modern Gatling guns) which fired about 4000-6000 rounds per minute. I was directing fire, by listening for the sound made by hundreds of thousands of rounds, ripping through the trees to our south. At daylight the next morning, I moved my unit in the general direction of the remainder of the Company. During that movement, we encountered six NVA soldiers, who were shooting at helicopters trying to resupply our Company. We killed four and wounded two.

During the interrogation of the two wounded NVA soldiers by Battalion intelligence units, it was reported that my little unit was engaged by a "regiment 31" (approximately fifteen hundred NVA infantrymen). The interrogation of the wounded enemy soldiers revealed that they believed their casualties were very, very high; possibly as many as between four hundred fifty, and five hundred; all inflicted by the Spooky gunships. They were not sure; because it was dark, and because of all the confusion trying to take cover from the deadly airplanes. During the remainder of the operation, we mostly patrolled. One day, while leading a patrol, when I bent over to refill my canteen from a mountain stream, I was knocked off my feet, and thought someone had pushed me hard into the water. What really happened, is that a sniper shot at me; hitting the canteen hooked to my pistol belt. We eventually killed the sniper; but what I was most upset about was the loss of the scotch in my canteen!

At the conclusion of Operation Oklahoma Hills (which started out for my platoon, as a three-day reconnaissance in force patrol, but wound up as a forty-six day combat operation) the Battalion was ordered to relocate south, to Fire Support Base (FSB) Ross, between 11 and 15 August 1969. FSB Ross was located about sixty miles south of Da Nang, and directly west of the large US base at Chu Lai. Most of the move was via US Army truck convoy, and we were under fire many times. FSB Ross was a small, isolated trash heap of dilapidated bunkers; inferior defensive positions, that were previously part of the US Army Americal (23rd Infantry) Division area of operations. Americal briefings reveled that there had been little or no enemy contact in the area of FSB Ross, over the previous few months.

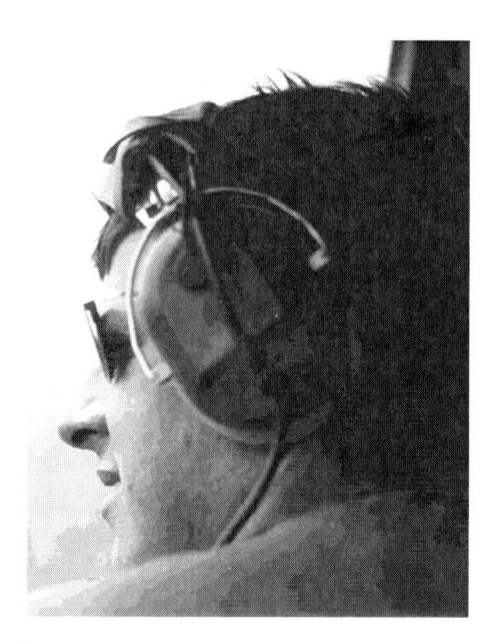

2nd Lt. Bill Warren on visual reconnaissance,
west of Chu Lai, Vietnam (1969)

However, we quickly found the enemy, and they retaliated; especially after our Companies were deployed to conduct aggressive combat patrols in the areas surrounding FSB Ross. FSB Ross was under constant mortar and recoilless rifle attack, and withstood one major night attack, that penetrated our defenses, and resulted in several instances of hand-to-hand combat with enemy soldiers, inside the perimeter of the FSB. After arriving at FSB Ross, I had to turn over my Platoon to a newer Platoon leader, and I was resigned to the Battalion staff as the S-4 (Logistics Officer), responsible for ensuring that the Battalion and all of its combat units were resupplied daily, with ammunition, food, water, radio batteries, uniforms, boots, mail and many other "necessities" to sustain active combat operations.

Additionally, I was given collateral duties as the Commander of the 106mm Recoilless Rifle Platoon, which was really run by my Platoon Sergeant. Interestingly, we had twelve recoilless rifles; but a normal platoon would only have eight of them. We did not have enough Marines to man twelve guns, but managed to borrow some off duty truck drivers. I personally manned one gun when necessary; and those who were there will remember the crazy Lieutenant named Warren, who conducted counter-recoilless rifle duels with enemy recoilless rifles, and won! It was almost a game each night, and enabled me to engage the enemy at a 1,000 – 1500 yard distance.

2nd Lt. Bill Warren sighting a 106mm recoilless rifle;
Dia Loc Pass, Vietnam (1969)

Beginning sometime around 21 August 1969, the Battalion was committed to a major operation, at the request of the 196th Army Infantry Brigade, in an area named "The Arizona Territory," more specifically, Hiep Duc. That offensive was recounted by Keith William Nolan in his book titled *Death Valley, the Summer Offensive, I Corps, August 1969,* published in 1987; which named the Arizona Territory in 1969 as one of the Vietnam War's bloodiest areas. Moving west from FSB Ross on foot, two of the four Battalion Companies became engaged in murderous fire from several locations. Another Company was helicoptered into the fray. The enemy stopped our Battalion, dead in its tracks, on 25 August.

On the second day of the operation, I was temporarily placed in command of the Battalion scout section. Flying out to the active combat area, and arriving in a "hot" (under enemy fire) landing zone, it occurred to me that besides using the scouts as a mini-reconnaissance unit, we could probably use some of my recoilless rifles to destroy enemy bunkers. The staff thought this was a great idea, and an appropriate use of our four "extra" recoilless rifles. We managed to get those four recoilless rifles, ammunition, and crews into the "hot" landing zones without any casualties or equipment losses, and were able deploy our assets quickly; even under heavy enemy fire. During the next few days, we were able to neutralize ten or eleven enemy bunkers, and provide supporting fire for the infantry Companies.

During this Operation, the Battalion sustained very high casualties. Someone finally figured out that our Battalion had engaged an NVA Division-size unit, and that we had walked into a well-planned and large scale enemy ambush. The fourth Company of the Battalion was landed in two different hot landing zones, under withering mortar fire. The Battalion Commander then committed all four Companies to the battle, and attempted to use the Battalion headquarters unit (including my small scout unit) as a maneuver element. This resulted in more heavy Marine casualties, and my old Company became surrounded, cut-off, and decimated. Through the heroic efforts of a group of Marine helicopter pilots, and the members of my scout unit, our air liaison officer, and the Battalion Sergeant Major (who later became the Sergeant Major of the Marine Corps), we were able to extract my old Company, and all their dead, and wounded, and equipment, in a night operation that was as complex as anything I had ever witnessed.

Our Battalion was pretty well chopped up. The Regimental Commander flew in, under enemy fire, and relieved our Battalion Commander. With no Commander, and units that were largely ineffective, because of the high casualty rates, we formed an awkward defensive position, from which we repulsed several attacks; and within a couple of days, we were relieved by elements of another Battalion of the 7th Marine Regiment.

After moving back to FSB Ross, the Battalion received a very seasoned, and highly respected, combat leader, as the new Commander. Within a couple of weeks, our Battalion was replaced at FSB Ross by another Battalion of the 7th Marine Regiment. We relocated to another, but much larger FSB, named "Baldy," which was where the 7th Marine Regiment was headquartered.

1st Lt. Bill Warren at Landing Zone "Baldy" (1969)

Our infantry Companies were brought back up to strength; and within a month were conducting continuous combat patrols, and small operations. The Companies were widely disbursed, and because of the longer than normal monsoon rainy season, became increasingly difficult to resupply.

Normally, supplies, replacement personnel, and ammunition were delivered by helicopter; but because of the monsoon weather, I often had to resort to resupplying by human transport, also known as "man-pack," secured by combat units; often composed of cooks, supply, clerical and any other personnel available. We would transport by trucks, and jeeps with trailers, (sometimes even using tanks, or other tracked vehicles, to get as close to the unit being resupplied and then deliver overland by man-pack. On the return trip, we would evacuate wounded and dead. One such operation was led by our Battalion Executive Officer; and it was not unusual, or hard to recruit, competent officers to lead such expeditions. Several times, these expeditions had to defend themselves against enemy attack; but not even one expedition failed in its mission. Truly, this was testament that every Marine is first, a rifleman; and trained for combat.

Being the Logistics Officer often required "creative" acquisition of necessary supplies. Once, I was able to trade a jeep, (which I suspected began as the property of the Air Force, then several Army units, before ending up in our Battalion), for a very large electric generator - about the size of a railroad engine, with enough power capability to run several small cities. It arrived on a low-boy trailer, was hooked up, and then destroyed a couple of days later, by a direct hit from an NVA mortar round. I lost the jeep, and the generator! Another time, after an NVA ground attack on FSB Baldy, we needed tons of razor-type concertina wire to replace what was damaged, and to beef up the defenses in our area. A classmate of mine from VMI, who was the S-4 for an Army Battalion, accepted my offer of one hundred sheets of ¾ inch plywood for as much concertina wire as he could provide. A couple of days later, ten tractor trailer rigs delivered enough concertina to us to beef up several miles of defensive positions.

      The landing zone at FSB Baldy was used by both the Marines and the Army. The Army maintained hundreds of Container Express (Conex) boxes (standardized military shipping containers, made of steel and aluminum) filled with supplies. After conducting a reconnaissance of those containers, certain ones containing supplies that Marines could not get were identified, and no one seemed to notice that all the locks had been cut. We offered to relieve the Army guards, so that they could go to an evening cook-out, and drink some beer. When they were out of sight, I had a rough-terrain forklift move the containers we wanted, to our side of the FSB. We "acquired" about 30 containers, and promptly emptied them. I thought there would be major repercussions; but the only flak I received was from an Army officer, who just wanted the containers back. He got them back, but they were empty, and I had a lot of very happy Marines!

      We seemed to have difficulty obtaining replacement uniforms, and even though they were made of rip-stop nylon, our combat units suffered torn, rotted, and filthy clothing. General Lewis Walt, Assistant Commandant of the Marine Corps, and the former Commander of all Marine forces in Vietnam was scheduled to visit the 7th Marine Regiment.[xxviii] My father worked for General Walt in Vietnam. I attended a meeting of the Regimental and Battalion staffs set up for General Walt, during which I was embarrassed by the Regimental Commander, pointing out the "creativity" of 1st Lieutenant Warren who so adeptly kept his Battalion resupplied, during very difficult times.

During a break in this briefing, General Walt asked me to take a walk with him. During that walk, he reminded me of past times, and asked me how I was doing. He also asked if I needed anything; and I told him about "acquiring" some Army uniforms, pillaging the medevac for usable utility uniforms, and even resorting to "rescuing" uniforms from various laundry facilities. He acknowledged that the "palace guard" at the FSB seemed to have new uniforms, but understood that a visiting General sometimes caused that. A week after his visit, hundreds of boxes of uniforms showed up at my field office. Sometimes it's nice to know a General!

I spent the remainder of my time in Vietnam as the S-4 of the Battalion, continuing to keep our Battalion units well-supplied; and I rotated back to the U.S. in February 1970. I still feel fortunate to have been so well-trained for combat, to have served with so many fine young Marines, and Corpsmen, and to have survived without any major physical injury. I am still in awe of the ability of a Marine Lieutenant to manage so much destructive power, and of the awesome destructive power of a Marine, and his rifle.

My subsequent assignments included a tour at HQMC, as a casualty notification officer. Of significance during that assignment, I was the funeral Officer for the burial of Lieutenant General Lewis B. "Chesty" Puller, in October of 1971 in Saluda, Virginia. Subsequently, I returned to the Fleet Marine Force, 2nd Marine Division, as the Commanding Officer of D Company, 1st Battalion, 6th Marine Regiment, deployed from Camp Lejeune, NC to the Caribbean (3 times), and Mediterranean Sea areas (2 times), as part of the expeditionary forces; and then I became the Commanding Officer of Service Company, 2nd Marine Division. After that, I was assigned to the staff of Amphibious Squadron 8, as a Combat Cargo Officer; and beyond that, I became the Commodore's liaison to the embarked USMC units.

Captain Bill Warren aboard USS Raleigh (LPD-1)
off the coast of Crete (1976)

Personally, and more importantly, I was intricately involved in the evacuations of U.S. citizens from Cyprus in 1974, and Lebanon in 1976.

Beirut, Lebanon evacuations (Jul 1976)

After duty with Amphibious Squadron 8, I was reassigned as the Inspector-Instructor of a Marine Corps Reserve Rifle Company, located in Madison, Wisconsin. I separated from the Marine Corps 30 November 1977.

General Lewis Walt awarding the Navy Commendation Medal to Lt. Bill Warren for combat in Vietnam (23 Oct 1970)

Epilogue

Bob and Millie enjoyed many happy years together in retirement – years blessed with the love of their many friends, and their beautiful and growing family. They remained in Tustin, California until 1989, enjoying many adventures, including forays into the world of business.

Bob founded Warren Systems (a street sweeping service) and later, with his long-time friend Cos, The First National Bank of Irvine, which was later sold to the Bank of America. During the 1980's, Bob was called back to active duty six times, by the Secretary of the Navy, to serve on The Advisory Committee on Retired Personnel.

Eventually, Bob and Millie moved to Palmetto, FL where they lived rich and full lives, making many new friends, and being involved in their church and community. Bob was very proud of being one of the founders, and a long-time volunteer with the Thrift Cottage associated with their church. The Thrift Cottage was extraordinarily successful; providing much needed goods to the community, while also providing the majority of the funding for a new larger church building, when the congregation outgrew their historic chapel.

Ever the Marine, Bob very much enjoyed belonging to the local Marine Corps League Detachment in Bradenton, FL; leading a team on trivia nights, and attending various events, including the annual Marine Corps Ball, where he was an honored guest.

On January 8th of 2010, the winter following their 65th Wedding Anniversary, Bob's beloved Millie died. After missing Millie for a long time, Bob married again, and found a wonderful companion and love in Rosemarie Wagner. They enjoyed the years they shared together until, following a brief illness, Bob died on

9 February 2021, at the age of 97. Until then, he was happy, healthy, optimistic, generous, gregarious, and devoted to his family, who he was endlessly proud of - especially his daughter Jeanne, and his son, Bill. May Bob and Millie rest in peace, and may their memories be a blessing.

On 21 May 2011, Bob was honored for his twenty-seven years of dedicated and excellent service in the United States Marine Corps, with enshrinement in the Michigan Aviation Hall of Fame.

Family Pictures

Bob and Millie Warren's home in Tustin, CA (1969-1989)

Helen (Warren) McKean and Millie Warren

Tustin, CA (1988)

Bob and Millie Warren's home in Palmetto, FL (1989-2021)

Bob Warren's restored 1930 Model A Ford

Palmetto, FL (1994)

Millie, Bob and Jan Warren; Bradenton, FL (26 Dec 2002)

Bill and Bob Warren at the WWII Memorial, Washington, DC (2013)

Bob and Rosemarie Warren, on the occasion of Bob's 95th Birthday, Bradenton, FL (2018)

Larry and Melanie Walt at the dedication of Walt Hall, in honor of General Lewis Walt, Quantico, VA (2013)

Bill and Jan Warren at Indian Land, SC (5 Dec 2014)

Conrad and Jeanne (Warren) Metz
Parrish, FL (Easter 2004)

Jeanne (Warren) and Conrad Metz
USMC Birthday Ball, Bradenton, FL (2010)

Bob and Millie with Bill and Jeanne, celebrating Millie's Birthday, and Bob & Millie's 60th Wedding Anniversary.
Palmetto, FL (April 2004)

Bob and Millie Warren, 2001

Acknowledgements

This book was written with the assistance of family, friends and colleagues. Without them, my memories would never have found their way into print. However, with their assistance and encouragement, my story was written, and can now be shared with my descendants. I also now realize that I should have started writing my book at least five years earlier. The list of names of those who have helped me is endless. Fearful that I may omit the names of important contributors, I've included only the names of my immediate family, and the professional writers who unselfishly edited my story, and prepared it for publication. To all who offered valuable assistance, I am most grateful.

My niece, Nancy (McKean) Reger provided inspiration, when she gifted me with my family genealogy, in a bound book; compiling years of her tireless research into our family's history. My son, Bill Warren, and his wife Jan, sent a micro-cassette tape recorder to me, with the admonishment to "start talking." Jan is a trained medical transcriber. She spent countless hours listening to, and transcribing my taped stories; then sent transcribed copies to me, for my review. Editing those copies sparked many more memories, that when recalled, became important additions to my story. I soon spent more time expanding the story, than in taping new story episodes. Jan's expertly transcribed texts were stacking up on my desk. Organization came, when our long-time friend, the Reverend Denise Terry, organized my semi-related stories into labeled chapters.

Throughout my writing, I repeatedly called my daughter, Jeanne (Warren) Metz, to verify the names, dates, and details of significant events. Also, through Jeanne, I met a talented lady named Pam Treme who was a highly skilled technical book author. She agreed to edit, and organize, my written story text, and to prepare it for publishing. Unfortunately, serious health issues in Pam's family required her constant attention, and she could not work on my manuscript.

At my request, Pam cheerfully mailed the manuscript to Denise, and she took over editing and fact-checking all of the text, editing and adding all of the pictures to the text, researching publishing options, and completing the book for publication.

I have really felt fortunate to have a talented "team" working on my behalf. Bill, Jan, Jeanne, Pam, and Denise have each contributed greatly, to turning my stories into what I hope will be an important resource for my descendants, to learn about my life, and our family, as well as some of the interesting details of many historical moments of the 20th century.

I am fully aware of the importance of my wife Rosemarie, who supports me daily in every possible way; by providing her warm and caring companionship, by meticulously keeping and decorating our two houses, by accepting full responsibility for driving and for maintaining our automobiles, by preparing delicious and healthy meals, and by bringing laughter and joy to my life, every day. Indeed, Rosemarie is a real gem, and I am truly thankful for her.

I would be remiss, if I did not also thank God, who has blessed me with a wonderful life, filled with opportunities and adventures, and the love of family and friends, who make every day a joy, and every story fun to tell.

Col. R.F. Warren, USMC (Ret)

Palmetto, FL (2020)

Appendix Items

- Letter from L. F. Chapman, Jr. (Gen., USMC), dated 22 Aug 1969
- Citation accompanying Air Medal awarded for "meritorious achievement in aerial flight" from 9-27 Apr 1945
- Citation accompanying Gold Star awarded in lieu of a second Air Medal awarded for "meritorious achievement in aerial flight" from 1-10 May 1945
- Citation accompanying Distinguished Flying Cross for "heroism and extraordinary achievement in aerial flight" from 7-16 June 1945
- Citation accompanying Gold Star awarded in lieu of a second Distinguished Flying Cross for "heroism and extraordinary achievement in aerial flight" on 27 Sep 1951
- Certification of Gold Star awarded in lieu of a fourth Air Medal for "meritorious achievement in aerial flight" from 1 Sep-1 Oct 1951
- Citation accompanying Gold Star in lieu of a fourth Air Medal
- Certification of Gold Star awarded in lieu of a fifth Air Medal for "meritorious achievement in aerial flight" from 12 Oct to 11 Nov 1951
- Citation accompanying Gold Star in lieu of a fifth Air Medal
- Citation accompanying Gold Star in lieu of a sixth Air Medal awarded for "meritorious acts while participating in aerial flights" from 11 Nov to 20 Dec 1951
- Certification of Gold Star awarded in lieu of a seventh Air Medal for "meritorious achievement in aerial flight" from 20 Dec 1951 to 10 Jan 1952
- Citation accompanying Gold Star in lieu of a seventh Air Medal

- Awards letter dated 3 Mar 1955 for Gold Stars in lieu of a second and third Distinguished Flying Cross, and Gold Stars in lieu of a 4th through 7th Air Medals for "heroism and extraordinary and meritorious achievements in aerial flights" during 1952 and 1953
- Letter from Mrs. Omar N. "Kitty" Bradley, dated 9 Sep 1967
- Certification of Meritorious Service Medal awarded for "outstanding meritorious service from 19 Jul 1968 to 31 Aug 1969
- Citation accompanying the Meritorious Service Medal
- Letter from R.G. Owens, Jr. (Maj. Gen., USMC), dated 25 Aug 1969
- Autographed picture of Sidney Mashbir (Col., US Army), dated 24 Aug 1972
- Certificate of Commendation in recognition of service as a member of the Advisory Committee on Retired Personnel
- Letter from Raymond F. L'Heureux, (Col., USMC) dated 23 Jul 2007

DEPARTMENT OF THE NAVY
HEADQUARTERS UNITED STATES MARINE CORPS
WASHINGTON, D. C. 20380

22 August 1969

Dear Colonel Warren,

I would like to take this opportunity to thank you for your many years of dedicated service to our Corps and to our Country. During your career of more than 27 years you have made a significant contribution in shaping the destiny of our Corps and in upholding those traditions which are so vital to its continuing reputation.

In reviewing your record, I am pleased to note among your awards the Legion of Merit with Combat "V" for exceptionally meritorious conduct in the Republic of Vietnam from June 1967 to June 1968; the Distinguished Flying Cross for heroism and extraordinary achievement in the Ryukyu Islands Area from 7 to 16 June 1945; Gold Stars in lieu of a second and a third Distinguished Flying Cross for heroism and extraordinary achievement in Korea on 27 September 1951 and 8 February 1952; the Air Medal with Gold Stars in lieu of a second and a third Air Medal for meritorious achievement against enemy Japanese forces during World War II; and Gold Stars in lieu of a fourth through a seventh Air Medal for meritorious acts in Korea during the period 1 September 1951 to 10 January 1952. I appreciate the manner in which you have carried out all of your assignments.

Please accept my very best wishes for much happiness throughout the years ahead.

Sincerely,

L. F. CHAPMAN, JR.
General, U. S. Marine Corps
Commandant of the Marine Corps

Colonel Robert F. Warren, USMC
3d Marine Aircraft Wing, FMF
Marine Corps Air Station
El Toro (Santa Ana), California 92709

THE SECRETARY OF THE NAVY
WASHINGTON

   The President of the United States takes pleasure in presenting the AIR MEDAL to

     SECOND LIEUTENANT ROBERT F. WARREN,
     UNITED STATES MARINE CORPS RESERVE,

for service as set forth in the following

  CITATION:

   "For meritorious achievement in aerial flight as Pilot of a Fighter Plane in Marine Night Fighter Squadron FIVE HUNDRED FORTY-THREE during operations against enemy Japanese forces in the Okinawa Shima, Nansei Shoto Area, from 9 to 27 April 1945. Completing his fifth combat air patrol during this period, Second Lieutenant Warren contributed materially to the success of his squadron in dispersing hostile enemy aircraft which were attempting to suicide-crash into our shipping and bomb and strafe personnel, ground installations and airfields. His courage and devotion to duty in the face of heavy antiaircraft fire were in keeping with the highest traditions of the United States Naval Service."

          For the President,

          Francis P. Matthews
          Secretary of the Navy.

THE SECRETARY OF THE NAVY
WASHINGTON

The President of the United States takes pleasure in presenting the GOLD STAR in lieu of a second AIR MEDAL to

FIRST LIEUTENANT ROBERT F. WARREN,
UNITED STATES MARINE CORPS RESERVE,

for service as set forth in the following

CITATION:

"For meritorious achievement in aerial flight as Pilot of a Fighter Plane in Marine Night Fighter Squadron FIVE HUNDRED FORTY-THREE during operations against enemy Japanese forces in the Okinawa Shima, Nansei Shoto Area, from 1 to 10 May 1945. Completing his tenth combat mission during this period, First Lieutenant Warren contributed materially to the success of his squadron in dispersing hostile enemy aircraft which were attempting to suicide-crash into our shipping. His courage and devotion to duty in the face of hostile antiaircraft fire were in keeping with the highest traditions of the United States Naval Service."

For the President,

Francis P. Matthews
Secretary of the Navy.

THE SECRETARY OF THE NAVY
WASHINGTON

The President of the United States takes pleasure in presenting the DISTINGUISHED FLYING CROSS to

FIRST LIEUTENANT ROBERT F. WARREN,
UNITED STATES MARINE CORPS RESERVE,

for service as set forth in the following

CITATION:

"For heroism and extraordinary achievement in aerial flight as Pilot of a Fighter Plane in Marine Night Fighter Squadron FIVE HUNDRED FORTY-THREE during action against enemy Japanese forces in the Ryukyu Islands Area, from 7 to 16 June 1945. Completing his twentieth mission during this period, First Lieutenant Warren contributed materially to the success of his squadron. His airmanship, courage and devotion to duty in the face of grave hazards were in keeping with the highest traditions of the United States Naval Service."

For the President,

Francis P. Matthews
Secretary of the Navy.

THE SECRETARY OF THE NAVY
WASHINGTON

The President of the United States takes pleasure in presenting the GOLD STAR in lieu of a second DISTINGUISHED FLYING CROSS to

CAPTAIN ROBERT F. WARREN,
UNITED STATES MARINE CORPS,

for service as set forth in the following

CITATION:

"For heroism and extraordinary achievement in aerial flight as Pilot of a Plane in Marine Helicopter Transport Squadron ONE HUNDRED SIXTY-ONE during operations against enemy aggressor forces in Korea on the night of 27 September 1951. Participating in a six-plane night air lift engaged in transporting a reinforced company from its reserve position to a combat area, Captain Warren piloted his helicopter through hazardous mountain passes and succeeded in safely landing the aircraft, heavily laden with fully equipped troops, in an area which was identified only by two hand signals. Maneuvering his helicopter with precise timing and compass headings to avoid the danger of collision with other planes during the high overcast and darkness which prevailed throughout the flights, he completed seven round trips, thereby contributing materially to the success of the mission. By his skilled airmanship, courage and unswerving devotion to duty, Captain Warren upheld the highest traditions of the United States Naval Service."

For the President,

C. S. Thomas

Secretary of the Navy.

THE UNITED STATES OF AMERICA

THIS IS TO CERTIFY THAT
THE PRESIDENT OF THE UNITED STATES OF AMERICA
HAS AWARDED THE

GOLD STAR IN LIEU OF A FOURTH

AIR MEDAL

TO

CAPTAIN ROBERT F. WARREN, UNITED STATES MARINE CORPS

FOR
MERITORIOUS ACHIEVEMENT
IN AERIAL FLIGHT

IN KOREA FROM 1 SEPTEMBER TO 1 OCTOBER 1951

C. S. Sherman
SECRETARY OF THE NAVY

UNITED STATES MARINE CORPS

HEADQUARTERS
1ST MARINE DIVISION (REINF) FMF
c/o FLEET POST OFFICE
SAN FRANCISCO, CALIFORNIA

In the name of the President of the United States, the Commanding General, 1st Marine Division (Reinf) FMF, takes pleasure in awarding a GOLD STAR IN LIEU OF THE FOURTH AIR MEDAL to

CAPTAIN ROBERT F. WARREN
UNITED STATES MARINE CORPS

for service as set forth in the following

CITATION:

"For meritorious acts while participating in aerial flight over enemy territory while serving with a Marine division in KOREA from 1 September to 1 October 1951. Serving as a pilot, Captain WARREN displayed outstanding professional skill and devotion to duty. During this period he participated in a total of twenty transportation flights in slow, unarmed aircraft at extremely low altitudes over areas where enemy anti-aircraft fire was received or could be expected. Missions accomplished during these flights contributed materially to the success of ground operations. Captain WARREN's courage and devotion to duty were an inspiration to all who served with him and his actions throughout were in keeping with the highest traditions of the United States Naval Service."

R. McC. PATE
Major General, U. S. Marine Corps
Commanding

Temporary Citation

THE UNITED STATES OF AMERICA

THIS IS TO CERTIFY THAT
THE PRESIDENT OF THE UNITED STATES OF AMERICA
HAS AWARDED THE

GOLD STAR IN LIEU OF A FIFTH

AIR MEDAL

TO

CAPTAIN ROBERT F. WARREN, UNITED STATES MARINE CORPS

FOR
MERITORIOUS ACHIEVEMENT
IN AERIAL FLIGHT

IN KOREA FROM 12 OCTOBER TO 11 NOVEMBER 1951

C. S. Thomas
SECRETARY OF THE NAVY

UNITED STATES MARINE CORPS

HEADQUARTERS
1ST MARINE DIVISION (REINF) FMF
c/o FLEET POST OFFICE
SAN FRANCISCO, CALIFORNIA

In the name of the President of the United States, the Commanding General, 1st Marine Division (Reinf) FMF, takes pleasure in awarding a GOLD STAR IN LIEU OF THE FIFTH AIR MEDAL to

CAPTAIN ROBERT F. WARREN
UNITED STATES MARINE CORPS

for service as set forth in the following

CITATION:

"For meritorious acts while participating in aerial flight over enemy territory in KOREA while serving with a Marine division from 12 October to 11 November 1951. Serving as a pilot, Captain WARREN displayed outstanding professional skill and devotion to duty. During this period he participated in a total of twenty transportation flights in slow, unarmed aircraft at extremely low altitudes over areas where enemy anti-aircraft fire was received or could be expected. Missions accomplished during these flights contributed materially to the success of ground operations. Captain WARREN's courage and devotion to duty were an inspiration to all who served with him and his actions throughout were in keeping with the highest traditions of the United States Naval Service."

R. McC. PATE
Major General, U. S. Marine Corps
Commanding

Temporary Citation

THE UNITED STATES OF AMERICA

THIS IS TO CERTIFY THAT
THE PRESIDENT OF THE UNITED STATES OF AMERICA
HAS AWARDED THE

GOLD STAR IN LIEU OF A SIXTH

AIR MEDAL

TO

CAPTAIN ROBERT F. WARREN, UNITED STATES MARINE CORPS

FOR
MERITORIOUS ACHIEVEMENT
IN AERIAL FLIGHT

IN KOREA FROM 11 NOVEMBER TO 20 DECEMBER 1951

C. S. Sherman
SECRETARY OF THE NAVY

UNITED STATES MARINE CORPS

HEADQUARTERS
1ST MARINE DIVISION (REINF) FMF
c/o FLEET POST OFFICE
SAN FRANCISCO, CALIFORNIA

In the name of the President of the United States, the Commanding General, 1st Marine Division (Reinf) FMF, takes pleasure in awarding a GOLD STAR IN LIEU OF THE SIXTH AIR MEDAL to

CAPTAIN ROBERT F. WARREN
UNITED STATES MARINE CORPS

for service as set forth in the following

CITATION:

"For meritorious acts while participating in aerial flight over enemy territory while serving with a Marine division in KOREA from 11 November to 20 December 1951. Serving as a pilot, Captain WARREN displayed outstanding professional skill and devotion to duty. During this period he participated in a total of twenty transportation flights in slow, unarmed aircraft at extremely low altitudes over areas where enemy anti-aircraft fire was received or could be expected. Missions accomplished during these flights contributed materially to the success of ground operations. Captain WARREN's courage and devotion to duty were an inspiration to all who served with him and his actions throughout were in keeping with the highest traditions of the United States Naval Service."

R. McC. PATE
Major General, U. S. Marine Corps
Commanding

Temporary Citation

THE UNITED STATES OF AMERICA

THIS IS TO CERTIFY THAT
THE PRESIDENT OF THE UNITED STATES OF AMERICA
HAS AWARDED THE
GOLD STAR IN LIEU OF A SEVENTH

AIR MEDAL

TO

CAPTAIN ROBERT F. WARREN, UNITED STATES MARINE CORPS

FOR
MERITORIOUS ACHIEVEMENT
IN AERIAL FLIGHT

IN KOREA FROM 20 DECEMBER 1951 TO 10 JANUARY 1952

SECRETARY OF THE NAVY

UNITED STATES MARINE CORPS

HEADQUARTERS
1ST MARINE DIVISION (REINF) FMF
c/o FLEET POST OFFICE
SAN FRANCISCO, CALIFORNIA

In the name of the President of the United States, the Commanding General, 1st Marine Division (Reinf) FMF, takes pleasure in awarding a GOLD STAR IN LIEU OF THE SEVENTH AIR MEDAL to

CAPTAIN ROBERT F. WARREN
UNITED STATES MARINE CORPS

for service as set forth in the following

CITATION:

"For meritorious acts while participating in aerial flight over enemy territory in KOREA while serving with a Marine division from 20 December 1951 to 10 January 1952. Serving as a pilot, Captain WARREN displayed outstanding professional skill and devotion to duty. During this period he participated in a total of twenty transportation flights in slow, unarmed aircraft at extremely low altitudes over areas where enemy anti-aircraft fire was received or could be expected. Missions accomplished during these flights contributed materially to the success of ground operations. Captain WARREN's courage and devotion to duty were an inspiration to all who served with him and his actions throughout were in keeping with the highest traditions of the United States Naval Service."

R. McC. PATE
Major General, U. S. Marine Corps
Commanding

Temporary Citation

DEPARTMENT OF THE NAVY
HEADQUARTERS UNITED STATES MARINE CORPS
WASHINGTON 25, D. C.

IN REPLY REFER TO
DLA-298-tl

3 MAR 1955

From: Commandant of the Marine Corps
To: Captain Robert F. WARREN 031417 USMC, Aircraft, Fleet Marine Force, Pacific, Marine Corps Air Station, El Toro, Santa Ana, California
Via: Commanding General, Aircraft, Fleet Marine Force, Pacific

Subj: Awards

Encl: (1) 2 Permanent citations
(2) 4 Certificates

1. I take pleasure in forwarding to you the enclosed permanent citation for the Gold Stars in lieu of a second and third Distinguished Flying Cross, and certificates for the Gold Stars in lieu of a fourth through seventh Air Medal previously presented to you in the name of the President of the United States for heroism and extraordinary and meritorious achievements in aerial flights during operations against enemy aggressor forces in Korea, during 1951 and 1952.

2. Be assured of my deep appreciation of your devotion to duty and gallant action which were in keeping with the highest traditions of the United States Marine Corps.

R. McC. PATE
Acting

Mrs. Omar N. Bradley
Room 2E 664, The Pentagon
Washington, D.C. 20310

September 9, 1967

Dear Colonel Warren,

I have just written to your wife and to your son, and thought I would take a moment to drop you a line to thank you for all the very special courtesies you extended General Bradley and me on our visit to Da Nang.

I assured both your wife and your son that you were well, so please stay that way!

When we returned to Saigon I mentioned your very special exuberance and your efforts regarding "Operation Soap" to General Westmoreland. He thought it was a fine effort you were extending toward the refugees, and when General Bradley and I mentioned that we would make every effort to channel soap in your direction General Westmoreland suggested that we channel it through him for wider distribution. I guess you might say that you have been out-ranked there, Colonel! We have already started several moves to get soap into Vietnam, and I have no doubt that your share will flow into the Da Nang area.

I tried to telephone your son at VMI the evening before last and was advised the the "rats" are not due to arrive until sometime next week. However, General Bradley and I are scheduled to be in Lexington in late October for an official function and will make every effort to see him at that time.

Stay happy and, once again, our thanks.

Sincerely,

Kitty Bradley
Mrs. Omar N. Bradley

Colonel Robert F. Warren, USMC
Hq III Marine Amphibious Force
FPO San Francisco 96602

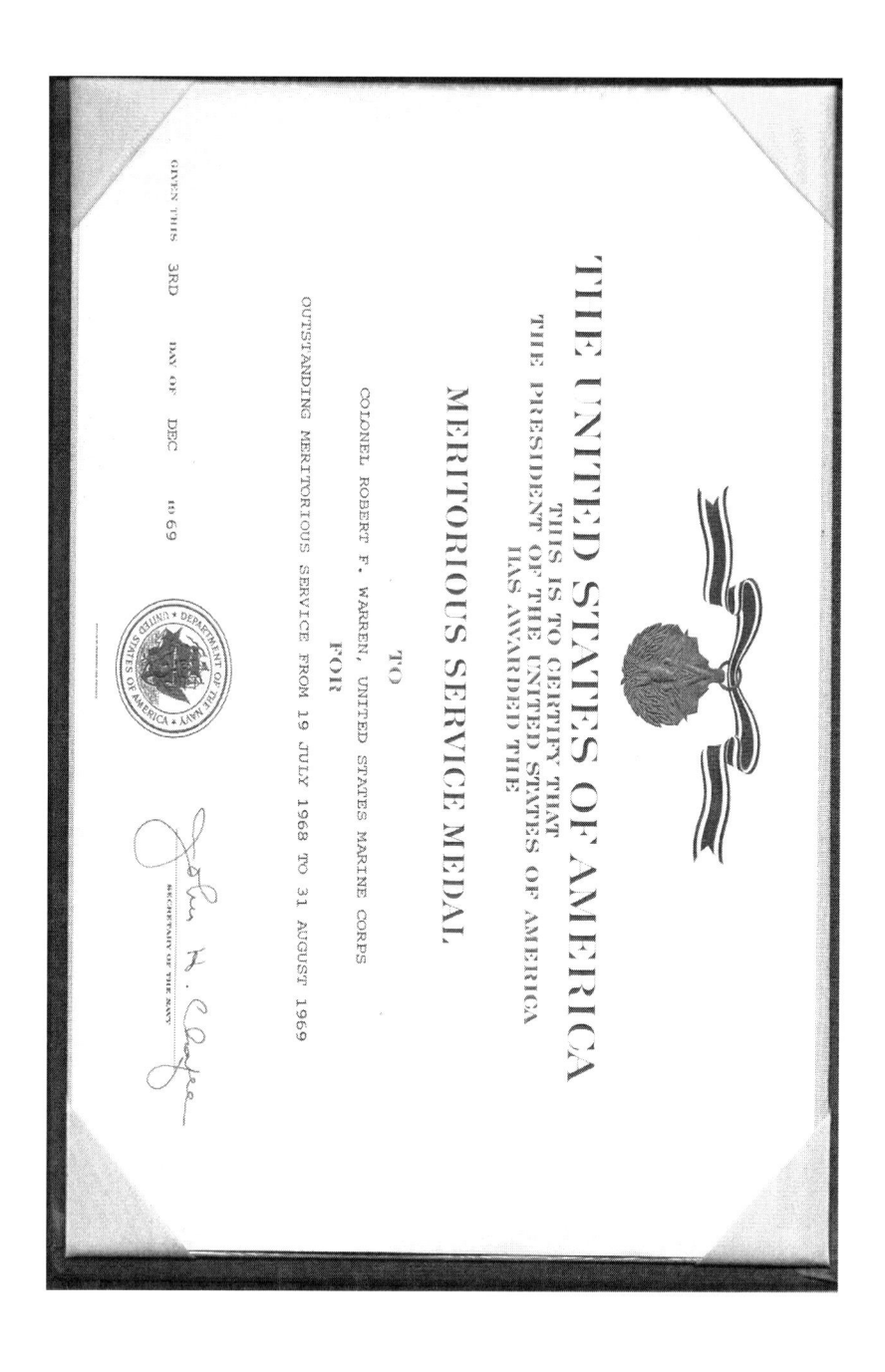

THE UNITED STATES OF AMERICA

THIS IS TO CERTIFY THAT
THE PRESIDENT OF THE UNITED STATES OF AMERICA
HAS AWARDED THE

MERITORIOUS SERVICE MEDAL

TO

COLONEL ROBERT F. WARREN, UNITED STATES MARINE CORPS

FOR

OUTSTANDING MERITORIOUS SERVICE FROM 19 JULY 1968 TO 31 AUGUST 1969

GIVEN THIS 3RD DAY OF DEC 19 69

SECRETARY OF THE NAVY

COMMANDER IN CHIEF
UNITED STATES PACIFIC FLEET

The President of the United States takes pleasure in presenting the Meritorious Service Medal to

Colonel Robert F. WARREN
United States Marine Corps

for service as set forth in the following:

CITATION

"For outstanding meritorious service while serving as the Commanding Officer of Marine Aircraft Group Fifty-Six, Third Marine Aircraft Wing, Fleet Marine Force, Pacific from 19 July 1968 to 31 August 1969. Colonel WARREN worked tirelessly and with superb resourcefulness, molding his unit into a well-coordinated effective force and providing consistently outstanding support to his command. Faced with the urgent task of preparing helicopter aviation units to meet tactical contingencies in the Western Pacific, he initiated a series of training activities which greatly enhanced the readiness posture of participating pilots and enlisted crewmen. Under his dynamic leadership, two helicopter squadrons and four observation detachments were organized, equipped, and prepared in a minimum amount of time and deployed to the Republic of Vietnam. He directed the reorganization of a CH-53 squadron, a CH-46 squadron, and an aircraft control unit, and was instrumental in training more than 1,500 Marines to fill deployment quotas. His resolute determination inspired all who served with him and contributed significantly to the accomplishment of his unit's mission. Colonel WARREN's leadership, superb professionalism and unwavering devotion to duty were in keeping with the highest traditions of the United States Naval Service."

For the President

JOHN J. HYLAND
Admiral, U. S. Navy
Commander in Chief U. S. Pacific Fleet

HEADQUARTERS
3d Marine Aircraft Wing
Fleet Marine Force, Pacific
U. S. Marine Corps Air Station
El Toro, (Santa Ana), California 92709

AUG 25 1969

Dear Colonel Warren,

As the end of your long and faithful tour of active duty approaches, may I take this opportunity to reflect with you on the honorable service you have rendered as a Marine to our Corps and nation.

From that day in June 1942, when you enlisted in the Marine Corps Reserve, to that day in June 1943 when you accepted your appointment as a Second Lieutenant, through the Second World War, then through the Korean and Vietnam conflicts, till the present, in your assignment as Commanding Officer, Marine Aircraft Group-56, you have demonstrated a dedication and professional competence which reflects credit upon yourself and is in keeping with the highest traditions of the Marine Corps.

Along with your many friends in the Marine Corps I extend, on behalf of myself and the officers and men of this Command, sincere best wishes for all your future endeavors.

R. G. OWENS Jr.
Major General, U. S. Marine Corps
Commanding General

It has been a signal honor to have served with you over the years — I wish you and your good health and happiness in coming years.

To Colonel Bob Warren a gallant Marine and to his gracious wife Millie a perfect hostess — with admiration and cordial regards,

Vinny T. Washbu[rn]
Emerald Bay 24 Aug '72

Department of the Navy
United States of America

Washington, D.C.

The Secretary of the Navy
takes great pleasure in presenting this

Certificate of Commendation

to

COLONEL ROBERT F. WARREN, USMC(RET)

in grateful recognition and appreciation
of outstanding service to the
Department of the Navy as a member of
The Advisory Committee on Retired Personnel

[signature]

Assistant Secretary of the Navy
(Manpower and Reserve Affairs)

July 23, 2007

Colonel Robert F. Warren, USMC (Ret.)
8425 Imperial Circle
Palmetto, Florida 34221

Dear Bob:

I want to thank you for your continued interest in HMX-1, for your nearly 30 years of service as an Officer of Marines and Naval Aviator. Your career as a Marine was most remarkable and your status as a veteran of World War II, Korea and Vietnam is reverently recognized by Marines who had gone before you and subsequent to your retirement as the Commanding Officer of Marine Air Group 56.

To the best of my knowledge, no Marine Aviator has ever commanded both a helicopter and jet attack squadron during their career. I understand also that except for an extension of your tour in the Far East, you would most likely have been one of my predecessors as the Commanding Officer of HMX-1 and as such, the helicopter pilot of the President of the United States.

We are honored that the United States Postal Service chose to commemorate Marine One with their Express Postage stamp first issued in Washington, DC on 13 June 2007. One of those stamps is affixed to this letter.

On behalf of all HMX-1 personnel, I am pleased to offer both you and your wife Millie our best wishes, many fond memories, and the thanks of a grateful nation for long and faithful service.

Respectfully,

Colonel Raymond F. L'Heureux
Commanding Officer
United States Marine Corps Squadron HMX-1
Quantico, Virginia

Acronyms and Abbreviations

1MARDIV	First Marine Division
3MARDIV	Third Marine Division
AES-9	Aircraft and Engineering Squadron Nine
AFB	Air Force Base
AGL	Above Ground Level
AMTRACS	Amphibian Tractors
ARCAV	Army Calvary
ARCP	Aerial Refueling Control Point
ARVN	Army of the Republic of Vietnam
AVGAS	Aviation Gas
AWS	Amphibious Warfare School
BAR	Browning Automatic Rifles
BOQ	Bachelor Officer Quarters
BUAER	United States Navy Bureau of Aeronautics
BUPERS	Bureau of Personnel (for U.S. Navy)
BUSANDA	Bureau of Supplies and Accounts (for U.S. Navy)
CAG	Carrier Air Group Commander
CAP	Combined Action Program
CARQUALS	Carrier Qualifications
CAS	Close Air Support
CAVU	Ceiling and Visibility Unlimited
CB	Construction Battalion
CFAD	Commander, Fleet Air Detachment
CG&A Box	Controlled Gyro and Amplifier Box
CIA	Central Intelligence Agency
CINCPAC	Commander in Chief, Pacific
COD	Carrier Onboard Delivery
COMUSMACV	Commander, United States Military Assistance Command, Vietnam
CORDS	Civil Operations and Revolutionary Development Support
CPT	Civilian Pilot Training
CTF	Commander of Task Force
CVE	Escort Aircraft Carrier
DEPCORDS	Deputy for Civil Operations and Revolutionary Development Support
DMZ	Demilitarized Zone

DFC	Distinguished Flying Cross
EPCOT	Experimental Prototype Community of Tomorrow
FACS	Forward Air Controllers
FBO	Fixed Base Operator
FCLP	Field Carrier Landing Practice
FMFPAC	Fleet Marine Forces Pacific
FRAG	Fragmentation
FCB	Fire Support Base
G	Gravity
GCA	Ground-Controlled Approach
H&MS	Headquarters and Maintenance Squadron
HAVR	High Velocity Aircraft Rocket
HMX-1	Helicopter Squadron at MCAS, Quantico; also the name of a helicopter, when the President of the United States is on-board
HP	Horsepower
HQMC	Headquarters, Marine Corps
JATO	Jet-Assisted Takeoff
JC	Junior Course
LAX	Los Angeles International Airport
LPH	Landing Platform Helicopter
LSO	Landing Signal Officer
LST	Landing Ship Tanks
LTA	Lighter Than Air
LZ	Landing Zone
MABS	Marine Air Base Squadron
MACV	Military Assistance Command, Vietnam
MAF	Marine Amphibious Force
MAG	Marine Air Group
MARTCOM	Marine Corps Air Reserve Training Command
MASH	Mobile Army Surgical Hospital
MAW	Marine Air Wing
MCAF	Marine Corps Air Facility
MCAS	Marine Corps Air Station
MCB	Marine Corps Base
MCDC	Marine Corps Development Center
MOS	Military Occupational Specialty
MPC	Military Payment Certificate

MSR	Main Supply Route
NAP	Naval Aviation Pilot
NAS	Naval Air Station
NATO	North Atlantic Treaty Organization
NAVSTAROTA	United States Naval Station, Rota, Spain
NCO	Non-Commissioned Officer
NVA	North Vietnamese Army
NWC	Naval War College
OCS	Officer Candidate School
OOD	Officer of the Deck
PAVN	People's Army of Vietnam
PaxRiver	Patuxent River Naval Air Test Center
PCS	Permanent Change of Station
PLC	Platoon Leaders Class
POW	Prisoner of War
PSP	Pierced Steel Planking
QHS	Quantico High School
R&R	Rest and Recuperation
ROK	Republic of Korea
RON	Remain Over Night
SATS	Short Airfield for Tactical Support
SDO	Squadron Duty Officer
SECNAV	Secretary of the Navy
SFO	San Francisco (California) International Airport
SOA	Speed of Advance
STOL	Short Takeoff and Landing
SVN	South Vietnam
TACA	Tactical Air Coordinator
TAD	Temporary Additional Duty
TBS	The Basic School
TO	Table of Organization
TPA	Tampa (Florida) International Airport
TRANSLANT	Trans-Atlantic
U.N.	United Nations
U.S.	United States
USAID	United States Agency for International Development
USNS	United States Naval Ship
USOM	United States Operations Mission

VC	Viet Cong
VMI	Virginia Military Institute
WDW	Walt Disney World
X-Corps	United States Army 10th Corps

Index

234 Mickey Mouse, 541
A Ride to Panmunjom, 233
Abrams, Creighton W., 522, 523, 524
Adak, Alaska, 261
Adams, Arthur H., 549, 550, 557
Air Force Aero Club, 381
Albright, Charlotte, 461, 464
Albright, Howard, 460, 461, 464
Albright, Walter L. "Walt", 465
Allen, Edward "Jack" and Daisy, *3*
Almeria, Spain, 394, 395, 396, 397
Amami Oshima, Japan, *105, 358*
An Angel with a Rotary Wing, 221
Anchorage, Alaska, 261
Angaur Island, 265
Arc Light Missions, 517, 518
Arizona Territory. *See* Hiep Duc
Arlington National Cemetery, *165, 274, 293*
Armstrong, Victor A. "Vic", 258, 335, 351, 363
Arndt, Gus, *110, 358*
Ascom City, 233, 237
Attu Island, 261
Austin Lake Airport, *36, 37, 38, 39, 41, 43, 44, 45, 120, 382*
Austin, Cal, 226
Axtell, George, *103, 104*

Bailey, Gwen, 270, 276, 294, 539, 559
Bailey, Kelvin "Kel", 260, 267, 270, 275, 276, 277, 283, 284, 292, 294, 539, 540, 541, 559
Ball, Vernon E. "Jack", 480
Bangkok, 329, 330, 332, 335, 337, 339, 341, 342
Barksdale Army Airfield, *88*
Barrow, Robert H., 370, 388
Basilone, John, 188
Beaufort High School, 391, 400, 435, 457, 458
Bennett (Floyd) Airfield, 408, 409
Berry, Sidney B. "Sid", 304, 370
Bierman, Bernie, *49*
Bitulok, Philippines, 310, 311
Black, Alice Schilt, 293
Black, Greg, 293
Bohn, Robert D. "Dewey", 431
Bolan, Charles, 174, 176
Bolling Field, 381
Bondi Beach, 511
Bonner, Bruce, *110, 358*
Bowman, George, 449, 450, 451
Bowser, Alpha L., 434, 435, 438, 449, 450
Boyington, Gregory "Pappy", 434
Bradley, "Kitty" Buhler, 488, 489, 490, 491, 495, 497, 498, 499, 500, 501, 503
Bradley, Omar, 139, 206, 463, 487, 488, 489, 490, 491, 492, 495, 496, 497, 498,

619

499, 500, 501, 502, 503, 504
Brewer, Robert "Bob", 482, 483, 519, 520
Brice, W. Oscar, 269
Brown Field, 280, 367, 376
Brown, Jessie, *58*
Brukner, Clayton J., *45*
Bryan, Toler, *157, 158*
Buckner, Simon Bolivar, Jr., *97, 113, 137*
Buie, Paul D., 322, 323, 324, 325
Bukove, Rolene, 321, 352
Bukove, Verdan (Buck), 321
Burke, Arleigh, 338, 531
Burke, Julian T., 431, 433
Buskirk, Bill, *163*
Butler, Smedley, *136, 378*
Byers, Clovis, 203, 206, 207, 208
Camp Kawae, 356
Camp Lejeune, 257, 372, 373, 375, 429, 434, 458, 574
Camp Nine Nails, 195, 210
Camp Pendleton, 181, 182, 183, 187, 188, 189, 257, 316, 317, 318, 375, 431, 548, 549, 550, 551, 552, 554, 555, 557, 562
Canoni, Tony, *31, 32*
Canoni Construction Company, *31*
Cape Batangan, 521
Cape Lookout, 405, 412
Carl, Marion, *163, 164, 165, 169, 257*
Carlson, Claude J., *85*
Carpenter, Stanley H. "Stan", 25, 58, 415, 416, 417

Cates, Clifton B., 139, 203, 206, 273
Chamberlain, Claire C., *85, 86*
Chapman, Leonard, Jr., 559
Chevron Hotel, 509, 513
China Beach, 516, 537
Chompawansic Creek, 376
Chosin Reservoir, 258
Chu Lai, 521, 535, 567
Chugie Bears, 198
Chuichi Nagumo, *118*
Chumunjim, 195, 196, 213
Clark Field, *114*
Cleland, Cook, 633
Collins, William R., 517
Coloma High School, *25, 26*
Combined Action Program, 490
Con Tien, 490
CORDS
   Civil Operations and Revolutionary Development Support (CORDS), 491, 505, 519, 520, 522, 523, 524, 525, 526, 527, 528, 529, 538
Corregidor Island, *114, 288*
Costello, Keith W. "Cos", 205, 219, 234, 546, 547, 555, 559
Costello, Marty, 560
Courtelyou, Stoddard, 417, 437
Covert Consolidated High School, 26, 27
Crone, Bob, *140, 159*
Cross, Charles, 527, 528, 538
Cushman, Robert E., Jr., 16, 164, 471, 484, 485, 487, 488, 489, 490, 491, 492, 494, 497, 503, 504, 505,

523, 524, 525, 526, 527, 528, 533, 534, 537
Da Nang, *16, 331, 339, 469, 470, 471, 472, 476, 478, 479, 480, 481, 483, 485, 487, 491, 493, 495, 497, 499, 503, 507, 513, 514, 516, 521, 522, 524, 525, 526, 527, 529, 530, 533, 536, 537, 538, 557, 562, 563, 565, 567*
Davis, Annie, 240
Davis, Carl, *117, 122, 240, 298, 359*
Davis, Dellwyn L. "Del", 397
Davis, Martha, 240, 298, 359
Dean, Dick and Lucille, 12
Dean, Gretchen, 240, 297, 544
Dean, Margaret, 96, 240, 297, 544
Dean, William F. "Bill", 12, 30, 35, 37, 65, 132, 133, 161, 240, 297, 544
Death Valley, the Summer Offensive, 569
Defourneaux, Rene, 341, 342
Demilitarized Zone (DMZ), 471, 473, 482, 483, 489, 490, 493, 514, 518, 519, 520, 523, 536
DePietro, Bill, 445
Di Loc Pass, 563
Dien Bien Phu, 332, 470, 493
Disney, Walt, 294, 540, 541, 559
Dominguez, Ron, 559
Don Mueang International Airport, 331, 337
Dong Ha, 482, 490, 494, 518, 519

Douglas, Paul, 226
Dunn, Ellie, 317, 319
Dunn, Elswin P. "Jack", 317, 318, 319, 320, 322, 337, 342, 343
Dwiggins, Bill, 295
Eisenhower, Dwight D., 139, 298, 300, 301, 315
Eisenhower, Mamie, 503
Ejungee, 211, 235
Ekiben, 350
Elmendorf Air Force Base, 261
Engman, Charles "Chuck", *110, 358*
Ennis, Thomas "Tom", 316, 317, 319, 320
Etheridge, Jim, *111, 357*
Evashevski, Forest, *49*
Felt, Harry D., 329, 342, 353, 354
Finn, E.V., 354
Fire Support Base (FSB) Baldy, 571, 572, 573
Fire Support Base (FSB) Ross, 567, 568, 569, 571
Fisher, Donald D., 390, 394, 399, 434, 435, 436, 437, 439, 440, 457
Fisher, John, 247
Flanagan, Richard "Dick", *147*
Formosa, 105, 310
Forrester, Annie Dillon, 240, 298, 359
Forrester, Roy, *122, 240, 298, 359*
Fort Richardson, 261
Fort Snelling National Cemetery, *166*
Freeney Field, 380
Fritz, Nick, 383, 384
Fusan, Ernest C., 298, 299

Gadsden Purchase, 264
Gadsden, James, 264
Garmisch-Partenkirchen, Germany, 462, 464
Gaudette, Eddie, *83*
Geiger Hall, *137*, 367
Geiger, Roy, *113*, *137*, *280*, *367*, *395*
Gibson, George A., 432, 433
Gilman, George "Gizmo", 59
Glockenspiel Show, 462
Goldwater, Barry, 294, 381
Grand Rapids Airport, *132*
Grant, Mack, 18, 19, 20
Green, Wallace M. Jr., 459, 517
Grootendorst's Flower Farm, *25*
Guam, *80*, *94*, *110*, *114*, *115*, *117*, *123*, *124*, *127*, *128*, *129*, *265*, *295*, *358*, *367*, *517*
H&MS-56, 548
Hai Van Pass, 483, 522
Hall, Barry, 378
Han River, 236, 469, 472, 473, 476, 477, 478, 488, 527, 530, 531
Hancock Lodge, 538
Haneda International Airport, 330, 335, 337, 345, 352
Harris, Field, 258
Hartsock, Edmund P. "Ed", 390, 394, 397, 399, 400, 406, 407, 418, 434
Havelock High School, 457, 458, 459, 467, 539, 543
Hawaii
  Pearl Harbor, *34*, *71*, *91*, *94*, *96*, *143*, *323*

Hawkins, Harold "Hal", 44, 120
Haynes, Fred, 484, 487, 489, 505
Heinemann, Ed, *71*, *421*
Heintges, John, 332, 334
Helgoland, 528, 529, 530, 531
Herrin, Bert, 221
Herring, George, 193, 225, 321, 322, 326, 329, 335, 337, 354, 363, 460, 550
Hiep Duc, 569
Hillan, Donald D., 197, 208, 211
Hirohito, Emperor, *127*, *352*
Hiroshima, Japan, *126*, *127*
HMR(L)-363, 297, 298, 307, 312, 313
HMR-161, 179, 182, 185, 187, 196, 201, 204, 207, 209, 221, 225, 230, 232, 233, 236, 237, 258, 259, 266, 297, 321, 363, 368, 502, 546, 549, 550
HMR-363, 322, 337
HMRI-363, 313, 318
Ho Chi Minh, 342, 470
Ho Chi Minh Trail, 492, 514
Hochmuth, Bruno, 514
Hodde, Gordon V., 453, 454, 455, 457
Hofbrauhaus, 462
Hokkaido, Japan, 261
Holland, Percy, 143
Holland, Roxy, 143
Honey Buckets, 358
Honshu Island, 350
Hood, Harlen E. "Tex", 145, 147, 157
Hood, William "Bill", 103

622

Horgan, Jack, 479, 480, 491, 504, 533
Hubka, Frank J., 347, 356
Hue, Thua Thien Province, 479, 483, 514, 515, 516, 519, 520, 521, 523
Huering, Francis E. "Ed", 379
Hughes, Fred, 354, 355
Hunters Point Naval Shipyard, 496
Hurd, Doug, 460
I Corps, 471, 472, 476, 479, 480, 483, 491, 492, 494, 496, 505, 514, 516, 520, 521, 522, 523, 525, 531, 536, 537
Ie Shima Island, *97, 104*
III MAF, *16, 388, 467, 469, 470, 472, 473, 475, 476, 477, 478, 479, 483, 484, 487, 489, 490, 491, 492, 494, 501, 502, 503, 504, 505, 514, 516, 517, 518, 520, 521, 522, 523, 524, 525, 526, 527, 528, 529, 531, 532, 533, 535, 536, 537, 557*
Imjin River, 230, 236
Indian Spring, Nevada, 262
Ing, Herbert, 497, 498, 499
Ingraham School, *7, 9, 10, 11, 545*
Isamu Cho, *114*
Ishagaki, Japan, *105*
Isley Field, *120, 126*
Itami Airfield, 633
Iverson, Edwin T. "Ivy", *108*
Iwo Jima, *118, 121, 188*
Jacks, Edgar K. "Ken", 419, 420, 430, 445
Jaskilka, Samuel "Sam", 371

Jensen, Charlotte, *76*
Jerome, Clayton C., 206
Johnson, Bill, 478, 525
Johnson, Louis A., 257
Johnson, Lyndon B., 303, 475, 490, 492, 517, 524, 525
Johnson, Robert, 313
Joy, C. Turner, 230, 236
Kadena Airfield, *97, 98, 99, 100, 103, 104, 110, 111, 112, 114, 288, 330, 355, 356, 358, 469, 518, 538*
Kaesong, 236
Kagman Airfield, 117, 120, 122, 123, 124, 126, 127, 128
Kai Tak Airport, 265, 330, 337
Kamakura, Japan, 346
Kang Nung airfield, 195, 210, 233
Kelley, Richard E. "Doc", *109*
Kelly, Robert E. "Tex", 185
Kennedy, Edward, 536, 537
Kerama Retto, *100*
Khe Sanh, 479, 483, 490, 514, 518, 519, 520
Kimball, Dan, 235
Kimpo Airfield, 266
Kindley Air Force Base, 438, 441, 443, 452, 453
King Ranch, *60, 61*
Komer, Robert W. "Blowtorch Bob", 504, 525
Koren, Barney, 475, 476, 477, 478, 480, 482, 483, 487, 491, 492, 493, 494, 503, 504, 505, 523, 525, 526, 527, 536, 537
Koster, Samuel W. "Sam", 521
Krueger, Walter, 366
Kunz, Charles, *149*

Kuzian, Angeline Louise (Allen), 3
Kuzian, Frank, 3
Kuzian, John, 3
Kuzian, Mary (Urie), 3
Kuzian, Robert Frank, 3
Kuzian, Walter Fred, 3
Kuzian, Walter Fred Jr., 3, 12
Kyoto, Japan, 347, 348, 349, 633
Lajes Air Force Base, 283, 286, 397, 438, 452, 453
Lake Eibsee, 465
Lam, Hoang Xuan, 472, 480, 484, 491, 521, 523, 525, 526, 527, 537
Lang, Frank C., 389
Laos, *1*, *329*, *331*, *332*, *333*, *334*, *335*, *337*, *338*, *340*, *341*, *342*, *343*, *353*, *354*, *363*, *471*, *480*, *492*, *514*, *518*, *519*
Larissa Air Base, 438, 439, 445, 446, 447, 449, 451
Larson, 'Mom', 386
Le Chi Cuong, 471, 491, 525, 538
Lee Roskay's Flying School, *30*
Leeward Point Field, *154*
Lejeune, John A., 256
LeMay, Curtis E., 381
Leonard, Gene, 378, 379, 383, 384
Ie-Shima, *103*
Lewis, Mack, 419, 421
Leyte, *96*
Little Paw Paw Lake, *7*
Little Paw Paw River, *25*
Lownds, David E., 518
Luang Prabang, Laos, 334
Ludden, Charles H. "Chuck", 539
Lustron house, 364, 384
Lutz, Charlie, *92*
Luzon Island, 297, 307, 310, 313, 366
Lynch, Robert "Terry", 247
Lyster bags, 340
MacArthur, Douglas, *96*, *114*, *230*, *237*, *257*, *288*
Magicienne Bay, *121*, *125*
Mahon, John, 469
Mainhart, Lillian, 270, 273, 287
Malaga, Spain, 398
Mangrum, Richard C., *68*, *69*, *361*
Marble Mountain, 479, 489, 532, 534
Marine Air Base Squadrom 56 (MABS-56), 548
Marine Air Group 11 (MAG-11), *145*
Marine Air Group 14 (MAG-14), *145*, *164*, *165*, *167*
Marine Air Group 16 (MAG-16), 242, 321, 322, 329, 335, 342, 347, 354
Marine Air Group 31 (MAG-31), 98, 390, 394, 395, 396, 397, 398, 399, 400, 419, 434, 435, 436, 439, 453, 457
Marine Air Group 36 (MAG-36), 317, 532, 534
Marine Air Group 56 (MAG-56), 485, 546, 547, 548, 549, 550, 551, 552, 554, 555, 556, 557, 559
Marine Corp Air Facility

Santa Ana, 182, 183, 185, 187, 189, 191, 193, 194, 242, 243, 244, 245, 246, 248, 250, 251, 295, 297, 299, 303, 321, 322, 354
Marine Corps Air Station
Beaufort, 389, 393, 394, 398, 406, 415, 422, 423, 443, 453, 454, 457
Cherry Point, 77, 78, 79, 80, 84, 85, 86, 87, 89, 142, 143, 145, 146, 147, 155, 157, 159, 160, 161, 163, 164, 165, 167, 169, 170, 171, 247, 250, 257, 272, 275, 290, 362, 373, *375*, 383, 388, 389, 393, 394, 401, 403, 405, 407, 409, 411, 412, 421, 422, 427, 432, 434, 437, 438, 448, 449, 451, 452, 453, 457, 458, 459, 460, 465, 466, 469, 476, 538
El Centro, 87, 88, 89, 90, 91
El Toro, 88, 110, 179, 182, 183, 191, 242, 245, 248, 249, 250, 252, 253, 255, 257, 260, 261, 262, 263, 267, 269, 270, 279, 287, 288, 290, 292, 295, 317, 319, 361, 362, 375, 420, 431, 476, 540, 545, 546, 549, 550, 554, 555, 557
Ewa, *91, 92, 93*
Iwakuni, 288, 295, 352
Kaneohe Bay, 260, 287, 295
Miramar, *91, 130, 131*
New River, 275, 373, 388, 389, 406
Quantico, *138*, 139, 279, 280, 381, 383
Tustin, 172, 182, 237, 298, 304, 313, 485, 546, 548, 554, 555, 559
Yuma, 263
Marine Corps Base
Quantico, *131, 135, 136, 137, 139, 140, 142, 143, 145, 169, 170, 171, 173, 174, 177, 178, 179, 180, 181, 185, 187, 194, 196, 225, 244, 252, 258, 270, 278, 279, 280, 293, 300, 335, 338, 351, 358, 360, 361, 362, 363, 364, 365, 367, 369, 370, 372, 373, 375, 378, 381, 382, 385, 386, 387, 388, 389, 390, 394, 420, 432, 434, 466, 467, 469, 475, 477, 502, 544, 550, 561, 562*
Marpi Point, *118*
Marshall, Bill, 287, 378, 380
Mashbir, Sidney "Sid", 559
Mast, Claude, *25, 162*
Mast, Emma, *162*
Matsushima Bay, 351
McCalla Field, *154, 155*
McCaul, Verne J., 295
McCausley, Kay, 272
McCutcheon, Keith B., 173, 177, 178, 225, 229, 234, 362, 363, 364, 549, 550
McKean
Don, *141, 208, 427*
Eugene "Gene", 85, 141, 385, 423
Helen, *85, 141, 385*
Nancy, *141, 385, 386*
McQueen, John C., 284
Megee, Vernon, 247
Mekong River, 334

Merchant, Clark E., 412
Michigan
   Benton Harbor, *15*, *16*, *17*, *103*, *132*, *135*, *139*, *161*, *162*, *163*
   Coloma, *3*, *11*, *17*, *18*, *25*, *26*, *47*, *385*, *544*, *545*
   Covert, *26*, 29, 31, 304, 544
   East Lansing, *33*, *34*, *45*
   Grand Rapids, 132, 381
   Kalamazoo, *34*, *37*, *40*, *43*, *44*, *45*, *56*, *120*, *408*
   Lansing, *34*
   Niles, *30*, *161*, *162*
Michigan Aviation Hall of Fame, *45*, *72*
Michigan State College, *33*, *34*, *35*, *45*, *325*
Mighty Mite Sawmill Company, 532, 533
Mitchell, William P. "Mitch", 95, 96, 185, 193, 231, 232, 297
Mitsuru Ushijima, *114*
Miyako Hotel, 347, 633
Mog Mog, *95*
Monkey Mountain, 521
Montgomery, E.A., *13*, *78*
Moorer, Thomas H., 428, 437
Mortimer, Walt, 232
Mountbatten, Lord Louis, *1*, *283*, *284*
Mt. Fujiyama (Fuji), 349
Mt. Tapochau, *117*, *122*
Munich, Germany, 462, 465
Munsan, 230, 235, 236
Myers, George, 477, 478
Nagasaki, Japan, *126*, *127*
Naha, Okinawa, 265, 307, 308, 310, 313

National Memorial Cemetery of the Pacific, *103*, *165*
Naval Air Station
   Agana, *115*, *124*
   Alameda, 189, 279, 299, 300, 301, 303, 460
   Anacostia, 276, 286, 292
   Argentia, 283, 286
   Atsugi, 260, 288, 353
   Barber's Point, 260
   Barbers Point, *92*, *287*, *290*
   Beeville, *60*
   Cabaniss, *60*
   Cecil Field, *70*, *71*, *73*, *76*, *77*
   Columbus, *161*, *163*
   Corpus Christi, *59*, *60*, *63*, *67*, *361*
   Cubi Point, 287
   Cuddihy, *60*, *61*, *62*, *63*
   Dallas, 292
   El Centro, *156*
   Fallon, 425
   Grosse Ile, Michigan, 256
   Jacksonville, *71*, *73*, *165*
   Lajes, 397
   Lakehurst, 54, 171, 172, 173, 174, 176, 177, 180, 225, 363, 550, 552, 633
   Memphis, 293
   Miami, *69*, *70*, *71*, *167*
   New York, 408
   Norfolk, 415
   North Island, *89*, *91*, *191*, *550*, *551*
   Oppama, 307, 308, 321, 325
   Ottumwa, 52, 53, 54, 55, 57, 58, 59, 60, 63, 76
   Pensacola, *159*, *293*, *407*, *425*, *552*, *633*

Point Mugu, 292
Port Lyautey, 285
Quonset Point, 277
San Diego, 190
Sangley Point, 265, 287, 295
Vero Beach, *77, 78, 79, 82, 84*
Whidbey Island, 267
Naval Base Norfolk, *149, 155, 362, 385, 415, 434, 449*
Naval Station
    Guantanamo Bay, 154, 167, 275, 322, 437
    Roosevelt Roads, *146, 275, 399, 427, 428, 435, 436, 437, 438, 449, 633*
Ngo Dinh Diem, 470
Nguyen Cao Ky, 470, 482, 493, 526
Nguyen Van Thieu, 526, 527
Nickerson, Herman, 479, 521
Nimitiz, Chester, *118*
Nitze, Paul H., 459
Nixon, Richard, 58, 294, 524
Nolan, Keith William, 569
Numba-69, 210, 220
Oberammergau, Germany, 461, 462, 463, 464, 465
Okinawa, *86, 93, 94, 95, 97, 98, 99, 101, 102, 103, 104, 105, 106, 110, 113, 114, 119, 133, 134, 137, 191, 193, 240, 256, 265, 288, 295, 297, 307, 308, 310, 313, 329, 330, 341, 342, 347, 354, 355, 357, 358, 367, 398, 420, 469, 518, 538, 562*
Oktoberfest, 462
Olson, Virgil D., 300, 301, 302, 303
Opeka, Francis "Rocky", *139, 140, 147, 152, 153, 155*
Operation Blackbird, 203
Operation Bumblebee, 207
Operation Bushbeater, 209
Operation Forager, *117*
Operation Hotfoot, 333
Operation Iceberg, *113*
Operation Oklahoma Hills, 565, 567
Operation Rabbit Hunt, 210, 213
Operation Ripple, 229, 230
Operation Steel Pike, 394, 396, 398, 406
Operation Switch, 214, 233
Operation Windmill I, 199
Operation Windmill II, 201
Osmena, Sergio, *96*
Ou Mountains, 350
Overhuel, Jim, *31*
Owens, Robert G. Jr, 473
Owens, Robert G. Jr., 559
Owens, Robert G., Jr., 475, 479
Packard
    George, *26*
Panmunjom, 230, 233, 235, 236, 237, 266
Parsons, J. Graham, 338, 341, 342
Passion Play, 463
Pate, Mary Elizabeth "Bunty", 416, 417
Pate, Randolph M., 277, 416
Pathet Lao, 332, 333
Patton, George S., 462, 463, 501

Patton, George S. Hotel, 462, 464
Peleliu, *114*, *265*
Pendleton, Joseph H., 188
Peninsula Hotel, 330, 335
Phu Bai, 479, 523
Plotkin, Lou, 210
Pohang, Korea, 193, 194, 259, 265, 266
Power, Tyrone, *85*, *120*
Puller, Lewis B. "Chesty", 574
Pusan, Korea, 170, 194, 196, 213, 257, 496
Putnam, Paul A., 253
Quang Nam Province, 471, 492, 521
Quang Ngai Province, 16, 471, 492, 521, 531, 532
Quang Tin Province, 471, 482, 492, 521
Quang Tri Province, 471, 479, 518, 519, 520, 521, 522
Quantico High School, 376, 377, 378
Radford, Arthur W., 206
Rattan, Donald V., 519
Rawlings, Art, 200, 201, 206, 359, 539, 540
Rawlings, Audrey, 359
Redallen, Duane "Red", 315
Reed, Edwin, 363
Reger, Dean, 386
Reger, Nancy (McKean), 589
Renner, Joseph "Joe", 308
REO Speed Wagon School Buses, *26*
Rhee, Syngman, *1*, *266*
Ridgeway, Matthew B., 206, 237
Roberts, Carson A., 329, 337
Robertson, Donn J., 379, 497, 498, 499, 502, 503, 521
Rosenberg, Anna, 206, 502
Roskay, Lee, *30*, *161*
Rota, *451*
Rota, Spain, 117, 124, 128, 438, 446, 449, 450, 451, 452, 453, 616
Ryukyu Islands, *119*
Saigon, 471, 480, 500, 503, 504, 515, 521, 522, 523, 526, 527, 528, 529, 533, 534, 535
Saipan, *1*, *44*, *80*, *115*, *117*, *118*, *119*, *120*, *121*, *122*, *123*, *124*, *125*, *126*, *127*, *128*, *129*, *133*, *134*, *240*, *256*, *298*, *420*
Sakhalin Island, 261
Savannakhet, Laos, 339
Schilt, Christian, *138*, *194*, *206*, *249*, *250*, *251*, *252*, *253*, *255*, *256*, *257*, *258*, *259*, *260*, *261*, *263*, *264*, *265*, *266*, *267*, *269*, *270*, *273*, *274*, *275*, *276*, *277*, *278*, *279*, *280*, *281*, *283*, *284*, *285*, *286*, *287*, *288*, *289*, *290*, *291*, *292*, *293*, *294*, *295*, *297*, *317*, *325*, *361*, *383*, *393*, *416*, *417*, *420*, *429*, *431*, *476*, *487*, *540*
Schilt, Mrs. Elizabeth W., 292, 293
Schous, Mozell, *76*
Schriver, Richard J. "Jake", 249, 250, 258, 259
Schutter, Allen "Al", *108*, *111*, *117*, *128*, *129*, *256*
Selden, John T., 213, 431

Sendai, Japan, 350, 351
Sexton, Martin "Stormy", *138*
Shakaski, Howard, 37
Sheehan, Bob, 419, 420, 432, 445
Shell, Sergeant, 497, 498, 499
Shepherd, Lemuel, 188, 225, 247
Shifflett, Ed, 382
Shifflett, Martha, 382
Shifflett, Evelyn (Missy), 382
Sikorsky, Igor, 277, 278, 633
Simmons, "Tex", *117*
Simmons, Gloria " Simmons", 538
Simmons, Robert L. "Bob", 538
Simpson, Ormand R., 277, 429, 430, 435, 437, 438, 633
Smith, Andrew "Andy", 389
Smith, Charles Kingsford, 508, 509, 511
Smith, Holland M. "Howlin' Mad", *118*, *119*
Smith, Oliver P., 258
Snedeker, Edward W., 379, 382, 383, 387
Sparrow, Herbert G., 332, 333, 334
SS *Great Falls Victory*, 190, 194
St. Paul Winter Carnival, 264
Steele, "Rocky", 110, 358
Sterling, Jan, 226
Strandlund Carl, 364
Street, Lewis, 181
Sturdevant Lodge, *31*, *32*
Subic Bay Naval Base, 287
Sydney Opera House, 511
Tachikawa Air Force Base, 355

Taiwan, 265, 267, 295, 310
Tan Son Nhat Airport, 504, 533, 535
Tanapag Harbor, *126*
Tay Loc Airfield, 483
Teen Club, 385, 386
Temple, Charles F. "Chuck", *69*, *76*, *82*, *84*, *99*, *108*, *357*
Terry, Reverend Denise, 589
Tet Offensive, 515, 516, 517, 519, 520, 524, 525, 536
The Basic School, 137, 362, 365, 467, 475, 544, 561, 562
The Hague, 283, 284
Third Marine Aircraft Wing (3rd MAW), *145*, *546*, *547*, *549*, *550*, *551*, *555*, *557*, *559*
Thomas, Gerald C., 203, 207, 213, 259
Thorin, Duane, 232, 233
Thrash, William Gay, 545, 546
Thua Thien Province, 471, 479, 482, 522, 523
Tinian, *80*, *117*, *119*, *121*, *126*, *127*
Tinikling, 311
Titterud, Stanley V. "Stan", 526
Tojo, Hideki, *127*
Tolson, John J., 520
Tope, Lyle, 315, 317
Torii Gates, 347
Torrejon Air Force Base, 438, 440, 443, 445
Totten, Forrest E., *10*, *11*, *545*
Tra Bong, Quang Ngai Province, 531, 532, 533, 534, 535
Treme', Pam, 589

Twining, Merrill B., 290
Twining, Nathan F., 290
U. S. Agency for International Development (USAID), 340, 477, 478, 493, 532, 535
Ulithi atoll, *93, 94, 95*
Upschulte, Phillip P. "Phil", 549, 550
USNS *Geiger*, 395, 396, 398
USS *Achernar, 96, 99, 100*
USS *Akron*, 174, 184
USS *Badoeng Strait*, 243, 258, 368
USS *Consolation*, 200, 529
USS *Forestall*, 407, 415
USS *Haven*, 31, 35, 200
USS *Lexington*, 324
USS *Leyte, 58*
USS *Los Angeles*, 184
USS *Macon*, 174
USS *Manchester*, 231, 232
USS *Missouri, 60, 118, 127, 181, 257*
USS *Ranger, 71, 322, 323, 325, 326*
USS *Repose*, 200, 489, 494, 495, 496, 504, 529
USS *Ronquil*, 325, 326, 327
USS *Sanctuary*, 529
USS *Siboney, 147, 149, 153, 154, 155, 156, 157, 249*
USS *Sitkoh Bay, 93, 94, 97, 98, 100, 103, 190, 191, 193, 194*
USS *St. Paul*, 326
USS *Thetis Bay*, 307, 308, 309, 310, 311, 312, 313, 315, 337, 338, 339, 342, 343
USS *Valley Forge*, 245
USS *Wisconsin*, 140, 142, 226, 227, 229, 291

Van Fleet, James A., 206, 233, 237
Vandegrift, Alexander Archer, 188
Verdan (Buck) Bukove, 352
Vientiane, Laos, 331, 332, 334, 335, 337, 338, 339, 341
Vieques, Puerto Rico, *146, 430, 431, 433*
Virginia Military Institute (VMI), 188, 365, 388, 390, 391, 400, 406, 416, 435, 458, 466, 467, 475, 501, 503, 507, 510, 543, 558, 561, 562, 573
Vischer, Betty, 43, 44
VMA-331, 407, 415, 416, 417, 419, 427, 430, 433, 435, 436, 437, 438, 439, 446, 453, 454, 455, 457
VMCJ-1, 460
VMF (N)-542, 95
VMF(N)-534, *115*
VMF(N)-541, *114*
VMF(N)-543, 96, 97, 100, 191
VMF-122, 257
VMF-225, *147, 149, 152, 153, 154, 155*
VMF-312, *94, 97, 98, 103*
VMF-323, *103, 104, 111*
VMF-451, 397, 398, 400, 432, 433, 434
VMF-653, 633
VMGR-252, 260
VMO-6, 170, 196, 197, 259, 354, 355, 368, 555
VMP-354, *145, 147, 155, 157, 159, 160, 163, 247, 362, 389, 427*
VMT-1, 401, 402, 407, 412

Vo Nguyen Giap, 470, 515
Wainwright, Johnathan "Skinny", *114*
Wake Island, 70, 253, 260, 265, 287, 288, 291, 295
Walt Disney World, 294, 540
Walt, Larry, 378, 387
Walt. Lewis W. "Lew", 387, 388, 467, 469, 470, 472, 473, 475, 476, 477, 478, 479, 480, 482, 484, 485, 492, 502, 517, 521, 557, 573, 574
Warren
  George, *5, 13, 27*
  Helen, *5, 14, 27*
  Jan, 226, 589, 590
  Jeanne, *59, 143, 170, 171, 181, 182, 190, 239, 271, 272, 276, 293, 294, 295, 321, 345, 351, 352, 359, 361, 376, 377, 378, 382, 384, 385, 388, 391, 400, 416, 435, 457, 458, 459, 467, 507, 510, 539, 541, 543, 544, 558, 559, 589, 590*
  Joseph R. "Joe", 435
  Millie Weber, 27, 29, 31, 33, 34, 43, 44, 45, 46, 54, 58, 59, 69, 76, 81, 82, 84, 87, 89, 90, 91, 131, 133, 134, 135, 139, 140, 141, 142, 143, 159, 162, 165, 170, 171, 177, 181, 182, 186, 187, 190, 239, 249, 269, 276, 293, 304, 305, 321, 334, 335, 343, 345, 346, 347, 349, 350, 351, 352, 359, 360, 361, 364, 378, 382, 383, 384, 385, 400, 416, 435, 436, 447, 453, 457, 458, 461, 464, 465, 467, 469, 475, 501, 507, 510, 538, 540, 541, 543, 544, 557, 558, 559, 560
  Ruth, *3, 4, 5, 14, 15, 17, 18, 19, 21, 22, 26, 131, 162*
  Tom, *3, 5, 13, 16, 17, 19, 20*
  William " Bill", *139, 141, 142, 143, 156, 159, 165, 171, 181, 190, 239, 240, 271, 272, 276, 293, 294, 295, 305, 321, 345, 351, 352, 359, 360, 361, 376, 377, 378, 379, 380, 381, 382, 383, 384, 385, 388, 390, 391, 400, 406, 416, 435, 458, 459, 466, 467, 469, 475, 477, 501, 507, 510, 524, 538, 543, 556, 557, 558, 559, 561, 589, 590*
Weber
  Cindy, 360, 385
  Marnie, *91, 135, 359, 360, 361, 385*
  Millie, 29, 81, 162, 170, 305, 400
  Patricia "Tish", 360, 385
  Rudy, *27, 28, 32, 131, 162, 304*
  Walt, 33, 135
  Walter, *91*
Westmoreland, William C., 470, 471, 484, 485, 500, 503, 504, 517, 520, 522, 523, 524, 525, 526, 534
Wilson, Louis H. Jr., 366, 367
Witt, William T. "Bill", *156*
Wolfe, David C., 361, 362

Woodham, Irving, *37*
Yaiko, 345, 346, 350, 351, 352
Yang Yang, 195
Yeager, Chuck, *164*, *633*
Yokohama, Japan, 321, 350
Yokosuka, Japan, 312, 321, 323, 325, 326, 327, 337, 346, 350, 351, 496
Yokota Air Base, 353
Yontan Airfield, *97*, *98*, *103*, *104*, *108*, *111*, *114*, *357*
Yoshitsugu Saito, *118*
Young Radiator Company, 291
Yungdun-po, 236
Zugspitze, 464
Zushi, Japan, 346, 352

Notes

[i] The Navy later moved its helicopter training program from Lakehurst to NAS, Pensacola, Florida.

[ii] Years later, I saw a large photograph of HR-69 flying. It was hanging on the wall of the Commandant of The Marine Corps' outer office, in Washington, D.C.

[iii] 1st Marine Air Wing pilots were granted a week-long R&R in Japan about every six weeks. We were flown from Korea to Itami Airfield, near the Japanese cities of Osaka and Kyoto. While in Kyoto, we stayed at the beautiful Miyako Hotel, which was designated our R & R Hotel.

[iv] Captain Cook Cleland, USN was the commander of the Navy F4U (Corsair) squadron covering us (VMF-653. He had been recalled to active duty during the Korean War. During his civilian life he had become a famous racing pilot, who had won the annual Thompson Trophy at the Cleveland Air Races in 1947 and 1949; flying modified Corsairs both years.

[v] Enfilade and defilade are concepts in military tactics used to describe a military formation's exposure to enemy fire. A formation or position is "in enfilade" if weapons fire can be directed along its longest axis. A unit or position is "in defilade" if it uses natural or artificial obstacles to shield or conceal itself from enfilade.

[vi] Years later, Brigadier General Simpson visited me at Roosevelt Roads, Puerto Rico, where I had taken my jet aircraft squadron for training.

[vii] At the Tampa, Florida International Airport (TPA), one of the four banks of elevators in the central airport terminal is named after Igor Sikorsky. At the rear of each elevator, there is a large picture of him. When entering one of those elevators, I never tire of telling my wife (loudly) that I had lunch with Igor Sikorsky. I doubt that the other elevator passengers within earshot believe me or even care. The other three banks of elevators at TPA are named after famous aviators Chuck Yeager, Amelia Earhart, and Neil Armstrong.

[viii] Several squadrons of CH-53 helicopters were later purchased for the Marine Corps; and similar "Jolly Green Giants" were built for the U.S. Air Force, to support its downed pilot rescue mission in Vietnam. Advanced models of the CH-53 included adding a third turbo-shaft jet engine, and a nose-mounted aerial (in-flight) refueling probe. The latest version of the

CH-53 has lifted more than ten tons externally, and now has several external cargo attachment hooks, and seven main rotor blades.

[ix] Major Redallen related the brutal tactics of the Haitian dictator, Francois "Papa Doc" Duvalier. Duvalier held the wretchedly poor black citizens in the Republic of Haiti in a state of terror, for fourteen years. His tactics included murdering many of his suspected political opponents. His secret police called Tontons Macoutes (Creole, for "bogey men") also collected unofficial taxes and tribute from cowed businessmen. He cast his spell using voodoo, which, in effect, is the official language of Haiti. He was backed financially by United States grants for his anti-communist stance, and by the U.N. International Monetary Fund.

[x] General Officers and Admirals often had small flags, with the appropriate number of stars, mounted and flying from the front fender of the vehicle they were riding. Sometimes, the front license plate of their vehicle had the stars mounted on the plate. On transport aircraft a small, license plate size receptacle was permanently mounted outside the aircraft cockpit, making it easy for the pilot to slide a Flag Officer's license plate, from the open cockpit window down into the receptacle.

[xi] The reason our HUS helicopters were limited to Visual Flight Rules, was that the Controlled Gyro and Amplifier (CG&A) Box, which controlled the helicopter attitude instruments, often failed. The sealed box, measuring approximately twelve inches by twelve inches, was bolted to the transmission deck, above the pilot's cockpit. The box rested on four small external shock-absorbing springs, but was still subjected to ten Gs (ten times gravity), due to sustained vibrations. The CG&A Box was seriously affected by vibration, which in turn caused failure of some electronic components, inside the sealed Box. Opening the sealed boxes for local repairs was not permitted. Each CG&A Box had to be removed, and returned to the Sikorsky company plant in Connecticut, for inspection and repairs.

[xii] When in port, U.S. Navy ships fly the American Flag from the ship's stern. At sea, the flag is flown above the ship's bridge.

[xiii] Lyster bags are canvas water bags, usually with a thirty-six-gallon capacity. The bags are used to supply troops with chemically purified drinking water. In hot climates, the canvas bags sweat, cooling the water.

[xiv] See Chapter 15 for a MABS organization and responsibilities.

[xv] Months later I was transferred from Oppama to Okinawa. I located the language school headquarters, and was presented a clipboard, through a bank teller type glass window. The clipboard had a form that included who I wanted to see. I wrote his name code identification, which was "Rene D-4-No" and pushed the clipboard back through the same glass window. A buzzer sounded, and I entered through a door, to an Army Lieutenant Colonel's office. After explaining our brief association in Laos, I asked where Rene Defourneaux might be. I was told that he was well, and still on special assignment in Southeast Asia. Nothing more was revealed. I heard nothing further from Rene Defourneaux until after we had both retired. I was reading the Retired Officer Magazine, which includes a section devoted to books written by member authors. I spotted a reference to a new book entitled *The Winking Fox,* authored by Rene Defouneaux. I purchased a copy, and found out that Rene lived in Indianapolis, Indiana. I contacted him, by telephone, from my retirement home in California. He told me that the motivation to write his book was urging from his family, which is not too different from my motivation for writing this book.

[xvi] General McCutcheon's service on active duty as a General was short. In order to be promoted, a Marine has to pass a physical. General McCutcheon could not; as he unfortunately had cancer. However, by special Act of Congress, his physical requirement was waived. General McCutcheon was permitted to serve only one day on active duty before he was physically retired.

[xvii] In his honor, a section of Highway Route 8 in Connecticut, from Stratford to Ansonia, has been named "General Samuel Jaskilka Highway." Sam was born, and raised, in Ansonia, CT. His children were schoolmates of my children, Bill and Jeanne, at Quantico.

[xviii] The FBI Academy was once on Barnett Avenue, but has since been moved west to the base Impact Area, where its training facilities and technical expertise have all been greatly expanded.

[xix] Ed Huering would go on to serve in the Marine Corps for 23 years, including in Vietnam, before retiring a Lieutenant Colonel, in 1983.

[xx] NAS,Lajes was also the Supply Depot for the U.S. Sixth Fleet air operations in the Mediterranean Sea area.

[xxi] At, and above 24,000 feet, altitudes were referred to as Flight Levels.

[xxii] Admiral Moorer was later appointed Chairman of the Joint Chiefs of Staff. That appointment made him the most senior member, and placed him in charge of all the U.S. Armed Forces. As Chairman of the Joint Chiefs, he reports to the President's Secretary Of Defense.

[xxiii] A "buddy store" is a an aircraft that has the same probe and drogue refueling system carried in a KC-130 tanker aircraft, except that only one wing tank, housing the hose reel array is used. Aboard aircraft carriers, the "buddy store" aircraft is commonly used to refuel aircraft in emergency situations. Its normal call sign is "Texaco."

[xxiv] Marine sniper, Gunnery Sergeant Carlos Hathcock, had 93 confirmed "kills" in Vietnam. After being wounded, he was treated aboard the hospital ship, USS *Repose*.

[xxv] When Anna Rosenberg was sworn in as the Assistant Secretary of Defense, in November of 1950, hers was the highest position ever held, by a woman in the Defense Department.

[xxvi] Part of the sixty thousand Korean Forces sent to SVN.

[xxvii] The description of his visit to Bill in Vietnam is included in a succeeding chapter that I asked Bill to write.

[xxviii] General Walt's son, Larry, and I had been co-captains of our high school football team, at Quantico. General Walt had summoned me to his quarters at the Marine Barracks, 8th and I streets in Washington, DC, just prior to my deployment to Vietnam, and had talked at length to me, one-on-one, about leadership and taking care of the troops.

Made in the USA
Monee, IL
20 July 2022